Introduction to International Transitional Justice Law

# International Criminal Law Series



VOLUME 23

The titles published in this series are listed at *brill.com/icls*

# Introduction to International Transitional Justice Law

*By*

Emmanuel Guematcha

BRILL | NIJHOFF

ISSN 2213-2724
ISBN 978-90-04-76662-4
ISBN 978-90-04-76665-5 (PDF)
DOI https://doi.org/10.1163/9789004766655

Library of Congress Cataloging-in-Publication Data
A CIP catalog record for this book has been applied for at the Library of Congress.



Brill Nijhoff and Koninklijke Brill BV are part of De Gruyter Brill.
www.degruyterbrill.com

Questions about General Product Safety Regulation: productsafety@degruyterbrill.com

# Contents

# Acknowledgments

Writing this book would not have been possible without the collaboration and support of many individuals. I would like to thank all those who have created courses on transitional justice and given me the opportunity to teach this subject for many years, in particular, Professor Marina Eudes at the University of Paris Nanterre, Professor Sebastien Touzé at the International Institute of Human Rights (René Cassin Foundation), and Ismaël Tahirou at the Swiss UMEF University. Many thanks to the students and all those who attended these courses, which provided an opportunity to exchange ideas that have helped me envisage new insights on the complexity of transitional justice. I would like to thank the French transitional justice experts Magalie Besse and Professors Jean-Pierre Massias, Xavier Philippe, Pascal Plas, and Marina Eudes with whom I co-edited the French journal *Annuaire de justice transitionnelle* (Yearbook of Transitional Justice). This editing collaboration introduced me to many critical aspects of transitional justice. My thanks also go to Professors Mutoy Mubiala and Mouloud Boumghar who provided me with informative details on some of the topics covered in the book; Professor Sandra Szurek who first gave me the opportunity to study transitional justice by supporting me in writing a PhD dissertation on truth commissions and international law; Professor François Tanguay-Renaud of Osgoode Hall Law School and Professor Mary Shariff of Robson Hall who gave me the opportunity to conduct research at York University and the University of Manitoba on the implementation of transitional justice in established democracies.

I would also like to thank the reviewers for their constructive criticism and suggestions, which improved the first draft of the manuscript; Beth McAuley for all her helpful editorial corrections; and the Brill publishing team, particularly Selma Hoedt and Akiko Hakuno, for their support, advice, and suggestions throughout the review and publication process.

Any errors or mistakes remain my own.

*Emmanuel Guematcha*

# Abbreviations

| | |
|---|---|
| ACHPR | African Charter on Human and Peoples' Rights |
| ACHR | American Convention on Human Rights |
| AComHPR | African Commission on Human and Peoples' Rights |
| ACtHPR | African Court on Human and Peoples' Rights |
| AI | Amnesty International |
| ArCHR | Arab Charter on Human Rights |
| AU | African Union |
| CAT | Committee against Torture |
| CED | Committee against Enforced Disappearances |
| CEDAW | Committee on the Elimination of Discrimination against Women |
| CERD | Committee for the Elimination of Racial Discrimination |
| CESCR | Committee on Economic, Social and Cultural Rights |
| CFREU | Charter of Fundamental Rights of the European Union |
| CRC | Committee on the Rights of the Child |
| CRPD | Committee on the Rights of Persons with Disabilities |
| Doc. | Document |
| EAC | Extraordinary African Chambers |
| ECHR | European Convention on Human Rights |
| ECOWAS | Economic Community of West African States |
| ECtHR | European Court of Human Rights |
| ESCR | Economic, Social and Cultural Rights |
| EU | European Union |
| HRC | Human Rights Committee |
| IACHR | Inter-American Court of Human Rights |
| IAComHR | Inter-American Commission on Human Rights |
| ICC | International Criminal Court |
| ICCPR | International Covenant on Civil and Political Rights |
| ICESCR | International Covenant on Economic, Social and Cultural Rights |
| ICJ | International Court of Justice |
| ICL | International Criminal Law |
| ICRC | International Committee of the Red Cross |
| ICTR | International Criminal Tribunal for Rwanda |
| ICTY | International Criminal Tribunal for the former Yugoslavia |
| IHL | International Humanitarian Law |
| IHRL | International Human Rights Law |
| ILC | International Law Commission |
| IMT | International Military Tribunals |

| | |
|---|---|
| NGOs | Non-governmental Organisations |
| OAS | Organization of American States |
| OAU | Organization of African Unity |
| OHCHR | Office of the High Commissioner for Human Rights |
| Res. | Resolution |
| SCSL | Special Court for Sierra Leone |
| TRC | Truth and Reconciliation Commission |
| UN | United Nations |
| UNHCHR | United Nations High Commissioner for Human Rights |

# Introduction

Today, transitional justice has taken on unprecedented proportions. It is being invoked as a response to large-scale abuses, gross violations of human rights, violations of international humanitarian law and international crimes. The aim of this book is to demonstrate that with the development of transitional justice, international transitional justice law has been growing and has become a branch of international law. International transitional justice law is a set of international rules that are mobilised and applied in the field of transitional justice. On the one hand, practices and mechanisms, mainly to respond to international law violations in times of transition or after an armed conflict, have been feeding this branch of international law. On the other hand, international law has been progressively defining international obligations of states in the field of transitional justice even if there is still room for improvement.

This book proposes an understanding of transitional justice as a global phenomenon that has influenced international law, raised new legal issues and led to a new branch of international law. It critically reviews and assesses the emergence, international diffusion, processes and mechanisms of transitional justice, and the international rules that have been mobilising in that field. The book is divided into three main parts.

Part 1 is a general introduction to the concept of transitional justice. It presents the emergence and international spread of transitional justice. It shows how transitional justice has developed internationally and examines its origins, definition, history, the contributions of international organisations to its development, and theoretical approaches in this field.

Part 2 examines the main mechanisms of transitional justice that have been created by states and the international community. These mechanisms are responses to violations of international law and have gradually contributed to the emergence of international transitional justice law. They include judicial processes such as international and national criminal tribunals. They also include non-judicial procedures such as truth commissions, reparations programmes, vetting initiatives and institutional reforms. Part 2 describes these mechanisms, their creation, composition, mandate, operation, and contributions to international transitional justice law.

Part 3 analyses the sources and rules of international transitional justice law. Building on the developments in Part 2 on transitional justice mechanisms, Part 3 identifies the international sources of transitional justice, examines and discusses the international obligations of states implementing tran-

HTTPS://DOI.ORG/10.1163/9789004766655-002

sitional justice or confronted with transitional justice. It particularly links transitional justice to branches of international law and shows that international transitional justice law relies on these branches to exist.

The book concludes that there is still room for improvement in this branch of international law, which tends to have its own peculiarities and faces challenges.

# PART 1

# Introducing Transitional Justice: The International Appearance and the Diffusion of the Concept

# Introduction to Part 1

Part 1 examines how the term "transitional justice" has emerged, developed and spread internationally. The first chapter examines the origins and definition of transitional justice. The second chapter looks at the history of transitional justice and the gradual implementation of transitional justice. The third chapter looks at the dissemination of the concept of transitional justice by international organisations, and the fourth chapter presents the main theoretical approaches to the field of transitional justice in relation to dealing with past violations of international law.

CHAPTER 1

# Origins, Definition and Contents of the Term "Transitional Justice"

Where does the term "transitional justice" come from and when was it born? This question has provoked some debate among scholars. Ruti Teitel, born in Argentina and a law professor in the United States, wrote that she coined the term in 1991 and used it to refer to problems in the field of justice during the radical political changes that follow in the wake of dictatorial regimes.[1] Arthur Paige noted that the term was used before 1991.[2] According to Paige, it was used in 1948 in the title of a book chapter on the American occupation of New Mexico.[3] He added that in 1989, two years before Teitel, the philosopher Milton Fisk used the term to refer to transitions to socialism. Indeed, in his book, Fisk used the term *transitional justice* once,[4] and referred several times to what he called the *transitional state*.[5]

There are other references in the literature to *transitional justice* after 1948 and before 1989. In an article on criminological theory published in the journal *Insurgent Sociologist* in 1975, James P. Brady used the term in relation to the need to reform the American criminal justice system. He stated: "Our *transitional justice* reform measures must provide for the direct self-defense of the community against crime, and must include social services for offenders and the general public."[6] In Brady's article, transitional justice referred to the transition from an existing criminal justice system to one that was considered more appropriate and just.

In 1983, in an issue of *The Monist*, Robert Simon used the term "justice in transition" in an article in which he questioned the applicability at the inter-

1 Ruti Teitel, 'Editorial Note – Transitional Justice Globalized' (2008) 2(1) *International Journal of Transitional Justice* 1, 1. See also, Ruti Teitel, 'Globalized Transitional Justice' (2010) Working paper n°8, Center for Global Studies, 1. The author states that in 1991, she used the term in an application for research project funding to the United States Institute of Peace.

2 Arthur Paige, 'How 'Transitions' Reshaped Human Rights: A Conceptual History of Transitional Justice' (2009) 31(2) *Human Rights Quarterly* 321, 329–330, note 23.

3 *Ibid.*

4 Milton Fisk, *The State and Justice: An Essay in Political Theory* (Cambridge University Press 1989) 305.

5 For example, *Ibid.*, 304 and 306.

6 James P Brady, 'The Talking Stone: Evolution and Action of People's Criminology' (1975) 5(4) *Insurgent Sociologist* 73, 78. Emphasis added.

 | HTTPS://DOI.ORG/10.1163/9789004766655-004

national level of a theory of social justice generally implemented within the state.[7] The article focused on the conditions that would have to be met in the context of a transition from the internal order (state system) to the international order (global level).[8] Acknowledging his failure to find a theory applicable to this issue, Simon referred to *transitional justice*: "although I have not been able to provide a theory of justice in transition, perhaps enough has been said to show that the issues of transitional justice need special attention in international affairs."[9] It would not be surprising to find other uses of the term "transitional justice" used elsewhere in the literature.

It is clear that the term was used several times before the 1990s. However, given the current state of knowledge about the origins of transitional justice, the meaning that was given to the term prior to 1990 was very different from the meaning that Teitel claimed to have adopted in the early 1990s.

Transitional justice was first used as the title of a book in 1995. The United States Institute of Peace published a compilation entitled *Transitional Justice*.[10] Initiated in 1991,[11] edited by Neil Kritz and comprising three volumes, it brought together doctrinal works and articles – some already published in journals or books, as well as case studies and legal documents on justice in the context of political transitions. These massive volumes on transitional justice make it clear that transitional justice refers to implementing justice in a political transition and the problem such a transition poses.

The birth of the concept of transitional justice, understood as the application of justice in times of transition, can therefore be dated to the early 1990s. However, identifying the first uses of the term is not enough to understand the dynamics that influenced its emergence and promoted its use. The invention of transitional justice and the issues it describes are the result of research on political transitions, which have been the subject of growing interest, especially since the 1970s. Doctrinal scholarship in political science developed a theory called *transitology*, and other legal scholars began to take an interest in the process of justice after the fall of an authoritarian regime (discussed in Section 1). Meanwhile, civil society organisations and their actions against

7 Robert L Simon, 'Global Justice and the Authority of States' (1983) 66(4) *The Monist* 557, 567.

8 *Ibid.*

9 *Ibid.*, 569.

10 Neil J Kritz (ed), *Transitional Justice, How Emerging Democracies Reckon with Former Regimes*, 3 vol., (United States Peace Institute 1995).

11 Neil J Kritz, 'The Dilemmas of Transitional Justice' in Neil J Kritz (ed), *Transitional Justice, How Emerging Democracies Reckon with Former Regimes*, vol. 1 (United States Peace Institute 1995) xix.

authoritarian rules, and the United Nations, faced with human rights violations in many states, became interested in dealing with the past (discussed in Sections 2 and 3). This gave transitional justice an international audience, influencing its definition and content (discussed in Section 4), although competing phrases emerged (discussed in Section 5).

## 1 Doctrinal Scholarship: From Transitology to the Invention of Transitional Justice

Transitology is defined as "the study of the systemic change process from authoritarian regimes to democracies or to postauthoritarian regimes."[12] Developed by political scientists, it is devoted to political change, particularly transitions from authoritarian to democratic regimes, and the dynamics that explain them. So defined, it can be considered the closest ancestor of transitional justice, since the latter, when it began to be used, was intended to describe processes of justice during political transitions. This theory is sometimes traced back to Niccolò Machiavelli, who is considered its founder because of his interest in the dynamics of change in political regimes.[13] However, it was not until the 1970s that the theory gained prominence in the United States and, later, became associated with the birth of transitional justice.

Dankwart Alexander Rustow, a professor of political science in the United States, is generally regarded as the author of one of the first modern studies of transitology. In a famous article published in 1970, entitled "Transitions to Democracy," he studied the process of transition from an authoritarian regime to a democratic one, mainly using the cases of Sweden and Turkey.[14] He found that national unity is a prerequisite for the dynamics of democratisation, which then goes through a preparatory phase marked by struggles between political actors, a decision-making phase in which the actors and leaders accept their diversity in unity and agree to institutionalise the democratic process and the rules of the game, before the final phase in which the actors get used to democracy.[15]

12 Jiri S Melich, 'Transitology' in *Encyclopedia of Political Science* 5 (2011) 1683.

13 Philippe C Schmitter and Terry Lynn Karl, 'The Conceptual Travels of Transitologists and Consolidologists: How Far to the East Should They Attempt to Go?' (1994) 53(1) *Slavic Review* 173, 174.

14 Rustow A Dankwart, 'Transitions to Democracy: Toward a Dynamic Model' (1970) 2(3) *Comparative Politics* 337, 350–361.

15 *Ibid.*

As the number of political transitions increased in the context of the Cold War, other studies followed, including a 1982 book on political transitions in the south of Europe and in Latin America[16] and, in particular, the publication in 1986 of *Transitions from Authoritarian Rule*, a four-volume book on political transitions from authoritarian to democratic regimes.[17] The first two volumes were devoted mainly to political transitions in Southern Europe and Latin America. The third volume examined aspects of political transitions from a comparative perspective, and the final volume drew conclusions. Based on many case studies, the general assumption of transitologists was that transitions from authoritarian regimes mostly led to democracies. As pointed out by the book's editors, Guillermo O'Donnell and Philippe C. Schmitter:

> Transition in regime type implies movement from something toward something else. For the countries we have been concerned with, the initial something has been (or still is) authoritarian rule, although of differing social base, configuration, longevity, severity, intent, and success. The subsequent something else may be a political democracy, although present-day Turkey and the recent past of Bolivia, Argentina, and, in a different way, contemporary Nicaragua demonstrate that other outcomes are possible.[18]

In general terms, this assumption that political transitions from authoritarian rule lead to democracies has been criticised by many scholars who insist that the outcomes of political transitions are uncertain and unpredictable.[19]

---

16 Julián Santamaría, (Compilación de), *Transición a la democracia en el sur de Europa y América Latina* (Centro de Investigaciones Sociológicas, 1982).

17 Guillermo O'Donnell, Philippe C Schmitter and Laurence Whitehead (eds), *Transitions from Authoritarian Rule: Southern Europe* (The Johns Hopkins University Press 1986); Guillermo O'Donnell, Philippe C Schmitter and Laurence Whitehead (eds), *Transitions from Authoritarian Rule: Latin America* (The Johns Hopkins University Press 1986); Guillermo O'Donnell, Philippe C Schmitter and Laurence Whitehead (eds), *Transitions from Authoritarian Rule: Comparative Perspectives* (The Johns Hopkins University Press 1986); Guillermo O'Donnell and Philippe C Schmitter, *Transitions from Authoritarian Rule. Tentative Conclusions about Uncertain Democracies* (The Johns Hopkins University Press 1986).

18 Guillermo O'Donnell and Philippe C. Schmitter, *Transitions from Authoritarian Rule. Tentative Conclusions about Uncertain Democracies, Ibid.*, 65.

19 See, for example, Guy Hermet, 'Rethinking Transitology' in Aurel Braun and Zoltan Barany (eds), *Dilemmas of Transition: The Hungarian Experience* (Rowman and Littlefield 1999) 33, who wrote that "it is widely understood that transitions correspond only with the extremely varied and unpredictable period of time that elapses between the fall of a regime and the moment when the wheels of power come under the complete control of the political order replacing it- in the best circumstances democracy."

Examples of political transitions that have "failed" or led to regimes that are far from democratic can be found in Africa, for example.

These studies, despite their critics, have pointed to the fact that there are many difficulties that need to be overcome during political transitions, as would be the case later in the transitional justice discourse. The authors of these studies were mainly concerned with the political dynamics of regime change. They did not often include elements of justice for the victims of crimes perpetrated during authoritarian rule or elements of accountability for those accused of crimes. These transitologists were more concerned with the political dynamics and establishing models to explain transitions to democracy. However, as these political scientists insisted on the political dynamics of transitions, some scholars who were also interested in political transitions from a dictatorship to a democracy decided to address the issue of justice and the legacy of authoritarian regimes.

In 1979, John Herz, a professor of political science, organised a conference at the Graduate Center of the City University of New York. The conference dealt with the legacy of authoritarian and totalitarian regimes, and led to the publication of a collective volume in 1982, edited by Herz.[20] Many contributions of that book analysed the denazification and reconstruction of Germany,[21] and the democratic regimes that arose from the Second World War in Italy,[22] Austria,[23] France[24] and Japan.[25] The last three contributions of the book were dedicated to political transitions of the 1970s in Spain,[26] Portugal[27] and Greece.[28]

Although the contributors to this book were interested in the political and social dynamics that influenced and shaped transitions, they also devoted

20 John H Herz (ed), *From Dictatorship to Democracy: Coping with the Legacies of Authoritarianism and Totalitarianism* (Greenwood 1982).

21 *Ibid.*, see Part I of the book entitled 'How West German Democracy Was Rebuilt', with the contributions of: John H Herz, 'Denazification and Related Policies' in *Ibid.*, 15; Karlheinz Niclauss, 'Political Reconstruction at Bonn' in *Ibid.*, 39; Michael Fichter, 'Non-State Organizations and the Problems of Redemocratization' in *Ibid.*, 57; Jutta-B Lange-Quassowski, 'Coming to Terms with the Nazi Past: Schools, Media, and the Formation of Opinion' in *Ibid.*, 83.

22 Giuseppe Di Palma, 'Italy: Is There a Legacy and Is It Fascist?' in John H Herz (ed.), *Ibid.*, 107.

23 Frederick C Engelmann, 'How Austria Has Coped with Two Dictatorial Legacies' in *Ibid.*, 135.

24 Roy C Macridis, 'France: From Vichy to the Fourth Republic' in *Ibid.*, 161.

25 Arthur E Tiedemann, 'Japan Sheds Dictatorship' in *Ibid.*, 179.

26 Edward Malefakis, 'Spain and Its Francoist Heritage' in *Ibid.*, 215.

27 Kenneth Maxwell, 'The Emergence of Portuguese Democracy' in *Ibid.*, 231.

28 Harry J Psomiades, 'Greece: From the Colonels' Rule to Democracy' in *Ibid.*, 251.

parts of their writings to justice and accountability after the Second World War, the trials and purges that took place, and the obstacles and limits that these processes faced – all issues that would later become central to transitional justice. A few examples will illustrate the "avant-garde" achievement of this collective work. Herz, for example, analysed the trials that attempted to enforce criminal accountability of the Nazis after the Second World War and showed that, in the end, few Nazis were convicted. Despite this, he insisted that these trials were important. "To some extent, [he wrote,] at least, the prosecution of Nazi criminality, however flawed, contributed to such an assumption of responsibility. And in any event, the trials constitute one of the rare instances in which a nation has found it possible to try 'its very own' for crimes committed during war."[29] He also examined many issues that are relevant to transitional justice studies today, such as reparations and the "personnel purge" in Germany, and their practical limits – reparations awarded to only a few victims, the issue of replacing purged Nazi personnel, etc. – that this country faced.[30] In his contribution on Italy, Giuseppe Di Palma presented the first efforts to bring some Fascists to justice and the purge in the administration after the Second World War, pointing out that this did not hide the fact that many ultimately escaped accountability in the context of the adoption of an amnesty.[31] Roy C. Macridis explained that accountability after the Second World War was marked by purges in many sectors of French society, including the administration.[32] In Greece, Harry Psomiades pointed out that trials and purges were used after the fall of the dictatorship, although, as in Italy, many of those once in government escaped justice and accountability.[33]

Years after the publication of Herz's book, and following a conference organised by the Aspen Institute, another collective book was published, dealing with issues related to what would later be included in transitional justice.[34] Published in 1988, this collection differed from previous edited volumes in that it did not focus primarily on analysing the political dynamics of transi-

29 John H Herz, 'Denazification and Related Policies' in *Ibid.*, 20–21.

30 *Ibid.*, 21–29.

31 Giuseppe Di Palma, 'Italy: Is There a Legacy and Is It Fascist?' in John H Herz (ed), *From Dictatorship to Democracy: Coping with the Legacies of Authoritarianism and Totalitarianism* (Greenwood 1982) 122.

32 Roy C. Macridis, 'France: From Vichy to the Fourth Republic' in *Ibid.*, 169–177.

33 Harry J Psomiades, 'Greece: From the Colonels' Rule to Democracy' in *Ibid.*, 262–265.

34 *State Crimes: Punishment or Pardon*, papers and report of the conference, November 4–6, 1988, (Aspen Institute 1989). John Herz contributed to the conference, John H Herz, 'An Historical Perspective' *Ibid.*, 11.

tions but rather on justice and the legal dimensions of dealing with past crimes and human rights violations after the fall of a dictatorship.[35] This collective book explored issues such as "punishment," the state's minimum obligation to establish the truth after human rights violations, and the difficulties of bringing former dictators and the military to justice.[36] The book included contributions from people who had played a role in defending human rights in their countries undergoing political change. For example, José Zalaquett, a prominent Chilean human rights defender, wrote a paper on dealing with past human rights violations committed by governments that lost power.[37] Jaime Malamud-Goti, an Argentinian law professor, examined the dilemma facing transition governments.[38]

The early 1990s also saw publications on issues that will be relevant to transitional justice. For example, although she didn't use the term "transitional justice" in her paper, Ruti Teitel published an article in 1990 on the fate of human rights in Latin America after the fall of dictatorships and the advent of democracies.[39] Jaime Malamud-Goti published a paper that was discussed at the 1988 Aspen Institute conference, insisting both on the importance of punishing military officers and on the need to set some limits on prosecutions.[40] Naomi Roht-Arriaza published a detailed article on the obligation of new governments formed after a transition to prosecute and punish those who have violated human rights.[41] On the same subject, there was also an

---

35 Alice H Henkin, 'Conference Report' in *State Crimes: Punishment or Pardon* (The Aspen Institute, 1989) 1–7, reprinted in Neil J Kritz (ed), *Transitional Justice, How Emerging Democracies Reckon with Former Regimes*, vol. 1 (United States Peace Institute 1995) 184–188.

36 *Ibid.*

37 José Zalaquett, 'Confronting Human Rights Violations Committed by Former Governments: Principles Applicable and Political Constraints' in *State Crimes: Punishment or Pardon*, papers and report of the conference, November 4–6, 1988, (Aspen Institute 1989) 26–65; reprinted in Neil J Kritz (ed), *Ibid.*, 3–31.

38 Jaime Malamud-Goti, 'Trying violators of human rights: The dilemma of transitional democratic governments' in *State Crimes, Ibid.*, 71–88.

39 Ruti Teitel, 'How are the New Democracies of the Southern Cone Dealing with the Legacy of the Past Human Rights Abuses' (Paper presented to the Council on Foreign Relations Latin America Project, New York, May 17, 1990), excerpt reprinted in Neil J Kritz (ed), *Transitional Justice, How Emerging Democracies Reckon with Former Regimes*, vol. 1 (United States Peace Institute 1995) 146–153.

40 Jaime Malamud-Goti, 'Transitional Governments in the Breach: Why Punish State Criminals?' (1990) 12(1) *Human Rights Quarterly* 1. Excerpt Reprinted in Neil J Kritz (ed), *Ibid.*, 190.

41 Naomi Roht-Arriaza, 'State Responsibility to Investigate and Prosecute Grave Human Rights Violations in International Law' (1990) 78 *California Law Review* 449.

interesting debate in the *Yale Law Journal* between Diane Orentlicher and Carlos Nino, two prominent scholars.[42] The former argued that there was an obligation under international law to prosecute human rights violations committed by the previous government, and the latter disagreed, pointing to the complex context of transitional government and the constraints faced by new governments, for example, in Argentina.[43] Also interested in the complexities of political transitions, in one of his major books, the political scientist Samuel Huntington analysed "transitions to democracy between 1974 and 1990," which he called a "third wave of democratization," distinguishing this wave from the first one, between 1828 and 1926, and the second one, between 1943 and 1962.[44] After examining the experiences and dilemmas of holding accountable perpetrators in times of political transitions in many European and Latin American countries since the 1970s,[45] Huntington designed the "Guidelines for Democratizers" when it comes to "Dealing with Authoritarian Crimes," weighing up the options available for states in transition such as prosecuting, punishing or forgiving, and forgetting.[46] Even if they are not based on an analysis of inter-

42 Diane F Orentlicher, 'Settlings Accounts: The Duty to Prosecute Human Rights Violations of a Prior Regime' (1991) 100 *Yale Law Journal* 2537; Carlos S Nino, 'The Duty to Punish Human Rights Violations of a Prior Regime: The Case of Argentina' (1991) 100 *The Yale Law Journal* 2619; Diane F Orentlicher, 'A Reply to Professor Nino' (1991) 100 *The Yale Law Journal* 2641.

43 *Ibid.*

44 According to Huntington, "It is often arbitrary to attempt to specify precisely when a regime transition occurs. It is also arbitrary to attempt to specify precisely the dates of democratization waves and reverse waves. It is, nonetheless, often useful to be arbitrary, and the dates of these waves of regime changes are more or less as follows:

"First, long wave of democratization 1828–1926 // First reverse wave 1922–1942 // Second, short wave of democratization 1943–1962 // Second reverse wave 1958–1975 // Third wave of democratization 1974," Samuel P Huntington, *The Third Wave. Democratization in the Late Twentieth Century* (Adarsh Books 1991) 16."

45 *Ibid.*, 211–231.

46 He wrote:

(1) If transformation or transplacement occurred, do not attempt to prosecute authoritarian officials for human rights violations. The political costs of such an effort will outweigh any moral gains.

(2) If replacement occurred and you feel it is morally and politically desirable, prosecute the leaders of the authoritarian regime promptly (within one year of your coming into power) while making clear that you will not prosecute middle- and lower-ranking officials.

(3) Devise a means to achieve a full and dispassionate public accounting of how and why the crimes were committed.

(4) Recognize that on the issue of "prosecute and punish vs. forgive and forget," each alternative presents grave problems, and that the least unsatisfactory course may

national law, Huntington's considerations of options and decision-making concerning prosecutions will lie at the heart of the implementation of transitional justice and the debates on the role of law, both domestically and internationally, in times of transition.

Interested in the role of international law and the human rights discipline in 1992, the French Commission Nationale Consultative des Droits de l'Homme and the International Commission of Jurists organised an international conference under the auspices of the United Nations, in order to discuss impunity of perpetrators of severe human rights violations.[47] Published in 1993, the edited volume presented the contributions of many scholars and experts to this international conference.[48] Even though they did not use the phrase "transitional justice," many of these contributions analysed political transitions in many countries that had experienced authoritarian rule, and examined to what extent justice was delivered regarding past gross human rights violations.[49]

In the same vein, in 1992, the Project on Justice in Times of Transition held its inaugural meeting in Salzburg, Austria, where the question of accountability for gross human rights violations was discussed and the term "transitional justice" was employed. The summary of what happened during the meeting was written by Mary Albon, who used the term "transitional justice" several times. She wrote: "The Project on Justice in Times of Transition was established by the Charter 77 Foundation-New York in an effort to provide perspective, guidance and direction to the decision-makers currently grappling with the grave and complicated issues connected with transitional justice."[50] The project looked at "justice in times of transition," particularly in Latin America and Europe, which had just experienced the fall of communism and were faced with the question of how to turn the page. The project was in the spirit of the conference organised by the Aspen Institute in 1988. But in contrast to

---

well be: do not prosecute, do not punish, do not forgive, and, above all, do not forget. *Ibid.*, 231.

47 Commission nationale consultative des droits de l'homme et Commission internationale des juristes, *L'impunité des auteurs de violations graves des droits de l'homme* Rencontres internationales, 2–5 novembre 1992 (Dijon-Chenôve, 1993).

48 *Ibid.*

49 For example, Emmanuel Decaux, 'Droit international et expériences nationales', *Ibid.*, 27–66.

50 Mary Albon, 'Project on Justice in Times of Transition: Report of the Project's Inaugural Meeting' in Neil J Kritz (ed), *Transitional Justice, How Emerging Democracies Reckon with Former Regimes*, vol. 1 (United States Peace Institute 1995) 42: excerpts from Mary Albon, The Charter Seventy-Seven Foundation – New York, Project on Justice in Times of Transition (Report of the Project's Inaugural Meeting, Salzburg, March 7–10, 1992), 5–18.

what happened at that conference, the term "transitional justice" was used during the inaugural Salzburg meeting, marking one of the very first academic uses of transitional justice to refer to the problem of justice after the fall of a political regime.

In the same year, Juan E. Corradi, Patricia Weiss Fagen and Manuel Antonio Garretón used the phrase "transitional justice" in the introduction to a book they edited, *Fear at the Edge: State Terror and Resistance in Latin America*.[51] They held: "The tension between punishment and reconciliation – the thorny issue of political justice under successor regimes – leads us to explore new notions, such as that of transitional justice."[52] More interestingly, in the same book, Juan Corradi, one of the editors, wrote an article in which he used the phrase several times, describing transitional justice as "a particular and intensive type of political justice: the trial by fiat of a previous regime."[53] He also explained what he considered to be transitional justice, stating:

> Transitional justice is both more and less than ordinary justice. It is more because it aims beyond the simple ordering of human relations: it seeks to achieve moral and political regeneration. It is less than ordinary justice because it is subject to serious irregularities, it is a political formula for the formal elimination of a scapegoat, it is imbued with problematic judgments by the power holders of the moment on the qualities and policies of their predecessors, and it is a constitutive act of a new regime.[54]

In a 1994 article, Ruti Teitel referred explicitly to the phrase "transitional justice" when examining what she called "paradoxes in the revolution of the rule of law."[55] Analysing the difficulties and dilemmas in the field of justice in Hungary and Unified Germany in the context of political transitions in the beginning of the 1990s, she wrote: "The dilemma of successor justice faced by the Hungarian and German courts forms part of a rich dialogue on the

51 Juan E Corradi, Patricia Weiss Fagen, and Manuel Antonio Garretón, 'Introduction: Fear: A Cultural and Political Construct' in Juan E Corradi, Patricia Weiss Fagen, and Manuel Antonio Garretón (eds), *Fear at the Edge: State Terror and Resistance in Latin America* (University of California Press 1992) 10.

52 *Ibid.*

53 Juan E Corradi, 'Toward Societies without Fear' in Juan E Corradi, Patricia Weiss Fagen, and Manuel Antonio Garretón (eds), *Ibid.*, 285.

54 *Ibid.*, 285–286.

55 Ruti G Teitel, 'Paradoxes in the Revolution of the Rule of Law (Symposium: Constitutionalism in the Post-Cold War Era)" (1994) 19(239) *Yale Journal of International Law* 239, 241.

nature of law. H.L.A. Hart and Lon Fuller's debate on transitional justice wrestles with the relationship between law and morality, between positivism and natural law."[56] With the development of commissions mandated in some states to investigate past human rights violations, Priscilla Hayner published a paper on the subject,[57] later followed by Margaret Popkin and Naomi Roht-Arriaza,[58] as well as by an interdisciplinary discussion at Harvard Law School on the same topic.[59] After decommunisation, many papers began to be written on the subject, analysing the political transitions and accountability initiatives, such as purges and lustration laws that some Eastern European states underwent.[60]

So, by 1995, there were many analyses and publications on how to deal with human rights violations after the fall of an authoritarian regime. All these papers and books on political transitions and justice were quite diverse, and they were generally written by political scientists and legal specialists, most of whom were members of the human rights movement. At the time, there was no academically accepted term to name the field of these new developments focusing on political transitions and justice.

It was in this context that the three-volume book *Transitional Justice*, edited by Neil Kritz from the United States Institute of Peace, was published in 1995.[61] As though he were aware of the broad dimensions of transitional justice, Kritz added the subtitle *How Emerging Democracies Reckon with Former Regimes*. As Charles Duryea Smith explained in the introduction, the book was limited to "the way that emerging *democratic* societies address the legacy of their repression of their own people," and did not include analyses on "non-democratic successor states," on "the transition policies of occupation authorities (such as post-World War II Japan)" or on "the process of democratization."[62] With editor's notes included on many of the topics, the book brought together

---

56 *Ibid.*

57 Priscilla B Hayner, 'Fifteen Truth Commissions-1974 to 1994: A Comparative Study' (1994) 16(4) *Human Rights Quarterly* 597.

58 Margaret Popkin and Naomi Roht-Arriaza 'Truth as Justice: Investigatory Commissions in Latin America' (1995) 20(1) *Law & Social Inquiry* 79.

59 *Truth Commissions: A Comparative Assessment. An Interdisciplinary Discussion Held at Harvard Law School in May 1996*, Organized by the Human Rights Program Harvard Law School and the World Peace Foundation, (Harvard Law School Human Rights Program, 1997).

60 For example, Herman Schwartz, 'Lustration in Eastern Europe' (1994) 1(2) *Parker School of East European Law* 141. For more on lustration and purges, see Part 2 of this book.

61 Neil J Kritz (ed), *Transitional Justice. How Emerging Democracies Reckon with Former Regimes*, 3 vol., (United States Institute of Peace 1995).

62 Charles Duryea Smith 'Introduction', Neil J Kritz (ed), in *Ibid.*, vol. 1, xvi.

hundreds of articles and documents, many of which had been published previously and elsewhere, on the subject of justice in times of political transitions.[63]

Volume I of the book was devoted to "general considerations" on, for example, the role of justice in times of transitions, moral issues relating to the need for accountability, criminal and non-criminal sanctions, truth commissions and redress for victims.[64] That volume contained many papers published in the 1980s and early 1990s. For example, it reprinted excerpts of articles by Guillermo O'Donnell and Philippe C. Schmitter, John Herz, Ruti Teitel, Diane Orentlicher, José Zalaquett, Priscilla Hayner, Carlos Nino[65] and others. Volume II dealt with country studies of twenty-one transition processes, mainly in Europe and Latin America: Germany (after Nazism and after communism), France, Denmark, Belgium, Italy, South Korea, Greece, Portugal, Spain, Argentina, Uruguay, Brazil, Chile, Uganda, Czechoslovakia, Hungary, Bulgaria, Albania, Russia and Lithuania.[66] Volume III brought together documents, many of them legal, relating to transitional justice processes in many countries, mainly in Europe and Latin America, but also in Asia and Africa.[67]

This edited volume was very important for the development and recognition of transitional justice for three main reasons. First, it brought under the umbrella of "transitional justice" many previous scholarly publications, legal documents, reports, and national and international practices. The use of this term as the title of an edited volume was unprecedented at a time when the term was still unknown to the general public and most social scientists.

Second, it gave "transitional justice" a wider audience. The concept, which had been circulating only among a few scholars, became known to a wider scholarly community and beyond. This international audience for transitional justice was also influenced by current developments in the 1990s in dealing with past crimes and serious human rights violations. The publication of the book in 1995 coincided with reconciliation efforts in South Africa that attracted international attention. South Africa, a state long criticised and in part ostracised by the international community for its apartheid policies, faced transitional justice dilemmas (such as whether or not to prosecute for-

---

63 *Ibid.*, xvii.

64 *Ibid.*

65 For their articles, see above, this section of Chapter 1.

66 Neil J Kritz (ed), *Transitional Justice. How Emerging Democracies Reckon with Former Regimes*, vol. II, Countries Studies, (United States Institute of Peace 1995).

67 Neil J Kritz (ed), *Transitional Justice. How Emerging Democracies Reckon with Former Regimes*, vol. III, Laws, Rulings, and Reports (United States Institute of Peace 1995).

mer rulers) and established a truth and reconciliation commission to deal with its past. Nelson Mandela, who was a famous and well-known long-term political prisoner who became president of South Africa, wrote the foreword to the book.[68] The publication also coincided with the first experience of international criminal justice since the Second World War. The United Nations Security Council established the International Criminal Tribunals for the former Yugoslavia and for Rwanda to deal with the accountability of those responsible for international crimes committed in those two countries.[69]

Third, the book's publication demonstrated that although transitional justice was rooted in the question of dealing with past violations or crimes committed by previous regimes, it was a multidisciplinary field, as many of the contributions and analyses collected in the book came from different disciplines such as law, political science, history, sociology, theology, psychology and anthropology. Thus, it is not an exaggeration to say that *Transitional Justice* actually promoted the emergence of transitional justice as a new and distinct field in the social sciences. Other publications on transitional justice followed, such as *Transitional Justice and the Rule of Law in New Democracies*, edited by A. James McAdams in 1997,[70] and most notably, in the early 2000s, Ruti Teitel's book, *Transitional Justice*.[71]

This scholarly momentum marked the beginning of a non-stop expansion of the notion of transitional justice, with several more articles and books on the subject being published since the early 2000s. While these scholarly publications were interested in analysing justice in times of transition, civil society organisations were also fighting for the rights of victims of dictatorships and armed conflicts, contributing to the emergence and diffusion of transitional justice.

68 Nelson Mandela, 'Foreword' in Neil J Kritz (ed), *Ibid.*, vol. I, xi.

69 For The former Yugoslavia, UN Security Council Resolution 827, UN doc. S/RES/827 (1993) and UN Security Council Resolution 808, UN doc. S/RES/808 (1993); for Rwanda, UN Security Council, Resolution 955, UN doc. S/RES/955 (1994), 8 November 1994.

70 A James McAdams (ed), *Transitional Justice and the Rule of Law in New Democracies* (University of Notre Dame Press 1997).

71 Ruti G Teitel, *Transitional Justice* (Oxford University Press 2000).

## 2 Civil Society and the Emergence and Diffusion of Transitional Justice

Civil society organisations, including NGOs and private organisations, have played a significant role in the development and dissemination of the concept of transitional justice, as well as its implementation. For example, while the concept of transitional justice was first introduced in academic scholarship, the International Center for Transitional Justice, an NGO founded in New York in 2001, helped to promote it.[72] This private organisation, which provided transitional justice expertise to many states, was founded by Alex Boraine who was the deputy chair of the South African Truth and Reconciliation Commission and had published on transitional justice issues in South Africa;[73] Paul Van Zyl who acted as executive secretary of the South African Truth and Reconciliation Commission; and Priscilla Hayner, specialist of truth commissions who has published on that subject.[74]

However, prior to the establishment of this organisation, civil society organisations in many states under dictatorships were fighting for accountability and respect for victims' rights, which would later become central to the implementation of transitional justice. Transitional justice would not have developed internationally after the 1970s without the involvement of these organisations and their fight for the rights of victims in countries subject to authoritarian rule or armed conflict. Historically, the gradual implementation of transitional justice has generally been forged through the multidimensional actions of groups of victims and various civil society organisations, including NGOs, which have campaigned for justice for victims and accountability for perpetrators.

Many civil society organisations in states in transition and in the international arena have been proposing solutions to deliver justice, participating in shaping transitional justice, and calling for national and international legal action against perpetrators. They have also insisted on national and international compliance with the rule of law and respect for victims' rights. In most countries that have undergone transitional justice, civil society has

72 ICTJ, 'Annual Report', 2001–2002, 7.

73 Alex Boraine, Janet Levy and Ronel Scheffer (eds), *Dealing with the Past: Truth and Reconciliation in South Africa* (2nd edn, Institute for Democracy in South Africa 1997); Alex Boraine, *A Country Unmasked: Inside South Africa's Truth and Reconciliation Commission* (Oxford University Press 2000).

74 Priscilla B Hayner, 'Fifteen Truth Commissions-1974 to 1994: A Comparative Study' (1994) 16(4) *Human Rights Quarterly* 597; Priscilla B Hayner, *Unspeakable Truths: Facing the Challenge of Truth Commissions* (Routledge 2001).

played an important role in its implementation. In many cases, the involvement of state and international organisations in transitional justice implementation has been prompted by pressure and demands from civil society organisations, particularly groups representing victims and their defenders. Scholars have analysed and highlighted the role of civil society organisations in times of transition and in the implementation of transitional justice, or the role they should play.[75] Some publications have also focused on case studies of the role of these organisations in transitional or post-conflict states.[76]

Some few examples of the early and recent involvement of civil society organisations in transitional justice illustrate the instrumental role they have been playing. For instance, in the context of forced disappearances that occurred in Argentina's dictatorship in the late 1970s, the Mothers of the Plaza de Mayo emerged as a powerful civil society movement that drew attention to the fate of people who had disappeared.[77] The "Mothers" used to walk around the Plaza de Mayo in Buenos Aires, the capital of Argentina, to protest against the country's political authorities and demand information about the fate of their sons and daughters who had disappeared amid the context of political repression during the Argentina Junta. The Mothers of the Plaza de Mayo movement is considered to be one of the earliest examples of the call for the implementation

75 See, for example, Paul Gready and Simmons Robins, 'Rethinking Civil Society and Transitional Justice: Lessons from Social Movements and 'New' Civil Society', (2017) 21(1) *The International Journal of Human Rights* 956; David Backer, 'Civil Society and Transitional Justice: Possibilities, Patterns and Prospects' (2003) 2(3) *Journal of Human Rights* 297; Elin Skaar and Eric Wiebelhaus-Brahm, 'The Drivers of Transitional Justice: An Analytical Framework for Assessing the Role of Actors' (2013) 31(2) *Nordic Journal of Human Rights*, 127; Paige Arthur and Christalla Yakinthou, 'Refocusing on Civil Society: How to Make – Not Miss – Connections' in Paige Arthur and Christalla Yakinthou (eds), *Transitional Justice, International Assistance, and Civil Society: Missed Connections* (Cambridge University Press 2018); Eric Wiebelhaus-Brahm, 'Transitional Justice, Civil Society and the Development of the Rule of Law in Post-conflict Societies' (2007) 9(4) *International Journal of Not-for-Profit Law*.

76 Olivera Simić and Zala Volčič (eds), *Transitional Justice and Civil Society in the Balkans* (Springer 2013); Łukasz Bojarski, 'Civil Society Organizations for and with the Courts and Judges – Struggle for the Rule of Law and Judicial Independence: The Case of Poland 1976–2020' (2021) 22 *German Law Journal* 1344; Joanne Wallis and Lia Kent (eds), *Reconceiving Civil Society and Transitional Justice Lessons from Asia and the Pacific* (Routledge 2020); Hugo van der Merwe and Jasmina Brankovic (eds), *Advocating Transitional Justice in Africa. The Role of Civil Society* (Springer 2018).

77 On that movement, see Marguerite Guzman Bouvard, *Revolutionizing Motherhood: The Mothers of the Plaza de Mayo* (SR Books-Rowman & Littlefield Publishers 2002).

of the right to the truth and the right of families to know the fate of their loved ones, rights that lie at the heart of transitional justice.[78]

This movement and other civil society movements in Latin America helped draw the United Nations' attention to the need to combat "enforced or involuntary disappearances" in the late 1970s and early 1980s. Unsurprisingly, after the fall of the Argentinian dictatorship, the new political authorities created a truth commission, a mechanism of transitional justice, to investigate disappearances and address the past.[79] Thus, the establishment of this truth commission was rooted in civil society movements and was a response to calls for respect for the right to truth, an important right for victims in transitional justice and international law. There are other examples of the involvement of civil society in the early implementation of transitional justice in the 1990s. For example, Crocker writes that in South Africa "civil society – through conferences and public hearings – helped forge the idea of a truth commission."[80] A truth commission was established in 1995 in South Africa, drawing international attention to this mechanism, which would become one of the most widely used in transitional justice as a response to gross human rights violations. Sometimes, civil society organisations and NGOs had engaged in truth-seeking, just as truth commissions had, publishing voluminous reports on human rights violations during armed conflict or authoritarian rule.[81]

Transitional justice has also been developed through the role of civil society organisations in establishing criminal accountability in international and national criminal proceedings, in documenting human rights violations and

78 Patricia Naftali, 'Crafting a "Right to Truth" in International Law: Converging Mobilizations, Diverging Agendas?' (2013) XIII *Champ pénal/Penal field*, online: http://journals.openedition.org/champpenal/9245 (last accessed, 11 February 2026). All the websites cited in this book were accessed on 11 February 2026.

79 On that commission, see below Chapter 6, Section 1.2.2, of this book.

80 David A Crocker, 'Truth Commissions, Transitional Justice, and Civil Society' in Robert I Rotberg and Dennis Thompson (ed), *Truth v. Justice. The Morality of Truth Commissions*, (Princeton University Press 2000) 110.

81 See, for example, the report of the Catholic Church in Guatemala, REMHI, *Informe del Proyecto Interdiocesano de Recuperación de la Memoria Histórica Guatemala: Nunca Más*, IV Tomos (Oficina de Derechos Humanos del Arzobispado de Guatemala 1998); on the authoritarian rule in Chad during the regime of Hissein Habré, see Olivier Bercault (Écrit en collaboration avec Reed Brody), *La Plaine des Morts. Le Tchad de Hissène Habré 1982–1990*, Basé sur les recherches de Olivier Bercault, Reed Brody, Maria Koulouris, Martien Schotsmans, Human Rights Watch; Avec la participation de: Fédération Internationale des ligues des Droits de l'Homme, Association des Victimes des Crimes du Régime de Hissène Habré, Association Tchadienne pour la Promotion et la Défense des Droits de l'Homme, Human Rights Data Analysis Group (Black Print Cpi Ibérica, Human Rights Watch, 2013).

international crimes, in highlighting the situation of victims and in advocating for prosecutions and reparations. For example, civil society organisations have been involved in the creation and activities of the International Criminal Court, which is today an instrument of transitional justice, pushing for prosecutions in case of perpetrations of international crimes committed in post-conflict states, and for the awarding of reparations to many victims of these crimes.[82] In Rwanda, civil society organisations played a part in using the Gacaca, a traditional Rwandan mechanism, to address crimes of genocide committed in the country.[83]

Against the backdrop of the role played by international organisations and states in the implementation of transitional justice, the actions of civil society and groups of victims should not be overlooked in the emergence of international transitional justice law. Thus, in terms of its origins and dissemination, transitional justice appears to be both a new concept used by doctrine (especially American) to describe the problems of justice in the context of transitions, and a network made up of individuals, civil society organisations defending victims' rights and NGOs, including the International Centre for Transitional Justice, which offer their services to states wishing to respond to crimes and serious violations committed on their territory. While these developments were taking place, the United Nations was also engaged in work to address human rights violations, which was inextricably linked to transitional justice and encouraged its emergence and institutionalisation.

---

82 On this topic, see for example, Marlies Glasius, *The International Criminal Court: A Global Civil Society Achievement* (Routledge 2006). See, for example, the 2025 annual report of the Office of the Prosecutor (OPP) which mentions that: "During 2025, the Office continued strengthening its work with CSOs through active engagement and collaboration," ICC, 'Office of the Prosecutor Annual Report 2025', 75. See pages 75–78 for more details on this work with civil society organisations (CSOs). Reports on the activities of the ICC Trust Fund for victims generally mentions the involvement of civil society organisations regarding the awarding of reparations to victims of international crimes; see, for example, Trust Fund for Victims, 'Realising reparative programmes in challenging times. Annual Report 2021', at 35; ICC, *The Prosecutor v. Thomas Lubanga Dyilo*, Public Redacted Version of Trust Fund for Victims' Fifth Update Report on the implementation of reparations in the Lubanga and Ntaganda cases, submitted on 28 October 2025, no. ICC-01/04-01/06-2927-Conf., para. 103.

83 Paul Gready, ' 'You're Either with Us or Against Us': Civil Society and Policy Making in Post-genocide Rwanda' (2010) 109(437) *African Affairs* 637.

## 3 The United Nations and the Emergence and Diffusion of Transitional Justice

The United Nations did not use the term "transitional justice" extensively before the early 2000s. However, the work done within the organisation prior to that date contributed to the birth of the concept and its international recognition. Indeed, since its creation at the end of the Second World War, the United Nations has been somewhat involved in the human rights movement and the fight against international crimes, following the end of the Nuremberg and Tokyo trials. Within the UN, the International Law Commission (ILC), created in 1947,[84] was interested in the formulation of the *Principles of International Law Recognized in the Charter of the Nürnberg Tribunal and in the Judgment of the Tribunal*, and in the creation of an international criminal tribunal that would deal with international crimes such as those committed during the Second World War.[85] This work of the ILC was a precursor to the legal establishment of the criminal accountability of perpetrators of international crimes at the international level, including, of course, criminal accountability in times of political transition. But despite these new studies on accountability and the means to establish criminal accountability at the international level, the project was blocked by the Cold War and it was not until the 1990s that new international criminal tribunals were established, as we will see.

Within the UN, however, some work, particularly in the field of human rights and the fight against enforced disappearances, was interested in what would later become core elements or issues of transitional justice. The UN was interested in enforced disappearances – which consisted of dictatorial regimes abducting people, giving no information about their fate and thus making them "disappear" – which was a common practice, especially in Latin America countries, in the 1970s and early 1980s.[86] These countries underwent political transitions after the fall of authoritarian regimes, which, as we have seen, have been analysed by transitologists and political scientists. The new political regimes in these countries were also faced with social demands from families,

84 Resolution 174(II). Establishment of an International Law Commission, UN doc. A/RES/174(II), 21 November 1947.

85 ILC, 'Yearbook of the International Law Commission', vol. II, Part II, 1950, 374–379, paras. 95–145.

86 See 'Question of Human Rights of all Persons Subjected to any Form of Detention or Imprisonment, in Particular: Question of Missing and Disappeared Persons', Report of the Working Group on enforced or involuntary disappearances, UN doc. E/CN.4/1435, 26 January 1981, 21, para. 45.

who urged them to reveal the truth about the fate of their loved ones who had disappeared during various dictatorships. The first truth commissions, now known as transitional justice mechanisms, were set up to investigate and tell the truth about disappearances and forced disappearances in Uganda (1974), Bolivia (1982), Argentina (1983) and Zimbabwe (1985).[87]

In this context, a resolution on the fight against "enforced or involuntary disappearances" was adopted in 1981 by the UN Sub-Commission on Prevention of Discrimination and Protection of Minorities,[88] which was part of the UN Commission on Human Rights. This resolution echoed a provision already known in international humanitarian law. The 1977 Additional Protocol I to the 1949 Geneva Conventions of 12 August 1949, and relating to the protection of victims of international armed conflicts, insisted on "the right of families to know the fate of their relatives" after armed conflicts and on the obligation of states to search for the missing.[89] In the human rights field, this Sub-Commission reiterated "the right of families to know the fate of their relatives"[90] and recommended the Human Rights Commission "to urge States in which persons have been reported to have disappeared, to repeal or refrain from adopting laws which could impede inquiries concerning such disappearances."[91] This was one of the first formulations of the recognition of what would later be called the right to truth, and be considered an important element of transitional justice.[92]

In the same vein, in 1983, faced with the questions of amnesties that had arisen in Europe and Latin America in the 1970s, the Sub-Commission asked a special rapporteur, the French magistrate Louis Joinet, to draw up a report on amnesty laws and their role in safeguarding and promoting human rights.[93]

---

87 See below Chapter 6, on truth commissions.

88 Resolution 15 (XXXIV), Question of human rights in the case of persons under any form of detention or imprisonment (932nd meeting of the Sub-Commission, 10 September 1981), UN doc. E/CN.4/1512, 28 September 1981, 88.

89 Articles 32 and 33 of the Protocol Additional to the Geneva Conventions of 12 August 1949, and Relating to the Protection of Victims of International Armed Conflicts (Protocol I), of 8 June 1977.

90 Resolution 15 (XXXIV), Question of human rights in the case of persons under any form of detention or imprisonment (932nd meeting of the Sub-Commission, 10 September 1981), UN doc. E/CN.4/1512, 28 September 1981, 88.

91 *Ibid.*, 89.

92 See below Part 3, for various details on the right to know.

93 'Study on Amnesty Laws and their Role in the Safeguard and Promotion of Human Rights', Report by Louis Joinet, Special Rapporteur of the Sub-Commission on Prevention of Discrimination and Protection of Minorities, UN doc. E/CN.4/SUB.2/1985/16, 21 June 1985, para. 1.

Joinet submitted his report, which was limited to amnesties for political offences, in 1985.[94] The report considered amnesties as the legal expression of a political act aimed at promoting or protecting human rights, and in some cases securing the return or consolidation of democracy.[95] Amnesty was seen here as a positive and necessary act, far from the disapproval that it would later arouse, especially in the human rights community, as an act that marked the beginning of democracy, promoted national consensus or played an important role in defusing or stopping hostilities in the event of armed conflict.[96] The report contained a section entitled "Amnesty and the Transition to Democracy"[97] that looked at the adoption of amnesty laws in the context of political transitions. However, it distinguished between the unilateral amnesties adopted in Chile in 1978 and in Argentina in 1983, which were aimed at forgetting the abuses committed, and the amnesty adopted in Uruguay in 1985, which was the result of a broad consensus among the political class.[98] The 1985 Joinet report also excluded crimes against humanity from the political offences (the main subject of the report) for which amnesty could be granted.[99]

Many other important elements of transitional justice today are actually rooted in the work of the United Nations on human rights violations and the international obligations of states, in particular the UN Human Rights Commission and its Sub-Commission on Prevention of Discrimination and Protection of Minorities. In 1989, Theo Van Boven, was mandated by the Sub-Commission to undertake "a study concerning the right to restitution, compensation and rehabilitation for victims of gross violations of human rights and fundamental freedoms"; simply put, to undertake a study on the right to reparation.[100] He issued a report in 1993 that contained "proposals concerning reparation to victims of gross violations of human rights," which identified restitution, compensation, rehabilitation, satisfaction and guarantees of non-repetition as forms of reparation.[101] Later, he issued another report on the

94 *Ibid.*, See paras. 5–6 dedicated to the "scope of the study."

95 *Ibid.*

96 *Ibid.*, para. 7. On amnesties and its rejection by some international human rights bodies, see below Chapters 8 and 9.

97 *Ibid.*, paras. 30–32.

98 *Ibid.*

99 *Ibid.*, paras. 62–64.

100 'Study Concerning the Right to Restitution, Compensation and Rehabilitation for Victims of Gross Violations of Human Rights and Fundamental Freedoms', Final report submitted by Mr. Theo van Boven, Special Rapporteur, UN doc. E/CN.4/Sub.2/1993/8, 2 July 1993, para. 1.

101 *Ibid.*, para. 137.

same subject on the request of the same Sub-Commission.[102] Within the UN, Cherif Bassiouni continued the work of Theo Van Boven and also produced reports on reparation.[103] Reparation will come to be considered later as one of the "pillars" of transitional justice, and transitional justice actors will rely on this research published by the UN.[104]

In the same vein, in 1991, Louis Joinet was again mandated by the Sub-Commission on Prevention of Discrimination and Protection of Minorities "to undertake a study on the impunity of perpetrators of human rights violations."[105] In 1997, he published a report in which he identified several principles within the main elements of the fight against impunity: the right to know (that includes the "inalienable right to the truth"), the right to justice and the right to reparation (including guarantees of non-repetition of violations).[106] Within the UN, Diane Orentlicher continued the work and included the principles in her published report in 2004.[107] These main elements of these principles (the right to the truth, the right to justice, the right to reparation and guarantees of non-repetition of violations), known as the "Joinet principles," would later be labelled "pillars of transitional justice."[108]

With the development of the concept in scholarship and the important role that the International Centre for Transitional Justice began to play in providing assistance to states emerging from armed conflict or dictatorship, the United Nations also began to use the term transitional justice and played an important role in its dissemination. The term transitional justice was quickly

---

102 'Revised Set of Basic Principles and Guidelines on the Right to Reparation for Victims of Gross Violations of Human Rights and Humanitarian Law', prepared by Mr. Theo van Boven pursuant to Sub-Commission decision 1995/117, Annex Basic Principles and Guidelines on the Right to Reparation for Victims of Gross Violations of Human Rights and Humanitarian Law, UN doc. E/CN.4/SUB.2/1996/17, 24 May 1996.

103 For example, 'The Right to Restitution, Compensation and Rehabilitation for Victims of Gross Violations of Human Rights and Fundamental Freedoms', Final report of the Special Rapporteur, Mr. M. Cherif Bassiouni, submitted in accordance with Commission resolution 1999/33, Annex, Basic Principles and Guidelines on the Right to a Remedy and Reparation for Victims of Violations of International Human Rights and Humanitarian Law, UN doc. E/CN.4/2000/62, 18 January 2000.

104 On these pillars, see below the introduction of Part 2.

105 'Question of the Impunity of Perpetrators of Human Rights Violations (Civil and Political)', Revised final report prepared by Mr. Joinet pursuant to Sub-Commission decision 1996/119', UN doc. E/CN.4/Sub.2/1997/20/Rev.1, 2 October 1997, para. 1.

106 *Ibid.*, Annex II.

107 See also, 'Independent Study on Best Practices, Including Recommendations, to Assist States in Strengthening their Domestic Capacity to Combat all Aspects of Impunity', by Professor Diane Orentlicher, UN doc. E/CN.4/2004/88, 27 February 2004, 2.

108 On these pillars, see below the introduction of Part 2.

adopted in English in United Nations documents in early 2000,[109] and later, a number of reports on transitional justice were published on that topic.[110]

However, in French – another official language of the UN – the translation of the expression was marked by variations that left uncertainties. The translation of the first word, "justice," did not pose any particular problem. On the other hand, the translation of the word "transitional" varied from *transitoire* to *de transition*. For example, in a 2002 United Nations document, the name of the organisation International Center for Transitional Justice was translated by the United Nations services as "*Centre international de justice transitoire*."[111] The following year, in a speech to a UN Security Council meeting on the rule of law and justice, the Secretary-General used the term "transitional justice mechanisms," which the UN translation services translated into French as *mécanismes transitoires mis en place aux fins de l'administration de la justice*.[112] The UN also used the phrase *administration de la justice dans les pays sortant d'un conflit*.[113]

In 2004, the United Nations used the literal translation of "transitional justice," translating the International Center for Transitional Justice into French as "*Centre international pour la justice transitionnelle*."[114] But it also moved away from the literal translation of the expression "transitional justice," pre-

109 See, for example, a draft resolution of the third Committee of the General Assembly, Human rights in the administration of justice, UN doc. A/C.3/56/L.60, 20 November 2001, para. 14 that "welcomes the role of the Office of the United Nations High Commissioner for Human Rights in supporting the establishment and functioning of transitional justice mechanisms in post-conflict situations."

110 See, for example, 'Rule of Law and Transitional Justice in Conflict and Post-conflict Societies', Report of the Secretary-General, UN doc. S/2004/616, 23 August 2004; 'Study by the Office of the United Nations High Commissioner for Human Rights on Human Rights and Transitional Justice Activities undertaken by the Human Rights Components of the United Nations system', UN doc. E/CN.4/2006/93, 7 February 2006; 'Annual Report of the United Nations High Commissioner for Human Rights and Reports of the Office of the High Commissioner and the Secretary-General, Analytical study on human rights and transitional justice', UN doc. A/HRC/12/18, 6 August 2009.

111 Letter dated 12 June 2002 from the Permanent Representative of Norway to the United Nations addressed to the President of the Security Council, UN doc. S/2002/663, 13 June 2002, 8.

112 Security Council, 4833rd meeting Wednesday, 24 September 2003, UN doc. S/PV.4833, p. 3 (see the English and French versions of the document).

113 Draft Resolution XVII Human Rights in the Administration of Justice, UN doc. A/58/508/Add.2, 15 December 2003, 101, para. 17.

114 Annex to the note verbale dated 30 June 2004 from the Permanent Mission of Chile to the United Nations addressed to the President of the Security Council Summary of the work of the Security Council during the presidency of Chile (January 2004), UN doc. S/2004/524, 6.

ferring other phrases such as "*Administration de la justice pendant la période de transition*,"[115] and "*Institutions judiciaires de transition*."[116] The notion of transitional justice prevailed over time, with the United Nations eventually adopting the French translation *justice transitionnelle*, which is literally close to the English phrase. Transitional justice/*justice transitionnelle* has fully entered the vocabulary of the United Nations and is used today without hesitation. These translation problems show how difficult it was at the time to use and translate a term that was new to the United Nations vocabulary and that was gradually becoming established. This diverse and multidimensional emergence of the concept of transitional justice reflects the difficulty of finding a clear and precise definition.

## 4 The Definition of Transitional Justice and Its Main Characteristics

There are many ways to define transitional justice.[117] First of all, it is possible to define the two words of the phrase: justice and transition (from which the word "transitional" is derived).

Defining justice in the context of transitional justice sometimes boils down to mobilising theoretical developments on justice and contextualising these developments by bringing them closer to the problems of political transitions. For example, it is possible to draw on the concepts of justice of certain philosophers or theorists in order to understand the meaning of justice in the term "transitional justice."[118] This tendency would lead one to believe that there could be as many definitions of transitional justice as there are definitions or concepts of justice. Here, it is appropriate to stick to justice as an institution within the state, or instituted by states, whose functions include adjudicating

---

115 'The Rule of Law and Transitional Justice in Conflict and Post-conflict Societies', Report of the Secretary-General, UN doc. S/2004/616, 23 August 2004.

116 'Estimates in Respect of Special Political Missions, Good Offices and Other Political Initiatives Authorized by the General Assembly and/or the Security Council', Report of the Secretary-General, Addendum, UN doc. A/59/534/Add.1, 23 November 2004, 76.

117 On the definition of transitional justice, see in particular Oleksii Plotniko, 'Defining Transitional Justice: Scholarly Debate and UN Precision' (2017) 1(3) *Lex Portus* 50.

118 See, for example, Kora Andrieu, 'Political Liberalism after Mass violence: John Rawls and a 'theory' of Transitional Justice' in Susanne Buckley-Zistel, Teresa Koloma Beck, Christian Braun and Friederike Mieth (eds), *Transitional Justice Theories* (Routledge 2013) 85; Helen Gyr, 'Transitional Justice Process and the Justice Theory of Roland Dworkin' (2023) 12(3) *Laws* 35. For more details on transitional justice and theoretical approaches, see below Chapter 4.

disputes, responding to violations of the law and preventing them. This institution may provide for punitive and non-punitive, judicial and non-judicial, contentious and non-contentious mechanisms. Here, however, justice must also be understood in a broader sense than that of the classical judicial institution, which refers exclusively to the courts.[119] Indeed, transitional justice mechanisms are not limited to courts. They also include truth commissions, reparations, traditional justice mechanisms and reform programmes, and so on.[120]

With regard to the definition of transition, it insists on the timing of the implementation of justice. In their book published in 1986, Guillermo O'Donnel and Philippe C. Schmitter wrote: "What we refer to as 'transition' is the interval between one political regime and another."[121] Understanding "transition" is somewhat difficult and poses many problems. Indeed, it is not always easy to place political transition in a precise temporal framework. Transition, in the field of transitional justice, should be understood as a dynamic of change after a dark period marked by large-scale violations. The timeframe of this dynamic does not need to be determined from the moment it is evident that political authorities or other official actors implicated in the political transitions are engaged in examining past violations in order to establish accountability and prevent future violations.

Second, the definition of transitional justice can be determined by examining the scholarship and institutional publications that have used the phrase since the 1990s. Ruti Teitel, a leading scholar in transitional justice, discussed past crimes and responses to them in a 1990 article.[122] She noted that she used

---

119 See, for example, Kai Ambos, 'The Legal Framework of Transitional Justice: A Systematic Study with a Special Focus on the Role of the ICC' in Kai Ambos, Judith Large and Marieke Wierda (eds), *Building a Future on Peace and Justice: Studies on Transitional Justice, Peace and Development* (Springer 2009) 19. He analyses the "contents of the justice element in" the expression transitional justice and held that: "Justice in this sense is to be understood broadly, going beyond mere criminal justice and including certain key elements such as accountability, fairness in the protection and vindication of rights and the prevention and punishment of wrongs."

120 See below Part 2, for details on the mechanisms of transitional justice.

121 Guillermo O'Donnell and Philippe C Schmitter, *Transitions from Authoritarian Rule. Tentative Conclusions about Uncertain Democracies* (The Johns Hopkins University Press 1986) 6.

122 Ruti Teitel, 'How are the New Democracies of the Southern Cone Dealing with the Legacy of the Past Human Rights Abuses' (paper presented to the Council on Foreign Relations Latin America Project, New York, May 17, 1990, excerpt Reprinted in in Neil J Kritz (ed), *Transitional Justice, How Emerging Democracies Reckon with Former Regimes*, vol. 1 (United States Peace Institute 1995) 146–153.

the term in a 1991 application for research funding,[123] and stated in a 2008 article that when she proposed the phrase, her "aim was to account for the self-conscious construction of a distinctive conception of justice associated with periods of radical political change following past oppressive rule."[124] In her book *Transitional Justice*, published in 2000, Teitel emphasised the specificity of the political context and circumstances in which transitional justice is implemented.[125] As we have seen, Juan Corradi, in his 1992 book, also set out to explain what transitional justice consisted of, writing that it was "both more and less than ordinary justice."[126]

Significantly, the first three-volume work, published in 1995 under the title *Transitional Justice*, which brought together numerous contributions on the subject of transitional justice, did not provide a clear definition of the concept.[127] In the introduction, the book's editor Neil Kritz addressed the dilemmas of transitional justice that dealt with "basic components of 'transitional justice,'"[128] referring to criminal sanctions,[129] non-criminal sanctions,[130] recognition of the past,[131] compensation, restitution and rehabilitation.[132] So, the definition we have to be satisfied with is an enumerative one, a definition of transitional justice by identifying components whose definitions are inescapable. This enumerative definition was repeated in several subsequent works and became common in debates on transitional justice. For example, the International Center for Transitional Justice, established in 2001, argued that transitional justice referred to judicial and non-judicial mechanisms, listing the following: prosecution, reparations, truth-telling, institutional reform and the removal of human rights violators from political power.[133]

---

123 Ruti Teitel, 'Globalized Transitional Justice' (2010) Working paper n°8, Center for Global Studies, 1.

124 Ruti Teitel, 'Editorial Note-Transitional Justice Globalized' (2008) 2(1) *International Journal of Transitional Justice* 1, p. 1.

125 Ruti G Teitel, *Transitional Justice* (Oxford University Press 2000) 6.

126 Juan E Corradi, 'Toward Societies without Fear' in Juan E Corradi, Patricia Weiss Fagen, and Manuel Antonio Garretón (eds), *Fear at the Edge: State Terror and Resistance in Latin America* (University of California Press 1992) 285.

127 Neil J Kritz (ed), *Transitional Justice, How Emerging Democracies Reckon with Former Regimes*, 3 vol., (United States Peace Institute 1995).

128 Neil J Kritz (ed) 'The Dilemmas of Transitional Justice' in Neil J Kritz (ed), *Ibid.*, vol. 1, xxi and ff.

129 *Ibid.*

130 *Ibid.*, xxiv.

131 *Ibid.*, xxvi.

132 *Ibid.*

133 ICTJ, 'Annual Report 2001–2002' 1.

It now appears that it was the entry of transitional justice into the United Nations vocabulary that influenced the emergence of a commonly accepted definition. In 2003, the Security Council took an interest in the role of the United Nations in the field of justice and the rule of law and organised meetings on these issues.[134] The UN Secretary-General proposed to prepare a report to inform the Council's "further consideration of these matters."[135] On 23 August 2004, the Secretary-General issued a report entitled *Rule of Law and Transitional Justice in Conflict and Post-conflict Societies*. This report defined "transitional justice" as follows:

> The notion of "transitional justice" discussed in the present report comprises the full range of processes and mechanisms associated with a society's attempts to come to terms with a legacy of large-scale past abuses, in order to ensure accountability, serve justice and achieve reconciliation. These may include both judicial and non-judicial mechanisms, with differing levels of international involvement (or none at all) and individual prosecutions, reparations, truth-seeking, institutional reform, vetting and dismissals, or a combination thereof.[136]

According to this definition, transitional justice is a set of judicial and non-judicial processes and mechanisms with multiple objectives: to address massive past violations and to contribute to accountability, justice and reconciliation. Without claiming to be exhaustive, the definition identifies mechanisms that pursue these objectives. These include prosecutions, compensation, truth-telling and institutional reforms. The definition allows for the possibility of a combination of these mechanisms. This enumerative definition has gradually become the most cited definition of transitional justice. However, it is not free from criticism.

First, after reading some of the elements of the definition, one wonders what is so special about transitional justice and whether it is not just justice. After all, the mechanisms envisaged exist in all states governed by the rule of law. One might respond to this criticism by saying that if these mechanisms exist in all rule-of-law states, they do not necessarily deal with mass abuses.

---

134 Security Council, 4833rd meeting Wednesday 24 September 2003, UN doc. S/PV.4833; Security Council, 4835th meeting Tuesday 30 September 2003, UN doc. S/PV.4835.

135 'The Rule of Law and Transitional Justice in Conflict and Post-conflict Societies', Report of the Secretary-General, UN doc. S/2004/616, 23 August 2004, para. 1.

136 *Ibid.*, para. 8.

Second, developments in transitional justice today show that the mechanisms do not always focus on mass abuses. This is the case, for example, of a truth commission set up in Honduras in 2010 to investigate a coup d'état.[137] There is no evidence that all truth commissions, which are part of transitional justice, have investigated massive abuses.

Third, some elements that are now recognised as transitional justice mechanisms are not included in this definition. For example, the definition does not explicitly list traditional justice mechanisms. It does not provide details on the forms of reparations that have been implemented in the field of transitional justice. As we will see, reparations in transitional justice include not only compensation but also other forms of reparations recognised under international law, such as restitution, rehabilitation, satisfaction and guarantees of non-repetition.[138]

Fourth, it is difficult to say that all transitional justice mechanisms have reconciliation as an objective. For example, not all truth commissions and international criminal tribunals have reconciliation on their agendas, and reconciliation is a difficult objective to measure.

This definition was later supplemented by the UN Secretary-General and other UN bodies. For example, in 2006, in a new report in which the term "transitional justice" was used, the UN Secretary-General noted that within the framework of the United Nations,"[ ]he activities under Transitional justice will include the following: national transitional justice consultation processes, truth and reconciliation processes, reparations, international and hybrid tribunals, national human rights institutions, vetting processes and ad hoc investigations, fact-finding and commissions of inquiry."[139] In 2011, the Human Rights Council created a position of Special Rapporteur on the promotion of truth, justice, reparation and guarantees of non-recurrence.[140] This Special Rapporteur, Pablo de Greiff at the time, defined transitional justice as "a strategy for the realization of the rights to justice, truth, reparations and guarantees of non-recurrence in the aftermath of gross violations of human rights and serious violations of international humanitarian law."[141] These rights were

137 Honduras, Decreto Ejecutivo Nùmero PCM 011-2010, 13 Abril 2010.

138 See below Chapter 7, Section 3, for details on reparations.

139 'Uniting our strengths: Enhancing United Nations support for the rule of law', Report of the Secretary-General, UN doc. A/61/636-S/2006/980, 14 December 2006, para. 41.

140 Resolution 18/7 of the Human Rights Council, Special Rapporteur on the Promotion of Truth, Justice, Reparation and Guarantees of Non-recurrence, UN doc. A/HRC/RES/18/7, 25 September 2011.

141 'Report of the Special Rapporteur on the Promotion of Truth, Justice, Reparation and Guarantees of Non-repetition' UN doc. A/67/368, 13 September 2012, 3, note 1.

considered the four pillars of transitional justice, before a new Special Rapporteur added memorialization as the fifth pillar of transitional justice.[142]

All these UN definitions and other elements refer to five main elements that help to determine the main characteristics of transitional justice:

- Transitional justice is a set of identified mechanisms, judicial or non-judicial. These mechanisms include judicial processes, truth commissions, traditional justice, reparations programmes including memorialization processes, guarantees of non-repetition including institutional reforms, lustration and vetting.
- Transitional justice is implemented in response to specific abuses that are considered serious.
- Transitional justice has five pillars: justice, truth, reparation, guarantees of non-repetition and memorialisation.
- The ultimate goal of transitional justice generally is to achieve lasting peace and/or reconciliation.
- Transitional justice is closely linked to violations of human rights and international humanitarian law, covers transitions from authoritarian rule to democracy, from armed conflict to peace, from a dark past to a better future.

In short, transitional justice is a set of identified mechanisms, with defined objectives, implemented after serious violations of human rights and international humanitarian law. This book adopts this deliberately simplified definition. While this book prefers the term "transitional justice," which has gradually gained currency, it is useful to recall that other terms have been used in relation to transitional justice.

## 5 Competing Phrases: Other Phrases that Emerged around Transitional Justice

Some terms are used either as synonyms for transitional justice or to describe specific aspects of transitional justice.

### 5.1 Post-conflict Justice: Synonymous with Transitional Justice?

Post-conflict justice is a term that has emerged as the main competitor to transitional justice in a context where there has been a gradual interest in

142 'Memorialization Processes in the Context of Serious Violations of Human Rights and International Humanitarian Law: The Fifth Pillar of Transitional Justice', Report of the Special Rapporteur on the Promotion of Truth, Justice, Reparation and Guarantees of Non-recurrence, UN doc. A/HRC/45/45, 9 July 2020.

the question of armed conflict and post-conflict accountability. As we have seen, although there were some reflections about the post–Second World War era and the trials that followed, the first studies that would be labelled transitional justice focused mainly on post-dictatorial regimes in Europe and Latin America. In the late 1990s and early 2000s, however, a number of private organisations and scholars began to consider the question of justice in the aftermath of armed conflict, drawing on the experiences of the post–Second World War era and the 1990s, which saw bloody armed conflicts in the former Yugoslavia and Rwanda, as well as the UN Security Council's decision to establish international criminal tribunals to bring to justice those responsible for violations of international humanitarian law. In 1997, for example, the Stanley Foundation sponsored two conferences on post-conflict justice. The first was the Stanley Foundation Conference on Post-conflict Justice, held in Queenstown, Maryland, in April 1997, on "the role of the international community." According to the conference report, the conference participants, which included international law professors Diane Orentlicher and Cherif Bassiouni, analysed "the role of the international community" by discussing issues such as prosecutions by the newly established International Criminal Tribunal for the former Yugoslavia (ICTY) and the International Criminal Tribunal for Rwanda (ICTR) as well as alternatives to criminal sanctions such as truth commissions.[143]

The second conference was the 38th Strategy for Peace, US Foreign Policy Conference, held in Warrenton, Virginia, in October 1997, on the theme "Accountability and Judicial Response: Building Mechanisms for Post-conflict Justice." The report of this conference noted that the definition of "post-conflict" was debated:

> For purposes of this conference, the phrase "post-conflict justice" is assumed to refer to the period immediately after hostilities have ceased – or, in the words of one participant, "post-bullets." The immediate threat of harm is over and there probably are international peacekeeping forces on the ground deployed by the United Nations, a coalition of governments, or by a single donor government. There may or may not be a formal peace agreement, but there is a strong likelihood that hostilities will not rekindle in the foreseeable future and that peace will prevail.[144]

143 Eliot Goldberg and Mary C. Theisen (Rapporteurs), 'Post-conflict Justice: The Role of the International Community: Report of a Vantage Conference', Stanley Foundation, April 4–6 1997, 17–23.

144 Mary Theisen (Rapporteur), 'Accountability and Judicial Response: Building Mechanisms for Post-conflict Justice', 38th Strategy for Peace, US Foreign Policy Conference, Warrenton, Virginia, October 23–25, 1997, 4–5.

Participants to the conference discussed international and national prosecutions in the aftermath of armed conflict as well as truth commissions and lustration.[145]

In the same vein, Cherif Bassiouni, who participated in the April 1997 Stanley Foundation conference, edited a collective book entitled *Post-conflict Justice*, which was published in 2002.[146] This edited volume brought together articles on a wide range of topics such as international and national prosecutions, experiences of transition from armed conflict to peace in many countries, truth commissions, lustration, and so on, and included contributions on national and international judicial accountability and non-judicial mechanisms. The volume bore a striking resemblance to Neil Kritz's 1995 book *Transitional Justice*,[147] which marked a decisive turning point in the use and dissemination of the term "transitional justice." Issues covered by Kritz under the category of transitional justice were also covered in Bassiouni's book. This suggests that the terms "transitional justice" and "post-conflict justice" had begun to overlap. However, the term "post-conflict justice" seemed to be mainly concerned with what happened in the aftermath of an armed conflict.

The same impression continued with a project led by Bassiouni between 1997 and 2007 that brought together many experts who identified what were called the "principles of post-conflict justice."[148] The principles, which were published in 2007 in the volume *The Chicago Principles on Post-conflict Justice*, referred to the need for prosecution, truth-seeking and truth-disclosure, redress for serious violations, administrative sanctions, reform and more generally the need to respond to serious violations committed in the past,[149] all of which were also found in the debates on transitional justice. In an analysis that preceded the publication of the principles, Cherif Bassiouni and Daniel Rothenberg acknowledged that other terms were used to describe the same issue, citing the term "transitional justice," but insisted that the term "post-

145 *Ibid.*

146 Cherif Bassiouni (ed), *Post-conflict Justice*, (International and Comparative Criminal Law Series, Transnational Publishers 2002).

147 Neil J Kritz (ed), *Transitional Justice, How Emerging Democracies Reckon with Former Regimes*, 3 vol., (United States Peace Institute 1995).

148 Cherif Bassiouni (Project director), Daniel Rothenberg (Executive editor), Etelle Higonnet and Michael Hanna (Contributors), 'The Chicago Principles on Post-conflict Justice' (International Human Rights Law Institute 2007) 16–17, https://law.depaul.edu/about/centers-and-institutes/international-human-rights-law-institute/projects/Documents/chicago_principles.pdf.

149 *Ibid.*, 16–17 and 29–60. See below Chapter 8, Section 3.3, for more details on these principles.

conflict justice" covered dealing with violations committed during armed conflict. They wrote:

> The term "post-conflict justice" is used with an understanding that there exist a number of similar or related concepts including "transitional justice," "strategies for combating impunity," "peace building," and "post-conflict reconstruction." These terms and their definitions overlap and their diversity reflects both the evolving nature of the field and links with particular institutions rather than substantial differences in understanding or ideology. The term post-conflict justice is therefore intended to highlight the responses of states and the international community to violations committed during armed conflict.[150]

The term "post-conflict justice" is not without its critics. Alex Boraine, a founding member of the International Center for Transitional Justice and a former member of the South African Truth and Reconciliation Commission, has argued that the term is reductive because it does not cover post-dictatorship or post-apartheid contexts in states that have not experienced armed conflict in the strict sense of the word.[151] Nevertheless, the two terms (transitional justice and post-conflict justice) have sometimes been used "interchangeably."[152] However, if we stick to their literal meaning, the concept of transitional justice is much broader than that of post-conflict justice. Today, transitional justice is concerned with both post-conflict and post-authoritarian regimes, as well as with situations that are not always linked to clear political transitions, but in which a painful part of the state's past is being addressed.

### 5.2 Phrases Describing Particular Aspects or Reflecting the Evolution of Transitional Justice

#### 5.2.1 Reconstructive Justice and Restorative Justice

The notion of reconstructive justice (in French, *justice reconstructive*), rather than transitional justice, is used in the work of French scholars Antoine Garapon and Gérard Cahin, who insisted that transitional justice seeks to recon-

150 See Cherif Bassiouni and Daniel Rothenberg, 'Facing Atrocity: The Importance of Guiding Principles on Post-conflict Justice' in Cherif Bassiouni et al. (ed), *Ibid.*, 3.

151 Alex Boraine, 'Transitional Justice as an Emerging Field', Presentation at the symposium, *Repairing the Past: Reparations and Transition to Democracy*, Ottawa, Canada, 11 March 2004, 2.

152 Rachel Kerr and Eirin Mobekk, *Peace and Justice. Seeking Accountability after War* (Policy Press 2007) 3.

struct the whole state and the victims of the atrocities committed.[153] Gérard Cahin wrote that rather than using the term "transitional justice," it is better to use the term "reconstructive justice" because this justice is "less concerned with punishing individuals than with repairing the whole political group."[154] The term "reconstructive justice" used by French scholars is very close to the term "restorative justice," which also insists on the restoration of victims and has been used to describe some mechanisms and operations in transitional justice.

The main ideas at the heart of restorative justice are the participation of victims and the association of the offenders and their victims in the search for the consequences of the offence committed.[155] This type of justice is implemented in the criminal justice systems of many developed countries that are not in transition.[156] As the term "transitional justice" began to be used by scholars, the term "restorative justice" also began to be used in the context of political transition, in relation to the establishment and activities of truth commissions, notably the South African Truth and Reconciliation Commission.[157] After the end of the apartheid regime in South Africa, the Truth and Reconciliation Commission was set up to establish and disseminate the truth about serious human rights violations and to achieve reconciliation. To this end, it organised public hearings in which perpetrators and victims could interact. It provided a forum for victims and perpetrators to come together. Victims could freely share their stories and the abuses they had suffered. Perpetrators could also "confess" their crimes. They were promised amnesty if

153 Antoine Garapon, *Des crimes que l'on ne peut ni punir ni pardonner* (Ed. Odile Jacob 2002) 296–297; Gérard Cahin, 'L'impact des tribunaux pénaux internationalisés sur la (re)construction de l'état de droit' in Hervé Ascensio, Elisabeth Lambert-Abdelgawad and Jean-Marc Sorel (ed), *Les juridictions pénales internationalisées* (*Cambodge , Kosovo, Sierra Leone , Timor Leste*) (Société de législation comparée 2006) 300.

154 Translation from French, Gérard Cahin, *Ibid.*

155 On restorative justice, Daniel W Van Ness and Karen Heetderks Strong, *Restoring Justice: An Introduction to Restorative Justice* (5th edn, Routledge 2015); Daniel Van Ness and Gerry Johnstone (ed), *Handbook of Restorative Justice* (Willan Publishing 2007).

156 *Ibid.*

157 See, for example, Jennifer J Llewellyn and Robert Howse, 'Institutions for Restorative Justice: The South African Truth and Reconciliation Commission' (1999) 49(3) *The University of Toronto Law Journal* 355; Stephan Parmentier, 'The South African Truth and Reconciliation Commission. Towards restorative justice in the field of human rights' in Ezzat Fattah and Stephan Parmentier (eds) *Victim Policies and Criminal Justice on the Road to Restorative Justice. Essays in Honour of Tony Peters* (Leuven University Press 2001) 401–428; Carrie J Niebur Eisnaugle, 'An international truth commission: Utilizing restorative justice as an alternative to retribution' (2003) 36 *Vanderbilt Journal of Transnational Law* 209. For more on truth commissions, see below Chapter 6.

they told the whole truth about the crimes they had committed, and prosecution if they did not. The South African Truth and Reconciliation Commission introduced a model of victim participation in a national truth and reconciliation process. As such, truth commissions, such as the South African one, have been seen as alternatives to retribution and prosecution, and thus, according to many, as the implementation of restorative justice.

However, it is not possible to conclude that restorative justice and reconstructive justice are synonymous with transitional justice. They only describe elements of transitional justice. Reconstruction is generally at the heart of transitional justice, as is the idea of restoration. Transitional justice, through truth commissions as one of its mechanisms, sometimes draws on the principles of restorative justice to provide a forum for victims and perpetrators, to enhance victim participation and to promote reconciliation.

### 5.2.2 Transitional Justice in Ongoing Armed Conflict

In some situations, the implementation of transitional justice, whether through judicial or non-judicial mechanisms, takes place when an armed conflict has not really ended. For example, transitional justice mechanisms have been implemented in Colombia and Mali – two countries that have experienced bloody armed conflict – even though hostilities have not ended. Because of the increase in this type of situation, some scholars have used the term "transitional justice in ongoing armed conflict," a term that better describes these situations.[158] Some have even argued for the inclusion of societies facing armed conflict in the scope of transitional justice.[159] The phrase "transitional justice in ongoing armed conflict" highlights the difficulty of identifying the end of a conflict in order to be able to say that the period of transitional or post-conflict justice has begun. The inclusion of this phrase in transitional justice gives transitional justice a broader scope. This inclusion should not be ruled out, as there are a number of ongoing armed conflicts – such as in Ukraine – where justice processes related to these armed conflicts have been initiated (e.g., before the International Criminal Court). Thus, the term "transitional

---

158 For example, Thomas Unger and Marieke Wierda, 'Pursuing Justice in Ongoing Conflict: A Discussion of Current Practice' in Ambos Kai, Large Judith, Wierda Marieke (eds), *Building a Future on Peace and justice. Studies on Transitional Justice, Peace and Development* (Springer 2009).

159 Stephen Winter, 'Theorising Transitional Justice in Ongoing Conflict' in Tine Destrooper, Line Engbo Gissel and Kerstin Bree Carlson (eds), *Transitional Justice in Aparadigmatic Contexts Accountability, Recognition, and Disruption* (Routledge 2023).

justice in ongoing armed conflicts" reflects the development of transitional justice in the context of armed conflicts.

### 5.2.3 Transitional Justice after Transition or Post-transitional Justice

The use of the term "transitional justice after transition" or "post-transitional justice" is intended to describe the implementation of justice to deal with crimes committed during dictatorships or armed conflicts, when the political transition initiated several years earlier has been successful. The state concerned by this "transitional justice" is generally no longer in transition but has established a relatively consolidated democracy. States that have passed the stage of political transition sometimes decide to deal with serious human rights violations committed before the transition. It is therefore difficult to speak of transitional justice because the state is no longer in transition. Several Latin American countries that have passed the stage of political transition, such as Argentina, El Salvador and Chile, have conducted trials of perpetrators of crimes committed during dictatorships (especially in the 1970s or 1980s). These trials have been studied by scholars who have used the terms "transitional justice after transition" and "post-transitional justice" to refer to these legal processes.[160] The use of these terms signals that transitional justice is a dynamic that can take place long after political transitions.

### 5.2.4 Transitional Justice without Transition

This is undoubtedly one of the expressions that expresses the success of transitional justice. It has been used to describe two situations: the first is that of a state that has dealt with an armed conflict or a dictatorship, that has not undergone a political transition, but that either faces calls and pressure from the international community and other actors to engage in transitional justice, or has decided to engage in transitional justice by creating its mechanisms. Cases analysed from this perspective have included, for example, Syria[161]

160 Cath Collins, *Post-transitional Justice: Human Rights Trials in Chile and El Salvador* (Pennsylvania State University Press 2010); Elin Skaar, *Judicial Independence and Human Rights in Latin America* (Palgrave Macmillan 2011); Nicola Palmer, Phil Clark and Danielle Granville, *Critical Perspectives in Transitional Justice* (Series on Transitional Justice, Intersentia 2012) xi;.

161 Ben Van Schaack, 'Transitional Justice Without Transition: The International Community's Efforts in Syria' in Hilli Moodrick-Even Khen H, Nir T. Boms and Sareta Ashraph (eds), *The Syrian War: Between Justice and Political Reality* (Cambridge University Press 2020).

and Colombia.[162] The second is that of states that are not in transition, that have not had to deal with an armed conflict or a dictatorial regime in their recent history but that are using transitional justice mechanisms, or are under pressure to do so, to deal with past crimes and injustices. Many Western industrialised countries have engaged in such transitional justice processes. The most emblematic case is that of Canada, which established a Truth and Reconciliation Commission (TRC) to investigate the violations committed in the context of residential schools, where Indigenous children were placed and suffered numerous abuses, even death.[163] Norway, Sweden and Finland have also set up truth commissions to deal with the abuses experienced by Indigenous peoples on their territories.[164]

What is clear today is that transitional justice has become a very successful term, used to describe situations far beyond its original meaning and context in the 1990s. Therefore, in order to get a clearer picture of transitional justice, it is important to briefly trace the history of its implementation.

---

162 Nelson Camilo Sánchez and Rodrigo Uprimny Yepes, 'Transitional Justice Without Transition? The Colombian Experience in the Implementation of Transition Measures' in *Contribution of Truth, Justice, and Reparation Policies to Latin American Democracies* (Inter-American Institute of Human Rights 2011).

163 Jung Courtney, 'Canada and the Legacy of the Indian Residential Schools: Transitional Justice for Indigenous Peoples in a Non-Transitional Society', April 8, 2009. Available online: https://ssrn.com/abstract=1374950.

164 For more, see below Chapter 6, on truth commissions.

CHAPTER 2

# The History and Evolution of Transitional Justice

The concept of transitional justice as it is understood today emerged in the 1990s. However, it is now common for transitional justice to be used to describe mechanisms that were implemented before the term was coined and given its current meaning. In fact, throughout human history, human societies or groups have used legal mechanisms and tools that are now included in transitional justice. For this reason, the history of transitional justice goes back much farther than the 1990s.

As many writings on transitional justice suggest, the end of the Second World War is a landmark in the history of international criminal law because, as we will see, it established individual criminal responsibility under international law. The fact that the first steps of international criminal responsibility are now being incorporated into transitional justice makes the end of the Second World War a landmark in transitional justice. In the field of transitional justice and the implementation of its mechanisms, there is "a before" and "an after" the Second World War. The other important element in this history is the end of the Cold War, which saw the expansion of the use of transitional justice mechanisms. Since the 2000s, the utilisation of transitional justice has been broadened beyond the scope of post-authoritarian regimes and armed conflicts where it has been primarily employed. It is therefore useful to divide the history of transitional justice into three main periods: before the Second World War (discussed in Section 1), after the Second World War (discussed in Section 2) and after the end of the Cold War (discussed in Section 3), before examining the current limitless use of the concept of transitional justice (discussed in Section 4).

## 1 Transitional Justice before the End of the Second World War

Among the authors who have written on transitional justice, Jon Elster and Ruti Teitel appear to be those who have most extensively described the existence of transitional justice before the Second World War. However, the work of these authors remains mainly geographically focused on the Western world, leaving open the question of the use of such mechanisms in other geographical areas.

 | HTTPS://DOI.ORG/10.1163/9789004766655-005

## 1.1 The Research of Jon Elster and Ruti Teitel on the History of Transitional Justice

Jon Elster considers that "[d]emocratic transitional justice is almost as old as democracy itself."[1] Drawing on the work of two authors, Martin Ostwald and Mogens Herman Hansen, who did a great deal of work on the political structures of antiquity but without referring to transitional justice,[2] Elster traces the first use of institutional tools, now considered to be part of transitional justice issues.[3] He points out that Athens experimented with a number of transitional justice measures in ancient times, during political transitions that were aimed at restoring democracy: in 411 BC, retributive measures such as the prosecution of oligarchs ousted from power, and in 403 BC, an amnesty and a desire for reconciliation.[4] Referring to amnesties and the dilemmas in transitional contexts, Ruti Teitel also refers to the Athenian experience of justice. According to her: "Transitional amnesties appear often to be the precursors to, or coincident with, liberalizing political change. An ancient illustration appears in the account in the Athenian Constitution of the reconciliation following Athens's defeat in the Peloponnesian War. Transitional oligarchic rule and the subsequent restoration of democracy (though not, to be sure, democracy of modern times) raised the question of whether and to what extent to punish the prior despotic regime."[5]

After these Athenian episodes, we had to wait more than 2,000 years to see the resurgence of transitional justice measures, with the restoration of the English monarchy from 1660 onwards, followed by the restoration of the French monarchy in 1814 and 1815.[6] These restorations were accompanied by

1 Jon Elster, *Closing the Books: Transitional Justice in Historical Perspective* (Cambridge University Press 2004) 3.

2 Martin Ostwald, *From Popular Sovereignty to the Sovereignty of Law: Law, Society, and Politics in Fifth-Century Athens* (University of California Press 1986). See also, Martin Ostwald, *Nomos and the Beginnings of the Athenian Democracy* (Oxford University Press 1969); Mogens Herman Hansen, *The Athenian Democracy in the Age of Demosthenes. Structure, Principles, and Ideology* (Blackwells 1991).

3 Jon Elster, *Closing the Books: Transitional Justice in Historical Perspective* (Cambridge University Press 2004) 3–16.

4 Jon Elster, *Ibid.*

5 Ruti G Teitel, *Transitional Justice* (Oxford University Press 2000) 52.

6 Jon Elster, *Closing the Books: Transitional Justice in Historical Perspective* (Cambridge University Press 2004) 24–46.

amnesty, retributive and reparative measures in the case of the UK,[7] and purges and reparations in the case of France.[8] Elster notes that the reparations and restitutions provided for in the Anglo-American Peace Treaty of 1783, adopted in the United States in the context of the transition to independence, are part of transitional justice.[9] He highlights the difficulties involved in implementing these measures.[10] Ruti Teitel also argues that dilemmas related to transitional issues have been present throughout the history of transitions, particularly in the eighteenth century in the context of the transition from a monarchy to a republic.[11]

Elster is often quoted and criticised by scholars writing on the history or early implementation of transitional justice. He is criticised for the "anachronistic" nature of his approach, which is to apply a recently created concept to the distant past.[12] In particular, he is criticised for applying a new concept to a distant past that was shaped by contexts very different from those that would prevail after the concept was created. These criticisms can also be directed at Teitel, and they are not unfounded. For example, the question of the universality of human rights and international crimes as we understand them today, did not exist in antiquity or during the English, American or French historical experiences of transitional justice.

Despite these criticisms, the work of Elster and Teitel shows that current developments in transitional justice are not so recent, that humanity has always faced the dilemma of political transitions, even if the context was different and the term "transitional justice" did not exist. Their work also helps us to better observe humanity's evolution over the centuries in responding to abuses after an armed conflict or the fall of an authoritarian regime. It provides an opportunity to see what is recurrent in human behaviour with regard to responsibility after abuses, and what is not recurrent or what has (or has not) evolved. Some comparative studies on transitional justice have shown that it is possible to compare contemporary transitional justice mechanisms with some practices that took place after abuses a very long time ago, and which can be called transitional justice if we consider the content of transi-

7 *Ibid.*, 49–51.
8 *Ibid.*, 24–46.
9 *Ibid.*, 52.
10 *Ibid.*, 53.
11 Ruti G Teitel, *Transitional Justice* (Oxford University Press 2000) 12.
12 See, for example, Marcos Zunino, *Justice Framed: A Genealogy of Transitional Justice* (Cambridge University Press 2019) 9–10; Arthur Paige, 'How 'Transitions' Reshaped Human Rights: A Conceptual History of Transitional Justice' (2009) 31(2) *Human Rights Quarterly* 321, 328.

tional justice today. For example, in her dissertation, Elizabeth Marie Alexion compared transitional justice in Ancient Greece with transitional justice in Rwanda after the 1994 genocide.[13] Adriaan Lanni examined the possibility of relying on the example of the Athenian experience of transitional justice to draw lessons that may be useful in contemporary transitional justice.[14] She wrote:

> The Athenian case provides some mid-level observations about factors that may contribute to a successful transition. The Athenian experience suggests (1) the importance of granularity, that is, letting individual victims at the local level decide whether to prosecute their antagonists; and (2) that uncovering the truth is not always the best way to ensure peace and reconciliation following atrocities. These observations from the Athenian case offer insight into prominent contemporary issues in transitional justice. First, the Athenian experience suggests that attention to local resentments and ordinary victims and perpetrators may be just as important as centralized, exemplary justice or the exposure of the command structure behind atrocities. Second, the Athenian experience invites us to reexamine whether the focus on truth seeking (so common in contemporary transitional justice institutions) is well founded.[15]

Thus, these findings on pre–Second World War transitional justice can be useful in building a bridge between the past and contemporary transitional justice. However, this historical approach is generally limited to a geographical boundary, parts of Europe and, to some extent, North America. So, the question is whether other regions experienced similar events centuries ago, either as to what happened in parts of Europe and North America, or as to what has happened in the field of transitional justice since the 1990s.

## 1.2 Other Historic Developments from Other Regions

Historical developments related to contemporary transitional justice mechanisms have been identified in other regions and contexts within sacred religious texts. Links have been established between transitional justice and religions that were created many centuries ago, such as Buddhism, Christianity, Islam

13 Elizabeth Marie Alexion, *"The Judge Will Be Your Neighbor": Transitional justice in Ancient Athens and Post-genocide Rwanda*, Dissertation (Wesleyan University, 2016).

14 Adriaan Lanni, 'Transitional Justice in Ancient Athens: A Case Study' (2010) 32 *University of Pennsylvania Journal of International Law* 551, 589.

15 *Ibid.*, 589–590.

and Judaism, using rhetoric of reconciliation and/or forgiveness that are sometimes found within these religions.[16] Hakeem Yusuf, for example, has written that "it is also possible to discern transitional justice practices in the texts, traditions and historical accounts of religious communities, especially of the Abrahamic faiths: Judaism, Christianity and Islam. While there have been applications of some other mechanisms of transitional justice, reconciliation practices, in particular, have very strong roots in and feature prominently in the texts and historical traditions of numerous religions."[17] He gives an example from the Quran, a case in which Prophet Mohammed decided to pardon some of his enemies after a war, and his declaration of a general amnesty for the vanquished except "the most culpable criminals in the city," and his call for reconciliation.[18]

Similarly, in her book dedicated to transitional justice, Ruti Teitel makes references to the Old Testament of the Bible, to the Israelites and Egypt. For instance, she draws parallels between reparations, a mechanism of transitional justice, and the biblical account of the Exodus of the ancient Israelites from Egypt. According to Teitel, this "biblical account of the political shift – from oppression to freedom – of the Israelites in Egypt offers an ancient story of transition."[19] She writes that the biblical account of the Israelites, who after being freed from Egyptian oppression, "stripped" clothing, silver and gold objects from them, "suggests the valuables were not taken by force but willingly given up by the Egyptians," even if there may be other interpretations.[20] The account holds that the objects "stripped" by Israelites from the Egyptians were destined to be worn by the Israelites' "sons and daughters."[21] According to Teitel, "The stripping of the Egyptians and the 're-dressing' of the Israelites signifies more than a material settlement, it is a setting straight, a ceremonial redressing, a rehabilitation in the public eye," and it is an "ancient symbolic aspect of reparatory measures."[22] However, Teitel writes that there are various interpretations of this account.[23] It would not be surprising to find elsewhere

16 For a deep analysis on this topic, Thomas Brudholm and Thomas Cushman (eds), *The Religious in Responses to Mass Atrocity Interdisciplinary Perspectives* (Cambridge University Press 2009).

17 Hakeem O Yusuf, 'Origin, Context and Development of Transitional Justice' in Hakeem O Yusuf and Hugo Van der Merwe (eds), *Transitional Justice. Theories, Mechanisms and Debates* (Routledge 2022) 12.

18 *Ibid.*, 12–13.

19 Ruti G Teitel, *Transitional Justice* (Oxford University Press 2000) 120.

20 *Ibid.*

21 *Ibid.*

22 *Ibid.*, 120–121.

23 *Ibid.*, 121.

ancient accounts or practices similar to what is now referred to as components of transitional justice.

## 1.3 Other Evidence of Transitional Justice in the History before the Second World War: The Progressive Establishment of Accountability in the Field of Armed Conflicts

In terms of accountability for abuses committed during an authoritarian regime or armed conflict, there are not many references to post-conflict or transitional justice, as we now understand it, in early writings on military strategy, war and political change. There seemed to be little interest in the post-war period, in spite of the fact that, as written by Ibn Khaldoum, "[w]ars and different kinds of fighting have always occurred in the world since God created it."[24] War, seen as "politics by other means" according to Carl von Clausewitz's *On War*,[25] was sometimes a means of settling disputes. In such a context, post-conflict analysis, establishing responsibilities or reporting on serious abuses seemed unthinkable. For example, there are no references to post-conflict justice in Sun Tsu's *Art of War*[26] or in Kautilya's *Arthashastra*, which deal with the dynamics of change at the political level,[27] or much later in Carl Von Clausewitz's *On War*. The victory of a conqueror or sovereign was sometimes enough to install or consolidate the new power, the old one being vassalised, condemned to the sword or exiled, as the case may be. However, in the works of Niccolò Machiavelli in the sixteenth century, failure to render justice after violations of the law or armed conflict had sometimes been seen as a political risk, as an event likely to provoke unrest. Machiavelli highlighted the need for rulers to dispense justice, as the absence of justice could foster a desire for vengeance that is harmful to a country's integrity.[28] He wrote that the Gauls were outraged because some envoys who had violated the law of nations had not been punished by Rome, despite a request to that effect. Instead, they were honoured by Rome. The Gauls attacked Rome and occupied much of its terri-

24 Ibn Khaldun, *The Muqaddimah. An Introduction to History* (first published 1377, Translated and Introduced by Franz Rosenthal, Abridged and Edited by N. J., Bollingen Series, Princeton University Press 2005), 223.

25 Carl Von Clausewitz, *On War* (first published 1832), Book 8, Chapter 6, Section B.

26 Sun Tzu [544–496 B.C.], *The Art of War*, (Oxford University Press 1963).

27 Kautilya, *The Arthashastra*, (written in the 2nd Century, Edited, Rearranged, Translated and Introduced by L.N. Ranga Rajan, Penguin books 1992).

28 Niccolò Machiavelli, *Discourses on the First Decade of Titus Livius* (first published 1531, Lexington KY 2013), Book II, XXVIII, 123–124.

tory, with the exception of the Capitol. According to Machiavelli, "This disaster overtook the Romans entirely from their disregard of justice."[29] He continued:

> This should make us reflect, how carefully all princes and commonwealths ought to refrain from committing like wrongs, not only against communities, but also against particular men. For if a man be deeply wronged, either by a private hand or by a public officer, and be not avenged to his satisfaction, if he live in a republic, he will seek to avenge himself, though in doing so he bring ruin on his country; or if he live under a prince, and be of a resolute and haughty spirit, he will never rest until he has wreaked his resentment against the prince, though he knows it may cost him dear.[30]

Rendering justice is seen here as a necessity for social peace, a condition for avoiding future unrest and guaranteeing the integrity of a territory. This topic – guaranteeing justice to avoid revenge that would jeopardise peace, and guarantees of non-repetition – lies at the heart of transitional justice today. However, this link between the work of Machiavelli and transitional justice may not be so convincing. Here, it is what might be called a lack of justice that provoked an armed conflict, which is quite different from the pursuit of justice after wars.

In the field of international law, the seventeenth-century arguments of Hugo Grotius – who is considered the "father of international law" – on the end of war and the necessity of building peace,[31] have been interpreted by several transitional justice scholars as indicating that "in the aftermath of war, it was not fitting to follow up former wrongs in peace."[32] Sometimes, amnesties were granted after armed conflicts. This was the case, for example, after the Thirty Years' War in Europe. It was ended by the two Peace Treaties of Westphalia in 1648. One of the treaties provided for a general amnesty: "There shall be on the one side and the other a perpetual oblivion, amnesty,

---

29 *Ibid.*, 124.

30 *Ibid.*, 123–124.

31 Hugo Grotius, *The Law of War and Peace* (first published 1625, Translated into English by Francis W. Kelsey, Lonang Institute 2005), Book III, Chapter XX, para. XVII, 539: "The same principle does not apply to the right to inflict punishment.' For this right, in so far as it concerns kings or peoples, ought to be considered as held in abeyance, from fear that the peace will not be a perfect peace if it leaves the old causes for war".

32 Anja Seibert-Fohr, 'Transitional Justice in Post-conflict Situations' in *Max Planck Encyclopedia of Public International Law* (Oxford University Press 2019), para. 2; Christina Binder, 'Introduction to the Concept of Transitional Justice' in Walter Feichtinger, Gerald Hainzl and Predrag Jurekovic (eds), *Transitional Justice: Experiences from Africa and the Western Balkans* (Landesverteidigungsakademie 2013) 11.

or pardon of all that has been committed since the beginning of these troubles […]."[33]

Nevertheless, before the twentieth century, there are references to accountability and the need to prosecute and punish those responsible for crimes committed after wars. Some developments on accountability and the necessity to render justice occurred as early as the 1400s and 1500s. The trial of Peter von Hagenbach in 1474 is considered by many experts in international criminal law to be the first international criminal trial of crimes that would later be recognised as war crimes,[34] or crimes against humanity.[35] Peter von Hagenbach was tried by a tribunal of twenty-eight judges from different parts of the Holy Roman Empire for crimes, including rapes and murders, "allegedly perpetrated as governor of the Duke's Alsatian territories from 1469 to 1474."[36]

When he dealt with the behaviour of victors after an armed conflict, Francisco Vitoria noted that it was not necessary to put all defeated enemies to death, and insisted on the proportionality of the punishment to the offence committed, and on the fact that vengeance should not go beyond this.[37] Here,

---

33 Para. II of the Peace Treaty between the Holy Roman Emperor and the King of France and their respective Allies, The Peace of Westphalia, Münster, 24 October 1648.

34 Gregory S Gordon, 'The Trial of Peter von Hagenbach: Reconciling History, Historiography and International Criminal Law' in Kevin Jon Heller and Gerry Simpson (eds), *The Hidden Histories of War Crimes Trials* (Oxford University Press 2013) 13; William Schabas, *Introduction to International Criminal Court* (4th edn, Cambridge University Press 2011), 1.

35 Georg Schwarzenberger, *International Law as Applied by International Courts and Tribunals: The Law of Armed Conflict*, vol. II, (Steven and Sons Limited 1968) 466. This scholar holds that "Hagenbach's crimes had been committed before the outbreak of open war between Burgundy and her enemies. Thus, in a strict sense, they were not war crimes. At that time, the borderline between peace and war was, however, even more fluid than in the centuries to come". *Ibid.*, He adds that "broadly, these crimes fall into the category of what, since 1945, would be termed crimes against humanity, rather than war crimes in the strict sense of the term". *Ibid.*, For more details on the trial and its context, see *Ibid.*, at 462–466.

36 Gregory S Gordon, 'The Trial of Peter von Hagenbach: Reconciling History, Historiography and International Criminal Law' in Kevin Jon Heller and Gerry Simpson (eds), *The Hidden Histories of War Crimes Trials* (Oxford University Press 2013).

37 Franciscus De Vitoria, *De Indis Et De Ivre Belli Relectiones* (first published in 1557, Edited by Ernest Nys. A Translation of the Text by John Pawley Bate, Oceana Publications 1964) 183, para. 457: "as it needs must be that scandals come (St. Matthew, ch. 18) and also wars between princes, it would involve the ruin of mankind and of Christianity if the victor always slew all his enemies, and the world would soon be reduced to solitude, and wars would not be waged for the public good, but to the utter ruin of the public. The measure of the punishment, then, must be proportionate to the offense, and vengeance ought to go no further, and herein account must be taken of the consideration that, as said above, subjects are not bound, and ought not, to scrutinize the causes of a war, but can follow their prince to it in reliance on his authority and on public."

although it was not clearly stated what form of punishment should be chosen, it was implicitly accepted that there should be punishments for the vanquished after an armed conflict, provided that these were proportionate to the offenses committed.

In the context of the progressive construction of international humanitarian law, the nineteenth century provided some examples of legal documents and proposals insisting on accountability for crimes committed during wars. National military legislations providing for the punishment of those who committed military offenses in the context of wars emerged. The 1863 US Lieber Code, written in the context of the US Civil War, provided punishment for American soldiers who committed some offenses against the inhabitants of an invaded country.[38] This made it clear that after wars, there could be some form of accountability for offenses.

After the battle of Solferino and the adoption of the first Geneva Convention, the 1864 Convention for the Amelioration of the Condition of Military Wounded in Armies in the Field, Gustave Moynier foresaw the anomaly of turning the page on serious violations of the laws of war without establishing judicial responsibility. According to the author, the creation of an international tribunal was an appropriate response to these violations.[39] This was the first attempt to envisage post-conflict justice at international level. However, it was only in theory. Moynier was pragmatic, recognising the shortcomings of the law of nations, which did not envisage such a possibility at the time, and felt that "rescue committees" could play a role in alerting and denouncing violations of the laws of war, a denunciation that would enable offenders to be "ostracized by civilized nations."[40]

---

38 USA, General Orders No. 100, Instructions for the Government of Armies of the United States in the Field (Lieber Code), 24 April 1863. "Art. 44. All wanton violence committed against persons in the invaded country, all destruction of property not commanded by the authorized officer, all robbery, all pillage or sacking, even after taking a place by main force, all rape, wounding, maiming, or killing of such inhabitants, are prohibited under the penalty of death, or such other severe punishment as may seem adequate for the gravity of the offense". The expression "invaded country" here does not seem to mean another State. It seems to mean other geographical territories invaded, including within the USA.

39 Gustave Moynier, *Etude sur la Convention de Genève pour l'amélioration du sort des militaires blessés dans les armées en campagne (1864–1868)* (Librairie de Joël Cherbuliez 1870) 302.

40 *Ibid.*, translation, "Moreover, the guilty cannot flatter themselves to escape this punishment, now that the relief committees are placed under observation like vigilant sentinels, and would not let a violation of the laws of war go by without pointing it out and scourging it. The prospect, for those concerned, of being brought before the tribunal of public conscience, if they fail in their commitment, and of being ostracized by civilized

Moynier also played an important role in drafting the *Oxford Manual* that was published by the International Law Institute in 1880. This manual provided for the possibility of punishing those who had violated the law of wars, stating that "[o]ffenders against the laws of war are liable to the punishments specified in the penal law."[41] This also made it clear that criminal punishment against wrongdoers could be envisaged domestically at the end of an armed conflict.

Notwithstanding these elements of post-war sanctions prior to the twentieth century, it was during the twentieth century that some of the mechanisms that are now part of transitional justice were developed. Prior to the First World War, the 1906 Convention for the Amelioration of the Condition of the Wounded and Sick in Armies in the Field referred to national penal law and the need for states parties to act and punish misconduct during wars.[42] This could also mean that after wars, those accused of misconduct could be prosecuted and punished.

After the First World War, the Allied Powers planned to try William II, the "German Emperor" who was considered to be responsible for the war. Article 227 of the Treaty of Versailles, which sealed the end of the First World War, stipulated the following:

> The Allied and Associated Powers publicly arraign William II of Hohenzollern, formerly German Emperor, for a supreme offence against international morality and the sanctity of treaties.
>
> A special tribunal will be constituted to try the accused, thereby assuring him the guarantees essential to the right of defence. It will be composed of five judges, one appointed by each of the following Powers: namely, the United States of America, Great Britain, France, Italy and Japan.
>
> In its decision the tribunal will be guided by the highest motives of international policy, with a view to vindicating the solemn obligations of international undertakings and the validity of international morality. It will be its duty to fix the punishment which it considers should be imposed.

---

nations, constitutes a sufficiently powerful brake for us to believe that no other would be worth it".

41 Article 84, The Laws of War on Land, Oxford, 9 September 1880.

42 Article 28, Convention for the Amelioration of the Condition of the Wounded and Sick in Armies in the Field, 1906.

> The Allied and Associated Powers will address a request to the Government of the Netherlands for the surrender to them of the ex-Emperor in order that he may be put on trial.

These provisions marked the birth of an unprecedented awareness of the need to punish individuals accused of violations of law in the aftermath of international armed conflict. However, the birth of this awareness expressed in the provisions of a treaty did not translate into effective action. William II was never brought to trial. The Netherlands, where the deposed sovereign had taken refuge, refused to hand him over to the victorious Allied Powers.[43] A few rare trials did take place in Germany after the First World War, but they were not aimed at senior German officials, but at the executors.[44] In the same post–First World War context, another treaty between the Allied Powers and Turkey, the 1920 Treaty of Sèvres, provided for trials of individuals who had violated the laws and customs of war, stating:

> The Turkish Government recognises the right of the Allied Powers to bring before military tribunals persons accused of having committed acts in violation of the laws and customs of war. Such persons shall, if found guilty, be sentenced to punishments laid down by law. This provision will apply notwithstanding any proceedings or prosecution before a tribunal in Turkey, or in the territory of her allies.[45]

The treaty also added:

> The Turkish Government undertakes to hand over to the Allied Powers the persons whose surrender may be required by the latter as being responsible for the massacres committed during the continuance of the state of war on territory which formed part of the Turkish Empire on August 1, 1914.
>
> The Allied Powers reserve to themselves the right to designate the tribunal which shall try the persons so accused, and the Turkish Government undertakes to recognise such tribunal.

---

43 See on this case, William A Schabas, *The Trial of the Kaiser* (Oxford University Press 2018) 269 ff.

44 On these trials, see Claud Mullin, *The Leipzig Trials – An Account of the War Criminals' Trials and a Study of German Mentality* (Witherby 1921).

45 Article 226, The Treaty of Peace between The Allied and Associated Powers and Turkey, Signed at Sèvres, 10 August 1920.

> In the event of the League of Nations having created in sufficient time a tribunal competent to deal with the said massacres, the Allied Powers reserve to themselves the right to bring the accused persons mentioned above before such tribunal, and the Turkish Government undertakes equally to recognise such tribunal.

Despite this courageous attempt to prosecute war criminals, the treaty was not ratified by Turkey and was never applied. It was later replaced by the Treaty of Lausanne, which provided for an amnesty and prevented any trials.[46]

These attempts to establish individual criminal responsibility at the international level, and the few trials held after the First World War were followed by the adoption of treaties in international humanitarian law. Some of them advocated accountability and the punishment by states of those who violate the law of wars. For example, the 1929 Geneva Convention for the Amelioration of the Condition of the Wounded and Sick in Armies in the Field proposed: "The Governments of the High Contracting Parties shall also propose to their legislatures should their penal laws be inadequate, the necessary measures for the repression in time of war of any act contrary to the provisions of the present Convention."[47] These efforts were interrupted by the Second World War and its atrocities. The end of that war marked a crucial stage in the implementation of accountability after armed conflicts.

## 2 Early Developments after the Second World War

The end of the Second World War gave states the opportunity to contradict the experience of the end of the First World War and to engage the international criminal responsibility of individuals accused of international crimes. The Allies created two international military tribunals: the Nuremberg International Military Tribunal and the Tokyo International Military Tribunal.[48] These two tribunals were charged with judging those accused of having committed serious crimes during the war. This first implementation of international criminal justice was the first experience of transitional justice in the

46 Treaty of Peace, signed at Lausanne, 24 July 1923. See VIII, Declaration relating to the Amnesty.

47 Article 29, Convention for the Amelioration of the Condition of the Wounded and Sick in Armies in the Field, Geneva, 27 July 1929.

48 For all the judicial elements presented in this section, see, for more details, Part 2, Chapter 5, of this book.

twentieth century, and legal scholars consider the International Military Tribunals to be its starting point.[49] The birth of transitional justice, as we understand it today, must therefore be dated from 1945 onwards.

The International Military Tribunals established the criminal responsibility of several individuals. Other trials were held to establish responsibility for acts committed during the Second World War.[50] The Allied Powers held trials in the regions of Germany they occupied. In the period following the end of the Second World War, several European states also held trials at national level, and responsibility was sought by national courts in Europe, which convicted many individuals accused of crimes. At the domestic level, trials against individuals who participated in the commission of crimes during the Second World War have continued over time. In the twentieth and twenty-first centuries, the hunt for "Nazis" continued, resulting in arrests and trials, including in the 2020s, in what is sometimes referred as "late transitional justice." At the end of the Second World War, the configuration of criminal justice for the repression of international crimes began to take shape.

The first elements of transitional justice after the Second World War were not limited to judicial proceedings. In parallel with national trials, several European countries[51] initiated administrative procedures known as purges to dismiss people who had collaborated with the German Nazi regime, which are now considered part of issues studied in transitional justice.

Transitional justice, as projected onto the post–Second World War period, is therefore, above all, a post-conflict punitive justice that combines judicial sanctions, prosecutions and criminal penalties, with administrative sanctions and the removal of those who collaborated in the commission of crimes.

The decades following the end of the Second World War were marked by a relative lull on the transitional justice front. This does not mean, however, that states did not experiment with procedures or issues known to be related to transitional justice. To cite just a few examples, in the 1970s, the end of the colonels' dictatorship in Greece and the fall of the Franco regime in Spain raised the question of how to deal with the past and punish individuals who had violated human rights under a previous regime or as part of a regime change. In the former case, the fall of the colonels' dictatorship in

---

49 See, for example, Ruti G Teitel, *Transitional Justice* (Oxford University Press 2001) 12.

50 For more details on these trials, see Part 2 of this book.

51 Notably in France, see François Rouquet and Fabrice Virgili, *Les Françaises, les Françaises et l'Épuration. De 1940 à nos jours* (Folio 2018), chapter VI. For more on purges, see below Chapter 7, Section 2.

1977 led to the opening of criminal proceedings and administrative purges.[52] In the second case, a controversial amnesty law was passed which prevented accountability for crimes committed under Franco's regime in Spain.[53]

Despite a few examples here and there, after the Second World War and the sanctions imposed on defeated nations accused of serious crimes, there was a general shelving of criminal prosecutions in cases of serious, large-scale crimes. In the 1970s, against the backdrop of the Cold War between the East and the West, a number of armed conflicts, notably in Vietnam, Indochina and Korea, did not give rise to the same level of criminal responsibility as had been the case after the Second World War. In spite of the accusation of violations of human rights and of crimes in numerous dictatorships around the world, many perpetrators did not face trials for these violations and crimes.

However, as seen earlier in this book, especially in Latin America, social and international demands became more pressing in the late 1970s and 1980s. The question of how to respond to serious human rights violations was increasingly raised. It was then that an original response, somewhere between silence and prosecution, gradually emerged. This new response, considered today as a transitional justice mechanism, is known as "truth commissions" and was created in Latin America and Africa in the 1970s, 1980s and beyond.[54] These truth commissions were in fact the result of the transformation of an existing mechanism at national and international levels, commissions of inquiry, into a mechanism for responding to serious, large-scale human rights violations. Indeed, commissions entrusted with various tasks by the executive or created as part of parliamentary proceedings have long existed within many states. The same is true of commissions of inquiry set up at international level by states to examine the circumstances of an incident to which states attach the utmost importance. The perpetration of serious crimes in states which are unwilling to prosecute the perpetrators, but which must at the same time respond to a national or international demand for a response to these crimes, leads states to reinvent these commissions in a way, by entrusting them with the task of, among others, investigating serious human rights violations, publishing the truth and making recommendations. Such commissions were set up in Uganda (1974), Bolivia (1982), Argentina (1983) and again in Uganda (1986), before expanding in the early 1990s.

---

52 Harry J Psomiades, 'Greece: From the Colonels' Rule to Democracy' in Neil J Kritz (ed), *Transitional Justice, How Emerging Democracies Reckon with Former Regimes*, vol. II (United States Peace Institute 1995) 253–268.

53 Spain, Ley 46/1977, de 15 de octubre, de Amnistía.

54 See below Chapter 6 on truth commissions.

## 3 Decisive Developments after the End of the Cold War

A new and dynamic era of transitional justice began in the 1990s and continued into the 2000s. Indeed, in the 1990s and 2000s, transitional justice experienced a kind of golden age in the context of the end of the Cold War, with acceleration in the creation of punitive and non-punitive transitional justice mechanisms.[55] International criminal courts were once again set up on an *ad hoc* basis to examine international crimes committed in former Yugoslavia and Rwanda (the International Criminal Tribunal for Rwanda and the International Criminal Tribunal for former Yugoslavia). These were followed by other criminal tribunals such as the permanent International Criminal Court and numerous hybrid tribunals combining national and international elements. National courts were also responsible for prosecuting and punishing those responsible for serious crimes committed in the context of dictatorships or armed conflicts, and were positioned as tools of transitional justice. At the same time as this spread of national and international prosecutions, which scholars have characterised as a "justice cascade,"[56] truth commissions continued to be set up in several states, and the South African Truth and Reconciliation Commission, created in 1995, was highly reputed and the subject of unprecedented international interest, giving a boost to the development of this type of mechanism.

Other transitional justice mechanisms also emerged in response to serious violations. Lustration procedures appeared, which were a kind of purging of the public administration as part of the decommunisation of Eastern European states. Traditional justice bodies that existed in certain states before colonisation, were reactivated or reinvented in certain states, such as Rwanda, which in the context of the aftermath of genocide, used the traditional mechanism of *Gacaca* courts (traditional courts), to respond to serious crimes. Reparations were offered as part of the activities of transitional justice mechanisms (criminal justice or truth commissions) or outside them. There was also increasing talk of guarantees of non-repetition, in particular institutional reforms to prevent mass crimes or serious violations.

Transitional justice became popular only a few years after the Cold War ended. Its mechanisms "seduced" many states in transition or experiencing armed conflict. Today, there are no cases of transitions in which transitional

---

55 All these mechanisms are studied in Part 2 of this book.

56 Kathryn Sikkink, *The Justice Cascade: How Human Rights Prosecutions Are Changing World Politics* (W. W. Norton & Company 2010); Ellen Lutz and Kathryn Sikkink, 'The Justice Cascade: The Evolution and Impact of Foreign Human Rights Trials in Latin America' (2001) 2 (1) *Chicago Journal of International Law* 1.

justice is not implemented, or at least envisaged. Quite unexpectedly, some of its mechanisms also appealed to states that were not in transition, including developed states, but which wished to shed light on serious violations committed on a large scale on their territory. The implementation of transitional justice has grown significantly. It is no longer a question of its existence. Rather, it is a question of its contours, which appear to be limitless as time goes on.

## 4 The Limitless Use of Transitional Justice: Multiplications of Fields Connected to Transitional Justice

The scope of transitional justice has expanded beyond its previous focus on human rights and international humanitarian law violations in the context of authoritarian regimes and/or armed conflicts. However, even if the new topics connected to transitional justice are outside its traditional context, they are generally related to human rights violations, and sometimes even international crimes. The use of transitional justice outside its traditional and classical framework has been growing over the past many years and has met the scrutiny of scholars.[57]

This new implementation includes the use of transitional justice in established democracies, as well as the utilisation of transitional justice, or calls for the use of transitional justice, to address some contemporary global challenges. However, closer inspection of these new developments and topics in the field of transitional justice reveals that these topics are not ignored by the classical or traditional framework of transitional justice.

### 4.1 Implementation of Transitional Justice outside of Its Classical Framework

This category illustrates the evolution of transitional justice. The violations analysed within its framework are generally those committed in or by consolidated democracies, or before the twentieth century, whose effects are still vivid. Many consolidated democracies have been experiencing the use of transitional justice and many scholars have used transitional justice to analyse

57 See, for example, Stephen Winter, *Transitional Justice in Established Democracies. A Political Theory* (Palgrave Macmillan 2014); Nicola Henry, 'From Reconciliation to Transitional Justice: The Contours of Redress Politics in Established Democracies' (2015) 9 *International Journal of Transitional Justice* 199.

topics related to violations committed in these states. As mentioned earlier, in consolidated democracies such as Canada, Finland, Sweden and Norway, truth and reconciliation commissions have been used to address violations of Indigenous peoples' rights, the crimes committed against them and the legacy of discrimination they have endured.[58] There are many academics analyses and calls for transitional justice to be used to deal with racism in many states,[59] including developed states like the USA. In that country, truth commissions have been created to deal with racism and/or slavery.[60] Transitional justice has also been used to analyse and address the legacies of crimes committed during colonialism by many former colonial powers that are now consolidated democracies. This is in relation to post-colonial justice and reparations for states and peoples that have experienced colonisation and its abuses.[61] This call to use transitional justice to address historical colonial wrongs have raised debates about decolonising international law to examine these wrongs. Pietro Sullo has well summarised the terms of these debates:

> When it comes to addressing the wrongdoings of the colonial past, international law, if traditionally interpreted, becomes an insurmountable obstacle to reach the main goals of transitional justice. It makes so by simply postulating that colonial wrongdoings, although unfair, were not prohibited by international law in force at the time. Breaching its link with Eurocentric and colonial bias by embracing a decolonized relationship with international law, can provide transitional justice with legal guidance and new pathways to address the legacy of historical colonial atrocities.[62]

---

58 On these truth commissions and these states, see below Chapter 6.

59 'Special Issue: Race, Racism and Transitional Justice' (2024) 18(1) *International Journal of Transitional Justice* 1; Andrew Valls, 'Racial Justice as Transitional Justice' (2003) 36(1) *Polity* 53; Hugo van der Merwe and M Brinton Lykes, 'Racism and Transitional Justice' (2020) 14(3) *International Journal of Transitional Justice* 415.

60 For details, see Part 2 of this book.

61 Hakeem O Yusuf, 'Transitional Justice and Colonialism', *Research Handbook on Transitional Justice*, (Edward Elgar Publishing 2023); Theresa Mair, 'Transforming Transitional Justice to Address Colonial Crime. The Nama's and Herero's Claim for Justice for Germany's Colonial Genocide in Namibia' in Norman Weiß (ed), *Transitional Justice Theoretical and Practical Approaches* (Universitätsverlag Potsdam 2022); Morten Bergsmo, Wolfgang Kaleck and Kyaw Yin Hlaing (eds), *Colonial Wrongs and Access to International Law* (Torkel Opsahl Academic EPublisher 2020).

62 Pietro Sullo, 'Taking Colonialism Seriously. A Decolonial Approach to International Law, Transitional Justice and the Restitution of Cultural Heritage' (2025) 16 *Deusto Journal of Human Rights* 275, 275.

Another example of transitional justice analysis being used to address past violations is how sexual violence and other abuses within the Catholic Church are dealt with, typically in well-established democracies. Proposals have been made to establish a truth and reconciliation commission to deal with these sexual violence abuses.[63] The dealing with these abuses perpetrated within the Catholic Church has been examined within the framework of transitional justice.[64] Thus, the particularity of these implementations of transitional justice or calls for implementation is that they are applied in developed countries.

The evolution of transitional justice has led to its use in dealing with global contemporary challenges, including those related to the environment and climate change.[65] The legal doctrine has occasionally addressed the relationship between transitional justice mechanisms and environmental issues. There are scholars who, while highlighting the opportunities for international criminal law, especially international criminal tribunals which are part of the implementation of transitional justice, to take environmental issues into account, almost immediately lament the inadequacy of this law and its shortcomings in this area.[66] Beyond international criminal justice, the specific question of the link between transitional justice and climate change has been explored by some scholars. For example, Sonia Klinsky and Jasmina Brankovic have examined the usefulness of transitional justice concepts in the field of climate change, and have analysed extensively how transitional justice instruments

63 For example, Kate Jackson-Meyer, 'A Clergy Abuse Truth and Reconciliation Commission' (2023) 3 *Journal of Moral Theology* 230.

64 James Gallen, *Transitional Justice and the Historical Abuses of Church and State* (Cambridge University Press 2023); Elizabeth B Ludwin King, 'Transitional Justice and the Legacy of Child Sexual Abuse in The Catholic Church' (2018) 81(1) *Albany Law Review* 121. There have been some private initiatives in this field. For example, in France, the Catholic Church's Congregation of Bétharram set up a commission of inquiry to address the physical and sexual violence that had been perpetrated within the Notre-Dame-de-Bétharram institution, following the public exposure of several cases of sexual and physical violence within the institution. The commission is chaired by Jean-Pierre Massias, a French law professor specialising in transitional justice. See the website of this commission: https://commission.betharram.ifjd.org/.

65 Some of developments that follows on climate change and transitional justice were included in Emmanuel Guematcha paper, "Transitional Justice and Climate Change", presented at the Annual Conference of the African Society for International Law, Cairo, 29 October 2022.

66 Christian Tshiamala Banungana, 'La judiciarisation des atteintes environnementales: la cour pénale internationale à la rescousse?' (2018) *Revue québécoise de droit international* 205.

can be used in the context of global climate change.[67] Olivier de Frouville engaged in a holistic approach by proposing the implementation of a global transitional justice that would also take into account environmental and climate issues.[68] Some other scholars have examined the relationships between nature and transitional justice.[69]

### 4.2 Links between the New Topics Examined and Classical Transitional Justice

The uses of transitional justice in many other fields such as the study of Indigenous peoples, racism, colonial crimes, environmental and climate change are not always separated from the classical and traditional contexts in which transitional justice is implemented. Racism and crimes committed against Indigenous peoples are not topics ignored by classical developments of transitional justice in the aftermath of dictatorships or armed conflicts. This is particularly true in the works of some truth commissions, one of the main mechanisms of transitional justice, created to investigate violations committed during armed conflicts and/or dictatorships. For example, the truth commission of Guatemala examined discrimination and racism against Indigenous peoples in that state and the violations of their rights, and concluded that genocide was perpetrated against some groups of Guatemala Indigenous peoples during the armed conflict.[70]

Regarding colonial crimes, the truth commission of Kenya has examined the crimes committed by the British during the colonialisation of Kenya, reporting "that between 1895 and 1963, the British Colonial administration in Kenya was responsible for unspeakable and horrific gross violations of human rights."[71]

With regard to environmental issues and climate change, it has been confirmed by numerous reports that armed conflicts have effects on the environ-

---

67 Sonia Klinsky and Jasmina Brankovic, *The Global Climate Regime and Transitional Justice* (Routledge 2018).

68 Olivier de Frouville, 'Towards Global Transitional Justice?' (2022) Working Papers, Geneva Academy 5.

69 Lieselotte Viaene, Peter Doran and Jonathan Liljeblad, 'Editorial Special Section: Transitional Justice and Nature: A Curious Silence' (2023) 17(1) *International Journal of Transitional Justice* 1. See also many articles published in the dossier of this issue of the journal International Journal of Transitional Justice.

70 Guatemala, Comisión para el Esclarecimiento Histórico, *Guatemala Memoria Del Silencio*, Tomo III, (Guatemala: Oficina de Servicios para Proyectos de las Naciones Unidas, 1999) 314–424.

71 Kenya, 'Report of the Truth, Justice and Reconciliation Commission', vol. 1, 2013, vii.

ment and on climate change, and problems generated by climate change are sometimes among the causes of armed conflicts, or at least contribute to exacerbating conflicts and worsening the situation of the most vulnerable.[72] In this regard, the 2022 report of the Intergovernmental Panel on Climate Change noted that "[c]limate hazards have affected armed conflict within countries but the observed influence of climate is small relative to socioeconomic, political and cultural factors"; it also clearly stated that "[a]dverse impacts of climate change threaten to increase poverty and inequality, [...] and place strain on civil institutions – all of which are factors that contribute to the emergence or worsening of civil unrest and conflict."[73] The link between climate change and unrest or armed conflicts has been established in several states, notably in Mali, Somalia, the Central African Republic, South Sudan, Yemen, Afghanistan, Iraq and in Latin American states.[74] In these contexts, transitional justice may be interested in environmental issues in post-conflict states or after authoritarian rule. Some truth commissions investigating violations committed during armed conflicts and/or authoritarian rule have not ignored environmental issues and even climate change issues in their investigations of past human rights and international humanitarian violations. In its final report, Kenya's Truth, Justice and Reconciliation Commission devoted some developments to environmental issues and climate change when addressing the Turbi massacre that took place in 2005. In analysing

72 ICRC, 'When Rain Turns to Dust. Understanding and Responding to the Combined Impact of Armed Conflicts and the Climate and Environment Crisis on People's Lives', Report 2020; CICR, 'Crise de l'eau, conflits armés et changement climatique', note d'information, 2022; Philippe Bou Nader, 'Le changement climatique comme multiplicateur de conflits armés' (2018) 1(No. 30 + Supplément) *Les Champs de Mars* 449.

73 IPCC, *Climate Change 2022: Impacts, Adaptation and Vulnerability. Contribution of Working Group II to the Sixth Assessment Report of the Intergovernmental Panel on Climate Change* [H.-O. Pörtner, D.C. Roberts, M. Tignor, E.S. Poloczanska, K. Mintenbeck, A. Alegría, M. Craig, S. Langsdorf, S. Löschke, V. Möller, A. Okem, B. Rama (eds)], (Cambridge University Press 2022) 1128.

74 ICRC, 'When Rain Turns to Dust. Understanding and Responding to the Combined Impact of Armed Conflicts and the Climate and Environment Crisis on People's Lives', Report 2020, 5; Human Rights Council, 'Report of the Office of the United Nations High Commissioner for Human Rights on the Relationship between Climate Change and Human Rights', UN doc. A/HRC/10/61 (2009) paras. 61–64; Tuiloma Neroni Slade, 'International Humanitarian Law and Climate Change' in Suzannah Linton, Tim McCormack and Sandesh Sivakumaran (eds), *Asia-Pacific Perspectives on International Humanitarian Law* (Cambridge University Press 2019) 643–655; Afshin Akhtarkhavari and Fiona Lubett, 'Nature's Access to Water in Post-conflict Peacebuilding Efforts in South Sudan' in Natalia Szablewska Sascha and Dominik Bachmann (eds), *Current Issues in Transitional Justice. Towards a More Holistic Approach* (Springer 2015) 303.

the causes, the commission noted the recurrent conflicts taking place between several communities over access to resources, which was made difficult because of climate change.[75] Here, climate change is a factor that exacerbates conflicts between communities, which in turn generates human rights violations. The Kenyan commission stated:

> There has also been a struggle over access to resources that are diminishing at a high rate because of climate change and the encroachment on pastoral lands by agriculturalists. Local communities thus often find themselves on a collision course as they negotiate for access to pasture and water. Increased population also puts more pressure on the dwindling resources, thus heightening conflicts, especially over water and pasture. Conflict increases during the dry spell when livestock tend to concentrate in the diminishing areas with water and pasture.[76]

According to the same commission, the marginalisation of the Coast Province in Kenya was a source of conflict. In analysing this marginalisation, the commission noted that there were environmental and serious problems of pollution affecting the province, pollution that was destroying the environment and becoming a source of frustration that fuelled human rights violations and conflict.[77]

In the same vein, the truth commission in Colombia has taken the issue of climate change into account in its recommendations to the Colombian state. When discussing peace in the rural territories of Colombia, the commission recalled the inequalities and serious problems of access to land and resources in Colombia's rural areas, and indicated that it had taken into account, among other things, the issue of climate change – a challenge, it wrote, that Colombia and the planet were facing.[78] The report stressed the importance of preventing

---

75 Kenya, 'Report of the Truth, Justice and Reconciliation Commission' vol. II A, 2013, 407, para. 783.

76 *Ibid.*

77 *Ibid.*, vol. II B 99, para 303, and 116, para. 360: "Areas served by sewage systems, however, also contribute to environmental degradation because treatment works are not operational and the sewage is disposed directly into the sea, threatening public health and marine life. The situation is compounded by the fact that Kenya does not yet have any effluent standards for discharge into the sea, and most water projects have been implemented without due consideration of sanitation and other complementary infrastructure. The main causes of the poor urban water systems in coastal regions include poor planning, mismanagement and lack of technical expertise."

78 Comisión para el Esclarecimiento de la Verdad, la Convivencia y la No Repetición, 'Hay futuro si hay verdad, Informe Final, Hallazgos y recomendaciones de la Comisión de la Verdad de Colombia', Bogotá, 22 de junio de 2022, 866. In particular, the commission

future conflicts over access to resources.[79] In its recommendations to the Colombian state for a strategy of sustainable development and peace at the rural level, the Colombian commission proposed to "[a]ddress the effects of armed conflict and legal and illegal economic activities on environmental degradation and climate change, through actions to contain them and to protect and care for ecosystems, water and land as fundamental goods for the general interest and the common good."[80] Thus, the Colombian commission insisted on the prevention of tensions that could, as a result of climate change, provoke conflicts or aggravate those conflicts already underway, and which could inevitably have dramatic human consequences.

The extension and the evolution of areas and contexts in which transitional justice is implemented or called on to be implemented is sometimes linked to classical and traditional implementation of transitional justice. Between the classical use of transitional justice and the evolution of transitional justice, there is a continuum, not a breakup. The implementation of transitional justice in different contexts that embrace limitless topics illustrates the variety of areas in which the rights of individuals and groups of individuals have been violated on a large scale. It is also a sign of the need to respond to these violations and of the reality of the success of a concept that continues to prevail.[81] This expansion of transitional justice may sometimes be a challenge because its limitless use has the potential of blurring the concept or letting it become a catch-all concept, raising continuous questions about what is and will be the next topic that can be included in transitional justice as time goes on. In this vein, even if transitional justice, its mechanisms and its analysis may be used in other contexts, one should not forget that its primary focus is on justice being applied in cases of gross human rights violations or international crimes in times of transition from authoritarian rule and/or after an armed conflict or efforts to end an armed conflict. Nonetheless, while focusing on these contexts, the use of transitional justice and its mechanisms in other contexts should be considered if it can help to improve victims' rights and find effective solutions to contemporary challenges. In the international sphere, this extraordinary development and prevalence of the field of transitional justice could not have been achieved without the actions of international organisations.

---

proposed to implement a strategy to ensure equitable access to land and better management of land and socio-environmental conflicts, see 865–866.

79 *Ibid.*, 866.

80 Translation from Spanish. *Ibid.*, 869.

81 See the "resources library" and regular compilation of news on the implementation of "transitional justice" in the world, according to the International Center for transitional justice, available online: https://www.ictj.org/.

CHAPTER 3

# International Organisations and Diffusion of Transitional Justice

Many international organisations are involved in the dissemination of transitional justice: the United Nations, European Union, Organization of American States, African Union and so on. At the international level, it is often within these organisations that transitional justice has taken off. Studying the institutionalisation of transitional justice at the international level, therefore, generally means studying the contributions and actions of international organisations in its implementation. In this field, the United Nations is the international organisation that used to play the main role (discussed in Section 1). Regional organisations have also been extensively involved in the implementation of transitional justice (discussed in Section 2).

## 1 The United Nations and Its Main Role in the Implementation of Transitional Justice

As we have seen, the United Nations, which is the largest international organisation in the world, has played a significant role in the birth and growth of transitional justice. It is an organisation that was created in 1945, in the aftermath of a major armed conflict. It is not surprising that it was involved from the beginning in matters that would later be categorised as transitional justice mechanisms. It is no exaggeration to say that without the UN, transitional justice would not have developed and spread as quickly as it did. The role of the UN goes far beyond these earlier developments and the definition of transitional justice. The UN has a mandate to maintain security and peace and therefore intervenes in many conflict and post-conflict transitional situations; today, the UN is an organisation whose many organs are involved in transitional justice. The UN participates in transitional justice by developing activities in several areas: creating or participating in the creation of criminal tribunals and truth commissions, contributing to strengthening the capacity of states to implement transitional justice, and defining the normative aspects of transitional justice.

 | HTTPS://DOI.ORG/10.1163/9789004766655-006

## 1.1 The Contribution to the Creation and Functioning of Criminal Tribunals

The UN's first contribution to the establishment of criminal tribunals came from the UN Security Council. In the 1990s, as transitional justice was being explored by scholars, the Security Council decided to use Chapter 7 of the UN Charter, which gives the Council the power to take action in the event of a threat to international peace and security, to create two *ad hoc* criminal tribunals. The first was the International Criminal Tribunal for the former Yugoslavia (ICTY),[1] and the second was the International Criminal Tribunal for Rwanda (ICTR).[2] These tribunals were both established in the context of an armed conflict characterised by international crimes. The two tribunals were part of the UN, which funded them and participated in their operation.

The UN also contributed to the creation of the International Criminal Court (ICC), which, unlike the two previous *ad hoc* tribunals, is a permanent court. Although the ICC is an independent tribunal created by several states, it was negotiated and shaped over many years within the UN. The process that led to the creation of the ICC dates back to the aftermath of the Second World War.[3] The International Law Commission, a body of international law experts within the UN, began considering the creation of an international criminal court in the late 1940s.The process was then frozen during the Cold War. In the 1990s, the process gained momentum within the UN when the UN General Assembly decided to examine the issue. This examination led to negotiations and the signing by many states in 1998 of the Rome Statute, which established the ICC. The ICC was set up to prosecute some international crimes and was not explicitly described as a transitional justice mechanism. However, as the crimes it investigated were generally committed by dictatorial regimes or during armed conflicts, it gradually became a strong transitional justice mechanism.[4]

Another key contribution of the UN to the establishment of judicial transitional justice mechanisms has been in the area of internationalised, mixed or hybrid tribunals, which are generally established in the context of ongoing or post-armed conflicts. These tribunals are called internationalised, mixed or hybrid because they combine both international and national elements.[5]

---

1 UN Security Council, Resolution 827, UN doc. S/RES/827 (1993) 25 May 1993.

2 UN Security Council, Resolution 955, UN doc. S/RES/955 (1994) 8 November 1994.

3 See on the process of the creation of the ICC, William Schabas, *An Introduction to the International Criminal Court*, (6th edn, Cambridge University Press 2020) 8–11 and 16–22.

4 See below Part 2 for details on the mechanisms of transitional justice.

5 For more details of these tribunals, see below Chapter 5.

The UN has been involved in the creation of some of these tribunals, either by setting them up with the transitional administration of a territory (e.g., Kosovo and East Timor) or by concluding bilateral agreements with the transitional states (e.g., Sierra Leone and Cambodia).

In Kosovo, the civil war pitting Kosovar Albanians against Serbs led to direct UN administration of a tribunal – the United Nations Mission in Kosovo (UNMIK). This tribunal was set up in 2000 and it was decided to appoint international judges and prosecutors who appeared first in the courts of Mitrovica, a city in Kosovo.[6] Later, the possibility of appointing international judges was extended to the entire territory of Kosovo.[7]

In East Timor, direct UN administration of the territory was established in the wake of a bloody war that saw Timorese fight for their independence from Indonesia.[8] The Special Representative of the Secretary-General (Transitional Administrator), head of the United Nations Transitional Administration in East Timor, created a hybrid tribunal in East Timor in 2000, which was established as the Panels with Exclusive Jurisdiction over Serious Criminal Offences.[9]

In 2002, after a peace agreement between the government of Sierra Leone and rebels failed to end the armed conflict in Sierra Leone, the UN and the government of Sierra Leone signed an agreement establishing the Special Court for Sierra Leone.[10] The Special Court was created to establish the criminal responsibility of those "who bear the greatest responsibility for serious violations of international humanitarian law and Sierra Leonean law committed in the territory of Sierra Leone since 30 November 1996, including those leaders who, in committing such crimes, have threatened the establishment of and implementation of the peace process in Sierra Leone."[11]

In Cambodia, the UN concluded an agreement with the Cambodian government for the establishment of the Extraordinary Chambers in the Courts of Cambodia.[12] The tribunal was set to prosecute those who committed serious

6 See, *inter alia*, UNMIK Regulation 2000/6, UN doc. UNMIK/Reg/2000/6, 15 February 2000, in UN doc. S/2000/177/Add.2, 28 March 2000; Mathieu Jacquelin, 'International Law' (2018) 1(1) *Journal of Criminal Science and Comparative Criminal Law* 229.

7 UNMIK Regulation 2000/34, UN doc. UNMIK/Reg/2000/6, 27 May 2000.

8 UN Security Council, Resolution 1272 (1999), UN doc. S/RES/1272, 25 October 1999.

9 Regulation No. 2000/15 on the Establishment of Panels with Exclusive Jurisdiction over Serious Criminal Offences, UN doc. UNTAET/REG/2000/15, 6 June 2000.

10 Agreement between the United Nations and the Government of Sierra Leone, 16 January 2002.

11 Article 1 (1), Statute of the Special Court for Sierra Leone.

12 Agreement between the United Nations and Cambodia for the Prosecution of Crimes Committed during the Period of Democratic Kampuchea, 2003.

crimes during a dictatorial regime that governed Cambodia between 1975 and 1979. The agreement was preceded by a Cambodian Law creating that tribunal in 2001 and which was revised in 2004.[13]

The UN was also instrumental in establishing the Special Tribunal for Lebanon (STL). Established following the entry into force of a Lebanese–UN agreement adopted by the UN Security Council,[14] the tribunal's main objective was "to prosecute persons responsible for the attack of 14 February 2005, resulting in the death of former Lebanese Prime Minister Rafiq Hariri and in the death or injury of other persons."[15] The author of these lines is of the opinion that this tribunal could not be considered a transitional justice mechanism, as it was not established in a post-armed conflict or post-dictatorship context, and was not mandated to deal with abuses that could be described as massive or large-scale.

The UN's contribution here also extended to the financing of these mechanisms. The UN funded the hybrid tribunals for Kosovo, Sierra Leone and East Timor, and contributed to the funding of the Extraordinary Chambers of the Cambodian Tribunals.

### 1.2 The UN Contributions to the Creation of Truth Commissions

The United Nations has played a leading role in the establishment of many truth commissions, non-judicial bodies mandated to investigate serious violations or crimes, usually in the context of post-armed conflicts.[16] Even though most truth commissions are national bodies, the UN has been involved in their establishment and operation, usually in post-conflict contexts. The UN's involvement is usually linked to its participation in the process leading to a peace agreement that provides for the establishment of a truth commission, as in El Salvador and Guatemala, or because the UN has decided to administer a territory that has been through a bloody war, as in East Timor.

The first truth commission in which the UN played a major role was the one established in El Salvador following the UN-backed peace agreement signed by the Salvadoran government and the rebels, which put an end to

13 Law on the Establishment of the Extraordinary Chambers in the Courts of Cambodia, 27 October 2004.

14 UN Security Council, Resolution 1757, UN doc. S/RES/1757, 30 May 2007, para. 1 (a).

15 *Ibid.*, see Annex: Agreement between the United Nations and the Republic of Lebanon on the Establishment of a Special Tribunal for Lebanon, article 1.

16 For more on truth commissions, see Part 2, Chapter 6, of this book.

the country's bloody civil war.[17] The peace agreement, signed under the auspices of the United Nations, provided for the establishment of a truth commission to tell the truth about the violence committed in El Salvador during the armed conflict.[18] The United Nations led the establishment of this truth commission. All three of its members were international appointments made by the UN Secretary-General, with a mandate to submit its final report to El Salvador and the United Nations.[19] Members of the staff were also international, and the commission was funded by a UN special fund to which the United States and the then European Community and others contributed.[20]

The truth commission of Timor Leste can also be considered as having been created by the UN. Indeed, the UN decided to establish the United Nations Transitional Administration in East Timor (UNTAET) with the task "to exercise all legislative and executive authority, including the administration of justice," and a Special Representative of the Secretary-General was appointed for that task.[21] That Special Representative decided to create a truth commission in Timor.[22] The truth commission was considered as part of the accomplishment of the UN in East Timor even if its members were national commissioners.[23]

In the same vein, the UN contributed to the establishment of the Guatemalan truth commission, which was created in the context of a UN-backed peace agreement between rebels and the government after a bloody civil war.[24] The parties agreed to the creation of a truth commission in one of the agreements crafted to restore a lasting peace.[25] According to that agreement,

---

17 Peace agreement signed at Mexico City on 16 January 1992 between the Government of El Salvador and the Frente Farabundo Martí para la Liberación National, in UN doc. A/46/664, S/23501, 30 January 1992.

18 *Ibid.*, para. 5. See in particular, the Mexico Agreements signed on 27 April 1991 by representatives of the Government of El Salvador and of the Frente Farabundo Martí para la Liberación Nacional, para. IV, and Annex: Commission on the Truth.

19 See the Mexico Agreements, *Ibid.*, para. IV. Thomas Buergenthal, 'The United Nations Truth Commission for El Salvador' (1994) 27(3) *Vanderbilt Law Review* 497, 504.

20 *Ibid.*

21 UN doc. S/RES/1272 (1999) 25 October 1999.

22 Regulation No. 2001/10 on the Establishment of a Commission for Reception, Truth and Reconciliation in East Timor, UN doc. UNTAET/REG/2001/10, 13 July 2001.

23 *Ibid.*, section 4.

24 Agreement on a firm and lasting peace, signed on 29 December 1996 by the Peace Commission of the Government of Guatemala (COPAZ) and the General Command of the Unidad Revolucionaria Nacional Guatemalteca (URNG), UN doc. A/51/796 S/1997/114, 7 February 1997.

25 Agreement on the establishment of the Commission to clarify past human rights violations and acts of violence that have caused the Guatemalan population to suffer, see UN doc. A/48/954, S/1994/751, 1994, Annex.

the commission consisted of three members and the UN Secretary-General appointed the "moderator" of the commission, who was to designate the two other members of the commission."[26] However, in spite of the UN implication in the creation and establishment of the Guatemala truth commission and unlike in El Salvador, the UN was not that implicated in the functioning of the truth commission, and as such it "was not a United Nations managed truth commission."[27]

The same kind of contribution of the UN to the creation of a truth commission was seen in Sierra Leone. In that country, in the context of an armed conflict, the UN backed the negotiations between the rebels and the Sierra Leonean government. The peace agreement signed by both parties provided that a truth commission be created.[28] Later, an act passed by the Sierra Leone Parliament provided that the UN High Commissioner for Human Rights participate in the choice and hiring of the members of the truth commission.[29] However, just as was the case with the Guatemala truth commission, the Sierra Leone truth commission was not managed by the UN.

In spite of this direct involvement in the creation of truth commissions, the contribution of the UN in that field falls into the broader multidimensional help that it has offered the states in post-conflict or transitional situations. The UN's contributions to transitional justice mechanisms include strengthening the capacity of some national procedures to deal with serious human rights violations and international crimes in transitional and post-conflict contexts.

### 1.3 Improvement of the Transitional and Post-conflict States Capacity

The office of the UN High Commissioner for Human Rights (UNHCHR) is the main UN body that offers its assistance to countries in transition. Since 2000, the annual reports of the UNHCHR have referred to the role of the Office of the High Commissioner in that field. In 2007, in order to stress the commitment of the High Commissioner on this topic, "the Human Rights Council decided, without a vote, to commend the Office of the United Nations High Commissioner for Human Rights for its efforts in developing the issue of

26 *Ibid.*, para. V.

27 Daniel Rothenberg, *Memory of Silence. The Guatemalan Truth Commission* (Palgrave Macmillan 2012) xxxvi.

28 Peace Agreement between the Government of Sierra Leone and Revolutionary United Front signed on 7 July 1999, article XXVI, UN doc. S/1999/777, 12 July 1999.

29 See the document: Schedule – (Subsection (1) of section 3), Procedure for the Selection of Nominees for Appointment to the Commission, in Truth and Reconciliation Commission: The Truth and Reconciliation Commission Act, February 2000.

transitional justice and human rights, *inter alia*, by expanding the presence of the Office in peacebuilding operations, and to encourage the Office to continue to strengthen its important practical and analytical work regarding this complex issue."[30]

UNHCHR's contributions range from supporting national transition processes, reparations programmes and institutional reforms to providing expertise to and strengthening the capacity of transitional states. For example, in 2021, the High Commissioner reported that it "contributed to strengthening the capacities of the CEV [Commission for the Clarification of Truth, Coexistence and Non-recurrence, the Colombian truth commission] to ensure it incorporated international standards into its final recommendations, including in relation to security, justice, extrajudicial executions, education and culture, state presence, corruption, victims and land. UN Human Rights also increased the understanding of regional and national officials of the CEV about human rights violations, with a territorial perspective, by facilitating 35 technical assistance sessions on international norms and standards."[31] It also helped to push for the operationalisation of transitional justice mechanisms in the Central African Republic, Maldives and Sudan.[32] In 2020, it provided "technical support" to the Central African Republic authorities, strengthened the capacities of human rights defenders in Kenya in the context of transitional justice, supported a campaign of information for the truth commission of Tunisia, supported the fight against impunity in the Democratic Republic of the Congo and drafted legislation on transitional justice in Sudan,[33] thus influencing the normative dimension and good practices in transitional justice.

### 1.4 Contributions to Establishing Rules and Good Practice Principles in Transitional Justice

With the help of many experts and scholars, the UN has contributed to establishing the normative aspects of transitional justice and to defining the rules or principles of transitional justice. It has done so because it has been interested in the accountability of those accused of violating human rights or international law, or of committing international crimes, since the term "transitional justice" began to be used.

30 'Report to the General Assembly on the Fourth Session of the Human Rights Council', UN doc. A/HRC/4/123, See 4/102, Transitional justice, 30 March 2007.
31 'United Nations Human Rights Report', 2021, 50.
32 'United Nations Human Rights Report', 2021, 50–51.
33 'United Nations Human Rights Report', 2020, 50–51.

First of all, when the UN created criminal tribunals in the 1990s (e.g., the ICTY and ICTR) or participated in the creation of the ICC and hybrid tribunals, it participated directly or indirectly in the elaboration of their statutes. Today, these tribunals' statutes constitute one of the core aspects of international criminal law, which is now part of transitional justice. Second, it was within the UN that the "pillars of transitional justice" were identified. Starting in the 2000s, many documents from the UN or from scholars and other actors started to refer to the pillars of transitional justice, generally without indicating where those pillars came from. Actually, as we have seen, these pillars came from the work of Louis Joinet, who was mandated by the Sub-Commission on Prevention of Discrimination and Protection of Minorities of the Commission on Human Rights to work on the principles relating to the fight against impunity. The report that Joinet issued in 1997 identified many principles and four main elements in the fight against impunity: the right to truth, the right to justice, the right to reparation and the guarantees of non-repetition.[34] These four elements drawn from the Joinet principles, which were updated by Diane Orentlicher in 2005,[35] were later labelled "pillars of transitional justice": justice, truth, reparation and guarantees of non-recurrence. The same elements could also be found in a 1996 report by Theo Van Boven, who was commissioned by the UN to report on the right to reparation.[36] The report listed five forms of reparations: restitution, compensation, rehabilitation, satisfaction and guarantees of non-repetition. The fifth form, guarantees of non-repetition, was one of the core elements of Joinet's report. Forms of satisfaction and guarantees of non-repetition included "judicial sanctions" and "judicial decisions,"

34 'Question of the Impunity of Perpetrators of Human Rights Violations (Civil and Political),' Revised final report prepared by Mr. Joinet pursuant to Sub-Commission decision 1996/119, Annex II Set of Principles for the Protection and Promotion of Human Rights through Action to Combat Impunity, UN doc. E/CN.4/Sub.2/1997/20/Rev.1, 2 October 1997.

35 See also, 'Report of the Independent Expert to Update the Set of Principles to Combat Impunity', Diane Orentlicher, Addendum Updated Set of principles for the protection and promotion of human rights through action to combat impunity, UN doc, E/CN.4/2005/102/Add.1, 8 February 2005.

36 'Revised Set of Basic Principles and Guidelines on the Right to Reparation for Victims of Gross Violations of Human Rights and Humanitarian Law,' prepared by Mr. Theo van Boven, pursuant to Sub-Commission decision 1995/117. Annex Basic Principles and Guidelines on the Right to Reparation for Victims of Gross Violations of Human Rights and Humanitarian Law, UN doc. E/CN.4/SUB.2/1996/17, 24 May 1996. This work was continued by Cherif Bassiouni, see 'The Right to Restitution, Compensation and Rehabilitation for Victims of Gross Violations of Human Rights and Fundamental Freedoms,' Final report of the Special Rapporteur, Mr. M. Cherif Bassiouni, submitted in accordance with Commission resolution 1999/33, UN doc. E/CN.4/2000/62, 18 January 2000.

which were referred to as "justice" in the Joinet report, and "full and public disclosure of the truth," which was referred to as "truth" in the Joinet report. So, there was an overlap between the work of Louis Joinet and that of Theo Van Boven. Justice, truth, reparations and guarantees of non-repetition, which in the 2000s became the pillars of transitional justice, came mainly from Joinet's work on the fight against impunity and also from Theo Van Boven's work on the right to reparations. Memorialisation, which will be considered the fifth pillar of transitional justice in 2020, was also taken into consideration in the Joinet Report and the Van Boven report. The Joinet Report referred, for example, to measures "aimed at preserving the collective memory from extinction and, in particular, at guarding against the development of revisionist and negationist arguments".[37] It also pointed out the need of "[c]ommemorative ceremonies, naming of public thoroughfares, monuments"; of "[p]eriodic tribute to the victims," and of "[a]cknowledgement in history textbooks and human rights training manuals of a faithful account of exceptionally serious violations."[38] The Van Boven report emphasised the necessity of "[c]ommemorations and paying tribute to the victims."[39] This created a clear link between the transitional justice discourse on the one hand, and the fight against impunity and reparations on the other.

In the same vein, the UN Secretary-General's report on transitional justice in 2004 was a decisive moment in explaining what transitional justice was.[40] That report gave an official recognition to the phrase that had emerged among scholars. Another report exploring transitional justice issues was published by the Secretary-General in 2011.[41] He also published *Guidance Notes on Transitional Justice* in 2010 and 2023.[42] These documents, elaborated by the Sec-

37 'Question of the Impunity of Perpetrators of Human Rights Violations (Civil and Political),' Revised final report prepared by Mr. Joinet, pursuant to Sub-Commission decision 1996/119, Annex II Set of Principles for the Protection and Promotion of Human Rights through Action to Combat Impunity, UN doc. E/CN.4/Sub.2/1997/20/Rev.1, 2 October 1997, Principle 2.

38 *Ibid.*, Principle 44 (c, d, e).

39 'Revised Set of Basic Principles and Guidelines on the Right to Reparation for Victims of Gross Violations of Human Rights and Humanitarian Law,' prepared by Mr. Theo van Boven, pursuant to Sub-Commission decision 1995/117. Annex Basic Principles and Guidelines on the Right to Reparation for Victims of Gross Violations of Human Rights and Humanitarian Law, UN doc. E/CN.4/SUB.2/1996/17, 24 May 1996, para. 15 (f).

40 'The Rule of Law and Transitional Justice in Conflict and Post-Conflict Societies,' Report of the Secretary-General, UN doc. S/2004/616, 23 August 2004.

41 'The Rule of Law and Transitional Justice in Conflict and Post-Conflict Societies,' Report of the Secretary-General, UN doc. S/2011/634, 12 October 2011.

42 See 'Guidance Note of the Secretary-General, United Nations Approach to Transitional Justice,' 2010; 'Guidance Note of the Secretary-General on Transitional Justice', 2023.

retary-General, dealt with the UN's approach to transitional justice. They stressed repeatedly the need for legal measures to be taken in transitional states in response to violations and abuses. For example, the 2023 *Guidance Note on Transitional Justice* held that consultations, truth, justice, reparation and guarantees of non-recurrence must be at the heart of the implementation of transitional justice. From 2006, a series of reports by the Office of the High Commissioner for Human Rights on rule-of-law instruments in societies emerging from armed conflict also gave a broad picture of the mechanisms of transitional justice and the issues they faced. These reports were dedicated to normative and practical aspects of prosecutions,[43] truth commissions,[44] vetting,[45] reparation programmes,[46] amnesties,[47] national consultations on transitional justice[48] and archives.[49] In 2011, the Human Rights Council created a position of a Special Rapporteur on the promotion of truth, justice, reparation and guarantees of non-recurrence,[50] which could simply be labelled as the Special Rapporteur on transitional justice. The Special Rapporteur was mandated, *inter alia*, to conduct research on transitional justice topics and recommend measures in that field.[51] As we have seen, he also decided to push for the addition of memorialisation as the "fifth pillar" of transitional justice in 2020.[52]

There is no doubt that many other agencies of the United Nations, such as the United Nations Development Program,[53] and other United Nations entities, including its field missions, are involved in transitional justice by intervening in post-conflict states, supporting transitional justice initiatives

43 OHCHR, 'Rule-of-Law Tools for Post-Conflict States: Prosecution Initiatives,' 2006.

44 OHCHR, 'Rule-of-Law Tools for Post-Conflict States: Truth Commissions,' 2006.

45 OHCHR, 'Rule-Of-Law Tools for Post-Conflict States. Vetting: An Operational Framework,' 2006.

46 OHCHR, 'Rule-Of-Law Tools for Post-Conflict States: Reparations programmes,' 2008.

47 OHCHR, 'Rule-Of-Law Tools for Post-Conflict States: Amnesties,' 2009.

48 OHCHR, 'Rule-Of-Law Tools for Post-Conflict States: National Consultations on Transitional Justice,' 2009.

49 OHCHR, 'Rule-of-Law Tools for Post-Conflict States: Archives,' 2015.

50 HRC, Resolution 18/7; Special Rapporteur on the Promotion of Truth, Justice, Reparation and Guarantees of Non-recurrence, UN doc. A/HRC/RES/18/7, 29 September 2011.

51 *Ibid.*

52 'Memorialization Processes in the Context of Serious Violations of Human Rights and International Humanitarian Law: The Fifth Pillar of Transitional Justice,' Report of the Special Rapporteur on the promotion of truth, justice, reparation and guarantees of non-recurrence, UN doc. A/HRC/45/45, 9 July 2020.

53 For the action of UNDP, see the document, 'From Justice for the Past to Peace and Inclusion for the Future. A Development Approach to Transitional Justice Lessons Learned from UNDP Policy and Practice,' November 2020.

and providing expertise or capacity-building. In the same vein, many human rights bodies established by human rights conventions adopted within the United Nations have also contributed to the development of the normative aspects of transitional justice, particularly with regard to defining the international obligations of states in responding to human rights violations.[54] This feature has also appeared in many regional organisations that deal with transitional processes.

## 2 Regional Organisations' Participation in Transitional Justice

### 2.1 The European Union

The European Union is an organisation that is the culmination of the European economic construction, which began after the Second World War with the creation of the European Communities in 1957 by the Treaty of Rome. In the beginning, the European Economic Community had an economic aim and was not concerned with the issue of human rights. Gradually, the question of respect for human rights was raised within this organisation, initially through the Court of Justice of the European Communities, which took human rights into account in its decisions from 1970 onward.[55]

After the creation of the European Union (EU) in 1992, which has among its aims the preservation of peace and international security, and the protection of human rights,[56] the organisation became much more involved in human rights issues. In the 2000s, as transitional justice gained momentum within the United Nations, the EU became interested in the matter. It began to contribute financially to transitional justice processes, including to international criminal justice, truth commissions, reparations and reforms.[57] It also offered capability-building support to transitional justice processes in many countries; for example, in Colombia, Haiti, Senegal and Guatemala.[58] In 2015,

54 See below, Part 3, on the international obligations of transitional states.

55 See CJEC, *Handelsgesellschaft*, 1970.

56 Article 3, Treaty on European Union, 1992.

57 See for an overview, Laura Davis, 'European Union and Transitional Justice,' ICTJ Report, 2010.

58 Laura Davis, *EU Foreign Policy, Transitional Justice and Mediation: Principle, Policy, Practice* (Routledge 2014). See also, James A. Sweeney, 'The EU's Promotion of Transitional Justice: External and Internal Dimensions of a Patchwork of Policies' (2026) *International Journal of Human Rights*.

aware of the necessity to give a framework to its contribution on transitional justice, the EU published a document entitled *The EU's Policy Framework on Support to Transitional Justice*.[59] The document pointed out the approaches, "positions," "guiding principles" and strategies for the EU in the area of transitional justice. The EU also played an important role in the creation of a hybrid tribunal in Kosovo that was set up to investigate crimes committed during the armed conflict.[60] The European Parliament has also been involved in the normative aspects of transitional justice, adopting numerous resolutions in this field.[61]

### 2.2 The Council of Europe

Since its creation in 1949, the Council of Europe, which had the "realisation of human rights and fundamental freedoms" among its aims, has taken strong positions in cases of violations of human rights by dictatorial regimes. For example, it did so regarding Greece during the colonel's dictatorship in 1970.[62] Recently, it expelled Russia from the organisation after "[r]eaffirming that the aggression of the Russian Federation against Ukraine constitutes a serious violation by the Russian Federation of its obligations under Article 3 of the Statute of the Council of Europe."[63] However, one of its decisive contributions to the field of transitional justice is the 2011 publication by the Committee of Ministers of the Council of Europe entitled *Eradicating Impunity for Serious Human Rights Violations*.[64] Although the document does not explicitly refer to the phrase "transitional justice," it does deal with issues of transitional justice, as it refers to the need of investigations, of complementary measures such as commissions and of reparations in cases of serious violations of human rights.[65] The European Court of Human Rights, which is part of the Council of

---

59 EU, 'The EU's Policy Framework on Support to Transitional Justice,' 2015.

60 Law No. 04/L-274 on Ratification of the International Agreement between the Republic of Kosovo and the European Union on the European Union Rule of Law Mission in Kosovo, 23 April 2014; Law No.05/L-053 on Specialist Chambers and Specialist Prosecutor's Office, 3 August 2015.

61 On that issue, see Part 3 of this book on the definition of international obligations of transitional states.

62 Resolution DH (70) 1 of the Committee of Ministers of the Council of Europe, The Greek case, 15 April 1970.

63 Resolution CM/Res(2022)2 on the cessation of the membership of the Russian Federation to the Council of Europe, 16 March 2022.

64 CE, 'Eradicating Impunity for Serious Human Rights Violations. Guidelines and Reference Texts,' 30 March 2011.

65 *Ibid.*

Europe and in charge of monitoring the respect of the European Convention of Human Rights by States Parties, has also been dealing with transitional justice issues in some of its judgments on post-conflict or post-dictatorship states.[66]

### 2.3 The African Union

Although Africa has been one of the most productive terrains of experimentation of transitional justice because of the many armed conflicts and dictatorial regimes it has experienced, it did not produce relevant documents on that issue before the 2010s. In 2013, a resolution on transitional justice was adopted by the African Commission on Human and Peoples' Rights, a body in charge of protecting and promoting human rights in Africa, in order to conduct a study on that issue in Africa.[67] The African Union has also contributed in creating a criminal tribunal to try individuals accused of perpetrating crimes during a dictatorship or an armed conflict. In 2012, the African Union concluded an agreement with Senegal for the creation of the Extraordinary African Chambers in Senegal, a hybrid court that tried Hissein Habré, the former head of the State of Chad, for international crimes.[68] In 2019–2021, it also participated in the efforts to create and operationalise a hybrid court for South Sudan.[69]

However, the decisive role of the African Union in transitional justice is the adoption on 12 February 2019 of a policy document on transitional justice.[70] The document explained the understanding, strategies and objectives of the African Union in the field of transitional justice.[71] In 2025, Strategic Programs on Transitional Justice were also adopted within the African Union.[72]

The African Commission on Human and Peoples' Rights and the African Court on Human and Peoples' Rights, which are in charge of monitoring the

---

66 See below, Part 3, of this book and the international obligations of states.

67 AcomHPR, Resolution on Transitional Justice in Africa, doc. ACHPR/Res.235(LIII)2013, 23 April 2013.

68 Agreement between the Republic of Senegal and the African Union on the Establishment of Extraordinary African Chambers in the Courts of Senegal, 22 August 2012.

69 Signed Revitalized Agreement on the Resolution of the Conflict in South Sudan (R-ARCSS), Addis Ababa, 12 September 2018, Section 5.3 Hybrid Court for South Sudan (HCSS).

70 AU, *Transitional Justice Policy*, 2019.

71 *Ibid.*

72 African Union, *Strategic Programs on Transitional Justice*, Transitional Justice Unit, Democracy, Election and Constitutionalism Division (DEC) Directorate of Governance and Conflict Prevention (GCPD) Department of Political Affairs, Peace and Security African Union Commission, Addis Ababa, Ethiopia, 2025.

respect of human rights in African states, have also participated in defining the obligations of states during post-conflict periods of transition.[73] For example, the African Commission on Human and Peoples' Rights has published the "Study on Transitional Justice in Africa and Human and Peoples' Rights" in Africa.[74] The study analyses transitional justice in Africa, identifies the mechanisms of transitional justice, examines the African experiences, reviews the relevant African legal and institutional framework and makes recommendations.[75]

### 2.4 The Organization of American States (OAS)

The Organization of American States (OAS) has two human rights bodies – the Inter-American Commission on Human Rights and the Inter-American Court of Human Rights – that have played a normative role in transitional justice, especially examining and upholding the international obligations of states when it comes to human rights violations in the wake of a dictatorship or an armed conflict.[76] In order to synthesise these developments, the Inter-American Commission on Human Rights has produced a document entitled "Truth, Memory, Justice and Reparation in Transitional Contexts."[77] This document identifies the obligations of the American states, mainly Latin American states, that have faced armed conflicts and authoritarian regimes.[78]

In 2017, the Inter-American Commission on human rights also established a Unit on Memory, Truth, and Justice,[79] which became the Rapporteurship on Memory, Truth, and Justice in 2019.[80] The mandate of the Rapporteurship, which is the same as that of the Unit that preceded it, is clearly linked to transitional justice, as memory, truth and justice are all elements of transitional justice.[81] The Rapporteurship's mandate "is to promote the processes of memory, truth, justice, comprehensive reparation and non-repetition of

73 See Part 3 of this book on international obligations of states.

74 AcomHPR, 'Study on Transitional Justice in Africa and Human and Peoples' Rights in Africa,' 2019.

75 *Ibid.*

76 See Part 3 of this book for more details on the Inter-American Commission and the Inter-American Court.

77 IAComHR, 'Compendium of the Inter-American Commission on Human Rights on Truth, Memory, Justice and Reparation in Transitional Contexts,' doc. OEA/Ser.L/V/II., Doc. 121, 12 April 2021.

78 See Part 3 of this book on international obligations of states.

79 IAComHR, Annual Report, 2017, chap. IV, para. 169.

80 IAComHR, Annual Report, 2019, chap. III, para. 7.

81 See below the introduction of Part 2.

human rights violations committed, in general, in contexts of serious human rights violations."[82] The mandate consists of protecting and ensuring "the rights of victims and their next of kin within the jurisdiction of the 35 member states of the Organization of American States."[83] The office of the Rapporteurship is the main organ of the Inter-American Commission on Human Rights in the field of transitional justice. The Inter-American Commission's annual reports contain several references to the Rapporteurship's activities, particularly in the areas of promotion and training in many Latin American countries that have implemented or are implementing transitional justice.[84]

The invention of the concept, its implementation at the national and international level, and its subsequent development by international organisations have sparked many theoretical approaches and debates, which sometimes involve international law and discussions about its role.

---

82 See the website dedicated to the Rapporteurship on Memory, Truth and Justice, https://www.oas.org/en/iachr/jsForm/?File=/en/IACHR/r/MVJ/mandato.asp.

83 *Ibid.*

84 For example, IAComHR, Annual Report 2024, chap. III, para. 201; IAComHR, Annual Report 2023, chap. III, para. 216.

CHAPTER 4

# Main Theoretical Approaches and Debates in Transitional Justice

In doctrinal scholarship, it has been argued that there is "a lack of a unified [transitional justice] theory,"[1] and some publications have been dedicated to efforts that conceptualise and examine the theoretical approaches in this field.[2] The exploration of the theories or theoretical approaches adopted by scholars is particularly important, as some specialists interested in the theorisation of transitional justice have explained: "theories improve our ability to explain and understand – and potentially predict – processes and developments. They do so by increasing the level of abstraction, synthesising insights and by conceptualising them in the form of models or paradigms, allowing for wider generalisations beyond a particular phenomenon."[3]

Theoretical approaches to transitional justice explored by scholars are characterised by their diversity. First, this diversity essentially stems from the words "justice" and "transition" used in the term transitional justice.[4] Indeed, there are many theories of justice developed over the centuries that can be used to analyse transitional justice.[5] Similarly, questions may be asked about the kind of justice delivered by transitional justice, resulting in conflict-

1 Anja Mihr, 'An Introduction to Transitional Justice' in Olivera Simić (ed), *An Introduction to Transitional Justice* (2nd edn, Routledge 2021) 21.

2 See, for example, Susanne Buckley-Zistel, Teresa Koloma Beck, Christian Braun and Friederike Mieth (eds), *Transitional Justice Theories* (Routledge 2013); Claudio Corradetti, Nir Eisikovitts Suffolk and Jack Volpe Rotondi (eds), *Theorizing Transitional Justice* (Ashgate-Routledge 2015); Colleen Murphy, *The Conceptual Foundations of Transitional Justice* (Cambridge University press 2017); Hakeem O Yusuf and Hugo Van der Merwe (eds), *Transitional Justice. Theories, Mechanisms and Debates* (Routledge 2022); Pablo De Greiff, 'Theorizing Transitional Justice' (2012) 51 *Nomos* 31; Stephen Winter, 'Towards a Unified Theory of Transitional Justice' (2013) 7(2) *International Journal of Transitional Justice* 224.

3 Susanne Buckley-Zistel, Teresa Koloma Beck, Christian Braun and Friederike Mieth, 'Transitional Justice Theories: An Introduction' in Susanne Buckley-Zistel, Teresa Koloma Beck, Christian Braun and Friederike Mieth (eds), *Ibid.*, 3.

4 Claudio Corradetti, Nir Eisikovitts Suffolk and Jack Volpe Rotondi, 'Introduction' in Claudio Corradetti, Nir Eisikovitts Suffolk and Jack Volpe Rotondi (eds), *Theorizing Transitional Justice* (Ashgate-Routledge 2015) 1; Susanne Buckley-Zistel, Teresa Koloma Beck, Christian Braun and Friederike Mieth, 'Transitional Justice Theories: An Introduction', in Susanne Buckley-Zistel, Teresa Koloma Beck, Christian Braun and Friederike Mieth, *Ibid.*, 5.

5 Claudio Corradetti, Nir Eisikovitts Suffolk and Jack Volpe Rotondi, *Ibid.*, 3.

 HTTPS://DOI.ORG/10.1163/9789004766655-007

ing responses by different scholars. For instance, regarding the question of whether transitional justice is an ordinary justice or an extraordinary/exceptional justice, Eric Posner and Adrian Vermeulle address the concept of "transitional justice as ordinary justice" and argue that "transitional justice is continuous with ordinary justice."[6] Although Kai Ambos acknowledges that transitional justice "structurally faces similar problems as ordinary justice," he argues that "it is distinct from the latter in that it has to deal with large-scale and particularly serious abuses committed or tolerated by a past, normally authoritarian regime within the framework of a military or at least violent socio-political conflict."[7]

The word "transition" has also been scrutinised by many scholars who have questioned its significance in the field of transitional justice.[8] As discussed earlier in this book, transitologists have analysed the dynamics of political transitions in various contexts, including Latin America and the south of Europe.[9] In the same vein, Joanna Quinn has questioned the meaning of "transition" in the field of transitional justice[10] and developed a "typology of transitions": the classical "Post-conflict Transitional States," "Pre-transitional States" where there is no "definite transition," and "Non-Transitional States" where transitional justice mechanisms have been utilised.[11] These analyses show that "transition" is a concept that can be interpreted in different manners in the field of transitional justice.

A link has also been established between political transitions and the theoretical views about the "state of nature" developed by classical authors like Thomas Hobbes and John Locke, and this can be extended to Jean-Jacques Rousseau.[12] Even if their views are not similar regarding what was the fate of

6 Eric A Posner and Adrian Vermeule, 'Transitional Justice as Ordinary Justice' (2004) 117(3) *Harvard Law Review* 761, 764.

7 Kai Ambos, 'The Legal Framework of Transitional Justice: A Systematic Study with a Special Focus on the Role of the ICC' in Kai Ambos, Judith Large and Marieke Wierda (eds), *Building a Future on Peace and Justice: Studies on Transitional Justice, Peace and Development* (Springer 2009) 22.

8 Susanne Buckley-Zistel, Teresa Koloma Beck, Christian Braun and Friederike Mieth, 'Transitional Justice Theories: An Introduction' in Susanne Buckley-Zistel, Teresa Koloma Beck, Christian Braun and Friederike Mieth (eds), *Transitional Justice Theories* (Routledge 2013) 5.

9 See above Section 1 of Chapter 1, dedicated to "doctrinal scholarship."

10 Joanna R Quinn, 'Whither the Transition of Transitional Justice' (2014–2015) 8 *Interdisciplinary Journal of Human Rights Law* 64.

11 *Ibid.*, 70–78.

12 David Dyzenhaus, 'Review Essays: Transitional justice' (2003) 1(1) *International Journal of Constitutional Law* 163, 164; Hakeem O Yusuf, 'Origin, Context and Development of

human beings in the "state of nature," these three classical authors have written that human societies, which were in a "state of nature," had later concluded a social contract establishing a new society that was different from that "state of nature."[13] A scholar writes that "Thomas Hobbes and John Locke talk about the transition from a state of general disorder and violence, which they refer to as a 'state of nature.'"[14] According to another scholar, the book by Thomas Hobbes, *Leviathan*, "contains both significant instruction about how to achieve reconciliation or civic harmony in the face of deep ideological division and an account of the construction of political and legal institutions in order to maintain that harmony."[15]

Second, the theoretical discourse on transitional justice is influenced by the various contexts in which it is implemented, as well as by the different theories that have been developed in many disciplines that have been interested in the subject,[16] such as law, philosophy, sociology, anthropology, political science and psychology.

The aim of this chapter of the book is not to present all the theoretical approaches in the field of transitional justice, but rather to provide a synthesis of some of the recurrent approaches that have been the subject of debates among scholars and practitioners, who sometimes question the role of international law in implementing transitional justice. In this vein, there are two main categories of theoretical approaches that share links in the field of transitional justice and its literature. The first category comprises "binary"[17] theoretical approaches, which generally examine two elements that are perceived

---

Transitional Justice' in Hakeem O Yusuf and Hugo Van der Merwe (eds), *Transitional Justice. Theories, Mechanisms and Debates* (Routledge 2022) 12.

13 Thomas Hobbes, *Leviathan*, 1651; John Locke, *The Second Treatise on Government*, 1690; Jean-Jacques Rousseau, *Du contrat social*, 1792.

14 Hakeem O Yusuf, 'Origin, Context and Development of Transitional Justice' in Hakeem O Yusuf and Hugo Van der Merwe (eds), *Transitional Justice. Theories, Mechanisms and Debates* (Routledge 2022) 12.

15 David Dyzenhaus, 'Review Essays: Transitional justice', (2003) 1(1) *International Journal of Constitutional Law* 163, 164.

16 According to Claudio Corradetti, Nir Eisikovitts Suffolk and Jack Volpe Rotondi: "The study of Transitional Justice in recent decades has been interdisciplinary, running the gamut from philosophy through theology, sociology, anthropology, law and recently even neuroscience". Claudio Corradetti, Nir Eisikovitts Suffolk and Jack Volpe Rotondi, "Introduction" in Claudio Corradetti, Nir Eisikovitts Suffolk and Jack Volpe Rotondi, *Theorizing Transitional Justice* (Ashgate-Routledge 2015) 2.

17 This notion of "binary" is used by Susanne Buckley-Zistel, Teresa Koloma Beck, Christian Braun and Friederike Mieth, 'Transitional Justice Theories: An Introduction' in Susanne Buckley-Zistel, Teresa Koloma Beck, Christian Braun and Friederike Mieth (eds), *Transitional Justice Theories* (Routledge 2013) 4.

as contradictory and/or opposed when it comes to implementing transitional justice (discussed in Section 1). The second category comprises non-binary theoretical approaches. In this category, scholars sometimes refer to the theoretical approaches of the first category. However, they tend to criticise transitional justice, proposing alternative conceptual insights for delivering justice in times of transitions and/or rejecting the concept of transitional justice entirely (discussed in Section 2). These two categories do not always primarily rely on international law, the importance of which needs to be asserted in theoretical approaches to transitional justice (discussed in Section 3).

## 1 The "Binaries" Category of Theoretical Approaches in the Field of Transitional Justice

The "binaries" category of theoretical approaches typically considers two elements that are viewed as options during periods of transition. These options may be concurrent or complementary. Questions are asked about how to respond to human rights violations and crimes committed during an armed conflict or a dictatorship, and about how this response meets the needs of societies in transition. Attempts to answer these questions include classical theoretical debates about justice versus peace or peace versus justice, truth versus justice, retributive justice versus restorative justice and top-down versus bottom-up approaches.

### 1.1 Peace versus Justice

The dilemma of opposing peace and justice during times of transition is not a new one and is well known within the international relations between states, including after an armed conflict.[18] In the field of transitional justice, the ques-

18 See on that topic, I William Zartmann et Victor Kremenyuk (ed), *Peace Versus Justice. Negotiating Forward-and Backward-Looking Outcomes* (Rowman and Littlefield Publishers 2005). In this book, see, for example, Paul W Meerts, 'Turning Point Wesphalia: Negociations Processes Establishing a New Political and Legal Order in Europe', 11–13. This scholar refers to the opposition of *Justice v. Peace* in the context of the 1648 Peace of Westphalia, writing: "The Peace of Wesphalia had many faces. It was a necessary instrument of transition from the old era to the new. As far as peace and justice are concerned, it stood for important elements both in backward-and forward- looking negotiations. For the old powers, the peace agreements acted as a safeguard against further decay. For the young powers, it was the place to obtain justice, to assume their rightful place in the community of States", 12–13. See also, Kenneth A. Rodman, 'Peace Versus Justice' in *Encyclopedia of Global Justice* (Springer 2011) 820–827.

tion that is generally asked is how justice should be served during this period when states may face a variety of constraints such as the difficulties in prosecuting perpetrators who still hold power or political influence; the risk of renewed armed conflict or the risk of the dictatorship resuming causing the transition to fail; the large number of victims and perpetrators; insufficient funding for justice initiatives; and the lack of personnel and infrastructure that can administer justice. These problems, and others, force transitional or post-conflict states to make a difficult choice: choosing peace, which means an end to hostilities and/or authoritative repression, or choosing justice, which means judicial processes involving mainly prosecutions and criminal accountability for perpetrators.

In this regard, peace and justice during periods of transition have often been viewed as conflicting and opposing concepts. On the one hand, engaging in judicial accountability processes for past violations and prosecuting those responsible for crimes committed in the past could hinder negotiations between opposing parties and lead to the destabilisation of a state trying to end an armed conflict or bring down an authoritative regime. This could undermine the lasting peace and the prevention of human rights violations that transitional justice aims to achieve. To this end, judicial and criminal processes should be avoided in the pursuit of peace. On the other hand, engaging in judicial processes to prosecute and punish perpetrators of crimes committed in the past could be a prerequisite for peace. Thanks to the prosecution and punishment of perpetrators, the transitional or post-conflict state would apply judicial sanctions, expel perpetrators from the administrative and political space, prevent the repetition of the crimes and build a new society based on accountability, the rule of law and human rights. In this context, justice is a prerequisite for lasting peace, and "there can be no peace without justice."[19]

The discourse among scholars regarding the peace versus justice debate – which can be analysed in terms of the well-known theoretical debate between realism and idealism in international relations[20] and as a debate that can be applied in times of political transition[21] – has been quite diverse since the birth of transitional justice. Many scholars advocate the use of national and

---

19 Part of a sentence from Dr. Martin Luther King Jr. in 1967 during a rally outside UN Headquarters, see online: https://news.un.org/en/story/2024/08/1152626. He said "there can be no peace without justice, and there can be no justice without peace".

20 Robert M A Crawford, *Idealism and Realism in International Relations* (Routledge 2000).

21 See for more details on that distinction between realism and idealism during political transitions, see Emmanuel Guematcha, *Les Commissions vérité et les violations des droits de l'homme et du droit international humanitaire* (Pedone 2014) 40–41.

international criminal prosecutions to achieve peace, arguing that international legal norms support their position.[22] These scholars hold that there is an obligation for the state to prosecute and punish those who have committed serious human rights and international humanitarian law violations, or international crimes. They reject pardons, blanket amnesties and any action, including legal action, that would prevent the prosecution of former perpetrators. Other scholars point out that international and national criminal justice can hinder peace, arguing that international law is not peremptory on the obligation to prosecute and/or punish perpetrators.[23] Some also suggest that there could be a middle ground between prosecutions and forgetting. Along these lines, the truth and reconciliation commission model with conditional amnesty – a feature of the South African TRC that offered amnesty to perpetrators of politically motivated crimes who revealed the full truth about their actions – is seen as an example of a third path between forgetting and judicial processes.[24] While some scholars defend criminal prosecutions and consider them to be necessary, they also acknowledge that in certain situations, such as post–South Africa apartheid, implementing them was difficult or even impossible.[25]

This opposition between peace and justice is also reflected in the transitional justice where there is a choice between punishment and forgiveness/or reconciliation, the former meaning that a society cannot actually turn the page on atrocities without applying punishment through judicial processes, and the latter holding that in times of transition, forgiveness and reconciliation should be favoured over punishment due to the risks it poses.

The peace versus justice debate is certainly one of the most complex issues in transitional justice. Peace is an objective that is, and should always be, at

22 Diane F Orentlicher, 'Settlings Accounts: The Duty to Prosecute Human Rights Violations of a Prior Regime' (1991) 100 *Yale Law Journal* 2537; Diane F Orentlicher, 'A Reply to Professor Nino' (1991) 100 *The Yale Law Journal* 2641; Richard Goldstone, 'Peace versus Justice' (2006) 6 *Nevada Law Journal* 421. This author wrote: "At the outset I would concede that prosecuting political leaders might hamper or even wreck peace negotiations. The converse is also true. In my experience the threat of prosecutions and the issue of indictments against senior political players have aided rather than retarded peace negotiations", 421. For details regarding international law obligations of post-conflict and/or transitional states, see Part 3 of this book.

23 Carlos S Nino, 'The Duty to Punish Human Rights Violations of a Prior Regime: The Case of Argentina' (1991) 100 *The Yale Law Journal* 2619.

24 Richard Goldstone, 'Past Human Rights Violations: Truth Commissions and Amnesties or Prosecutions', (2000) 51(2) *Northern Ireland Legal Quarterly* 164, 165.

25 Antonio Cassese, 'Clemency Versus Retribution in Post Conflict Situations' (2007) 46(1) *Columbia Journal of Transnational Law* 1.

the heart of transitional justice. In some situations, the practical difficulties in transitional states may be genuine, and it may be reasonable to argue that implementing judicial proceedings would be challenging at that time. However, even in these situations, judicial proceedings should not be completely ruled out. Even if it may be pragmatic to conclude that judicial proceedings are impossible at a given moment, this does not prevent reflection on how to achieve justice or judicial proceedings during difficult transitional periods. Actually, the challenge lies in determining when justice would be feasible and finding ways to achieve it in times of transition or after an armed conflict, rather than simply ruling it out. In this case, justice could also be achieved through local community initiatives, not always national or international legal proceedings. Such local initiatives could also be consistent with international law, while responding to crimes and taking into account the plight of victims seeking justice. Local initiatives such as the Rwandan Gacaca demonstrate inventiveness in the delivering of justice.[26] Rather than being seen as concurrent, justice and peace should be viewed as two complementary goals that must be achieved in societies in transition.

### 1.2 Truth versus Justice

The binary theoretical approaches that pit truth against justice also entail the risk that states in transition may be exposed to if they engage in judicial processes involving prosecutions and punishment. These approaches are based on two main ideas. First, because prosecutions may be perceived as detrimental to peace and/or may derail negotiations for a lasting peace, judicial processes should be avoided, and the search for the truth about past violations prioritised. Second, due to the crimes and violations committed in the past and the resulting harm suffered by many victims, it is essential to tell the truth about these exactions in order to restore the victims' dignity. The truth versus justice dichotomy assumes that the difficulties of transition can lead to a preference for searching for truth rather than pursuing judicial procedures and prosecutions, which are considered too difficult or risky. In the institutional framework, the truth versus justice dilemma has resulted in legal trials that oppose the process of truth commissions, both of which are mechanisms of transitional justice.

Indeed, this theoretical approach was discussed in particular in the context of establishing truth commissions in countries in transition, especially in Latin

26 See "Traditional Justice" in Part 2 of this book.

America and South Africa.[27] In the final report of the South Africa TRC, chairman Desmond Tutu wrote that in the context of political transition in South Africa, trials like the Nuremberg trials were "not a viable option,"[28] citing the fact that no party had defeated another in South Africa,[29] enumerating factors such as the lack of resources, funding and personnel.[30] He also mentioned the limitations of trial when it came to establishing the truth, writing that "legal proceedings rely on proof beyond reasonable doubt, the criminal justice system is not the best way to arrive at the truth. There is no incentive for perpetrators to tell the truth and often the court must decide between the word of one victim against the evidence of many perpetrators. Such legal proceedings are also harrowing experiences for victims, who are invariably put through extensive cross-examination."[31] He also emphasised the importance of understanding what happened in South Africa during the apartheid regime. He supported the system of a TRC established in South Africa and the granting of amnesty to perpetrators who come forward to tell the truth.[32] According to him, "dealing with the past means knowing what happened. [...]."[33] He added: "We also need to know about the past so that we can renew our resolve and commitment that never again will such violations take place. We need to know about the past in order to establish a culture of respect for human rights. It is only by accounting for the past that we can become accountable for the future."[34]

In the 1990s and early 2000s, truth commissions were sometimes seen as an alternative to judicial processes in transitional states. As their primary mandate was to reveal the truth, they were considered an alternative to prosecutions. For example, in their examination of numerous truth commissions, Amy Gutmann and Dennis Thompson have argued that "these commissions sacrifice the pursuit of justice as usually understood for the sake of promoting other social purposes, such as historical truth and social reconciliation."[35]

27 Robert I Rotberg and Dennis Thompson (eds), *Truth v. Justice. The Morality of Truth Commissions* (Princeton University Press 2000); Ruti G Teitel, *Transitional Justice* (Oxford University Press 2000) 88–92.

28 South Africa, 'Truth and Reconciliation Commission of South Africa Report', 1998, vol.1, chap. 1, 5, para. 23.

29 *Ibid.*, para. 21.

30 *Ibid.*, para. 23.

31 *Ibid.*, 6, para. 26.

32 *Ibid.*, 7, para. 29.

33 *Ibid.*, 7, para. 28.

34 *Ibid.*

35 Amy Gutmann and Dennis Thompson, 'The Moral Foundations of Truth Commissions' in Robert I. Rotberg and Dennis Thompson (ed), *Truth v. Justice. The Morality of Truth Commissions*, (Princeton University Press 2000) 22.

International law was also invoked in the debate surrounding truth versus justice. Truth commissions were viewed as a way for the transitional state to fulfil the victims' right to know the truth about the fate of their relatives, as set out in Articles 32 and 33 of the 1977 Additional Protocol I to the 1949 Geneva Conventions of 12 August 1949, as well as about the human rights violations that they have experienced.[36] However, for many years, it has been considered that truth commissions complement trials in times of transition or after an armed conflict. Justice and truth are not mutually exclusive. Trials also contribute to finding the truth, even if it is a judicial truth.[37] Truth commissions also help to deliver justice. They are a form of justice in transitional justice. Their works and/or final reports may sometimes be used in trials and judicial proceedings as part of the documents necessary to understand the historical context of perpetrations of crimes.[38] In short, truth and justice complement each other.

### 1.3 Retributive Justice versus Restorative Justice

In the field of transitional justice, the opposition between retributive justice and restorative justice is not far from options to be chosen between peace and justice, or truth and justice. In the context of transitional justice, retributive justice focuses on punishing perpetrators and is generally associated with criminal proceedings, prosecutions and trials.[39] Restorative justice, as discussed earlier in this book, focuses on victims and aims to restore their dignity, which was destroyed by the crimes committed against them.[40] The question here is which type of justice is most appropriate in times of transitions,

36 For details on the right to the truth, see below Part 3.

37 Leora Bilsky, 'The Right to Truth in International Criminal Law' in Kevin Jon Heller, Frédéric Mégret, Sarah M H Nouwen, Jens David Ohlin, and Darryl Robinson (eds), *The Oxford Handbook of International Criminal Law* (Oxford University Press 2020) 473–493; Bruno Cotte et Julien Seroussi, 'La manifestation de la vérité en droit pénal international' (2010) 53 *Archives de philosophie du droit* 86.

38 See, for example, the use of the Sierra Leone TRC final report by the Special Court for Sierra Leone, concerning some historical elements related to the armed conflict in Sierra Leone, SCSL, Trial Chamber II, *The Prosecutor v. Charles Ghankay Taylor*, No. 2003-01-T, Judgement, 18 may 2012, para. 18, note 58.

39 Colleen Murphy, 'Transitional Justice, Retributive Justice and Accountability for Wrongdoing' in Claudio Corradetti, Nir Eisikovitts Suffolk and Jack Volpe Rotondi, *Theorizing Transitional Justice* (Ashgate-Routledge 2015) 59–68; Patrick Lenta, 'Transitional Justice and Retributive Justice' (2019) 22(2) *Ethical Theory and Moral Practice* 385.

40 Kerry Clamp and Jonathan Doak, 'More Than Words: Restorative Justice Concepts in Transitional Justice Settings' (2012) 12 *International Criminal Law Review* 339.

retributive justice involving trials and punishment of perpetrators, or restorative justice involving truth commissions, reparations and reconciliation or other mechanisms that are mainly focused on victims?[41] This long-discussed dichotomy in transitional justice has been criticised because of the shared links between restorative and retributive justice. For instance, restorative elements such as reparations can be found in criminal proceedings that are considered retributive. Conversely, truth commissions, which are restorative in nature, may also have retributive aspects.[42] For example, providing the names of perpetrators of crimes and violations in their final reports imposes a somewhat social accountability in the form of *naming* and *shaming*. A scholar has highlighted this potential link between restorative justice and retributive justice by mentioning that "gacaca could be experienced as both retributive and restorative at the same time."[43] Therefore, when implementing international law during transitions, the challenge is not to choose between retributive and restorative, but to consider how the mechanisms of transitional justice can contribute to both.

### 1.4 Top-Down versus Bottom-Up and Local versus Global Approaches

As seen earlier in this book, the implementation of transitional justice has gradually involved the international community, mainly the United Nations, other international organisations and Western developed states, and to a greater extent many transitional or post-conflict states. From this perspective, international norms about delivering justice have been standardising in the field of transitional justice, making it a high institutionalised field. International experts, often with the support of international organisations or Western states, have played a significant role in defining the terms of transitional justice. According to Eduardo Gonzalez, a transitional justice expert, transitional justice "is dominated by a legalistic human rights perspective,

---

41 See Oliver Bačanovikj, 'Transitional Justice between Retributive and Restorative Justice', *Dialogues Security*, 2015; Wendy Lambourne, 'Transitional Justice after Mass Violence: Reconciling Retributive and Restorative Justice' in Helen Irving, Jacqueline Mowbray and Kevin Walton (eds), *Julius Stone: A Study in Influence* (Federation Press-Annandale 2010) 214.

42 Stephan Landsman, 'Alternative Responses to Serious Human Rights Abuses: of Prosecution and Truth Commissions' (1996) 59(4) *Law and Contemporary Problems* 81, 89.

43 Wendy Lambourne, "Transformative Justice, Reconciliation and Peacebuilding" in Susanne Buckley-Zistel, Teresa Koloma Beck, Christian Braun and Friederike Mieth (eds), *Transitional Justice Theories* (Routledge 2013) 21. On Rwanda Gacaca, see below Chapter 7, Section 1.1.

with very concrete roots in Western philosophies."[44] All this has led to the understanding that transitional justice is a field dominated by a top-down, global/universal and predominantly Western approach, with the international community and certain states pushing to implement their own ideas of transitional justice and the associated norms that they believe transitional states should respect, as well as the mechanisms that these states should establish to address past international crimes and violations of human rights and international humanitarian law.

Many scholars have criticised this top-down approach, in which transitional justice comes from the "top" (mainly the international community) and is to be implemented "down" (by states in transition and the local communities of these states).[45] Some of them have also called for, or analysed, the decolonisation of transitional justice.[46] Even if these scholars do not entirely reject the role and positive impact of international institutions in implementing transitional justice within transitional states, they have sometimes referred to the relevance of "transitional justice from below" and their criticisms highlight that the implementation of transitional justice should rely on a bottom-up approach focused on local dynamics or on what "the local" wants.[47] This approach emphasises the importance of placing victims, local communities and grassroots organisations at the heart of transitional justice implementation, rather than international, and sometimes national, institutions. From this perspective, international criminal justice, which is one way to implement transitional justice in many contexts, has also been criticised for its top-down

---

44 Eduardo Gonzalez, 'The End of Transitional Justice? Potentials and Limitations of Our Position in the Decolonization Debate', 21 November 2022, online: https://frient.de/en/artikel/the-end-of-transitional-justice/.

45 See, for example, Kieran McEvoy and Lorna McGregor (eds), *Transitional Justice from below : Grassroots Activism and the Struggle for Change* (Hart Publishing 2008); Patricia Lundy and Mark McGovern, 'Whose Justice? Rethinking Transitional Justice from the Bottom Up' (2008) 35(2) *Journal of Law and Society* 265. See also for a synthesis of explanations of these criticisms, and their limits, Fiona McGaughey, Rachel Rafferty and Amy Maguire, 'Transitional Justice from Above and Below: Exploring the Potential Glocalising Role of Non-governmental Organisations through a Northern Ireland Case Study' (2023) 74(3) *Northern Ireland Legal Quarterly* 472.

46 See, for example, Tecla Namachanja Wanjala, 'Transitional Justice in Post-conflict Societies: A Call for Decolonization and Peace Sustainability' in Elias O Opongo, David Kaulem, Susan M. Kilonzo and Sarah Njeri (eds), *The Palgrave Handbook of Peace, Conflict and Security Studies in Africa* (Palgrave Macmillan 2025) 97–114; M. Brinton Lykes and Colleen Murphy, 'Decolonizing Transitional Justice: Soft, Radical or Beyond Reform' (2023) 17(3) *International Journal of Transitional Justice* 361.

47 Kieran McEvoy and Lorna McGregor (eds), *Transitional Justice from below : Grassroots Activism and the Struggle for Change* (Hart Publishing 2008).

approach. Marc Drumbl writes: "Instead of building accountability and restoration from the bottom-up through integration of Indigenous laws, customs, personalities, politics, and practices, international criminal law interventions drop from the top-down."[48] In this vein, he criticises the "democratic deficits and externalization of justice" and proposes "to rescript the division of labor toward greater inclusiveness of *in situ* sociolegal institutions and bottom up input."[49]

Criticisms of the top-down approach also target the "state centric" and institutional logic of transitional justice and point out its failure to deliver justice effectively. For example, Kieran McEvoy writes that "'state-centric' grand schemes [...] may fail to take sufficient account of local customs and practical knowledge and to engage properly with community and civil society structures. Such failures, often justified in the name of efficiency, professional expertise or simply 'getting the job done,' may in turn lead to incompetence or maladministration and encourage grassroots resistance to such state-led initiatives."[50]

Even though they do not entirely reject the role of law and international law in transitional justice, the supporters of "transitional justice from below" also criticise the "legalism" that characterises the top-down approach to transitional justice.[51] Kieran McEvoy argues that "the tendency of international lawyers to eulogise the glory and majesty of international law being 'brought to' previously war-torn regions often renders them oblivious to the strong evidence of a disconnect between such imperious aims and their perception in the communities affected by such violence."[52] He calls for a "legal humility,"[53] holding that "[l]egal institutions associated with transitional justice can and should operate most effectively if they run in conjunction with properly managed, effective and accountable local or indigenous processes, which comply with basic international human rights standards."[54] Similarly, Lorna McGregor highlights the importance of a "bottom-up" approach in transitional justice, and provides examples of situations in which a local initiative has yielded

48 Mark A Drumbl, *Atrocity, Punishment, and International Law* (Cambridge University Press 2007) 133.

49 *Ibid.*, 181.

50 Kieran McEvoy, "Letting Go of Legalism: Developing a 'Thicker' Version of Transitional Justice" in Kieran McEvoy and Lorna McGregor (eds), *Transitional Justice from below : Grassroots Activism and the Struggle for Change* (Hart Publishing 2008) 28.

51 *Ibid.*, 29.

52 *Ibid.*, 30.

53 *Ibid.*, 29.

54 *Ibid.*, 32.

positive results in the field of justice.[55] She refers to, for instance, the Gacaca in Rwanda, the report on human rights violations produced by the Catholic Church in Guatemala, and the work of the Greensboro Truth and Reconciliation Commission, a private initiative that investigated some exactions committed against Black Americans by the Ku Klux Klan in the United States.[56] However, she also acknowledges the potential issues with local initiatives, citing, for example, the criticism addressed to the Gacaca in Rwanda for its lack of due process and for not including human rights standards.[57]

The criticisms of the top-down approach to transitional justice are certainly consistent. After all, if justice is designed to be served for victims, it is hard to understand why the delivery of justice ignores the wishes of these victims and the affected local communities, disregards indigenous processes that victims and local communities are familiar with, and belittles the efforts and proposals of local civil society groups or organisations that have been working with the victims at a local level. For sure, a justice system that does not primarily consider the needs of victims and local communities affected, nor pays attention to indigenous processes and local wishes for the future after a dark period, is doomed to fail, either now or later. Any transitional justice process should always place victims at its core, with strong connections between local, national and international measures adopted in this field. The practice and implementation of international law in the field of transitional justice should always meet the needs of victims, take into consideration local communities affected and rely on and include indigenous processes and mechanisms, rather than ignoring them.

The link between the local, the national and the international levels must be effective. As clearly and strongly noted by Lorna McGregor, "the choice between local and 'international' approaches should not be viewed as exclusive. Rather, [...] it is the challenge for both to meet the requirements of international law in ensuring the rights of victims and traditionally marginalised groups."[58] In the same vein, Dustin Sharp warns of the need to "be careful not to romanticize local justice," and mentions that "transitional justice scholars, practitioners and policy-makers ignore local preferences and conceptions of justice at their own peril. While greater use of local modalities of justice

55 Lorna McGregor, "International Law as a 'Tiered Process': Transitional Justice at the Local, National and International Level" in Kieran McEvoy and Lorna McGregor (eds), *Transitional Justice from below : Grassroots Activism and the Struggle for Change* (Hart Publishing 2008) 60.

56 *Ibid.*

57 *Ibid.*, 62.

58 *Ibid.*, 72–73.

will require a fairly robust 'margin of appreciation' and acceptance of a degree of legal pluralism that may make some international human rights lawyers uncomfortable, the striking of a better balance between global and local modalities of justice is ultimately required if we are to make transitional justice into more of a true global project."[59]

Of course, this list of selected binary theoretical approaches is not exhaustive. There are other binary theoretical approaches in the field of transitional justice. For example, Jeremy Weber distinguishes between retrospective justice or backward-looking justice and prospective justice or forward-looking justice.[60] He also holds that transitional justice is about the adjustment of legal order and political order, which are in conflict with each other.[61] Hugo van der Merwe and Richard Chelin have examined "impartial versus selective justice" in the field of transitional justice.[62] Others have noted that many transitional justice "specialists implicitly adhere to a liberal, formal-legal, conception of justice, rather than a social-redistributive one. They favor procedural justice rather than social justice."[63] Some scholars also argue that there are multiple types of justice in the field of transitional justice. For example, Andrieu Kora distinguishes between retributive justice, restorative justice and social justice in transitional justice.[64]

These theoretical approaches tend to demonstrate that the implementation of transitional justice is complex and usually involves contradictory options. They make us aware that achieving justice after an authoritarian regime, an armed conflict or widespread human rights violations is a contradictory process that forces those involved to make difficult choices and recognise the complexities of finding suitable solutions. They also demonstrate that law and international law are not the only factors to consider when analysing transitional justice. Many other factors beyond legal considerations are at

59 Dustin N Sharp, 'Transitional Justice and 'Local' Justice' in Cheryl Lawther and Luke Moffett (eds), *Research Handbook on Transitional Justice* (Edward Elgard 2017) 143.

60 Jeremy Webber, 'Forms of Transitional Justice' (2012) 51 *Nomos* 98, 99.

61 *Ibid.*

62 Hugo van der Merwe and Richard Chelin, 'Impartial Versus Selective Justice: How Power Shapes Transitional Justice in Africa' (2020) 10(1) *African Conflict and Peacebuilding Review* 99.

63 Liora Israël and Guillaume Mouralis, 'General Introduction' in Liora Israël and Guillaume Mouralis (ed), *Dealing with Wars and Dictatorships – Legal Concepts and Categories in Action* (T.M.C. Asser Press-Springer 2013) 5.

64 Andrieu Kora, 'Transitional Justice: A New Discipline in Human Rights, Mass Violence & Resistance' (2010), online, http://bo-k2s.sciences-po.fr/mass-violence-war-massacre-resistance/fr/document/transitional-justice-new-discipline-human-rights, ISSN 1961-9898.

stake and should be taken into account by international lawyers and practitioners when implementing transitional justice. Non-binary theoretical approaches to transitional justice are also part of this perspective.

## 2 Non-binary Theoretical Approaches in Transitional Justice

In this category, there are many theoretical approaches that either do not analyse international law in depth or simply minimise its role in times of transition. Some scholars in this category have criticised transitional justice, proposing different means of delivering justice during times of transition. Others have rejected the concept of transitional justice altogether.

### 2.1 Critics of Transitional Justice

The concept of transitional justice has been criticised, with some scholars proposing alternative approaches of justice in times of transition. In an edited volume, these critiques of transitional justice have been summarised well, pleading "for an evidence-based transitional justice, for a practice more in tune with the pulse of local, everyday needs rather than global fads and priorities; for a focus on socioeconomic rights to augment the prevailing emphasis on civil-political rights; and for a more politicized engagement with power and privilege."[65] Criticising the concept of transitional justice, these scholars have proposed something else and examined "the potential for transformative justice during political transition." According to them, the transformative justice that they support is a "transformative change that emphasizes local agency and resources, the prioritization of process rather than preconceived outcomes, and the challenging of unequal and intersecting power relationships and structures of exclusion at both local and global levels."[66] They propose a new way of thinking during the transition period, emphasising the importance of combatting exclusion and taking local dynamics and needs into consideration. The proposal for the "transformation" of societies in transition, which will seek the well-being of the whole population and the non-recurrence of violence, also implies structural changes to repeal the old system that permitted violations. For example, Krista Thomason wrote: "First, the structures that contributed to the conflict or the violence must be examined and likely

65 Paul Gready, 'Introduction' in Paul Gready and Simon Robins (eds), *From Transitional to Transformative Justice* (Cambridge University Press 2019) 1–2.

66 *Ibid.*, 2.

repealed or abolish. Second, the new structures that are put into place must ensure that groups are not disenfranchised moving forward."[67]

Many theoretical approaches tend to explore "the limits of transitional justice."[68] Transitional justice is criticised because its implementation is usually highly politicised. Jelena Subotic, for example, considers that the objectives of states that implement transitional justice may not actually be primarily concerned with delivering justice.[69] She holds that "[c]arrying out a transitional justice project allows domestic elites to signal their respect of international institutions, while using justice mechanisms domestically to achieve other political goals, such as getting rid of domestic political opponents, obtaining financial aid, or gaining membership in prestigious international organisations."[70] In this context, states comply with transitional justice because the international consequence of non-compliance is severe, as is the compliance with transitional justice on a domestic level.[71] To solve these conflicting interests, "domestic political elites often choose to comply with international transitional justice requirements, avoiding sanctions, but repackaging transitional justice normatively to make it more acceptable to the domestic audience."[72] In short, the resistance to the implementation of transitional justice by some national political elites, and the politicisation of the transitional justice process, may lead to difficulties in adopting international human rights norms and standards in other transitional states, especially when international pressure to implement transitional justice elsewhere has not been successful.[73]

Other theoretical approaches have also criticised transitional justice and sometimes the top-down and institutional approach. These approaches call for transitional justice to be more inclusive and to take into account the needs of societies in transition. They also make propositions to improve the implementation of transitional justice. Examples of this include analyses of femin-

67 Krista K Thomason, 'Transitional Justice as Structural Justice' in Claudio Corradetti, Nir Eisikovitts Suffolk and Jack Volpe Rotondi, *Theorizing Transitional Justice* (Ashgate-Routledge 2015) 76.

68 See the different contributions on these limits in Susanne Buckley-Zistel, Teresa Koloma Beck, Christian Braun and Friederike Mieth (eds), *Transitional Justice Theories* (Routledge 2013) 125.

69 Jelena Subotić, 'Bargaining Justice. A Theory of Transitional Justice Compliance' in Susanne Buckley-Zistel, Teresa Koloma Beck, Christian Braun and Friederike Mieth (eds), *Ibid.*, 128.

70 *Ibid.*

71 *Ibid.*

72 *Ibid.*

73 *Ibid.*, 139–140.

ism and transitional justice,[74] post-colonial theory and transitional justice,[75] and development and transitional justice.[76]

## 2.2 The Rejection of the Notion of Transitional Justice

Some scholars have gone beyond criticisms and have rejected the notion of transitional justice. These scholars have often questioned the scientific nature of a catch-all concept, with vague contours, used by organisations to propose or implement their "expertise" services in states facing difficulties related to their past that is marked by serious abuses. One of the most elaborate criticisms in this field is that of the French political scientist Sandrine Lefranc in her important article "La justice transitionnelle n'est pas un concept" (Transitional justice is not a concept), published in 2008.[77] According to Lefranc, "Transitional justice is not so much a concept as a prescription, and it is all the worse for the participants in countless colloquia, which combine the concerns of the expert with those of the academic, to have believed it and to have tried to make it believe it, attempting to rationalise the expression *a posteriori* and to remove it from the political contexts in which it originated and in which it unfolds its effects."[78] She described this justice as "a justifying rhetoric interweaving truth commissions and international criminal law, to legitimize at the same time the constitution of an expertise."[79] Without criticising the

74 Martha Albertson Fineman and Estelle Zinsstag (eds), *Feminist Perspectives on Transitional Justice: From International and Criminal to Alternative Forms of Justice* (Series on Transitional Justice, Intersentia 2013); Christine Bell and Catherine O'Rourke, 'Does Feminism Need a Theory of Transitional Justice? An Introductory Essay' (2007) 1 *The International Journal of Transitional Justice* 23.

75 Khanyisela Moyo, 'Feminism, Postcolonial Legal Theory and Transitional Justice: A Critique of Current Trends' (2012) 1(2) *International Human Rights Law Review* 237.

76 Rama Mani, 'Dilemmas of Expanding Transitional Justice, or Forging the Nexus between Transitional Justice and Development' (2008) 2(3) *International Journal of Transitional Justice* 253.

77 Sandrine Lefranc, 'La justice transitionnelle n'est pas un concept' (2008) 53(1) *Mouvements* 61.

78 Translation from, Sandrine Lefranc, *Ibid.*, 62. Original text: "La justice transitionnelle est moins un concept qu'une prescription – et tant pis si les participants à d'innombrables colloques, imbriquant les soucis de l'expert et ceux de l'universitaire, l'ont cru et ont tenté de le faire croire en essayant de rationaliser *a posteriori* l'expression et en l'extrayant des contextes politiques dont elle tire ses origines et dans lesquels elle déploie ses effets".

79 *Ibid.*, Original text: "une rhétorique justificatrice imbriquant commissions de vérité et droit pénal international, pour légitimer dans le même temps la constitution d'une expertise".

term in such a direct way, another French public law scholar, Fabrice Hourquebie, questioned the definition of transitional justice and wondered whether it had any meaning in an article published in 2009.[80] However, in 2014, Hourquebie, drawing on recent experiences of transitional justice and echoing the UN Secretary-General's 2004 definition, noted that "transitional justice has a meaning."[81]

Despite criticisms of transitional justice at a theoretical level, its use has expanded considerably and the notion remains very popular in scholarship and practice. In this context, there is no doubt that scholars will continue to develop theoretical approaches to transitional justice in a world where calls for it are still prevalent due to ongoing violations of international law, international crimes, and human rights and international humanitarian law violations. Because these violations are at the core of international law, these theoretical approaches should not neglect this branch of law.

## 3 Considering International Law in Transitional Justice Theoretical Approaches

Many of the theoretical approaches do not consider international law when dealing with transitional justice. This raises questions about the importance of law during and after periods of transition or armed conflict. As is evident from most of these theoretical approaches to transitional justice, law and international law are not the only elements to be considered during transitions. Indeed, one could argue that legalisation has limits in post-conflict or transitional settings. The legal system is indeed challenged by the difficulties of transition and armed conflict, and stakeholders in transitional justice may be motivated by factors outside the legal system.

However, law, including international law which is the focus of this book, remains important when dealing with crimes and violations of rights. When crimes and violations are committed on a large scale, it has become unthinkable for societies not to rely on the norms provided within them to name these crimes and violations and to respond to them. International law contains many rules applicable to crimes and violations. Since the Second World War, particularly in the field of human rights and armed conflicts, international law

80 Fabrice Hourquebie, 'La notion de justice transitionnelle a -t-elle un sens' (2009) 398(90) *Les petites affiches* 6.

81 Fabrice Hourquebie, 'La justice transitionnelle a bien un sens' (2014) 250 (2) *Afrique contemporaine* 86.

has become central to naming rights that have been violated and crimes that have been committed, as well as finding responses to these violations. Writing in 1997 about the role of international law during political transitions, Ruti Teitel took a view that is still relevant today:

> In periods of political flux, international law offers a useful mediating concept. The framing of the rule-of-law dilemma easily shifts from the antinomies of positivism and natural law to those of national and international law. Grounded in positive law, but incorporating values of justice associated with natural law, international law mediates the rule-of-law dilemma. Moreover, in its normative circumscription of the most heinous abuses, international law offers a source of normative transcendence. Whereas international law preserves the ordinary understanding of the rule of law as settled law, it also enables transformation. In so doing, it mediates the transition.[82]

In this vein, international law is to be used as soon as it helps to justify prosecutions, telling the truth about violations, awarding reparations to victims, preventing future violations and remembering the past – all of which are at the core of transitional justice. Even if the role of international law may sometimes have limits in the field of transitional justice, even if international law is imperfect and sometimes ineffective because of its numerous violations and because of states' manipulations of selfish instrumentalisation, it is still extremely helpful in stigmatising past wrongdoings and proving that they were wrong and should never happen again. In this context, in the field of transitional justice, states and the international community have produced relevant mechanisms in response to crimes punishable under international law, to violations of rights which are enshrined in international law, or simply, to violations of international law rules. Thus, a positive approach of transitional justice, through a study of the mechanisms of transitional justice responding to international law violations, and the identification of the international obligations of states in transition or post-conflict states remain important.

82 Ruti G Teitel, "Transitional Jurisprudence: The Role of Law in Political Transformation" (1997) 106 *Yale Law Journal* 2029.

# Conclusion of Part 1

Formally born in the 1990s, the concept of transitional justice has spread internationally. States, international organisations, academics, non-governmental organisations and civil society organisations have been at the forefront of this diffusion. Today, for the most part, when a regime is overthrown, an authoritarian rule is brought into question, an armed conflict is ongoing or large-scale violations are perpetrated, it is almost quite certain that transitional justice will be invoked and debated.[1] Transitional justice has become so widespread that the question is no longer about its existence but about its limits. Throughout this diffusion, the central issue has been how to respond to violations of human rights, violations of international humanitarian law and international crimes. Thus, from the beginning, international law and some of its branches (international human rights law, international humanitarian law and international criminal law) have been at the centre of the development and diffusion of this concept, which led to the creation of transitional mechanisms to respond to these violations and crimes.

1 For example, on the armed conflict in Ukraine, Janine Natalya Clark, 'Transitional Justice and the Significance of More-Than-Human Worlds: Some Reflections from the Russia-Ukraine War' (2025) 17(3) *Journal of Human Rights Practice*; On Palestine, see Matiangai V S Sirleaf, 'Palestine as a Litmus Test for Transitional Justice' (2024) 18(1) *International Journal of Transitional Justice* 162; on North Korea, see Myung Jung Kim, 'Transitional Justice in North Korea' (2015) *Yonsei Journal of International Studies* 91; Sarah A Son, Nazanin Zadeh-Cummings, Danielle Chubb, 'Participatory Transitional Justice as Anticipatory Project: North Korea, Diasporas and Uncertain Futures' (2025) 19(2) *International Journal of Transitional Justice* 296; On Sudan and Darfur, Jibrin Ubale Yahaya, Conflict, Mass Atrocities, and the Quest for Transitional Justice in Darfur (2025) 1(5) *African Research Reports* 447; and on Yemen, Stacey Philbrick Yadav, *Yemen in the Shadow of Transition. Pursuing Justice Amid War* (Hurst & Company 2022).

# PART 2

# Mechanisms of Transitional Justice: Responses to the Violations of International Law

# Introduction to Part 2

Transitional justice mechanisms are the legal institutions, bodies or instruments established and used by states or international organisations to respond to serious and widespread violations or crimes committed in the past. As such, they are responsive to violations of the rules of international law, particularly those governing human rights, armed conflict and international crimes. There are many ways to identify and present transitional justice mechanisms.

First, they can be presented through the study of the "pillars of transitional justice," which are justice, truth, reparation, guarantees of non-repetition and memorialisation. As we have seen, the first four of these pillars were incorporated into transitional justice following a UN report by Louis Joinet, which identified principles and main elements of the fight against impunity.[1] The fifth pillar of transitional justice, memorialisation, was added by the UN Special Rapporteur on the promotion of truth, justice, reparation and guarantees of non-recurrence.[2] A UN report by Theo Van Boven on reparations also played a role in the identification of these pillars.[3] This enumeration of the pillars of transitional justice has become common discourse among transitional justice actors. However, even if the enumeration of the pillars has a pedagogical virtue in the sense that it helps to capture in a few words what transitional justice consists of, an analysis of the pillars sometimes reveals inconsistencies. The first pillar is justice, which refers to judicial bodies and is one of the words of "transitional justice." The inconsistency here is that the word "justice" is used twice, with different meanings. The second pillar is truth, which refers to truth commissions or commissions of inquiry that investigate and tell the truth, for example, about human rights violations. But the truth is that in the process of transitional justice, the truth is also revealed through other mechanisms, such as judicial bodies. When it comes to reparations, things are much more complex. Reparations are sometimes ordered by courts, and reparations programmes are proposed by truth commissions. Memorialisation, which is envisaged as the fifth pillar, is a form of reparation, as are guarantees of non-recurrence, which are the fourth pillar.

Meanwhile, judicial mechanisms and truth-telling by truth commissions can be seen as guarantees of non-recurrence. Judgments of courts and final reports of truth commissions can also be seen as forms of reparation. Thus,

1 See Part 1 above, on the contribution of the United Nations to transitional justice.
2 *Ibid.*
3 *Ibid.*

even if it is pedagogical to understand transitional justice through its pillars, there are so many interconnections between these pillars that it is very difficult to study each one of them in order to get a clear picture of the implementation of transitional justice as a response to violations of international law.

Second, one can distinguish between judicial and non-judicial mechanisms, a common categorisation in transitional justice mechanisms. However, it is not easy to determine what the term "judicial" covers and to categorise some transitional justice mechanisms. For example, reparations, which are considered a transitional justice mechanism, can be described as a judicial mechanism if reparations are ordered by a court, and as a non-judicial mechanism if reparations are not ordered by such a court or are awarded through administrative procedures or proposed by a truth commission. Similarly, traditional justice mechanisms in African countries, such as the Rwandan Gacaca courts, which dealt with genocide, among other things, can be characterised as both judicial and non-judicial.

In order to present the mechanisms of transitional justice, it is therefore much more appropriate to identify, without a global categorisation or "pillarisation," the mechanisms that have been used to ensure accountability for violations of international law. Observation of the development of transitional justice shows that, historically, there have been two main mechanisms in transitional justice: judicial bodies and truth commissions. These two mechanisms have been the most widely used in the field of transitional justice and have also contributed to a great deal of national and international development. However, there are other transitional justice mechanisms that are no less important and that are linked to the two main mechanisms, to punitive components or to judicial proceedings. These other mechanisms are reparations, traditional justice and administrative procedures. In this Part 2 of the book, Chapter 4 examines judicial bodies, Chapter 5 truth commissions and Chapter 6 the other mechanisms of transitional justice.

CHAPTER 5

# Judicial Bodies

Judicial bodies, which are mainly criminal tribunals, are one of the most important transitional justice mechanisms. States and the international community have used criminal tribunals in many cases of transition from dictatorships or armed conflicts to ensure criminal accountability for those responsible for crimes, including international crimes, serious violations of human rights and international humanitarian law. There are international and hybrid criminal tribunals on the one hand, and national courts on the other. There is a clear link between transitional justice and international criminal law, a branch of international law that comprises a set of rules applicable to international crimes. The purpose of this chapter is not to provide a detailed account of all of these criminal proceedings, a task already accomplished by numerous handbooks and manuals on international criminal law. Rather, the purpose of this chapter is to briefly introduce international criminal tribunals (discussed in Section 1), hybrid tribunals (discussed in Section 2) and national tribunals (discussed in Section 4) that are today an important part of the transitional justice mechanisms. This chapter presents how these tribunals have contributed to the development of transitional or post-conflict justice, how the rhetoric of peace or reconciliation is used in their implementation, and the contributions they have made to the development of international transitional justice law (discussed in Sections 3 and 5).

## 1 International Criminal Tribunals

Several international criminal tribunals have been established in the field of transitional justice. They fall into two categories. On the one hand, there are temporary and *ad hoc* tribunals, including the International Military Tribunals of Nuremberg and Tokyo (1945–1946) and the International Criminal Tribunals for the former Yugoslavia and Rwanda (1993–1994). On the other hand, there is a permanent criminal court, the International Criminal Court (1998). All temporary and *ad hoc* international criminal tribunals have been established in a post-conflict context. Indeed, the Second World War and the Yugoslav and Rwandan armed conflicts, in which international crimes were committed, preceded the establishment of these tribunals. These tribunals are therefore undoubtedly a transitional justice mechanism. As far as the

 | HTTPS://DOI.ORG/10.1163/9789004766655-010

International Criminal Court (ICC) is concerned, it is not a tribunal designed to deal exclusively with post-conflict or transitional justice. However, it appears that most of its cases to date have been opened to investigate and prosecute international crimes committed in the context of transition or armed conflict. The ICC has thus become an instrument of transitional justice.

These international criminal tribunals, analysed within the framework of international criminal law, are therefore part of transitional justice. The following developments may seem repetitive but are necessary for the sake of clarity. In chronological order, they present each of these tribunals, the context and objectives of their creation, which is linked to transitional justice, as well as their main characteristics.

## 1.1 The International Military Tribunal at Nuremberg

### 1.1.1 Creation: Context and Objectives

The context for the establishment of the International Military Tribunal at Nuremberg was the atrocities committed by the Nazis during the Second World War. The question of holding individual criminally accountable for atrocities was raised by the Allies before the end of hostilities of the war. One of the declarations of the Moscow Conference of October 1943 was the Statement on Atrocities, signed by the United States, the UK and the Soviet Union, which established the need to bring to justice those Nazis responsible for crimes committed during the war. It stated that "German officers and men and members of the Nazi party who have been responsible for or have taken a consenting part in the above atrocities, massacres and executions will be sent back to the countries in which their abominable deeds were done in order that they may be judged and punished according to the laws of these liberated countries and of free governments which will be erected therein."[1] According to its signatories, the Statement on Atrocities was "without prejudice to the case of German criminals whose offenses have no particular geographical localization and who will be punished by joint decision of the government of the Allies."[2] At the end of the war, the Nazis and the European Axis were defeated. The Allies – France, the Soviet Union, the United States and Great Britain – occupied German territory. The Allies decided to implement the idea of a criminal procedure and agreed on the trial of the Nazis as "major war

1 The Moscow Conference, Statement on Atrocities, signed by President Roosevelt, Prime Minister Churchill and Premier Stalin, October 1943.

2 *Ibid.*

criminals" The London Agreement of 8 August 1945, signed by the four powers, established an International Military Tribunal to try the main Nazi criminals.[3] The characteristics of this first *ad hoc* International Criminal Court, which sat in Nuremberg, are set out in detail in the London Agreement and, in particular, in the charter of the court, which is annexed to the Agreement.

### 1.1.2 Main General Characteristics

#### 1.1.2.1 Composition

The four Allied signatories to the London Agreement played a central role in the composition of the International Military Tribunal at Nuremberg. Article 2 of the charter of the tribunal provided that it shall be composed of four judges, each with an alternate, and that each of the four signatory states shall appoint one judge and one alternate. Pursuant to Article 14 of the tribunal's charter, the signatory states to the London Agreement also each appointed a "Chief Prosecutor."

#### 1.1.2.2 Jurisdiction

Article 6 of the tribunal's charter defined its personal and material jurisdiction. The tribunal was responsible for trying individuals considered to be "major war criminals of the European Axis," who had committed three international crimes provided for in Article 6: crimes against peace (Article 6-a), war crimes (Article 6-b) and crimes against humanity (Article 6-c).

Crimes against peace referred to, "namely, planning, preparation, initiation or waging of a war of aggression, or a war in violation of international treaties, agreements or assurances, or participation in a common plan or conspiracy for the accomplishment of any of the foregoing."

War crimes were defined as "violations of the laws or customs of war. Such violations shall include, but not be limited to, murder, ill-treatment or deportation to slave labor or for any other purpose of civilian population of or in occupied territory, murder or ill-treatment of prisoners of war or persons on the seas, killing of hostages, plunder of public or private property, wanton destruction of cities, towns or villages, or devastation not justified by military necessity."

---

3 Agreement by the Government of the United States of America, the Provisional Government of the French Republic, the Government of the United Kingdom of Great Britain and Northern Ireland, and the Government of the Union of Soviet Socialist Republics for the Prosecution and Punishment of the Major War Criminals of the European Axis. Agreement signed at London, 8 August 1945, with the charter of the International Military Tribunal. Entered into force 8 August 1945.

Crimes against humanity referred to "murder, extermination, enslavement, deportation, and other inhumane acts committed against any civilian population, before or during the war; or persecutions on political, racial or religious grounds in execution of or in connection with any crime within the jurisdiction of the Tribunal, whether or not in violation of the domestic law of the country where perpetrated."

From 1945 to 1946, the tribunals tried and convicted several Nazis convicted as "major war criminals", thus providing international criminal accountability after an international armed conflict.[4]

## 1.2 The International Military Tribunal for the Far East (Tokyo International Military Tribunal)

### 1.2.1 Creation: Context and Objectives

Like the Nuremberg Tribunal, the International Military Tribunal for the Far East was established in the aftermath of the Second World War. Japan was one of the Axis powers that opposed the Allies during the war. In 1945, the United States, Great Britain and China insisted on the need to bring war criminals to justice in the Potsdam Declaration on the Surrender of Japan.[5] The tribunal was established after the defeat, surrender and occupation of Japan. However, unlike the Nuremberg Tribunal, which was established by agreement between states, the International Military Tribunal for the Far East (Tokyo Tribunal) was established in 1946 by a Special Proclamation by the Supreme Commander for the Allied in Tokyo on 19 January 1946.[6] This Supreme Commander was Douglas MacArthur, an American national. The Special Proclamation held that the goal of the Tokyo Tribunal was to try "those persons charged individually, or as members of organizations, or in both capacities, with offenses which include crimes against peace."[7] The Supreme Commander also approved the charter of the Tokyo Military Tribunal of 1946, which was annexed to the

4 For a summary of trials, and the work, of the International Military Tribunal of Nuremberg, see "The Charter and Judgment of the Nürnberg Tribunal – History and Analysis," Memorandum submitted by the Secretary-General, UN doc. A/CN.4/5, 1949.

5 Proclamation Calling for the Surrender of Japan, approved by the Heads of Governments of the United States, China, and the United Kingdom, Postdam, 26 July 1945, para. 10: "stern justice shall be meted out to all war criminals, including those who have visited cruelties upon our prisoners."

6 Special Proclamation by the Supreme Commander for the Allied Powers at Tokyo, 19 January 1946.

7 *Ibid.*, Special Proclamation, art. 1.

Special Proclamation and contained many provisions similar to those of the statute of the Nuremberg Tribunal, although there were some differences.

### 1.2.2 Main General Characteristics

#### 1.2.2.1 Composition

According to Article 2 of the charter, the tribunal was to be composed "of not less than five nor more than nine Members, appointed by the Supreme Commander for the Allied Powers from the names submitted by the Signatories to the Instrument of Surrender," which were the United States, China, the UK, the Soviet Union, Australia, Canada, France and New Zealand.[8] Within this tribunal, a chief of counsel was appointed by the Supreme Commander to act as prosecutor under Article 8(a) of the charter. In addition, according to Article 8(b), an associate counsel could be appointed by any United Nation that was at war against Japan in order to assist the chief of counsel.

#### 1.2.2.2 Jurisdiction

Article 5 of the tribunal's charter defined the personal and material jurisdiction. The tribunal had jurisdiction over "Far Eastern war criminals" accused of the following crimes: (a) crimes against peace: "the planning, preparation, initiation or waging of a declared or undeclared war of aggression, or a war in violation of international law, treaties, agreements or assurances, or participation in a common plan or conspiracy for the accomplishment of any of the foregoing"; (b) conventional war crimes: "violations of the laws or customs of war"; and (c) crimes against humanity: "murder, extermination, enslavement, deportation, and other inhumane acts committed against any civilian population, before or during the war, or persecutions on political or racial grounds in execution of or in connection with any crime within the jurisdiction of the tribunal, whether or not in violation of the domestic law of the country where perpetrated. Leaders, organizers, instigators and accomplices participating in the formulation or execution of a common plan or conspiracy to commit any of the foregoing crimes are responsible for all 'acts performed by any person in execution of such plan.'"

From 1946 to 1948, the Tokyo Tribunal tried several individuals and sentenced them.[9]

---

8 Instrument of Surrender, 2 September 1945, 2.

9 Judgment of the International Military Tribunal for the Far East, November 1948.

## 1.3 The International Criminal Tribunal for the Former Yugoslavia

### 1.3.1 Creation: Context and Objectives

The International Criminal Tribunal for the former Yugoslavia (ICTY) was established in the context of the armed conflict and post-armed conflict in the former Yugoslavia. The post-Cold War period saw the break-up of Yugoslavia, which consisted of several national groups: Serbia, Slovenia, Croatia, Macedonia, Bosnia and Herzegovina, Montenegro and, later, Kosovo. These national groups gradually lost the desire to continue living together in the same state. Many of the national groups demanded independence from the Federal Republic of Yugoslavia,[10] and others, particularly the Serbs, refused to allow the disintegration of the former state. It was in this context that many armed conflicts between these groups broke out in the Balkans, starting in the 1990s.

The armed conflicts were characterised by numerous allegations of violations of human rights and international humanitarian law. The international community stepped in. At the request of the Security Council, the UN Secretary-General established a Commission of Inquiry to investigate international crimes committed in what is now the former Yugoslavia.[11] In an interim report, the Commission concluded that serious violations of international humanitarian law had been committed and proposed the establishment of an international criminal tribunal to try those responsible for these crimes. In 1993, in an unprecedented decision, the Security Council acted under Chapter VII of the UN Charter, which deals with "[a]ctions with respect to threats to the peace, breaches of the peace, and acts of aggression," and decided for the establishment of an international tribunal to prosecute "persons responsible for serious violations of international humanitarian law committed in the territory of the former Yugoslavia since 1991."[12] To realise this objective, and after

10 For example, Croatia and Slovenia declared their independence on 25 June 1991 and applied to join the United Nations as States in 1992. For Croatia: Application of Croatia for admission to membership in the United Nations, UN doc. A/46/912, S/23884, 7 May 1992 (on declaration of independence, see Annex, 2). For Slovenia: Application of the Republic of Slovenia for admission to membership in the United Nations, UN doc. A/46/913 S/23885, 7 May 1992. In March 1992, Bosnia-Herzegovina also declared its independence and later applied for membership in the UN, see Application of the Republic of Bosnia and Herzegovina for admission to membership in the United Nations, UN doc. A/46/921 S/23971, 19 May 1992.

11 UN Security Council, Resolution 780 (1992), UN doc. S/RES/780 (1992).

12 UN Security Council, Resolution 827, UN doc. S/RES/827 (1993). See also UN Security Council, Resolution 808, UN doc. S/RES/808 (1993).

a report by the UN Secretary-General,[13] the International Criminal Tribunal for the Former Yugoslavia (ICTY) was created by a UN Security Council Resolution, which also adopted the statute of the tribunal annexed to the UN Secretary-General's report.[14] This marked the first creation of an International Criminal Tribunal since the Second World War.

### 1.3.2 Main General Characteristics

#### 1.3.2.1 Composition

The ICTY consisted of sixteen judges assigned to three trial chambers and an appeals chamber. It also had an office of the prosecutor and a registry.[15]

#### 1.3.2.2 Jurisdiction

The statute of the tribunal provided that the tribunal had "to prosecute persons responsible for serious violations of international humanitarian law committed in the territory of the former Yugoslavia since 1991."[16] The tribunal had material jurisdiction over grave breaches of the Geneva Conventions of 1949, crimes against humanity, violations of the laws and customs of war, and genocide.[17] Its personal jurisdiction covered "natural persons."[18]

From 1993 to 2017, the ICTY tried and convicted several individuals accused of committing international crimes.[19]

## 1.4 The International Criminal Tribunal for Rwanda

### 1.4.1 Creation: Context and Objectives

The International Criminal Tribunal for Rwanda was established in a context of armed conflict, political regime change and serious crimes. In the context of tensions between the two main ethnic groups in Rwanda, the Tutsi minority and the Hutu majority, the assassination of the Burundian and Rwandan

---

13 "Report of the Secretary-General Pursuant to Paragraph 2 of Security Council Resolution 808 (1993)," UN doc. S/25704, 3 May 1993; for the Statute of the Tribunal created, see, in the same document, Annex-Statute of the International Tribunal.

14 UN doc. S/RES/827 (1993) 25 May 1993, para. 2.

15 See the Statute of the ICTY (updated version of the Statute, September 2009), art. 12 for the judges, art. 16 for the prosecutor and art. 17 for the registry.

16 Art 1, Statute of the ICTY.

17 Art. 2–5, ICTY Statute.

18 Art. 6, ICTY Statute.

19 See all the cases on the ICTY website: https://www.icty.org/.

presidents in a plane crash on 6 April 1994 triggered serious repression, massacres and genocide that had been in the making for many months.[20] These acts were mainly directed against the Tutsis, and the Hutus were accused of perpetrating these crimes.[21] Moderate Hutus were also victims of massacres.[22] After the plane crash, many Tutsis who had taken refuge in Uganda for years and formed an armed group, the RPF (Rwandese Patriotic Front), launched an armed offensive against the Hutu government forces and were also accused of carrying out raids and massacres.[23] The Hutu government was overthrown by the Tutsi rebellion in July 1994. The new government, which intended to repress the crimes committed by the Hutu leaders, requested in a letter addressed to the United Nations Security Council in September 1994 the "[s]etting up as soon as possible [of] an international tribunal to try the criminals."[24] Faced with allegations of serious violations committed in Rwanda, the UN Security Council had almost three months earlier requested the creation of a commission of experts to investigate the crimes committed in Rwanda.[25] The UN Secretary-General established this commission, which concluded in October 1994 that crimes had been committed[26] and that an international criminal tribunal was an appropriate instrument to try such crimes.[27] The commission noted, however, that rather than creating a new international criminal tribunal, the jurisdiction of the newly created ICTY should be extended to crimes committed in Rwanda.[28]

The Security Council preferred to create a new tribunal. Based on Chapter VII of the UN Charter, the Security Council established the International Criminal Tribunal for Rwanda and adopted its statute in November 1994.[29]

---

20 On the account of the context of the creation of the International Criminal Tribunal for Rwanda, see "Preliminary Report of the Commission of Independent Experts established pursuant to Security Council Resolution 935 (1994)," UN doc. S/1994/1125, para. 41.

21 *Ibid.*, para. 44.

22 *Ibid.*, para. 27.

23 See "Report of Secretary-General on the Situation in Rwanda," UN doc. S/1994/640, 31 May 1994, para. 12; see also UN doc. S/1994/1125, paras. 79–83.

24 Letter dated 28 September 1994 from the Permanent Representative of Rwanda to the United Nations addressed to the President of the Security Council (Annex), UN doc. S/1994/1115, 29 September 1994, 4.

25 United Nations Security Council, Resolution 935, UN doc. S/RES/935, 1er July 1994.

26 'Preliminary Report of the Commission of Independent Experts established pursuant to Security Council Resolution 935' (1994), UN doc. S/1994/1125 (Annex), 4 October 1994, paras. 42–83.

27 *Ibid.*, UN doc. S/1994/1125, para. 141.

28 *Ibid.*, para. 142.

29 United Nations Security Council, Resolution 955, UN doc. S/RES/955 (1994), 8 November 1994.

#### 1.4.2 Main General Characteristics

##### 1.4.2.1 Composition

The tribunal was composed of sixteen judges who were assigned to three trial chambers and an appeals chamber, which was shared with the ICTY, a prosecutor's office and a registry.[30]

##### 1.4.2.2 Jurisdiction

The tribunal was established to prosecute "persons responsible for genocide and other serious violations of international humanitarian law committed in the territory of Rwanda and Rwandan citizens responsible for genocide and other such violations committed in the territory of neighbouring States, between 1 January 1994 and 31 December 1994."[31] The statute of the tribunal provided that it had jurisdiction over genocide, crimes against humanity and violations of Article 3 common to the Geneva Conventions and Additional Protocol II.[32] Its personal jurisdiction covered "natural persons."[33]

From 1994 to 2015, the tribunal tried several persons and sentenced them.[34]

### 1.5 International Residual Mechanism for Criminal Tribunals

In order to finish the work of the ICTY and ICTR, an "International Residual Mechanism for Criminal Tribunals" was created by the Security Council in 2010.[35] The Security Council decided "to establish the International Residual Mechanism for Criminal Tribunals ('the Mechanism') with two branches, which shall commence functioning on 1 July 2012 (branch for the ICTR) and 1 July 2013 (branch for the ICTY), respectively ('commencement dates'), and to this end [decided] to adopt the Statute of the Mechanism in Annex 1 to this resolution."[36] In 2012, the "Residual Mechanism" became operational, and since the closure of the ICTR and ICTY, it has continued to examine the "residual" cases of individuals accused of international crimes committed in

30 See the Statute of the ICTR (last version, 31 January 2010): art. 11 for the judges, art. 15 for the prosecutor and art. 16 for the registry.

31 *Ibid.*, UN doc. S/RES/955, para. 1. See also Art. 1 of the Statute of the ICTR.

32 Art. 2–4 of the Statute of the ICTR.

33 Art. 5, *Ibid.*

34 For all the cases, see the "legacy website" of the ICTR, https://unictr.irmct.org/.

35 UN doc. S/RES/1966, 22 December 2010.

36 *Ibid.*, para. 1.

the context of armed conflicts in the former Yugoslavia and in Rwanda in the 1990s. This mechanism was not, as such, a new autonomous tribunal, but a new procedure invented to complete the work of the ICTY and ICTR.

## 1.6 The International Criminal Court

### 1.6.1 Creation: Context and Objectives

The process that led to the creation of the International Criminal Court is not similar to the process that led to the creation of the *ad hoc* international criminal tribunals mentioned above. The context of the creation of the ICC is neither transitional nor post-conflict. The creation of the ICC began after the Second World War. From the early 1950s, the UN General Assembly began to consider the establishment of a permanent international criminal court.[37] The UN International Law Commission (ILC) also played a significant role because it considered the creation of that tribunal in its work.[38] However, the process did not encounter success until the decisions of the UN General Assembly to consider the question in the late 1980s.[39] Negotiations were led between states based on a statute project established by the ILC.[40] In 1998, several states adopted the Statute of Rome, creating the International Criminal Court, and its statute entered into force in 2002.[41] This ICC was established as a permanent tribunal to "be complementary to national criminal jurisdictions"[42] and to try individuals accused of committing international crimes in accordance with its statute.

---

37 See, for example, UN doc. A/RES/489(V), 12 December 1950 on the establishment of a committee to elaborate a draft project of a permanent international criminal jurisdictions; on the same matter, UN doc. A/RES/687(VII), 5 December 1952.

38 See, for example, "Yearbook of the International Law Commission 1983," vol. I, UN doc. A/CN.4/SER.A/1983, paras. 22–24; "Yearbook of the International Law Commission 1983," vol. II, 1983, UN doc. A/CN.4/SER.A/1983/Add.l (Part 2), para. 69 (c); "Yearbook of the International Law Commission 1986," vol. II, UN Doc. A/CN.4/SER.A/1986/Add.l (Part 2), para. 185.

39 UN doc. A/RES/44/39, 4 December 1989.

40 "Yearbook of the International Law Commission 1994," vol. II, UN doc. A/CN.4/SER.A/1994/Add.l (Part 1), paras. 90–91.

41 Rome Statute of the International Criminal Court, 17 July 1998, entry into Force: 1 July 2002.

42 See the preamble, *ibid.*

### 1.6.2 Main General Characteristics

#### 1.6.2.1 Composition

The court consists of eighteen judges,[43] assigned to three "divisions" (appeals, trial and pre-trial),[44] a prosecutor's office, and a registry. The court also has a presidency composed of judges.[45]

#### 1.6.2.2 Jurisdiction

The ICC has jurisdiction over individuals accused of genocide, crimes against humanity, war crimes and crimes of aggression.[46] The crimes must have been committed after the entry into force of the Rome Statute on 1 July 2002.[47]

#### 1.6.2.3 Work and Links with Transitional Justice

The entry into force of the statute in 2002 and the subsequent work of the ICC have raised the question of its involvement in the field of transitional justice. Indeed, since its establishment, the ICC has investigated numerous crimes committed in the context of armed conflict, post-conflict or transitional situations. The ICC has conducted investigations and has brought cases against individuals for crimes committed during armed conflicts and sometimes during efforts to end them. The states concerned include: Uganda, the Democratic Republic of the Congo, the Central African Republic, Mali, Côte d'Ivoire, Israel, Palestine and Ukraine.[48] The ICC has thus become an important instrument of transitional justice.

## 2 Hybrid Criminal Courts

Since the beginning of the 2000s, hybrid criminal tribunals have been established in several states struggling to overcome a past armed conflict or dealing with international crimes committed during a dictatorship. These tribunals combine both national and international aspects. Almost all of them were established in a post-conflict and/or transitional context. They include the Mixed Courts of Kosovo (2000), the Special Panels for Serious Crimes in East Timor (2000), the Extraordinary Chambers in the Courts of Cambodia (2001),

43 Art. 39 para. 1, the Rome Statute of the International Criminal Court.
44 Art. 36(b), *ibid.*
45 Art. 36(a) and 38, *ibid.*
46 Art. 5, *ibid.*
47 Art. 11, para. 1, *ibid.*
48 See the cases and investigations on the website of the ICC, https://www.icc-cpi.int/.

the Special Court for Sierra Leone (2002), the Special Chambers for Bosnia and Herzegovina (2005, opened), the Extraordinary African Chambers in the Courts of Senegal (2012), the Special Criminal Court for the Central African Republic (2015), and the Specialised Chambers in Kosovo (2015).

### 2.1 Kosovo Courts of Mixed Composition and the Kosovo Specialised Chambers

The armed conflict in Kosovo during most of the 1990s and early 2000s was one of the consequences of the break-up of Yugoslavia. During this period, Kosovo, an autonomous province of the Republic of Yugoslavia (now Serbia), faced repressive rule, with Kosovo Albanians demanding independence, while Serbia, which had revoked the province's autonomous status, wanted to keep the province within its territory.[49] A violent armed conflict broke out in the late 1990s between Kosovo Albanian independence fighters and Serbs, and human rights abuses were widespread.[50] The armed conflict was marked by negotiations between the belligerents and saw direct NATO intervention, with air-strikes carried out against Serbian armed forces.[51] Subsequently, the territory of Kosovo was placed under UN administration by the Security Council, which, on the basis of Chapter VII of the UN Charter, "[d]ecides on the deployment in Kosovo, under United Nations auspices, of international civil and security presences, with appropriate equipment and personnel as required."[52] The United Nations Mission in Kosovo (UNMIK) was established. It took the decision in 2000 to appoint international judges and prosecutors, first in the courts of Mitrovica, a city in Kosovo,[53] before extending this possibility to the entire territory of Kosovo.[54] These courts tried individuals accused of committing, among other crimes, international crimes.[55]

---

49 Lord Robertson of Port Ellen (Secretary General of NATO), "Kosovo One Year On. Achievement and Challenge," 21 March 2000, 6.

50 OSCE, "Kosovo/Kosova. As Seen, As Told. An analysis of the human rights findings of the OSCE Kosovo Verification Mission, October 1998 to June 1999," 1999.

51 Lord Robertson of Port Ellen (Secretary General of NATO), "Kosovo One Year On. Achievement and Challenge," 21 March 2000, 7–15.

52 UN doc. S/RES/1244, 10 June 1999, para. 5.

53 See, *inter alia*, UNMIK Regulation 2000/6, UN doc. UNMIK/Reg/2000/6, 15 February 2000, in UN doc, S/2000/177/Add.2, 28 March 2000. Jacquelin, Mathieu, 'International Law' (2018) 1(1) *Journal of Criminal Science and Comparative Criminal Law* 229.

54 UNMIK Regulation 2000/34, UN doc. UNMIK/Reg/2000/6, 27 May 2000.

55 See Organization for Security and Co-operation in Europe, Mission in Kosovo, Department of Human Rights and Communities, "Kosovo's War Crimes Trials: An Assessment Ten Years on 1999–2009," May 2010, 11.

Years later, following a Council of Europe report finding serious human rights violations in Kosovo,[56] another hybrid tribunal was set up in 2015 after negotiations between Kosovo, which declared its independence in 2008, and the European Union.[57] The tribunal, named the Kosovo Specialist Chambers and the Specialist Prosecutor's Office, was responsible for investigating crimes committed in Kosovo between 1 January 1998 and 31 December 2000,[58] dates which cover the period during which the territory of Kosovo was the scene of an armed confrontation. The tribunal has jurisdiction over crimes against humanity, war crimes and other crimes provided for under Kosovo law.[59] Trials are currently underway before this tribunal.[60]

### 2.2 Special Panels in the Courts of Dili in East Timor

The Special Panels in the courts of Dili in East Timor were a tribunal created in the context of armed conflict and its aftermath. East Timor, a territory once colonised by Portugal, experienced a war for independence. Many Timorese demanded independence after colonisation and were confronted by the Indonesians, who considered the Timorese territory to be an integral part of Indonesia. Armed conflict began in the mid-1970s and culminated in the late 1990s, pitting the pro-independence Timorese against the anti-independence Indonesians, against a backdrop of serious human rights violations and a catastrophic humanitarian situation.[61] After negotiations, agreements and a referendum that saw the Timorese voting overwhelmingly for independence, the armed conflict did not end, and human rights continued to be violated.[62] In this context, the United Nations Security Council, on the basis of Chapter VII of the United Nations Charter, had established "a United Nations Transitional Administration in East Timor (UNTAET), which will be endowed with overall

56 Council of Europe, Parliamentary Assembly, "Inhuman treatment of people and illicit trafficking in human organs in Kosovo," 7 January 2011, doc. 12462.

57 Law No. 04/L-274 on Ratification of the International Agreement between the Republic of Kosovo and the European Union on the European Union Rule of Law Mission in Kosovo, 23 April 2014; Law No.05/L-053 on Specialist Chambers and Specialist Prosecutor's Office, 3 August 2015.

58 Art. 7 and 8, Law No.05/L-053.

59 Art. 13, 14 and 15, *ibid.*

60 See the website of the tribunal, https://www.scp-ks.org/en.

61 On the armed conflict and the situation in East Timor, see UN Security Council resolutions: UN doc. S/RES/38425, December 1975; S/RES/1272, 25 October 1999.

62 See, for example, the UN Security Council Resolutions: UN doc. S/RES/1236, 7 May 1999, S/RES/1272, 25 October 1999. See also, reports of the UN Secretary-General, UN doc. S/1999/513, 5 May 1999; S/1999/595, 22 May 1999.

responsibility for the administration of East Timor and will be empowered to exercise all legislative and executive authority, including the administration of justice."[63] It is within the framework of this administration that the UN Special Representative, as part of the administration of justice, set up the "Panels With Exclusive Jurisdiction Over Serious Criminal Offences," composed of national and international judges and mixing other aspects of national and international law.[64] These Special Panels were tasked with trying individuals accused of committing, "in the period between 1 January 1999 and 25 October 1999,"[65] genocide, war crimes, crimes against humanity, murder, sexual offences and torture.[66] These courts indicted and tried many individuals and sentenced several of them.[67]

### 2.3 Extraordinary Chambers in the Courts of Cambodia

In the context of the Cold War, the Communist Party of Kampuchea, the Khmer Rouge, came to power in Cambodia in 1975 after years of armed struggle against Cambodian governments, which had started in the 1960s.[68] Many crimes were committed during the years the Khmer Rouge were in power between 1975 and 1979.[69] Years after the fall of the Khmer Rouge regime, the dark past of Cambodia was still vivid, and, after the end of the Cold War, the Cambodian government wrote a letter to the UN Secretary-General "to ask for the assistance of the United Nations and the international community in bringing to justice those persons responsible for the genocide and crimes against humanity during the rule of the Khmer Rouge from 1975 to 1979."[70]

63 UN Security Council, Resolution 1272, UN Doc. S/RES/1272, 25 October 1999, para. 1.

64 See: Regulation No. 2000/11 on the Organization of Courts in East Timor, UNTAET doc. UNTAET/REG/2000/11, 6 March 2000; Regulation No. 2000/15 on the Establishment of Panels with Exclusive Jurisdiction over Serious Criminal Offences, UNTAET doc. UNTAET/REG/2000/15, 6 June 2000; Regulation 2001/18 on the Amendment of UNTAET Regulation No. 2000/11 on the Organization of the Courts in East Timor, UNTAET doc. UNTAET/REG/2001/18, 21 July 2001.

65 UNTAET/REG/2001/18, *ibid.*, para. 10.2.

66 *Ibid.*, para. 10.1.

67 For more on the judgments of the Special Panels, see the website on the Virtual Tribunals collection of the Center for Human Rights and International Justice of the University of Stanford, "Special Panels for Serious Crimes in Timor," online: https://exhibits.stanford.edu/virtual-tribunals/feature/spsc-cases.

68 "Report of the Group of Experts for Cambodia established pursuant to General Assembly resolution 52/135," 18 February 1999, para. 14.

69 *Ibid.*, paras. 46–83.

70 Letter dated 21 June 1997 from the First and Second Prime Ministers of Cambodia addressed to the Secretary-General, UN doc. A/51/930, S/1997/488, 24 June 1997, Annex.

The UN and Cambodia negotiated to establish a court to try those responsible for crimes committed during the Khmer Rouge regime. In this context, on 10 August 2001, Cambodia adopted a law establishing the Extraordinary Chambers in the Courts of Cambodia, which was later revised in 2004.[71] In 2003, the United Nations and Cambodia signed an agreement establishing the Extraordinary Chambers in the Courts of Cambodia.[72] The Extraordinary Chambers were composed of Cambodian and international judges and prosecutors,[73] and were set to try individuals who committed certain national and international crimes "during the period from 17 April 1975 to 6 January 1979."[74] They had jurisdiction over crimes of genocide, crimes against humanity, grave breaches of the Geneva Conventions of 1949, and crimes defined by the agreement of 10 August 2001 establishing the Extraordinary Chambers.[75] The court has tried some individuals and sentenced them.[76]

## 2.4 The Special Court for Sierra Leone

The armed conflict that raged in Sierra Leone in the early 1990s prompted the creation of the Special Court for Sierra Leone. A 1999 peace agreement between the Sierra Leonean government and the Revolutionary United Front (RUF) rebels failed to end the conflict.[77] It was in this context that, in 2000, the Sierra Leone president at the time asked the UN Security Council for the creation of a special court for Sierra Leone that would "try and bring to credible justice those members of the Revolutionary United Front (RUF) and their accomplices responsible for committing crimes against the people of Sierra Leone and for the taking of United Nations peacekeepers as hostages."[78] The Security Council then passed a resolution asking the UN Secretary-General to

71 Law on the Establishment of the Extraordinary Chambers in the Courts of Cambodia, 27 October 2004.

72 Agreement between the United Nations and Cambodia for the Prosecution of Crimes Committed during the Period of Democratic Kampuchea, 6 June 2003.

73 Art. 3 for the judges and Art. 6 for the prosecutors, *ibid.*

74 Art. 1, *ibid.*

75 Art. 9, *ibid.*

76 See on the website of the Extraordinary Chambers in the Court of Cambodia, online: https://www.eccc.gov.kh/en/case-load.

77 Peace Agreement signed between the Government of Sierra Leone and the Revolutionary United Front of Sierra Leone in Lomé on 7 July 1999, UN doc. S/1999/777, 12 July 1999, Annex.

78 Annex to the letter dated 9 August 2000 from the Permanent Representative of Sierra Leone to the United Nations addressed to the President of the Security Council, UN doc. S/2000/786, 10 August 2000.

open negotiations with Sierra Leone on the matter.[79] In 2002, these negotiations resulted in an agreement that provided for the establishment of the Special Court for Sierra Leone (SCSL).[80] The statute of the SCSL, which was annexed to the agreement, provided that the SCSL had jurisdiction over crimes against humanity, genocide, violations of Article 3 common to the Geneva Conventions of 12 August 1949 and Additional Protocol II, other serious violations of international humanitarian law, and crimes under Sierra Leonean law.[81] The SCSL was composed of judges appointed by the Government of Sierra Leone and the UN Secretary-General.[82] The prosecutor and the registrar of the tribunal were appointed by the UN Secretary-General.[83] The SCSL tried several individuals, including the former head of state of Liberia, Charles Taylor, and sentenced them.[84]

### 2.5 The War Crimes Section of Bosnia and Herzegovina

This "court" was set up in the context of the post-war conflict in the former Yugoslavia. It was part of a desire to relieve the workload of the ICTY by allowing it to complete its trials, while providing Bosnia and Herzegovina, one of the states that emerged from the ashes of the former Yugoslavia, with the means to establish criminal responsibility for crimes committed during the armed conflict. The initiative for the establishment of the court came from the conclusions of the Office of the High Representative for the former Yugoslavia and the ICTY on the need to establish criminal proceedings to determine the responsibility of war criminals.[85] After the adoption of several laws, the court was inaugurated on 9 March 2005.[86] It was composed of judges (international judges could be appointed and would gradually be replaced later by national judges).[87] The court held several trials and convicted many

---

79 UN Security Council, Resolution 1315, UN doc. S/RES/1315(2000), 14 August 2000.

80 Agreement between the United Nations and the Government of Sierra Leone, 16 January 2002.

81 Art. 2-5, Statute of the Special Court for Sierra Leone, 16 January 2002.

82 Art. 12, *ibid.*

83 Art. 15 and 16, *ibid.*

84 The judgments and decisions of the Special Court for Sierra Leone can be found on the website: https://rscsl.org/the-rscsl/rscsl-decisions/.

85 See ICTY website: https://www.icty.org/fr/outreach/renforcement-des-capacites-nationales/d%C3%A9veloppement-des-instances-judiciaires-nationales.

86 *Ibid.*

87 See Art. 24 "Transitional provisions," Law on Court of Bosnia and Herzegovina, – Consolidated Version, Official Gazette of Bosnia and Herzegovina, 49/09, 2009.

individuals.[88] As part of the same ICTY completion strategy, other such courts have been established in Serbia and Croatia.[89]

## 2.6 The Extraordinary African Chambers in the Senegalese Courts

This jurisdiction was the result of the struggle of the victims of the regime of Hissein Habré in Chad, a regime accused of being a dictatorship that committed serious crimes against individuals in the 1980s.[90] After the fall of his regime, Hissein Habré settled in Dakar, Senegal, while the victims of his regime continued to fight to bring him to justice for the crimes committed during his presidency of Chad. This struggle was successful when, on 22 August 2012, the African Union and Senegal agreed to establish the African Extraordinary Chambers in the courts of Senegal.[91] Composed of judges from Senegal and other African states, a prosecutor, a registry and an administrator,[92] these chambers were charged with trying those suspected of committing the crime of genocide, crimes against humanity, war crimes and crimes of torture in Chad between 1982 and 1990,[93] a period that coincided with the time when Hissein Habré was in power. They finally tried only Hissein Habré, the former head of state of Chad, and sentenced him to life imprisonment.[94]

## 2.7 The Central African Criminal Court

In a context of recurrent armed clashes between armed rebel groups or between armed rebel groups and the Government of the Central African Republic in the 2000s, the UN Security Council committed itself to restoring peace and security, and under Chapter VII of the UN Charter, decided to estab-

88 See, for example, the World Report of Human Rights Watch on Bosnia and Herzegovina, online: https://www.hrw.org/world-report/2018/country-chapters/bosnia-and-herzegovina.

89 See ICTY website: https://www.icty.org/fr/outreach/renforcement-des-capacites-nationales/d%C3%A9veloppement-des-instances-judiciaires-nationales.

90 Chad, "Les crimes et détournements de l'ex-président Habré et de ses complices. Rapport de la commission nationale d'enquête du ministère tchadien de la Justice," Paris, L'Harmattan, 1993.

91 Agreement between the Republic of Senegal and the African Union on the Establishment of Extraordinary African Chambers in the Courts of Senegal, 22 August 2012.

92 Art. 11, 12, 13 and 15 of the Statute of the Extraordinary African Chambers in the Courts of Senegal for the Prosecution of Crimes Committed in Chad during the Period from 7 June 1982 to 1st December 1990.

93 Art. 4, *ibid.*

94 CAE, *The Prosecutor v. Hissein Habré*, Judgment, 30 May 2016.

lish the United Nations Multidimensional Integrated Stabilisation Mission in the Central African Republic (MINUSCA) in 2014.[95] That same year, MINUSCA and the Government of the Central African Republic signed a *mémorandum d'entente* in which the government committed itself to establishing a special criminal court composed of national and international personnel, with MINUSCA contributing to many aspects of the court, notably the appointment of international judges and prosecutors.[96] The government created the court in a legislative act in 2015 to "investigate, prosecute and judge serious human rights violations and grave breaches of international humanitarian law committed on the territory of the Central African Republic since 1 January 2003, as defined by the Central African Penal Code and by virtue of the international obligations contracted by the Central African Republic in matters of international law, in particular the crime of genocide, crimes against humanity and war crimes, which are the subject of current and future investigations."[97] The court is composed of national and international judges,[98] a registry[99] and a special prosecutor.[100] Its work is underway, and it has indicted and prosecuted several individuals.[101]

### 2.8 Hybrid Court for South Sudan

In South Sudan, a peace agreement was signed in 2018, with the participation of the African Union, which provided for the establishment of the Hybrid Court for South Sudan.[102] But the tribunal has not yet been established.[103]

95 UN doc. S/RES/2149, 10 April 2014, para. 18.

96 "Mémorandum d'entente entre la Mission multidimensionnelle intégrée des Nations unies pour la stabilisation en Centrafrique et le gouvernement de la République centrafricaine," 2014, paras. 4–23.

97 Translation from French, Art. 3, Loi organique No. 15-003 portant création, organisation et fonctionnement de la Cour Pénale Spéciale, 3 June 2015.

98 Art. 11–14, *ibid.*

99 Art. 15, *ibid.*

100 Art. 18, *ibid.*

101 See the website of the Special Court: https://www.cpsrca.cf/detail-contenu-smenu/chiffres-cles-des-affaires/38/.

102 Signed Revitalized Agreement on the Resolution of the Conflict in South Sudan (R-ARCSS), Addis Ababa, 12 September 2018, Section 5.3: Hybrid Court for South Sudan (HCSS).

103 "Report of the Commission on Human Rights in South Sudan," UN doc. A/HRC/52/26, 31 January 2023; "Human Rights Watch Report 2024, South Sudan," online, https://www.hrw.org/world-report/2024/country-chapters/south-sudan.

## 2.9 Gambia's Special Accountability Mechanism

The authoritarian rule of Yahya Jammeh's regime in The Gambia came to an end in 2017. As the regime had been accused of committing several gross human rights violations, a truth commission was set up to investigate.[104] In order to deal with these past human rights violations and crimes, the Special Accountability Mechanism was created for The Gambia in 2024. It consists of "the Special Prosecutor's Office, the Special Tribunal founded in collaboration with ECOWAS and international partners, and the Special Criminal Division of the High Court."[105] The Special Prosecutor's Office was established by an Act in the same year, "as the first phase in establishing" this Mechanism.[106] According to the Act, the Special Prosecutor's Office will investigate and prosecute "cases of serious human rights violations and international and domestic crimes specified in or related to acts and omissions described in the TRRC Report, which occurred between July 1994 and January 2017."[107] The work and trials of this new hybrid tribunal are yet to begin.

## 2.10 Special Tribunal for the Crime of Aggression against Ukraine

In the context of the armed conflict between Russia and Ukraine, the Council of Europe and Ukraine adopted in 2025 the Agreement on Establishment of the Special Tribunal for the Crime of Aggression Against Ukraine, with the Statute of the Tribunal being annexed to the Agreement.[108] The special Tribunal's role is "to investigate, prosecute and try persons who bear the greatest responsibility for the crime of aggression against Ukraine".[109] There have been efforts to operationalise the special tribunal,[110] but its activities and the trials are, as in The Gambia, yet to begin.

The proliferation of these mixed national and international courts suggests that they will continue to be used in the future to address violations of inter-

104 See below Chapter 6 on truth commissions.

105 Section 2, Special Prosecutor's Office Act, 2024. See: "Special Accountability Mechanism."

106 Special Prosecutor's Office Act, 2024.

107 Section 3(1), *ibid.*

108 Agreement between the Council of Europe and Ukraine on the Establishment of the Special Tribunal for the Crime of Aggression Against Ukraine, Strasbourg, 25 June 2025.

109 Art. 1, para. 1, *Ibid.*

110 Resolution CM/Res(2026)5 establishing the Enlarged Partial Agreement on the Management Committee of the Special Tribunal for the Crime of Aggression against Ukraine, 15 May 2026, signed by 34 members of the Council of Europe, European Union, Australia and Costa Rica.

national law following armed conflict or authoritarian rule, thereby contributing to international transitional justice law.

## 3 International and Hybrid Criminal Tribunals and International Transitional Justice Law

International and hybrid criminal tribunals have built a new branch of international law. Indeed, they have constituted a pivotal aspect of the advent of international criminal law. While some international criminal trials were envisaged prior to this, it was the aftermath of the Second World War that saw the modern birth of international criminal law, with the creation of the International Criminal Tribunals of Nuremberg and Tokyo. As previously discussed in Part 1 of this book, this development occurred concurrently with the advent of transitional justice. Thus, the establishment of international criminal tribunals following the Second World War marked the advent of international criminal law, coinciding with a practice that would later be incorporated into the concept of transitional justice. Following the conclusion of the Cold War, these tribunals were re-established with the creation of the *ad hoc* international criminal tribunals for the former Yugoslavia and Rwanda. Their return marked a renewed development of international criminal law, as well as a resurgence in the field of transitional justice. The advent of hybrid tribunals contributed to this momentum, signifying a transformation in the landscape of international criminal institutions. These tribunals represented the tangible manifestation of the evolution of international criminal law, simultaneously constituting novel mechanisms for addressing serious international crimes and thus forming an integral part of the broader field of transitional justice.

International and hybrid criminal tribunals have also made a significant contribution to the development of norms within this branch of international criminal law, as well as to its interpretation. Each tribunal is bound by a statute or set of norms that provide guidance on its activities. Additionally, some of these tribunals, such as the ICC, the ICTY and the ICTR, have adopted Rules of Procedure and Evidence that are used in the course of their legal proceedings. These tribunals have been established to respond to international crimes, most notably genocide, crimes against humanity, war crimes and the violations of international humanitarian law – crimes and violations that are perpetrated in the contexts of authoritarian rule and armed conflict. In the wake of the Nuremberg trials, the International Law Commission drew upon the pivotal legal advancements emerging from these proceedings to establish the Nuremberg Principles, which remain a cornerstone of contemporary international criminal law.[111] The statutes, the rules of procedure and evidence, the rights that are recognised for the victims and accused in the proceedings, and the decisions of these tribunals have collectively informed the content of international criminal law, which is a field of international legal study that has been the subject of extensive examination by numerous scholars, resulting in the publication of a substantial body of literature on the topic. As these tribunals constitute an integral component of the mechanisms of transitional justice, the formal and substantive developments of international criminal law have now become an integral part of international transitional justice law. They help to establish the criminal accountability of the perpetrators, sometimes by filling in the gaps left by national courts or by supplementing them.

## 4 National Judicial Procedures

National judicial procedures are, in fact, the first common procedures to be mobilised in times of transition or after an armed conflict, since, in most cases, the state affected by the crimes committed has territorial jurisdiction over violations and crimes committed on its territory. Territorial states are the ones with primary jurisdiction, and international or hybrid procedures are, in principle, only used as a remedy because of the gaps at the state level.

However, the literature on transitional and post-conflict justice focuses on international or hybrid criminal proceedings. In the context of transitional justice, national judicial procedures often remain underexplored. This is understandable. There are several obstacles to the study of these procedures. First, access to information on national judicial decisions is not easy. Second, there is a language barrier for those who dare to try to identify all these procedures. While some decisions are translated into English and French, the two main international languages, this is not the case for many of the decisions taken as relating to serious and large-scale abuses.

In spite of these undeniable obstacles, it is rather impertinent to present the mechanisms of transitional justice without attempting to identify and analyse the national legal procedures used by states to hold accountable those who have violated the law during a dictatorship or an armed conflict. Obviously, this book cannot identify and present all the cases, jurisprudence and procedures that have been implemented in all states that have undergone

111 Principles of International Law Recognized in the Charter of the Nüremberg Tribunal and in the Judgment of the Tribunal, 1950. See "Report of the International Law Commission covering its Second Session," 5 June–29 July 1950, UN doc. A/1316, 11–14.

a transition or post-conflict accountability. It does, however, aim to identify, as far as possible, those states where there have been judicial proceedings in connection with a dictatorship or armed conflict during which serious abuses were recorded. This identification will focus on judicial, mainly criminal, procedures in states since the Second World War.

## 4.1 National Criminal Proceedings Related to the Second World War

The trials of the International Military Tribunals were "only the tip of the 'legal iceberg'" after the Second World War.[112] There were many national criminal proceedings against the Nazis and their supporters. It is not always easy to access original information, such as lists of judgments, on all the trials that took place in all European and even Asian countries after the end of the war. There are, however, a number of publications that identify these national trials and thus help to record them. These publications often select a few states and do not deal exhaustively with all procedures in all states. What is certain is that such procedures have been put in place and are a good illustration of the problems faced by states in a transitional or post-conflict context. On the one hand, the Allies occupying Germany had initiated criminal proceedings against the Nazis and their collaborators after the International Military Tribunal (IMT), and on the other hand, several states had initiated proceedings on their territory.

### 4.1.1 Trials by the Allied Occupiers of Germany against the Nazis and Their Collaborators

Before, during and after the Nuremberg judgment, numerous trials were conducted against the Nazis by the American, British, French and Soviet occupiers of Germany. A distinction must be made between the criminal proceedings conducted under Control Council Act No. 10 and other criminal proceedings focusing primarily on war crimes.

One of the legal bases for the post-Nuremberg IMT was the Control Council Act No. 10. This law allowed the Allied Powers to conduct trials against the Nazis in the parts of German territory they occupied.[113] The Americans seized this opportunity and held trials in Nuremberg after the Nuremberg IMT. The

112 David M Crowe, *War Crimes, Genocide, and Justice. A Global History* (Palgrave Macmillan 2014) 243.

113 Article III, Control Council Law No. 10. Punishment of Persons Guilty of War Crimes, Crimes Against Peace and Against Humanity, 20 December 1945.

Act No. 10 provided the same subject matter jurisdiction as that of the Nuremberg IMT. Persons accused of crimes against peace, war crimes and crimes against humanity could be tried.[114] The Americans held a dozen trials between October 1946 and April 1949, sentencing several Nazis to terms ranging from imprisonment to death.[115]

The Allied Powers also held numerous trials in the parts of German territory they occupied or on their own territory, usually on the basis of national legislation. These trials before "tribunals," or rather often "military commissions," concerned mainly persons accused of war crimes. Almost all of these proceedings were published by the United Nations War Crimes Commission.[116] On the part of German territory that they occupied, but also on their own territory, the United States held trials for war crimes within the framework of military commissions based on laws passed by the American Congress, in particular on a law of 4 June 1920, Chapter II of which was entitled "Articles of War."[117] The United States tried more than 2,000 Germans.[118] Trials were organised within the framework of American military commissions in Japan against Japanese individuals accused of violations of the laws and customs of war provided for, in particular, in the Hague Conventions of 1907 and the Geneva Conventions of 1929.[119]

In the same vein, the British organised trials on the basis of a national text called the Royal Warrant, which was adopted on 14 June 1945 and entered into force on 18 June of the same year. This text expressed the need to bring to justice those responsible for violations of the laws and customs of war in which the United Kingdom had been engaged since 1939.[120] This text was therefore limited to war crimes.[121] The British held trials against dozens of

---

114 Art. II, *ibid.*

115 See "Trials of War Criminals before Nuernberg Military Tribunals Under Control Council Law No. 10," Nuernberg October 1946–April 1949, 15 vols.

116 United Nations War Crimes Commission, "Law Reports of Trials of War Criminals," 1947–1949, 15 vols.

117 See *ibid.*, vol. 1, 52 and especially the annexes, 111–112.

118 David M Crowe, *War Crimes, Genocide, and Justice. A Global History* (Palgrave Macmillan 2014) 245.

119 See, for example, United Nations War Crimes Commission, "Law Reports of Trials of War Criminals," 1947–1949, vol. 1, 71–79.

120 The War Office, 18th June, 1945, Royal Warrant, 0160/2498, A.O. 81/1945, Regulations for the Trial of War Criminals.

121 *Ibid.*, para. 1: "'War Crime' means a violation of the laws and usages of war committed during any war in which His Majesty has been or may be engaged at any time since the 2nd September, 1939."

Nazis and their allies before and after the Nuremberg judgment, and many of the accused were sentenced to death or imprisonment.[122]

Several trials also took place in the Soviet-occupied zone and the Soviet Union. In his book, Jeffrey Herf estimates that 12,500 Germans were convicted of war crimes in East Germany by courts set up in the Soviet-occupied zone.[123] Other trials also took place in the Soviet Union against persons accused of collaboration.[124]

Using national law, including the Penal Code and ordinances,[125] the French held trials in the part of German territory they occupied, and on their own territory, mainly against those of their nationals who had collaborated with the German occupier during the war.[126]

#### 4.1.2 Trials Held in Other States after the Second World War

In the rest of Europe and elsewhere, particularly in Asia, trials of former Nazi collaborators also took place after the Second World War, in a general context of major administrative purges. A few examples illustrate this situation. In Belgium, research by Martin Conway found that investigations were opened against 405,067 people, of whom 57,254 were prosecuted, 2,940 were sentenced to death, 242 were executed and 2,340 were sentenced to life imprisonment.[127] In Poland, a Supreme National Tribunal was established to try Nazi criminals, and Polish courts tried many people accused of crimes during the war.[128] Trials against persons who committed crimes during the Second World

---

122 For more information, see United Nations War Crimes Commission, "Law Reports of Trials of War Criminals," 1947–1949, vols. 1 and 2; A P V Rogers, 'War Crimes Trials under the Royal Warrant: British Practice 1945–1949' (1990) 39(4) *International and Comparative Law Quarterly* 780.

123 Jeffrey Herf, *Divided Memory: the Nazi Past in the Two Germanys* (Harvard University Press, 1997), 72.

124 David M Crowe, *War Crimes, Genocide, and Justice. A Global History* (Palgrave Macmillan 2014), 257–259.

125 On this subject, see Fabrice Virgili and François Rouquet, *Les Françaises, les Français et l'Épuration* (Gallimard 2018), chapter IV.

126 David M Crowe, *War Crimes, Genocide, and Justice. A Global History* (Palgrave Macmillan 2014) 255–257; Paul Sérant, *Les vaincus de la libération. L'épuration en Europe occidentale à la fin de la Seconde Guerre mondiale* (Robert Laffont 1964) 202–229; Peter Novick, *L'épuration française. 1944–1949* (Balland 1985) 253–286.

127 Martin Conway, 'Justice in Postwar Belgium: Popular Passions and Political Realities' in István Deák, Jan T. Gross, and Tony Judt (eds), *The Politics of Retribution in Europe: World War II and Its Aftermath* (Princeton University Press 2000) 134.

128 Alexander V Prusin, 'Poland's Nuremberg: The Seven Court Cases of the Supreme National Tribunal, 1946–1948' (2010) 24(1) *Holocaust and Genocide Studies* 1.

War also took place in China,[129] the Netherlands,[130] Greece,[131] Hungary,[132] Czechoslovakia,[133] Denmark[134] and Italy.[135]

What is quite interesting is the fact that these movements of prosecutions of individuals accused of committing international crimes during the war went far beyond the period following the end of the war.

### 4.1.3 Trials That Went beyond the End of the Second World War

The national trials for the crimes of the Second World War are not limited to the trials that took place in the period just before the end of the war in 1945 or in the period immediately after its conclusion. Other trials took place in the 1970s, 1980s, 1990s and even the 2000s. There seems to be no limit to the end of these trials of the Nazis and their collaborators. These trials have become so symbolic for those Western states that want to identify the dark past and heinous crimes that were committed during the war. There are examples of high-profile trials of Nazis and their collaborators. For example, Adolf Eichmann, a former Nazi leader, was tried in Israel,[136] and Klaus Barbie, another Nazi leader, was tried in France.[137] Maurice Papon, a French citizen who held a high position during the German occupation in France and participated in crimes, was also tried in France.[138] In Germany, many trials were held and

---

129 David M Crowe, *War Crimes, Genocide, and Justice. A Global History* (Palgrave Macmillan 2014) 265–282.

130 Peter Romijn, 'Restoration of Confidence: The Purge of Local Government in the Netherlands as a Problem of Postwar Reconstruction' in István Deák, Jan T. Gross, and Tony Judt (eds), *The Politics of Retribution in Europe: World War II and Its Aftermath* (Princeton University Press 2000) 186.

131 Mark Mazower, 'The Cold War and the Appropriation of Memory: Greece after Liberation' in István Deák, Jan T. Gross, and Tony Judt (eds), *ibid*, 212.

132 Laszlo Karsi, 'The People's Court and Revolutionary Justice in Hungary, 1945–46' in *ibid*, 233.

133 Bradley Abrams, 'The Politics of Retribution: The Trial of Josef Tiso in the Czechoslovak Environment' in *ibid*, 254–255.

134 Carl Christian Givskov, 'The Danish "Purge-Laws"' (1948) 39(4) *Journal of Criminal Law and Criminology (1931–1951)* 447.

135 Roy Palmer Domenico, *Italian Fascists on Trial, 1943–1948* (University of North Carolina Press 1991).

136 Hannah Arendt, *Eichmann in Jerusalem: A Report on the Banality of Evil*, (Viking Press 1963).

137 Bernard-Henri Lévy, *Archives d'un procès: Klaus Barbie* (Librairie générale française 1986).

138 See the book, Richard J Golsan, *Justice in Lyon: Klaus Barbie and France's First Trial for Crimes against Humanity* (University of Toronto Press 2022). The book refers many times to the trial of Maurice Papon.

continue to be held.[139] This dynamism in establishing the criminal responsibilities of the Nazis and their collaborators did not, curiously, extend to other serious crimes committed in other contexts of dictatorships or armed conflicts after the war and in the context of the Cold War.

### 4.2 National Procedures during the Cold War

The period of the Cold War is the time when two antagonistic blocs, the East and the West, led by the USSR and the United States, respectively, were pitted against each other in direct, unarmed confrontation on the international stage. The Cold War period can be placed between the late 1940s and the early 1990s, when the Berlin Wall fell and the Soviet Union collapsed. Throughout this period, while international criminal proceedings were "dormant," national proceedings took over, as we have seen in the trials for crimes committed during the Second World War. However, the effectiveness of national proceedings against crimes committed during armed conflicts or dictatorships has not gone very far. Criminal proceedings following dictatorships or armed conflicts were rather rare during this period, which is not lacking in dictatorial governments and armed conflicts where crimes were committed on a large scale. In Latin America, Southern Europe, Asia and Africa, there were numerous authoritarian political regimes accused of human rights violations that were not prosecuted.

Only a few states have decided to prosecute individuals accused of responsibility for crimes committed during periods of transition after the collapse of the previous regime. This was the case, for example, in Greece, Portugal and Argentina. In Greece, after the fall of the colonels' dictatorship, trials were organised against the former leaders. For the coup d'état they had organised to seize power, some leaders were sentenced to death before the sentence was commuted to life imprisonment.[140] Other Greek leaders were sentenced to prison terms, including life sentences.[141] However, these prosecutions were not widespread; most of the leaders' collaborators were not tried.[142] In Portu-

139 See on that topic, for example, Sabine Swoboda, 'Paying the Debts – Late Nazi Trials before German Courts: The Case of Heinrich Boere' (2011) 9(1) *Journal of International Criminal Justice* 243.

140 Nikiforos Diamandouros, 'Regime Change and the Prospects for Democracy in Greece' in Neil J Kritz (ed), *Transitional Justice*, vol. II (United States Peace Institute, 1995) 249–250. See also, Harry Psomiades, 'Greece: From the Colonels' Rule to Democracy' in Neil J Kritz (ed), *ibid*, 253–268.

141 *Ibid.*, 250.

142 *Ibid.*, 249. The author refers to these trials as "credible but restrained retribution."

gal, there were also some prosecutions, and purges, after the fall of a dictatorial regime in 1974.[143] However, the punitive measures against the former regime did not go further because they were either weak or later reformed or abandoned.[144] In fact, they were heavily criticised because they focused on prosecuting the executants rather than the leaders of the country involved in human rights violations. In Argentina in the 1980s, leaders of the dictatorship and many military officers were tried after a commission of inquiry revealed many crimes committed by the former leaders.[145] But amnesty laws halted this momentum in the late 1980s.[146]

With a few exceptions, states have generally been reluctant to prosecute former leaders of former regimes considered to be dictatorships accused of human rights violations. For example, Spain adopted an amnesty law after the collapse of the Franco regime.[147] Uruguay also adopted a similar amnesty law in 1985 after the fall of an authoritarian regime.[148] Chile followed the same path.[149] While trials for crimes committed during a dictatorship or after an armed conflict were rather rare during the Cold War period, just as for international criminal proceedings, this was no longer the case after the Cold War.

## 4.3 National Criminal Proceedings after the End of the Cold War

Since the end of the Cold War in the early 1990s, there has been a proliferation of national post-dictatorship and post-armed conflict criminal proceedings dealing with past crimes, parallel to the gradual emergence of international and then hybrid criminal proceedings. Some national courts, particularly in Latin America and sometimes under the pressure of international courts such as the Inter-American Court of Human Rights, have overturned amnesty laws and opened the possibility of trials for those accused of serious crimes com-

143 Antonio Costa Pinto, 'The Radical Right in the Contemporary Portugal' in Neil J Kritz (ed), *ibid*, 291–295.

144 *Ibid.*

145 Emilio F Mignone, Cynthia L Estlund and Samuel Issacharoff, 'Dictatorship on Trial: Prosecution of Human Rights Violations in Argentina' (1984) 10(1) *Yale Journal of International Law* 118.

146 Argentina, Ley de Punto Final, nº 23,492, 24 de diciembre de 1986, and Ley de Obediencia Debida, No. 23,521, 4 de junio de 1987.

147 Spain, Ley 46/1977, de 15 de octubre, de Amnistía.

148 Uruguay, Ley No. 15848, Ley de caducidad de la pretension punitiva del estado, Promulgación: 22/12/1986.

149 Chile, Decreto ley 2191 concede amnistia a las personas que indica por los delitos que señala, 18-ABR-1978.

mitted during dictatorships and/or armed conflicts.[150] National transitional justice proceedings are conducted either on the territory of the transitional states affected by the crimes committed or outside the territory of the states where the crimes were committed.

### 4.3.1 Domestic Proceedings Abroad under Universal Jurisdiction for Crimes Committed during Dictatorships and Armed Conflicts

It is in the context of universal jurisdiction that transitional justice has generated much debate since the 1990s. Universal jurisdiction is the ability of tribunals in states to deal with crimes committed abroad by foreigners. This jurisdiction is old and can be traced back centuries; for example, in the fight against piracy. However, since the end of the Cold War, victims and some NGOs have mobilised universal jurisdiction to seek accountability for alleged perpetrators of crimes committed in the context of dictatorships or armed conflicts. Indeed, in the absence of national prosecutions on the territory of states where international crimes were committed, victims of these crimes and many NGOs have not hesitated to take advantage of the possibilities for prosecution offered by the national legislation of certain foreign states or by international conventions. Many countries have dealt with proceedings for crimes committed abroad by foreigners. There are a few examples of how, over the years, universal jurisdiction has become a powerful form of transitional justice abroad after dictatorships and armed conflicts.

At the time when transitional justice began to be known in the academic field, the first trial that generated the most debate in the international community in the early to late 1990s was that of Augusto Pinochet, the former head of state of Chile, a state that had experienced a dictatorship and numerous crimes committed on a large scale in the 1970s and 1980s. Relying on the universal jurisdiction provided for by Spanish law,[151] victims of the Chilean

---

150 See, for example, the cases of Argentina (Corte Suprema de Justicia de la Nación, *Julio Héctor Simón and others*, 14 junio de 2005); of El Salvador (*Corte Suprema de Justicia, Incostitucionalidad* 44-2013/145-2013, San Salvador, 13 July 2016).

151 See Art. 23 para. 4, Spain, Ley Orgánica 6/1985, de 1 de julio, del Poder Judicial: "Igualmente será competente la jurisdicción española para conocer de los hechos cometidos por españoles o extranjeros fuera del territorio nacional susceptibles de tipificarse, según la ley penal española, como alguno de los siguientes delitos:
a) Genocidio.
b) Terrorismo.
c) Piratería y apoderamiento ilícito de aeronaves.
d) Falsificación de moneda extranjera.
e) Los relativos a la prostitución.

regime filed a complaint against the former Chilean head of state. While receiving medical treatment in the UK, Pinochet was arrested on an international arrest warrant issued by Spain, which requested his extradition.[152] A long legal battle ensued, involving Spain, the UK and Chile, culminating in Pinochet's release on health grounds,[153] and his return to Chile, where he would never be tried in spite of efforts to do so.

The failure of this criminal case did not mean that victims and human rights defenders gave up, as they suddenly discovered that it was possible to obtain justice through transitional justice abroad. In fact, this failure marked the beginning of a global movement to fight impunity through universal jurisdiction. Several other complaints relating to crimes committed during dictatorships or armed conflicts in Latin America have been filed in Spain and have led to the opening of criminal proceedings against the accused. For example, victims of grave violations committed during the armed conflict in Guatemala brought cases under universal jurisdiction before the Spanish courts.[154] These courts issued arrest warrants against several Guatemalan generals.[155] However, the proceedings did not succeed because Guatemala refused to extradite these generals after a decision by its Constitutional Court had judged the extradition request to be contrary to the sovereignty of Guatemala.[156]

In the same vein, complaints against certain crimes committed in El Salvador during the Salvadoran armed conflict, in particular the assassination of six Jesuit priests, five of whom were Spanish nationals, were also brought before the Spanish courts.[157] As in the case of Guatemala, for a long time, and despite

---

f) Tráfico ilegal de drogas psicotrópicas, tóxicas y estupefacientes.
g) Y cualquier otro que, según los tratados o convenios internacionales, deba ser perseguido en España."

152 All the proceedings in this case can be found in the judgment, Bartle and the Commissioner of Police for the Metropolis and Others, Ex Parte Pinochet, R v. [1998] UKHL 41; [2000] 1 AC 61; [1998] 4 All ER 897; [1998] 3 WLR 1456 (25th November, 1998).

153 See a Statement of the UK Home Secretary, Senator Pinochet, HL Deb, 02 March 2000, vol. 610 cc663-77. Online: https://api.parliament.uk/historic-hansard/lords/2000/mar/02/senator-pinochet.

154 A copy of the complaints is available in Spanish at: https://cja.org/wp-content/uploads/downloads/Guatemala_Complaint_Spanish.pdf, accessed on 23 July 2021.

155 Spain, Juzgado central de instruccion No. 1, Audiencia Nacional, Diligencias Previas 331/19996-10, 7 de julio 2006.

156 República de Guatemala, Corte de Constitucionalidad, expediente 3380–2007, 12 diciembre del 2007.

157 Cath Collins, *Post-Transitional Justice: Human Rights Trial in Chile and El Salvador* (Pennsylvania State University Press 2010) 180; Almudena Bernabeu and Carolyn Patty Blum, 'The Road to Spain: The Jesuit Massacre and the Struggle against Impunity in El Salvador' (2012) 18(1) *Peace and Conflict: Journal of Peace Psychology* 96.

the issuance of arrest warrants against Salvadorans, the Spanish justice system was unable to try the majority of the persons concerned, as El Salvador and its Supreme Court refused to authorise the extradition of Salvadorans.[158] However, one of the individuals targeted by the complaints, Colonel Orlando Inocente Montano, a former Salvadoran politician and military officer residing in the United States, was sentenced to twenty-one months in prison for having lied in documents relating to his immigration to the United States.[159] Spain subsequently requested his extradition from the United States, which granted it in 2017 after a long legal battle. The Spanish courts then tried and sentenced the former colonel to more than 133 years in prison for the five murders of Spanish Jesuit priests,[160] that is, for the facts mentioned in the extradition request to the United States. This sentence did not cover other crimes of which he may have been guilty against Salvadorans during the civil war.

As well, Spanish courts indicted Argentinians accused of having committed international crimes in Argentina in the 1970s and 1980s,[161] while Argentina responded by launching prosecutions against individuals who committed international crimes in Spain during Franco's regime.[162]

Indeed, Spain was only one illustration of that movement towards the growing use of universal jurisdiction to deal with the crimes of the past. In Belgium courts, many victims relied on the famous 1993 Belgium universal jurisdiction law[163] to seek criminal accountability of the individuals accused

158 Lisa Cohen, 'Salvadoran High Commanders Responsible for Jesuits Massacre in 1989 under Custody in El Salvador' *The Center for Justice and Accountability*, August 10, 2011; Elisabeth Malkin, "El Salvador: Court Denies Spain Request for Extradition of Suspects in Killings," *The New York Times*, 14 May 2012, A 14.

159 Department of Justice, U.S. Attorney's Office, District of Massachusetts, *Former Salvadoran Military Officer Sentenced for Perjury and Concealing Information from U. S. Government*, 27 August 2013.

160 Audiencia nacional, sala de lo penal, sección segunda, Rollo de sala procedimiento ordinario nº 4 / 2.015, procedimiento de origen: sumario nº 97 / 2.010, órgano de origen: juzgado central de instrucción núm. 6, 11 Septiembre 2020.

161 See, for example, the reference to the indictment of 98 Argentinians accused of committing crimes in Argentina during the dictatorship, Al Juzgado Central De Instruccion Nº 5 De La Audiencia Nacional, Sumario, 19/97-L, 6 septiembre 2000, Primero. See also a conviction: Audiencia Nacional (Sala De Lo Penal, Seccion Tercera, Sentencia NUM.16/2005, Adolfo Francisco Scilingo, 19 abril 2005; Tribunal Supremo, Sentencia Nº:798/2007, Adolfo Francisco Scilingo, 01 Octubre 2007.

162 See on these proceedings, Alejandro Lerena Garcia, 'Overview of the Argentine Lawsuit against the crimes of the Franco regime: outcomes and challenges' (2021) 9(12) *Journal of Political Sciences & Public Affairs* 1.

163 Belgium, *Loi relative à la répression des infractions graves aux Conventions de Genève du 12 août 1949 aux Protocoles I et II du 8 juin 1977*, 16 Juin 1993; Belgium, *Loi relative à la répression des violations graves du droit international humanitaire*, 10 février 1999.

of committing crimes against humanity, genocide, war crimes or torture in countries that experienced dictatorships or armed conflicts like Chad[164] and Rwanda.[165] Over the years, the number of cases have become countless. In spite of the reduction of the scope of some universal jurisdiction laws in Europe, namely in Belgium and Spain,[166] the movement has not stopped. Many countries have adopted universal jurisdiction laws and have prosecuted and sentenced people for crimes committed abroad in the context of dictatorships or armed conflicts. Just to enumerate a few examples: courts in France have convicted many Rwandese accused of committing genocide or crimes against humanity in Rwanda in the 1990s.[167] Courts in Germany and the Netherlands have convicted Syrians accused of committing crimes against humanity in Syria in the context of armed conflict.[168] Swiss courts have convicted a Liberian who violated the laws of war in the Liberian civil war in the 1980s and 1990s.[169] Every year since 2015, a consortium of NGOs publish an annual report on universal jurisdiction that identifies states in which universal jurisdiction has been used, mostly to deal with crimes committed during dictatorships or

164 See, for example, the complaint of a victim against Hissène Habré, former head of State of Chad, Souleymane Abdoulaye Tahir, Plainte contre Hissène HABRE, Bruxelles, 3 December 2001, online, https://www.hrw.org/legacy/french/themes/PlainteSouleymaneAbdoulaye.pdf. Hissein Habré was finally tried in Senegal by the African Extraordinary Chambers.

165 See, for example, the judgment Belgium, Assize Court of Brussels, verdict of 8 June 2001, which found four Rwandese guilty of war crimes committed in Rwanda in the context of the Rwanda genocide.

166 In Spain, the Scope of the 1985 law was reduced in 2009. For example, now, Spain has a universal jurisdiction only if the accused is in Spain, or the victim is a Spanish or there is a strong link between Spain and the crime. See *Ley Orgánica 1/2009*, de 3 de noviembre, complementaria de la Ley de reforma de la legislación procesal para la implantación de la nueva Oficina judicial, por la que se modifica la Ley Orgánica 6/1985, de 1 de julio, del Poder Judicial, Boletín oficial del estado, No. 266, 4 de noviembre 2009, sec. I, p. 92091. In Belgium, the scope of universal jurisdiction was limited in 2003. For example, Belgium has jurisdiction if the crime or part of it has been perpetrated in Belgium, or if the accused is a Belgian or has his main residence in Belgium, see Belgium, *Loi du 5 août 2003 relative aux violations graves du droit international humanitaire.*

167 See, for example, Cour d'assises de Paris, n°16/0066, 6 juillet 2018.

168 In Germany, see Anwar R. case, Koblenz Higher Regional Court (Oberlandesgericht Koblenz), 13 January 2022, Press release, Life imprisonment due to crimes committed against humanity and murder – sentencing of a suspected member of the Syrian secret service, 17 January 2022, online https://justiz.rlp.de/de/service-informationen/aktuelles/detail/news/News/detail/life-imprisonment-due-to-crimes-committed-against-humanity-and-murder-sentencing-of-a-suspected-me/. In the Netherlands, see, for example, Court of Appeal, The Hague, cause list number: 22-003926-19, 26 January 2021.

169 Switzerland, Tribunal Pénal fédéral, *Ministère public de la Confédération c. Alieu Kosiah*, Jugement du 18 juin 2021.

armed conflicts.[170] These reports show that universal jurisdiction has become one of the most widely used tools in criminal transitional justice.

More rarely, some national proceedings linked to dictatorships or armed conflicts have been implemented within the framework of passive personal jurisdiction, that is, in relation to the nationality of the victims. In France, for example, proceedings against Salvadoran soldiers were initiated by the relatives of a French nurse who was murdered during the armed conflict in El Salvador.[171] But this procedure did not conclude with the conviction of any person because of lack of evidence for a crime that was committed abroad. The proceedings were finally abandoned due to a lack of evidence that could lead to finding the individuals responsible for the murder.

Another particular aspect of transitional justice abroad has been what can be called civil universal jurisdiction, which has been performed mainly in the United States, when the alleged perpetrators live in that country. An eighteenth-century American law, the Alien Tort Statute (ATS) of 1789,[172] allowed foreigners to seize American jurisdictions to obtain compensation for violations of the law and international crimes committed abroad. In the same vein, the *Torture Victim Protection Act* adopted in 1991[173] allowed for the possibility of American judges hearing cases of torture and extra-judicial executions committed by people acting on behalf of foreign states, provided that the complainant had exhausted remedies in the state in whose territory the crime was committed and that the complaint had been filed within ten years of the commission of the crime.[174] Victims of armed conflicts or dictatorships have filed complaints in the United States, and some have been able to obtain convictions against perpetrators. This was the case for victims in Latin American countries. For example, Salvadorans obtained civil convictions against perpetrators residing in the United States.[175] Complaints also came from other parts

---

170 Universal Jurisdiction Annual Review, from 2015 to 2026.

171 See Archives Assemblée nationale française, Questions écrites, année 1990, No. 18 A.N. (Q), Lundi 30 Avril 1990, 2035, para. 27737.

172 Section 1350 of chapter 28 of the United States Code: "The district courts shall have original jurisdiction of any civil action by an alien for a tort only, committed in violation of the law of nations or a treaty of the United States."

173 The Torture Victim Protection Act, note to Section 1350 of the US Code (Alien Tort Claims Act).

174 *Ibid.*, section 2(b) and (c).

175 For El Salvador, see, for example, United States District Court, Southern District of Florida, *Juan Romagoza Arce v. Jose Guillermo Garcia and Carlos Eugenio Vides Casanova*, No. 99-8364 Civ-Hurley, Verdict, 23 July 2002; see also, for the amounts (tens of millions of dollars) awarded to the plaintiffs: *Juan Romagoza Arce v. Jose Guillermo Garcia and Carlos Eugenio Vides Casanova, Neris Gonzalez v. Jose Guillermo Garcia and Carlos Euge-*

of the world.[176] The US Supreme Court halted this process of the extraterritorial application of the ATS in 2013 when it decided "that the presumption against extraterritoriality applies to claims under the ATS, and that nothing in the statute rebuts that presumption."[177] Since then, cases have dropped dramatically, even though it is theoretically possible to use the *Torture Victim Protection Act* for some crimes committed abroad.

### 4.3.2 National Procedures on the Territory of States That Have Experienced Dictatorships and Armed Conflicts

At the national level, since the early 1990s, several trials have been launched against individuals accused of having violated human rights or committed serious crimes during dictatorships or armed conflicts. Countries in Latin America, Africa, Asia and Europe have been concerned by these proceedings, and a few examples from each can illustrate this trend.

In Latin America, several trials have taken place in countries that have experienced dictatorships or armed conflicts, including for crimes committed during the Cold War. Some studies have been published analysing the trials that have taken place, including in those countries less known for having experienced transitional justice, such as Guyana and Panama.[178] There are, however, some prominent state initiatives regarding trials in times of transition that can be mentioned. For example, Guatemala experienced an armed conflict in the 1970s and 1980s during which a number of crimes and human rights violations were committed. Following a peace agreement between the government and the rebels, and years after the armed conflict, the country began to prosecute individuals accused of committing these crimes and violations during the armed conflict. Initially, the prosecutions focused on low-level members of the military. Gradually, however, it included high-ranking officials such as the former head of state, Efrain Rios Montt. Not all of these prosecutions have been successful. For example, Montt was convicted, but his

---

*nio Vides Casanova, Carlos Mauricio v. Jose Guillermo Garcia and Carlos Eugenio Vides Casanova,* Final Judgement, 31 July 2002; United States District Court for the Western District of Tennessee, Western Division, *Ana Patricia Chavez, Cecicia Santos, Jose Francisco Calderon, Erlinda Revelo and Daniel Alvarado v. Nicolas Carranza,* No. 03-2932 ML/P, Judgement on Jury Verdict and Stipulation of Dismissal, 18 January 2006.

176 See Peter Henner, *Human Rights and the Alien Tort Statute: Law, History, and Analysis* (American Bar Association, 2009).

177 Supreme Court of United States, *Kiobel v. Royal Dutch Petroleum Co,* No. 10-1491, 17 April 2013.

178 See Kathryn Sikkink and Carrie Booth Walling, 'The Impact of Human Rights Trials in Latin America' (2007) 24(4) *Journal of Peace research* 427.

conviction was later ruled unconstitutional by the Guatemalan Constitutional Court, and he died without a new trial being completed.[179] But many other prosecutions resulted in convictions of individuals responsible for committing crimes during the armed conflict.[180]

El Salvador experienced armed conflict during the Cold War. Following the signing of a peace agreement between the government and the rebels, an amnesty law was passed in 1993, which, for years, prevented the prosecution of individuals accused of crimes committed during the armed conflict.[181] In 2016, the Salvadoran Supreme Court ruled that this amnesty law was unconstitutional and could no longer be used to block the prosecution of those accused of committing crimes during the armed conflict.[182] Following the El Salvador Supreme Court ruling, a special unit was created in 2018 within the Attorney General's Office to investigate these crimes, but some concerns have been expressed about the outcome of these criminal proceedings, and their success remains to be seen.[183]

Bolivia experienced a dictatorship between 1964 and 1982, during which a number of serious human rights violations were reported, in particular,

179 David Stoll, 'How the Guatemalan civil war became a genocide: Revisiting the 2013 trial of General Efraín Ríos Montt' (2022) 27 *The Journal of Latin American and Caribbean Anthropology* 528.

180 On these prosecutions in Guatemala, see: Naomi Roht-Arriaza, 'Making the State Do Justice: Transnational Prosecutions and International Support for Criminal Investigations in Post-Armed Conflict Guatemala' (2008) 9 *Chicago Journal of International Law* 79; Naomi Roht-Arriaza, 'Criminal Prosecutions for Genocide in Guatemala: Advances and Obstacles in Transnational and Domestic Cases' in Etelle Higonnet (ed), *Quiet Genocide. Guatemala 1981–1983* (Routledge 2009); Hanna Bosdriesz and Sander Wirken, 'An Imperfect Success–The Guatemalan Genocide Trial and the Struggle against Impunity for International Crimes' (2014) 14(6) *International Criminal Law Review* 1067; Susan Kemp, 'Guatemala Prosecutes Former President Ríos Montt: New Perspectives on Genocide and Domestic Criminal Justice' (2014) 12(1) *Journal of International Criminal Justice* 133.

181 El Salvador, Ley de Amnistía General para la Consolidación de la Paz, aprobada mediante Decreto Legislativo No. 486, de 20-III-1993, publicado en el Diario Oficial No. 56, tomo No. 318, del 22-III-1993.

182 El Salvador, *Corte Suprema de Justicia, Incostitucionalidad* 44-2013/145-2013, San Salvador, 13 July 2016.

183 On these prosecutions in El Salvador, see Committee against Torture, Concluding observations on the third periodic report of El Salvador, UN doc. CAT/C/SLV/CO/3, 19 December 2022, paras. 12–13; Human Rights Council (Working Group on the Universal Periodic Review Thirty-fourth session 4–15 November 2019), National report submitted in accordance with paragraph 5 of the annex to Human Rights Council Resolution 16/21, El Salvador, UN doc. A/HRC/WG.6/34/SLV/1, 20 August 2019, para. 30; Cath Collins, *Post-transitional Justice: Human Rights Trials in Chile and El Salvador* (Penn State University Press 2010) 168–175.

enforced disappearances. When the dictatorship collapsed, there was no immediate plan to prosecute. Several years later, the UN Committee on Enforced Disappearances reported that only seven cases of enforced disappearances had been dealt with in Bolivia, despite the fact that many thousands of enforced disappearances had occurred in the country.[184]

Uruguay was under a dictatorial regime between 1973 and 1985. When the regime fell, an amnesty law was passed in 1986 to prevent any prosecution of those who committed serious crimes during the dictatorship.[185] However, in the early 2000s, a truth commission was established, and following the publication of its public report, some prosecutions were initiated for crimes committed during the dictatorship. Some prosecutions have even been launched against former presidents Juan Maria Bordaberry and Gregorio Alvarez.[186] Some prosecutions were also open to investigate cases of enforced disappearances. However, the UN Committee on Enforced Disappearances has noted that the process of investigating the cases has been slow and that perpetrators have not yet been convicted.[187] The committee called on Uruguay to prosecute and punish the perpetrators.

Some final examples of trials across Latin America can also be mentioned. In Argentina, prosecutions were stopped after the adoption of amnesty laws but resumed after that law was repealed in 2005.[188] In Chile, an amnesty was adopted after the dictatorial Pinochet regime fell. However, beginning at the end of the 1990s, prosecutions were launched against Pinochet, and trials were held in Chile against persons accused of having violated human rights during the dictatorial regime.[189] In Paraguay, after the fall of the dictatorship in 1989,

184 On Bolivia, see Committee on Enforced Disappearances examines the report of Bolivia, hails the setting up of the truth commission, Press Releases, Treaty Bodies, 3 October 2019.

185 Uruguay, Ley de Caducidad de La Pretension Punitiva del Estado, No. 15848, 22 de diciembre de 1986.

186 On these prosecutions and transitional justice in Uruguay, see Francesca Lessa, *Memory and Transitional Justice in Argentina and Uruguay: Against Impunity* (Palgrave Macmillan 2013), 131. Both former presidents were found guilty of crimes.

187 Committee on Enforced Disappearances Concluding observations on the additional information submitted by Uruguay under article 29(4) of the Convention, UN doc. CED/C/URY/OAI/1, 20 October 2022, paras. 16–17.

188 Argentina, Corte Suprema de Justicia de la Nación, *Julio Héctor Simón and others*, 14 junio de 2005. See Francesca Lessa, 'Beyond transitional justice: Exploring continuities in human rights abuses in Argentina between 1976 and 2010' (2011) 3(1) *Journal of human rights practice* 25.

189 See Hugo Rojas and Miriam Shaftoe, *Human Rights and Transitional Justice in Chile. Memory Politics and Transitional Justice* (Palgrave Macmillan 2022) 137–154; Cath Collins,

some prosecutions, even if limited, were carried on.[190] In Peru, trials were held against some security forces personnel for crimes committed in the 1980s in the context of armed confrontation and dictatorship.[191] In Colombia, many investigations for trials have been held after the peace agreement in 2016 was signed, and a Special Jurisdiction for Peace was established.[192]

Turning now to the continent of Africa, international criminal proceedings such as those of the ICC, ICTR and hybrid tribunals have attracted the attention of scholars of transitional justice implementation. There are not many studies on national criminal procedures in Africa. However, there are some national criminal proceedings in the field of transitional justice. For example, in Chad, a trial related to the dictatorial regime of Hissein Habré in the 1980s was held and, in 2015, resulted in the convictions of several individuals.[193] In South Africa, some trials related to the apartheid regime were also held.[194] Uganda created an international crime division in its national criminal system in order to try perpetrators of international crimes, particularly committed during Uganda's armed conflict.[195] It is now common knowledge that during periods of transition, some African states have pursued criminal prosecutions on various charges, including human rights violations, against former heads of state and other individuals accused of committing crimes while in power.[196] Cases of trials in contexts of transition include those of Mengistu Haile, former head of state of Ethiopia, convicted in absentia; Moussa Traoré, former head of state of Mali, convicted and later pardoned; Jean-Bedel Bokassa, former head of state of the Central African Republic, convicted and sentenced to death, the sentence was later commuted to imprisonment; Pascal Lissouba, former head of state of the Democratic Republic of the Congo, convicted in absentia; Hastings Kamuzu Banda, former head of state of Malawi, acquitted; Pasteur Bizi-

*Post-transitional Justice: Human Rights Trials in Chile and El Salvador* (Penn State University Press 2010).

190 Cath Collins, 'Paraguay: Accountability in the Shadow of Stroessner' in Elin Skaar, Jemina Garcia-Godos and Cath Collins (eds), *Transitional Justice in Latin America: The Uneven Road from Impunity towards Accountability* (Routledge 2016) 157–158.

191 Rebecca K Root, *Transitional Justice in Peru* (Palgrave Macmillan 2012), 109–119.

192 For cases, see the website of the tribunal: https://www.jep.gov.co/Paginas/casos.aspx.

193 See Chad, Cour d'appel de N'Djamena, *Ministère Public et Ismael Hachim et autres c. Saleh Younous Ali, Waroun Fadoul ali et autres*, Répertoire n°01/15, 25 Mars 2015.

194 See Ole Bubenzer, *Post-TRC Prosecutions in South Africa: Accountability for Political Crimes After the Truth and Reconciliation Commission's Amnesty Process* (Brill 2009).

195 For Uganda, see the website of the division: https://judiciary.go.ug/data/smenu/18/International%20Crimes%20Division.html.

196 For some cases, Ellen L. Lutz and Caitlin Reiger (ed), *Prosecuting Head of States* (Cambridge University Press 2009) 301–303.

mungu, former head of state of Rwanda, convicted and later pardoned; Ben Ali, former head of state of Tunisia, convicted in absentia; and Hissein Habré, former head of state of Chad, convicted to death in absentia.

All these national cases were not uniform, of course, and the political regimes that tried individuals for serious violations committed during a period of dictatorship or armed conflict were not all democratic or trying to establish a new and democratic regime. Nevertheless, they are all cases in which these countries have tried to come to terms with the past, even if, as elsewhere, these trials may have been politically motivated.

In some Asian countries, there have been cases of national prosecutions to address past serious human rights violations. For example, South Korea has pursued prosecutions against former political leaders, including former heads of state, resulting in convictions and later pardons.[197] The Solomon Islands held trials in relation to atrocities committed on its territory in the context of tensions and several armed confrontations.[198]

European countries also experienced national criminal prosecutions, even if these were rare, in the context of transitions, notably in the 1990s when several Central and Eastern European states launched decommunisation. This was the case, for example, in the Czech Republic (part of the former Czechoslovakia),[199] Albania,[200] Bulgaria,[201] Romania[202] and Hungary.[203]

## 5 National Judicial Procedures and International Transitional Justice Law

As a transitional justice mechanism, national courts are linked to international law. They are a response to violations and crimes under national and international law. At the national level, these violations and crimes often constitute violations of international human rights law and international humanitarian

197 Hun Joon Kim, 'Transitional Justice in South Korea' in Renée Jeffery and Hun Joon Kim, *Transitional Justice in Asia-Pacific* (Cambridge University Press 2014) 247.

198 See Renée Jeffery, 'Reconciliation and the Rule of Law in the Solomon Islands' in Renée Jeffery and Hun Joon Kim, *ibid*, 209–211.

199 See Carmen González-Enríquez, 'De-Communization and Political Justice in Central and Eastern' in Alexandra Barahona de Brito, Carmen González-Enríquez and Paloma Aguilar (eds), *The Politics of Memory. Transitional Justice in Democratizing Societies* (Oxford University Press 2001) 228.

200 *Ibid.*, 230.

201 *Ibid.*, 232.

202 *Ibid.*, 236.

203 *Ibid.*, 242.

law. International crimes are also sometimes incorporated into national law, which allows national courts operating in a transitional context to prosecute the perpetrators of these crimes. Furthermore, when national proceedings are conducted on the basis of universal jurisdiction, they may be based on international conventions, such as the 1984 Convention against Torture. In their examination of violations and crimes, national courts have to respect the rights of victims, to effective remedy, for example, and the standards of trials that are recognised in international human rights law, notably the rights to defence.[204] Thus, national courts, as a transitional justice mechanism, help to hold accountable those who have violated international law and reaffirm the values of international law during a transition or after an armed conflict and, in this sense, contribute to the development of the implementation of international transitional justice law.

In conclusion, there are many judicial, mainly criminal, processes that have been used as transitional justice mechanisms, and they have all contributed to the development of international transitional justice law. They have been used to respond to human rights violations or crimes committed in the context of authoritarian rule or armed conflict. Of course, these criminal proceedings have been criticised. Some critics have generally focused on the fact that prosecutions are sometimes politically motivated and have referred to them as victors' justice because these prosecutions are undertaken by new political authorities that were generally opposed to the regime that fell or the one that lost the armed conflict. In the same vein, some critics target the selectivity of prosecutions, claiming that not all perpetrators are prosecuted and that the selectivity of cases is politically motivated. Whatever the reasons for prosecutions, prosecutions that result in trials of perpetrators are one of the core mechanisms of transitional justice. They are a way of establishing accountability so that mass crimes are not repeated, and they help to stigmatise the wrongs of the past, as does another key transitional justice mechanism, truth commissions.

---

204 On the international obligations of transitional states, see below Chapters 8 and 9.

CHAPTER 6

# Truth Commissions

Truth commissions are a particular form of commissions of inquiry that alone are one of the most visible tools of transitional justice. These commissions are best known at the national and international levels. Indeed, some authors have indicated that truth commissions are in line with the commissions of inquiry known in the Commonwealth and charged exceptionally with investigating a particular and urgent matter.[1] At the international level, commissions of inquiry and fact-finding commissions have long existed.[2] Truth commissions, which are generally a national mechanism of transitional justice, differ from other national or international commissions in that they deal with large-scale abuses (including international crimes, violations of human rights and international humanitarian law), although some may have dealt with smaller-scale events, and are also generally seen as institutions that aim to promote social peace or reconciliation.[3] A compilation of the various definitions given to truth commissions has led to defining them as non-judicial, official and temporary bodies charged with investigating past violations or serious crimes and making recommendations, sometimes in order to contribute to peace or reconciliation.[4]

The term "truth commissions" began to be disseminated in the 1990s when some commissions of inquiry were created to deal with human rights violations and had the terms "truth" and "commission" in their name. It was the case in Chile where in 1990 a Comisión Nacional de Verdad y Reconciliación (National Truth and Reconciliation Commission) was established,[5] and in El Salvador where in 1992 the United Nations participated in the creation of a

1 Mark Freeman, *Truth Commissions and Procedural Fairness* (Cambridge University Press 2006) 22.

2 Nicolas Politis, 'Les commissions internationales d'enquête' (1912) *Revue générale de droit international public* 149.

3 See below Chapter 6, for a list of truth commissions and the abuses and violations included in their mandates.

4 See in particular the definitions in: 'The Rule of Law and Transitional Justice in Conflict and Post-conflict Societies, Report of the Secretary-General', UN doc. S/2004/616, 23 August 2004, para. 50. Mark Freeman, *Truth Commissions and Procedural Fairness* (Cambridge University Press 2006) 18; Priscilla Hayner, *Unspeakable Truths Transitional Justice and the Challenge of Truth Commissions* (2nd edn, Routledge 2011) 11.

5 Chile, Supreme Decree No. 355 of 25 April 1990.

 | HTTPS://DOI.ORG/10.1163/9789004766655-011

"Commission on the Truth for El Salvador."[6] The use of the term was highly influenced by the work of Priscilla Hayner, one of the leading scholars in the field of truth commissions, who published an article in 1994 entitled "Fifteen Truth Commissions, 1974 to 1994," in which she used the term to designate some commissions of inquiry created in many states to deal with past violations or crimes.[7] Since this publication and the establishment of a truth and reconciliation commission (TRC) in South Africa in 1995,[8] which received international attention, the term "truth commission" has become widely used.

Truth commissions have been established in over fifty states. In the beginning, Uganda was considered the first state to establish a commission that would later be included in the category of truth commissions.[9] However, it is mainly in Latin America that these commissions were first created in the 1980s, notably in Bolivia and Argentina.[10] Then, there was a gradual expansion of these mechanisms and an incredible multiplication of them beginning in the 2000s in post-dictatorships, armed conflict or post-armed conflict contexts. Today, it is simply almost impossible to discuss political transitions or post-conflict situations in a state without reference to truth commissions. This success of truth commissions has influenced their use by states that have not experienced dictatorship or armed conflict in their recent history. Some established democracies have created truth commissions to deal with past injustices committed on their territory.[11]

Despite some commonalities, truth commissions are very often different and have very diverse characteristics in their composition, operations, activities and mandates. Because of this diversity, the presentation of truth commissions as transitional justice mechanism can be very challenging. The aim of this chapter is twofold: to present truth commissions as a global phenomenon and to identify those countries where they have been created (discussed in Section 1). While indicating that they are generally quite different from one another, the chapter delineates their general characteristics, such as details behind their creation, the authorities that create them (discussed in Section 2),

---

6 Peace Accords signed by representatives of the Government of El Salvador and the Frente Farabundo Martí para la Liberacíon Nacional (FLMN) in Mexico City, 27 April 1991, UN doc. A/46/553, S/23130, 9 October 1991, Annex, IV.

7 Priscilla Hayner, Fifteen Truth Commissions 1974 to 1994: A Comparative Study' (1994) 16(4) *Human Rights Quarterly* 597.

8 South Africa, Promotion of National Unity and Reconciliation Act, No. 34, 1995.

9 Priscilla Hayner, Fifteen Truth Commissions 1974 to 1994: A Comparative Study' (1994) 16(4) *Human Rights Quarterly* 597, 611.

10 On these truth commissions, see below Sections 1.2.1 and 1.2.2 in this chapter.

11 See below, Sections 1.2.13, 1.4.3, 1.4.4 and 1.4.5 in this chapter.

their composition (discussed in Section 3), their mandate (discussed in Section 4), their links with judicial bodies (discussed in Section 5) and their contributions to international transitional justice law (discussed in Section 6).

# 1 Truth Commissions as a Global Historical Phenomenon: The Creation of Truth Commissions

It can be summarised that the creation of truth commissions is generally linked to armed conflicts and dictatorships, whether or not they have ended. Most of the time, these truth commissions are located in developing countries. Recently, however, truth commissions have taken a new direction. States that have not experienced armed conflicts or dictatorships in their recent history have used truth commissions to find or tell the truth about historical violations or ongoing violations that have taken place on their territory. It is important to note that each of these truth commissions has been created in a particular or specific context. The specific context is worth discussing before studying the general characteristic of truth commissions. It is the reason why this section tries to identify and, when possible, briefly describe truth commissions created in several states across all the continents.

## 1.1 Africa

### 1.1.1 Uganda (1974 and 1986)

Africa is sometimes referred to as the cradle of truth commissions, with the first established in Uganda in 1974 by Idi Amin Dada, the then president of that country.[12] The commission was named Commission of Inquiry into the Disappearances of People in Uganda since 25 January 1971.[13] That commission was created in the context of a fierce repression put into place by the dictatorial regime of Idi Amin Dada who, after he came into power by a military coup, was accused of committing severe violations of human rights against his political opponents, who suffered enforced disappearance, and Asians residing in

12 See Priscilla Hayner, Fifteen Truth Commissions 1974 to 1994: A Comparative Study' (1994) 16(4) *Human Rights Quarterly* 597, 611–613. For the law establishing the Commission: Uganda, Commission of Inquiry into the Disappearances of People in Uganda since 25 January 1971: Charter, Legal Notice No. 2 of 1974.

13 *Ibid.*

Uganda, who were expulsed.[14] Even if its final report was not officially published, a confidential copy was presented to the Uganda's president; later, some organisations were able to get access to the report, photographed and published it in an electronic form (microfilm) that is now available.[15] The report detailed more than 300 cases of disappearances[16] and presented substantial evidence.[17] Part of the commission's mandate was to give examples of "what should the Government do to put an end to the criminal disappearances of people in Uganda."[18] As such, the commission recommended, *inter alia*, a reorganisation of the police,[19] the restriction of some security forces to their special mandate,[20] and a "program of legal training" for officers after it had noted that many of the problems arose because of their ignorance of the law.[21] The structure and content of this first final report of a truth commission is very common: findings on the one hand and recommendations on the other. It is important to remember that this first truth commission was not established after the fall of a dictatorial regime. The dictatorial regime created the truth commission to respond to criticisms of human rights violations.

However, the second truth commissions created in Uganda was established in the context of a transition after power was seized by a new president. Idi Amin Dada lost power in Uganda and was exiled in 1979. When the new political regime came to power, the military struggle between the government and armed groups continued. In 1986, Yuri Museveni, chief of the rebellion against the government of Uganda, took power and became the president of Uganda. The Minister of Justice of his new government, Joseph Nyamihana Mulenga, set up a new truth commission called Commission of Inquiry,[22] and mandated it to "inquire into all aspects of human rights, breaches of the rule of law and excessive abuses of power, committed against persons in Uganda by the regimes in government, their servants, agents or agencies whatsoever called,

14 On the repression of the regime of Idi Amin Dada, Commission of Jurists, 'Violations of Human Rights and the Rule of Law in Uganda', Study, 1974; Horace Campbell, *Four Essays on Neo-colonialism in Uganda: The Military Dictatorship of Idi Amin* (Afro-Carib Publications 1975) 42; James H Mittelman, *Ideology and Politics in Uganda: From Obote to Amin* (Cornell University Press 1975) 236–237; David Martin, *General Amin* (Faber 1974).

15 Uganda, Commission of Inquiry into Disappearances, 'Final Report', 1975.

16 See *ibid*, part V, see the table, 784.

17 See, for example, *ibid*, Part II, 556 ff. and Part III, 692 ff.

18 Charter, Legal Notice No. 2 of 1974 (g).

19 Uganda, Commission of Inquiry into Disappearances, 'Final Report', 1975, Part V, 799, para. 570.

20 For example, *ibid*, 801, para. 571, and 809, para. 578.

21 *ibid*, 814–815, para. 592.

22 Uganda, Commission of Inquiry Act Legal Notice No. 5, 16 May 1986.

during the period from 9th day of October 1962 to the 25th day of January 1986 and possible ways of preventing the recurrence of the aforesaid matters […].” In 1994, the commission issued its final report, detailing human rights violations and making recommendations.[23]

### 1.1.2 Zimbabwe (1983)

In Zimbabwe, the Zimbabwe Commission of Inquiry into the Matabeleland Disturbances was created in 1983[24] (also called the Chihambakwe Commission of Inquiry[25]). It was set up by the regime of Robert Mugabe, who came to power in 1979 and was accused of committing massacres in Matabeleland, a region of Zimbabwe whose people opposed the new regime. The commission's report was never published, despite growing calls for it to be. The Roman Catholic Church later published a report on the massacres.[26]

### 1.1.3 Chad (1990)

In 1990, after seizing power in a coup d'état and ousting former president Hissein Habré, a new Chadian president, Idriss Déby Itno, set up a truth commission called the Commission of Inquiry (*Commission nationale d'enquête*).[27] The regime of the former president Hissein Habré was called a dictatorship and he was accused of committing gross human rights violations.[28] The commission investigated these violations and rendered a final report in 1992, detailing the crimes committed by the Habré regime and making recommendations.[29]

---

23 Uganda, 'The Report of the Commission of Inquiry into Violations of Human Rights', Kampala, 1994, chap. 3–12.

24 For Zimbabwe, the decree establishing the commission in 1983 is not available. However, information on this decree is available in Article 19, 'Who Wants to Forget? Truth and Access to Information about Past Human Rights Violations', November 2000, 22–23.

25 Simplisius Chihambakwe was the name of the Commission's Chairman.

26 Catholic Commission for Justice and Peace in Zimbabwe, 'Breaking the Silence. Building true Peace. A Report on the Disturbances in Matabeleland and the Midlands, 1980 to 1988', February 1997.

27 Chad, Decree No. 014/P.CE/CJ/90 establishing the Commission of Inquiry into the crimes and misappropriations committed by the former President, his co-authors and/or accomplices, 29 December 1990.

28 See, for example, 'Amnesty International Annual Report 1989', 1 May 1989, Index Number: POL 10/0002/1989.

29 Chad, *Les crimes et détournements de l'ex-président Habré et de ses complices. Rapport de la commission nationale d'enquête du ministère tchadien de la Justice* (L'Harmattan 1993).

### 1.1.4 South Africa (1995)

In 1995, the South African Parliament created the South African Truth and Reconciliation Commission.[30] This commission attracted international attention and curiosity because it was the result of a political negotiated transition that put an end to the South African apartheid regime that had been in place in that country for years. It was established notably to investigate "gross violations of human rights, including violations which were part of a systematic pattern of abuse."[31] The particularity and originality of this commission was that it had the power to grant "amnesty in respect of acts associated with political objectives, by receiving from persons desiring to make a full disclosure of all the relevant facts relating to such acts."[32] Failing to provide full information allowed the possibility of prosecuting the perpetrators. In 1998, the South African Truth and Reconciliation Commission published its final report, which detailed the violations committed, and made recommendations.[33] The South African Truth and Reconciliation Commission is said to have played an important role in the spread of truth commissions as a transitional justice mechanism. In this sense, one scholar has argued that there was a before and after to the South African Truth and Reconciliation Commission.[34]

### 1.1.5 Nigeria (1999)

Nigeria has experienced many dictatorships and military regimes in its past and since the early years of independence in 1960. Following the return to a sustainable democracy in Nigeria in 1999, the newly elected president, Olusegun Obasanjo, decided to set up a Judicial Commission of Inquiry for the Investigation of Human Rights Violations to investigate past human rights abuses.[35] The commission was set up to "ascertain or establish the causes,

---

30 South Africa, Promotion of National Unity and Reconciliation Act, No. 34, 1995.

31 Section 4, a (i), *ibid.*

32 Section 4, c, *ibid.*

33 South Africa, 'Truth and Reconciliation Commission of South Africa Report', 7 vol., 1998.

34 Mark Freeman, *Truth Commissions and Procedural Fairness* (Cambridge University Press 2006) 26.

35 Nigeria, Instrument Constituting Judicial Commission of Inquiry for the Investigation of Human Rights Violations, 8 June 1999. This legal instrument is cited in the final report of the Nigerian truth commission, Nigeria, 'Human Rights Violations Investigation Commission: Aka Oputa Panel Report', vol. 1, 2002, 28, para. 2.34. The terms of reference of the mandate of the Nigerian truth commission were amended on some points. See the same volume of the final report, 30 ff.

nature and extent of all gross violations of human rights committed in Nigeria between the 15th day of January 1966 and the 28th day of May 1999."[36] The Nigerian truth commission published its reports in 2002, giving an account of human rights violations in Nigeria and making recommendations.[37]

### 1.1.6 Sierra Leone (2000)

The truth commission of Sierra Leone was created in the context of a bloody armed conflict that opposed the government of Sierra Leone and rebel armed groups, mainly the Revolutionary United Front (RUF). Under the auspices of the United Nations, both parties signed a peace agreement in 1999 that provided for the creation of a truth and reconciliation commission.[38] The commission was established by the Parliament of Sierra Leone in 2000.[39] The main objective of the Sierra Leone Truth and Reconciliation Commission was to "to create an impartial historical record of violations and abuses of human rights and international humanitarian law related to the armed conflict in Sierra Leone, from the beginning of the conflict in 1991 to the signing of the Lomé Peace Agreement; to address impunity, to respond to the needs of the victims, to promote healing and reconciliation and to prevent a repetition of the violations and abuses suffered."[40] The commission published its final report containing its findings and recommendations in 2004.[41]

### 1.1.7 Ghana (2002)

Ghana has experienced several authoritarian political regimes in the twentieth century, and its Parliament decided in 2002 to establish a national reconciliation commission.[42] The main task of the truth commission was to investigate human rights violations committed during these authoritative political

36 Nigeria, 'Human Rights Violations Investigation Commission: Aka Oputa Panel Report', *ibid*, 29, para. 2.36.

37 Nigeria, 'Human Rights Violations Investigation Commission: Aka Oputa Panel Report', 9 vol., 2002.

38 Art. XXVI of the Peace Agreement signed between the Government of Sierra Leone and the Revolutionary United Front, Lomé, 7 July 1999, UN doc. S/1999/777, 12 July 1999, Annex.

39 Sierra Leone, The Truth and Reconciliation Commission Act 2000, Supplement to the Sierra Leone Gazette, vol. CXXXI, No. 9, 10 February 2000.

40 Section 6.1, *ibid.*

41 Sierra Leone, 'Report of the Truth and Reconciliation Commission of Sierra Leone: Witness to Truth', 3 vol. and appendices, 2004.

42 Ghana, The National Reconciliation Commission Act, Act 611, 11 January 2002.

regimes. The commission was established "to seek and promote national reconciliation among the people of this country: (a) by establishing accurate, complete and historical record of violations and abuses of human rights inflicted on persons by public institutions and holders of public office during periods of unconstitutional government, namely from (i) 24th February 1966 to 21st August 1969 (ii) 13th January, 1972 to 23rd September 1979; and (iii) 31st December, 1981 to 6th January, 1993; and (b) by making recommendations to the President for redress of wrongs committed within the specified periods."[43] The truth commission published its final report in 2004, detailing human rights violations in Ghana and making recommendations.[44]

### 1.1.8 Morocco (2004)

Morocco, a monarchy, has experienced autocratic rule accompanied by serious human rights violations, but this has not led to a change of political regime. However, in the context of demands for justice following serious human rights violations, the king of Morocco decided to liberalise Morocco's political regime and set up a justice and reconciliation commission (Instance équité et réconciliation) in 2004. The main task of the commission was to investigate cases of enforced disappearances and arbitrary detention.[45] The truth commission published its final report in 2009, detailing cases of enforced disappearance, arbitrary detention and other human rights abuses, and proposing reparations for victims.[46]

### 1.1.9 Democratic Republic of the Congo (2004)

In the context of an armed conflict and political turmoil in the Democratic Republic of the Congo (DRC), various political parties or groups and the DRC government signed a transitional agreement in 2002 that provided for the establishment of a truth and reconciliation commission,[47] and the 2003 DRC transitional constitution did the same.[48] The DRC Parliament created the

43 Section 3 (1), *ibid.*

44 Ghana, National reconciliation Commission Report, 2004.

45 Art. 8, Morocco, Dahir No. 1.04.42 Du 19 safar 1425, 10 avril 2004, portant approbation des Statuts de l'Instance Equité et Réconciliation; see article 5 of this legal instrument for the definition of "serious human rights violations."

46 Morocco, 'Instance Equité et Réconciliation. Rapport', 6 vol., 2009.

47 Section V of the Accord global et inclusif sur la transition en République démocratique du Congo, signé à Pretoria (République d'Afrique du sud), 16 décembre 2002.

48 Art. 154, Democratic Republic of Congo transitional constitution, 2003.

truth commission in 2004.[49] The commission was set to promote justice, peace, reconciliation, pardon and reparation,[50] and to establish the truth about crimes and human rights violations committed in DRC from 30 June 1960 to the end of the transition.[51] Even if the final report was said to have been presented to the DRC Parliament in 2007,[52] a copy of that report is still not publicly accessible in 2026.

### 1.1.10 Liberia (2005)

Liberia has experienced a long and bloody armed conflict, particularly since the 1990s, involving the Liberian government and many armed opposition groups. Following negotiations under the auspices of the United Nations and regional organisations, the parties to the conflict signed a peace agreement in 2003, which included the establishment of a truth and reconciliation commission.[53] The Liberian Parliament created the truth commission in 2005.[54] It tasked the truth commissions to investigate "gross human rights violations and violations of international humanitarian law as well as abuses that occurred, including massacres, sexual violations, murder, extra-judicial killings and economic crimes, such as the exploitation of natural or public resources to perpetuate armed conflicts, during the period January 1979 to October 14, 2003."[55] The Liberian commission published its final report in 2009 with detailed information on violations and crimes, and made recommendations.[56]

49 DRC, Loi No./04/018 portant organisation, attributions et fonctionnement de la commission vérité et réconciliation, 30 juillet 2004.

50 Art. 5, *ibid.*

51 Art. 6, *ibid.*

52 See Elena Naughton, 'République démocratique du Congo: étude de cas' in ICTJ-KAF, 'À l'assaut des conventions Les commissions vérité peuvent-elles renforcer les processus de paix ?', 2014, 50.

53 Art. XIII, Peace Agreement between the Government of Liberia, the Liberians United for Reconciliation and Democracy, the Movement for Democracy in Liberia and the Political Parties, Accra, Ghana, 18 August 2003, UN doc. S/2003/850, Annex.

54 Liberia, An Act to Establish Truth and Reconciliation Commission of Liberia, 12 May 2005.

55 Section 4 (a), *ibid.*

56 Liberia, 'Report of the Truth and Reconciliation Commission', Monrovia, 2009.

### 1.1.11 Kenya (2008)

Following the disputed results of Kenya's 2007 presidential election, a violent conflict erupted between political opponents, with many human rights violations being committed. After the cessation of violence, the Kenyan Parliament decided to establish a truth, justice and reconciliation commission.[57] The truth commission was to establish "an accurate, complete and historical record of violations and abuses of human rights and economic rights inflicted on persons by the State, public institutions and holders of public office, both serving and retired, between 12th December, 1963 and 28th February 2008."[58] The commission rendered its final report in 2013 and gave information on the crimes and violations committed in Kenya, and made recommendations.[59]

### 1.1.12 Mauritius (2008)

Mauritius's truth commission was different from previous ones in that it was not set up to deal with a transition from armed conflict or dictatorship, but with its dark history linked to slavery and colonialism. Indeed, in 2008, Mauritius adopted a *Truth and Justice Commission Act*, which established a truth and justice commission "to make an assessment of the consequences of slavery and indentured labour during the colonial period up to the present,"[60] and to "make recommendations to the president on measures to be taken following its assessment and its findings with a view to achieving social justice and national unity."[61] The Mauritius truth commission published its final report in 2011, which provided an analysis of the complex issue of slavery and indentured labour and their impact on the Mauritian society, and made recommendations.[62]

### 1.1.13 Togo (2009)

In a context of human rights violations and political protest, the president of Togo decided to create a truth, justice and reconciliation commission in 2009,

57 Kenya, Truth, Justice and Reconciliation Commission Bill, 9 May 2008.
58 Section 5 (a), *ibid.*
59 Kenya, 'Report of the Truth, Justice and Reconciliation Commission', 4 vol., 2013.
60 Section 3 (1), Mauritius, Truth and Justice Commission Act, 22 August 2008.
61 Section 3 (2), *ibid.*
62 Mauritius, 'Report of the Truth and Justice Commission', 4 vol., November 2011.

even though the country had not experienced a political regime change.[63] The commission's mandate included investigating political violence and making recommendations,[64] and submitted its findings and recommendations in 2012.[65]

### 1.1.14 Côte d'Ivoire (2011)

The Côte d'Ivoire's truth commission was set up in the context of the violence that followed a disputed presidential election. After President Laurent Gbagbo was ousted from power, the new president, Alassane Ouattara, created a dialogue, truth and reconciliation commission.[66] The commission was to foster reconciliation and social cohesion between Côte d'Ivoire communities by, for example, telling the truth about past events, human rights violations and making propositions.[67] The commission published its small final report in 2014, reporting on violence in the country and making recommendations.[68]

### 1.1.15 Tunisia (2013)

The Tunisian truth commission was established in the aftermath of the Arab Spring, which saw huge street protests in some Arab countries. After the former president of Tunisia, Ben Ali, whose political regime was considered authoritative, was ousted, a new political regime was installed and decided to implement a transitional justice programme, of which a truth commission was an important part. Indeed, in 2013, the Tunisian Parliament adopted a law on transitional justice,[69] that provided for the establishment of the Truth and Dignity Commission (Instance de la vérité et de dignité),[70] which was a truth commission. Its role, among others, was to collect information about human

63 Togo, Décret No. 2009/046/PR portant création de la commission vérité, justice et réconciliation, 25 février 2009.

64 Art. 2, *ibid.*

65 Togo, Rapport final de la Commission vérité, justice et réconciliation, 2012.

66 Côte d'Ivoire, Ordonnance No. 2011-167 portant création, attributions, organisation et fonctionnement de la commission dialogue, vérité et réconciliation, 13 juillet 2011.

67 Art. 5, *ibid.*

68 Côte d'Ivoire, 'Commission Dialogue, vérité et réconciliation, Rapport final, 2014.

69 Tunisia, Loi organique 2013-53 relative à l'instauration de la justice transitionnelle et à son organisation, 24 décembre 2013.

70 Titre II, *ibid.*

rights violations and propose a reparation programme.[71] The commission presented its findings and recommendations in its 2019 final report.[72]

### 1.1.16 Burundi (2014)

Burundi is a country that has a long history of political turmoil and armed confrontation between armed rebel groups and the government. This unrest has been characterised by the perpetration of human rights violations, particularly in 1993, following the assassination of the elected president of the country during a political transition. An international commission of inquiry was set up by the UN Security Council in 1995 to investigate the assassination and its aftermath.[73] This was considered to be more of a classic international commission of inquiry than a truth commission. However, in 2014, the Parliament of Burundi decided to create a truth and reconciliation commission,[74] and mandated the commission to investigate and tell the truth about violations of human rights and international humanitarian law from the independence of Burundi on 1 July 1962 to 4 December 2008, the date the armed conflict ended, and to propose reparations.[75] The truth commission is still underway and has not yet produced the final report.

### 1.1.17 Mali (2014)

Mali has been facing an armed conflict since January 2012. In 2014, the president decided to create a truth, justice and reconciliation commission[76] in order, notably, to investigate serious human rights violations committed in Mali from 1960 to 2013.[77] The final report of the commission is not yet published.

---

71 Art. 39, *ibid.*

72 Tunisia, 'Instance Vérité et Dignité, Rapport final global', 2019 (translated from Arabic to French).

73 UN doc. S/RES/1012, 28 August 1995.

74 Burundi, Loi n°1/ 18 portant création, mandat, composition, organisation et fonctionnement de la commission vérité et réconciliation, 15 mai 2014.

75 Art. 6, *ibid.*

76 Mali, Ordonnance No. 2014-003 P-RM portant création de la Commission vérité, justice et réconciliation, 15 January 2014; Décret No 2014 0013 P-RM portant organisation et modalités de fonctionnement de la Commission vérité, justice et réconciliation, 15 January 2014.

77 Art. 2-3, Mali, Ordonnance, *ibid.*

### 1.1.18 Burkina Faso (2015)

After the fall of the long-time political regime of Blaise Compaoré and following the accusations of serious human rights violations, the new political authorities in Burkina Faso adopted a law that established a commission of reconciliation and reforms.[78] The commission consisted of several sub-commissions among which was the Sub-Commission of Truth, Justice and National Reconciliation.[79] This sub-commission is, in fact, a truth commission, mandated, among other things, to investigate blood and economic crimes and to make proposals in the field of justice and reconciliation.[80] The final report of the truth commission is yet to be published.

### 1.1.19 Gambia (2017)

In Gambia, after the ousting of President Yaya Jammeh and his authoritative regime, a political transition and a newly elected president, the Gambian Parliament decided to establish a truth, reconciliation and reparations commission in 2017.[81] The commission was mandated to "create an impartial historical record of violations and abuses of human rights from July 1994 to January 2017."[82] Its final report was published in 2021, detailing the human rights violations committed during the regime of Yaya Jammeh and making recommendations.[83]

### 1.1.20 Central African Republic (2020)

The Central African Republic is a country that has been facing political turmoil, armed conflicts between rebels and the government, and many political regimes. In 2020, after a new democratic president was elected, the Central African Republic decided to create a truth, justice, reparation and reconciliation commission.[84] Its mandate is to investigate crimes, establish the truth

78 Burkina Faso, Loi organique No. 003-2015/CNT portant attributions, composition, organisation et fonctionnement de la commission de la réconciliation nationale et des réformes, 23 January 2015.

79 Art. 4, *ibid.*

80 *Ibid.*

81 Gambia, Truth, Reconciliation and Reparations Commission Act, 2017.

82 Section 13 (a), *ibid.*

83 Gambia, 'Truth, Reconciliation and Reparations Commission. Report', 16 vol., 2021.

84 Central African Republic, Loi No. 20.009 portant création, organisation et fonctionnement de la commission justice, vérité, réparation et réconciliation (CVJR), 7 Avril 2020.

and determine responsibility for serious national events that occurred between 29 March 1959 and 31 December 2019.[85] The work of the truth commission is currently underway.

Other truth commissions have also been considered or proposed in the African countries of Libya,[86] South Sudan,[87] Sudan[88] and Guinea-Bissau.[89] Thus, out of the fifty-four or fifty-five states that make up the African continent, almost half have created or are considering creating a truth commission.

## 1.2 The Americas

### 1.2.1 Bolivia (1982 and 2016)

The first truth commission created in the Americas was in Bolivia in 1982, when, after many political authoritarian regimes, a new president decided to established a commission (Comisión Nacional de Investigación de Ciudadanos Desaparecidos) that was mandated to investigate forced disappearances.[90] But, the truth commission did not complete its mandate because it was disbanded, and the final report was not produced.[91] In 2016, the Parliament of Bolivia adopted a law that created a new truth commission (Comisión de la verdad).[92] This commission was also mandated to investigate forced disappearances, but its mandate was broadened to include assassinations,arbitrary detentions, torture and sexual violence – considered serious human rights violations for political and ideological reasons – that had been committed in Bolivia between 4 November 1964 and 10 October 1982.[93] In 2021, the truth commission presented its final report and an official executive final

85 Art. 1, *ibid.*

86 Libya, Law No. 29 on Transitional Justice, 2 December 2013.

87 Signed Revitalized Agreement on the Resolution of the Conflict in South Sudan (R-ARCSS), Addis Ababa, 12 September 2018, Section 5.2 Commission of Truth, Reconciliation and Healing (CTRH).

88 'Report of the International Commission of Inquiry on Darfur to the Secretary-General', UN doc. S/2005/60, 1 February 2005, para. 617.

89 AU, Peace and Security Council, 255th meeting, Addis Ababa, Ethiopia, 23 December 2010, AU doc. PSC/PR/COMM.2(CCLV), 1.

90 Bolivia, Decreto Supremo No. 19241, *Comisión Nacional de Investigación de Ciudadanos Desaparecidos*, 28 de Octubre de 1982.

91 See information on that truth commission online, https://www.usip.org/publications/1982/10/truth-commission-bolivia.

92 Bolivia, Ley No. 879, Ley de la comisión de la verdad, 23 de diciembre de 2016.

93 Art. 1, *ibid.*

report; the final report summarised the violations examined and proposed recommendations.[94]

### 1.2.2 Argentina (1983)

In Argentina, the end of the authoritarian regime and the arrival of a newly elected president accentuated the social demand for the truth about past human rights violations and about the many who had disappeared during the dictatorship. In 1983, in response to this urgent social demand, the newly elected president created the Argentinean National Commission on the Disappearance of Persons (Comisión Nacional sobre la Desaparición de personas) and charged it with investigating disappearances.[95] This truth commission was the first to receive international attention. In 1984, the truth commission published its final report, detailing thousands of forced disappearances and making recommendations.[96]

### 1.2.3 Uruguay (1985 and 2000)

In 1985, in a context of political transition in Uruguay after the fall of the dictatorship, two commissions of inquiry were set up within the Uruguayan Parliament to deal with forced disappearances.[97] These commissions found that there was a practice of forced disappearances in the country during the dictatorship, but these reports were largely ignored, or considered insufficient.[98] In 2000, the president of Uruguay decided to create the Commission for Peace, whose mandate was to examine forced disappearances committed during the dictatorship.[99] The Commission for Peace published its final report in 2003, presenting the results of its investigations and making recommendations.[100]

---

94 Bolivia, Comisión de la verdad, 'Memoria histórica de las investigaciones, Estado plurinacional de Bolivia, Informe ejecutivo', 2021.

95 Argentina, Decreto 187, *Comisión Nacional sobre la Desaparición de personas*, 15 de diciembre de 1983.

96 Argentina, 'Nunca Más (Never Again), Report of Conadep (National Commission on the Disappearance of Persons)', 1984.

97 See on that matter, Priscilla Hayner, Fifteen Truth Commissions 1974 to 1994: A Comparative Study' (1994) 16(4) *Human Rights Quarterly* 597, 616, and https://www.usip.org/publications/2000/08/truth-commission-uruguay.

98 *Ibid.*

99 Uruguay, Resolución de la Presidencia de la República No. 858/200, 9 de agosto de 2000.

100 Uruguay, 'Informe final de la comisión para la paz', 10 de abril de 2003.

### 1.2.4 Chile (1990)

After the fall of the dictatorship of General Pinochet, the newly elected president of Chile created a National Truth and Reconciliation Commission (Comisión Nacional de Verdad y Reconciliación)[101] to examine the serious human rights violations committed in Chile from 11 September 1973 to 11 March 1990.[102] The decree establishing the truth commission mandated it to investigate human rights violations, contribute to reconciliation and make recommendations.[103] The commission's report was published in 1996. It detailed human rights violations and made recommendations.[104]

### 1.2.5 El Salvador (1991)

After a long and bloody armed conflict, the government of El Salvador and the rebels of the Frente Farabundo Martí para la Liberacíon Nacional (FLMN) signed a peace agreement under the auspices of the United Nations that included the creation of a truth commission.[105] The truth commission was mandated to investigate "serious acts of violence that have occurred since 1980 and whose impact on society urgently demands that the public should know the truth."[106] The commission published its report in 1993, presenting its findings on acts of violence and recommending several measures.[107]

### 1.2.6 Guatemala (1994)

Just as in El Salvador, the truth commission of Guatemala was created in the context of efforts, under the auspices of the United Nations, to end a bloody civil armed conflict between the Government of Guatemala and the armed opposition group of the Unidad Revolucionaria Nacional Guatemalteca. In order to end the armed conflict, the two parties signed several agreements;

101 Chile, Decreto 355 crea comisión de verdad y reconciliación, Ministerio del interior; Subsecretaria del interior, 25 de abril de 1990.

102 Para 1, preamble, *ibid.*

103 Artículo primero, *ibid.*

104 Chile, 'Informe de la Comisión Nacional de Verdad y Reconciliación', 3 tomos, 1996.

105 Peace Accords signed by representatives of the Government of El Salvador and the Frente Farabundo Martí para la Liberacíon Nacional (FLMN) in Mexico City on 27 April 1991, UN doc. A/46/553, S/23130, 9 October 1991, Annex, 16, 'Commission on the Truth'.

106 *Ibid*, Annex, 16, para. 2.

107 El Salvador, 'Report of the Commission on the Truth for El Salvador, From Madness to Hope. The 12-Year War in El Salvador', UN doc. S/25500, 1 April 1993, Annex.

one of these was dedicated to the creation of a Commission of Clarification, mandated "[t]o clarify with all objectivity, equity and impartiality the human rights violations and acts of violence that have caused the Guatemalan population to suffer, connected with the armed conflict," and to make recommendations.[108] The final report of the commission was published in 1999. It gave a detailed account of human rights violations in Guatemala and made recommendations.[109]

### 1.2.7 Haiti (1994–1995)

The truth commission of Haiti was created in the context of the fall of the military dictatorship and the reinstallation at the presidency of Jean Bertrand Aristides. The president created the National Commission for Truth and Justice (Commission Nationale de Vérité et de Justice).[110] The commission was mandated to tell the truth about the most serious human rights violations committed from the 29 September 1991 to 15 October 1994, to contribute to the reconciliation of Haïtians[111] and to make recommendations.[112] The truth commission published its final report in 1998, with details on human rights violations and recommendations.[113]

### 1.2.8 Ecuador (1996 and 2007)

Ecuador has a long history of authoritative rule. In 1996, the government set up a truth commission to deal with the human rights violations.[114] But that commission did not go too far and did not produce a final report.[115] Another

---

108 Agreement on the establishment of the Commission to clarify past human rights violations and acts of violence that have caused the Guatemalan population to suffer, signed by the Government of Guatemala and the Unidad Revolucionaria Nacional Guatemalteca (UNRG) in Oslo on 23 June 1994, (UN Doc. A/48/954, S/1994/751, 1 July 1994, Annex II), see para. 2.

109 Guatemala, Comisión para el Esclarecimiento Histórico, *Guatemala Memoria Del Silencio,* 12 vol., (Guatemala: Oficina de Servicios para Proyectos de las Naciones Unidas, 1999).

110 Haiti, Arrêté créant la Commission Nationale de Vérité et de Justice, 17 décembre 1994. See also : Arrêté créant la Commission Nationale de Vérité et de Justice, 28 Mars 1995.

111 Art. 2, Haiti, Arrêté 28 Mars 1995, *ibid.*

112 Art. 7-8, *ibid.*

113 Haiti, Commission nationale de Justice et de Vérité, 'Si m pa rele', 29 septembre 1991–14 octobre 1994, Institute of Haïtian Studies, University of Kansas, 1998.

114 Ecuador, Ministerial Accord No. 012, 17 September 1996; Document cited in Inter-American Commission of Human Rights Report, Ecuador 1997 – chap. II, 3.

115 See https://www.usip.org/publications/1996/09/truth-commission-ecuador-96.

truth commission (Comisión de la Verdad "para impedir la impunidad) was set up in 2007 by the president.[116] That truth commission was mandated to investigate acts of violence, human rights violations that occurred between 1984 and 1988, as well as other periods.[117] In 2010, the commission issued a final report containing findings and recommendations.[118]

### 1.2.9 Panama (2001)

Panama experienced dictatorships over many decades and, in 2001, the newly elected president decided to create a truth commission (Comisión de la Verdad) to examine human rights violations against life, including disappearances, committed during these political regimes since 1968, and to make recommendations.[119] The commission's final report was published in 2002. It presented many cases of murders and disappearances, and made recommendations.[120]

### 1.2.10 Peru (2001)

Peru's truth commission was set up in the aftermath of the conflict that pitted the Shining Path rebels against the Peruvian government for many years, and in the context of a political transition when President Alberto Fugimori lost power. In 2001, the new president of Peru, Valentin Paniagua Corazao, created a truth commission (Comisión de la Verdad)[121] with the objectives, *inter alia*, of investigating and telling the truth about terrorist violence and violations of human rights in Peru from May 1980 to November 2000, and making recommendations.[122] In 2003, the truth commission published its findings and made recommendations in its final report.[123]

---

116 Ecuador, Presidente Constitucional de la República, Se creó la Comisión de la Verdad "para impedir la impunidad", 3 de mayo de 2007.

117 Art. 1, *ibid.*

118 Ecuador, 'Informe de la comisión de la verdad, Sin verdad, no hay justicia', 5 tomos, 2010.

119 Art. 1-2, Panama, Ministerio de Gobierno y Justicia, Decreto Ejecutivo No. 2, 18 de enero de 2001.

120 Panama, 'Informe Final de la Comisión de la Verdad de Panamá', 2002.

121 Peru, Decreto Supremo No. 065-2001-PCM, Crean Comisión de la Verdad, 2 de junio de 2001.

122 Art. 1-2, *ibid.*

123 Peru, Comisión de la Verdad y Reconciliación, 'Informe Final', 9 tomos, Lima, 2003.

### 1.2.11 Grenada (2001)

Against the backdrop of the Cold War, Grenada had experienced political turmoil from independence from Britain in 1974 until the 1990s, with authoritarian rule, several changes of government and an armed international intervention led by the United States. In order to establish the truth about these and other events, the Governor General of Grenada decided in 2001 to appoint a truth and reconciliation commission to "inquire into and record certain political events which occurred in Grenada during the period 1st January 1976 to 31st December 1991, and to report and make recommendations".[124] The Grenada Truth and Reconciliation Commission published its final report in 2006 detailing these events and making recommendations.[125]

### 1.2.12 Paraguay (2003)

Paraguay also experienced a dictatorship and the creation of a truth commission was a way to search and tell the truth about human rights violations. Indeed, in 2003, the Parliament of Paraguay adopted a law creating a truth and justice commission (Comisión de Verdad y Justicia),[126] and gave it a mandate to tell the truth about human rights violations committed from May 1954 to the present and to make recommendations.[127] The commission published its final report in 2008 with recommendations and accounts of human rights violations.[128]

### 1.2.13 Canada (2006)

After years of violations of their rights, Indigenous peoples of Canada filed judicial suits against the Canadian government and some churches regarding the practice of residential schools, which were established as early as the 1830s. Many Indigenous children were forcibly placed in residential schools by the Canadian authorities in order to assimilate them into Euro-Canadian culture. These law suits resulted in the signing of an agreement, which led to

124 Grenada, 'Truth and Reconciliation Report, Redeeming the Past. A Time for Healing, vol. 1, 2006, 11.

125 Grenada, 'Truth and Reconciliation Report, Redeeming the Past. A Time for Healing', 3 vol., 2006.

126 Paraguay, Ley nº 2225, Por la cual se crea la Comisión de Verdad y Justicia, 16 de octubre de 2003.

127 Art. 1, *ibid.*

128 Paraguay, Comisión de verdad y justicia, 'Informe Final, Anive haguã oiko' 3 tomos, 2008.

the creation of the truth and reconciliation commission of Canada to deal with the violations committed against Indigenous peoples in the context of residential schools.[129] The agreement was to be implemented under court supervision. The truth commission was later established by an Order in Council, signed by Governor General following the recommendation of the Canadian prime minister.[130] The commission published its final report in 2015, concluding that Canada had committed cultural genocide and making recommendations.[131]

#### 1.2.14 Honduras (2010)

Political turmoil, a military coup d'état against elected President Manuel Zelaya Rosales, and disputes over political power led the politicians of Honduras to agree on the creation of a truth commission.[132] The newly elected president created the National Truth and Reconciliation Commission (Comisión de la Verdad y la Reconciliación) to investigate the coup d'état and its consequences, and identify the means to prevent this kind of event from happening again.[133] This truth commission was unusual in Latin America because it did not have a mandate to examine serious human rights violations committed by a dictatorship, but rather to focus on an event, a coup d'état. The truth commission published its report in 2011, presenting details about the history of Honduras, the consequences of the coup d'état and recommendations.[134]

#### 1.2.15 Brazil (2011)

Brazil experienced authoritative and military regimes before the transition to a democracy and a civil regime in 1985. Since then, there had been calls from victims of these regimes and their relatives to tell the truth about the human

129 Canada, Indian Residential Schools Settlement Agreement (2006b, May 8); see Schedule "N" Mandate for the Truth and Reconciliation Commission.

130 Canada, Order-in-Council P.C. no. 2008-0793, 25 April 2008a.

131 Canada, 'Truth and reconciliation Commission of Canada, Canada's Residential Schools, Report', 6 vol., 2015.

132 Guaymuras Dialogue, Tegucigalpa/San Jose Agreement on national reconciliation and the strengthening of democracy in Honduras, see para. 6. On the Truth and Verification Committees, 30 October 2009. Document translated from Spanish by the University of Edinburg, see online: https://www.peaceagreements.org/viewmasterdocument/1940.

133 Art. 1, Honduras, Decreto Ejecutivo Nùmero PCM 011-2010, 13 de abril de 2010.

134 Honduras, 'Para que los hechos no se repitan: Informe de la Comisión de la Verdad y la Reconciliación', 2 tomos, julio de 2011.

rights abuses these regimes had committed. But it was many years after the dictatorship had ended that elected President Dilma Roussef decided to create a national truth commission (Comissão nacional da verdad) to deal with the serious human rights violations the regimes had committed.[135] The truth commission published its final report in 2014, with findings of its investigations and recommendations.[136]

### 1.2.16 Colombia (2017)

Colombia experienced a bloody armed conflict between the government and the rebels of the Fuerzas armadas revolucionarias de Colombia (FARC). Negotiations between the belligerents led to the signature of a peace agreement in 2016 that provided for the creation of a Commission for the Clarification of Truth, Coexistence, and Non-Recurrence (Comisión para el Esclarecimiento de la Verdad, la Convivencia y la No Repetición).[137] The commission was mandated, *inter alia*, to investigate serious human rights and international humanitarian law violations.[138] The commission published its final report in 2022, with findings and recommendations.[139]

## 1.3 Asia and Oceania

### 1.3.1 Nepal (1990 and 2006)

It was in Nepal, a country that had experienced a dictatorship accused of human rights violations, that the first Asian commission was created in 1990. This commission, called the Commission of Inquiry for the Location of Missing Persons, was dedicated to enforced disappearances, as were the first commissions in Latin America.[140] It was tasked with investigating human rights

135 Brazil, Art. 1, Lei No. 12.528, 18 de Novembro de 2011.
136 Brazil, 'Comissão nacional da verdade, Relatório', 3 vol., 2014.
137 Colombia, Final Agreement to End the Armed Conflict and Build a Stable and Lasting Peace, Part. 5.1.1.1. Truth, Coexistence and Non-recurrence Commission (Comisión para el Esclarecimiento de la Verdad, la Convivencia y la No Repetición), 24 November 2016.
138 Para. 5.1.1.1.2, Colombia, Final Agreement to End the Armed Conflict and Build a Stable and Lasting Peace.
139 Colombia, Comisión para el Esclarecimieto de la Verdad, la Convivencia y la No Repetición, 'Hay futuro si hay verdad. Informe Final, 2022.
140 The document creating the 1990 truth commission is not available. On that topic, see Carles Fernández-Torné, 'Still Disappeared': Reconstructing the 1990 'Truth Commission' in Nepal' (2022) 30(4) *Contemporary South Asia* 619.

violations committed by Nepal's previous dictatorial regime, namely, the dictatorial *panchayat* (non-party political system), which functioned in Nepal from 1961 to 1990.[141] Following an armed conflict between the government and armed rebels, a peace agreement was signed in 2006 and provided for the establishment of a "[h]igh-level Truth and Reconciliation Commission in order to probe into those involved in serious violation of human rights and crime against humanity in course of the armed conflict for creating an atmosphere for reconciliation in the society."[142] The truth and reconciliation commission was eventually created in 2014 and was mandated "to investigate into the incidents of the gross violation of human rights, and find out and record the truth and bring it out for the general public."[143] The truth commission's work is still ongoing and there are propositions to amend the legislation that created it.[144]

### 1.3.2 Sri Lanka (Various Dates)

Sri Lanka is a country that faced a bloody armed conflict between the Tamil rebels and the Government of Sri Lanka from 1983 to 2010; an armed conflict during which many crimes and human rights violations had been committed. Many commissions of inquiry were established in that country to deal with human rights violations. For example, in 1994, three commissions were created to investigate missing persons,[145] and another one was established in 1998.[146] In the context of the armed conflict, the president of Sri Lanka also appointed a Commission of Inquiry on the Lessons Learnt and Reconciliation in 2010,[147] and tasked the commission to investigate the failure of a ceasefire

---

141 *Ibid.*

142 Comprehensive Peace Agreement concluded between the Government of Nepal and the Communist Party of Nepal (Maoist), 21 November 2006, para. 5.2.5.

143 Section 13, Nepal, The Enforced Disappearances Enquiry, Truth and Reconciliation Commission Act, 2071 (2014), Nepal Gazette 2071/01/28, 11 May 2014.

144 See Binod Ghimire, 'Disputed bill to revise transitional justice law lands in House', *Kathmandu Post*, 17 February 2024. Available online : https://kathmandupost.com/politics/2023/03/20/disputed-bill-to-revise-transitional-justice-law-lands-in-house.

145 Sri Lanka, The Gazette of the Democratic Socialist Republic of Sri Lanka (Extraordinary), Charter 855/18, 1995, Ref. P.O. No. SP/6/N/191/94; Charter 855/19, 1995, Ref. P.O. No. SP/6/N/193/94; Charter 855/20, 1995, Ref. P.O. No. SP/6/N/192/94.

146 Sri Lanka, The Gazette of the Democratic Socialist Republic of Sri Lanka (Extraordinary). Charter 1060/13, 1998, Ref. No. SP/6/N/21/97.

147 See the document P.O. No. CA/3/3/24, 15 May 2010. The document is reprinted in Sri Lanka, 'Report of the Commission of Inquiry on Lessons Learnt and Reconciliation', 2011, ii-v.

and the events that followed. These commissions were a part of a global effort to force Sri Lanka to deal with its past, even if the establishment of multiple commissions in that country signalled that Sri Lanka was having difficulty giving a clear account of its past and of the human rights violations committed.

### 1.3.3 South Korea (2000 and 2005)

South Korea has also experienced multiple commissions. In 2000, for example, a truth commission was set up to deal with "suspicious deaths which have occurred in the course of democratization movement against any past authoritarian regime,"[148] and another one to investigate the "Jeju 4·3 Incident," events that happened between 1947 and 1954 and caused "'civilians' sacrifices in the process of armed conflicts."[149] In 2005, the South Korean Parliament created a Committee on Clearing up Past Incidents for Truth and Reconciliation, which was a large truth commission.[150] The truth commission's purpose was "to foster national legitimacy and reconcile the past for the sake of national unity by honoring those who participated in the anti-Japanese movements and investigating incidents regarding human rights abuses, violence and massacres occurring since the period of Japanese rule to the present time; specifically during the nation's authoritarian regimes."[151] It was mandated, *inter alia*, to investigate human rights violations.[152] In 2009, the commission published a report detailing three years of activities, and presenting its investigations and recommendations.[153] It also published its findings and recommendations in a

---

148 Art. 1, South Korea, Special Act to Reveal the Truth regarding Suspicious Deaths, Act n° 6170, 15 January 2000 (Amended by Act no. 6496, 24 July 2001; Act no. 6670, 25 March 2002; Act n°6750, 5 December 2002). See page 531 of the English and condensed version report of the commission: *A Hard Journey to Justice: First Term Report by the Presidential Truth Commission on Suspicious Deaths of the Republic of Korea* (*10.2000–10.2002*), (Samin Book 2004).

149 Art. 2, South Korea, The Special Law for Truth Investigation about the Jeju 4·3 Incident and Honoring Victims, Law no. 6117, 12 January 2000 (Revision Law no. 8264, 24 January 2007; Partial Revision Law no. 8435, 17 May 2007). See page 688 of the English version of the report: 'The National Committee for Investigation of the Truth about the Jeju April 3 Incident, Jeju 4·3', Peace Foundation, 2003.

150 South Korea, Framework Act on Clearing up Past Incidents for Truth and Reconciliation Enacted by Law No. 7542, 31 May 2005.

151 Art. 1, *ibid.*

152 Art. 2, *ibid.*

153 South Korea, Truth and Reconciliation Commission, 'Activities of the Past Three Years', 2009.

final report in 2010.[154] Another truth and reconciliation commission was set up by the South Korean parliament in 2020.[155] It was tasked "to investigate and uncover the truth about the anti-Japanese independence movement, overseas Koreans, mass atrocities during the Korean War, various human rights violations that occurred during Korea's authoritarian rule and killings by hostile forces."[156] Its work is still underway.

### 1.3.4 Timor Leste (2001)

In the context of an effort to end violence and an armed conflict between Timor's pro-independence resistance movement and the Government of Indonesia, the UN created a transitional administration to govern Timor in 1999.[157] The representative of the UN Secretary-General in Timor, invested among others with judicial powers, decided to create a Commission for Reception, Truth and Reconciliation in East Timor in 2001.[158] The truth commission's objective was mainly to inquire "into human rights violations that have taken place in the context of the political conflicts in East Timor," and to make recommendations.[159] It published its final report in 2005, providing an account of human rights violations and making recommendations.[160]

### 1.3.5 Indonesia–Timor (2004)

In the same context as the aftermath of the armed conflict between Timor's pro-independence movement and the Government of Indonesia, another truth commission was created. The Commission of Truth and Friendship was unique in that as it is was a bilateral truth commission, conjointly established by two states.[161] The Democratic Republic of Timor-Leste and the

154 South Korea, Truth and Reconciliation Commission, 'Comprehensive Report', 4 vol., 2010. Part 1 of vol. 1 of this report has been translated into English.

155 South Korea, Framework Act on Settling Past Affairs Truth and Reconciliation (Amended on June 9, 2020).

156 See the website of the truth Commission, online: https://www.jinsil.go.kr/en/bbm/bbs/selectBoardArticleView.do?nttId=23429.

157 UN Security Council, Resolution 1272 (1999), UN doc. S/RES/1272, 25 October 1999.

158 Regulation No. 2001/10, On the Establishment of a Commission for Reception, Truth and Reconciliation in East Timor, UN doc. UNTAET/REG/2001/10, 13 July 2001.

159 Section 3, *ibid.*

160 Timor Leste, '*Chega,* The Report of the Reception, Truth, and Reconciliation Timor Leste', 5 vol., 2005.

161 Agreement to establish a Commission of Truth and Friendship between Indonesia and Timor-Leste, 14 December 2004.

Republic of Indonesia agreed to set up the commission in order to, notably, "[r] eveal the factual truth of the nature, causes, and the extent of reported violations of human rights, that occurred in the period leading up to and immediately following the popular consultation in Timor-Leste in August 1999," to promote reconciliation, and to make recommendations.[162] The truth commission published its final report in 2008, providing its conclusions on human rights violations and making recommendations.[163]

### 1.3.6 Solomon Islands (2008)

The Solomon Islands experienced "ethnic" clashes between two main groups that resulted in human rights violations between 1998 and 2003. Efforts to restore peace were finally successful and, in 2008, the Solomon Islands Parliament created the truth and reconciliation commission. Notably, the commission was to investigate and examine "the nature, antecedents, root causes, accountability or responsibility for and the extent of the impact on human rights violations or abuses which occurred between 1st January 1998 and 23rd July 2003, including the destruction of property, deprivation of rights to own property and the right to settle and make a living," to promote reconciliation and unity, and to propose means to prevent the repetition of the violations.[164] The commission gave an account on human rights violations and made recommendations in its final report published in 2012.[165]

### 1.3.7 Taiwan (2017)

Taiwan endured a "[p]eriod of authoritarian rule" from 15 August 1945 to 6 November 1992,[166] and, in 2017, created a Transitional Justice Commission to deal with that period. The commission was mandated to provide "for public access to political archival records," remove "authoritarian symbols and preserving sites where injustices were committed," redress "judicial wrongs,"

162 Section 14 of Terms of Reference for The Commission of Truth and Friendship Established by The Republic of Indonesia and The Democratic Republic of Timor-Leste, 5 August 2006.

163 Indonesia-Timor-Leste, 'Final Report of the Commission of Truth and Friendship (Ctf)', 2008.

164 Section 5, Solomon Islands, Truth and Reconciliation Commission Act 2008.

165 Solomon Islands, Truth and Reconciliation Commission, 'Confronting the Truth for a better Solomon Islands, Final Report', 5 vol., 2012.

166 Art. 3 (1) of Taiwan, Act on Promoting Transitional Justice CH, Executive Yuan, (Creation and Statute of the Transitional Justice Commission), 27 December 2017.

restore "historical truth," promote "social reconciliation," settle and utilise "ill-gotten party assets," and handle "other matters pertaining to transitional justice."[167] As well, the commission was "to investigate the truth and, on the basis of the archival materials acquired in accordance with the provisions of this article, shall invite concerned parties to express their views, so as to uncover the facts surrounding human rights abuses and to ascertain the responsibility of perpetrators and participants in mechanisms of oppression."[168] The commission published its final report in 2022.[169]

## 1.4 Europe

### 1.4.1 Germany (1992 and 1995)

The German Parliament set up two commissions of inquiry after the fall of the Berlin Wall in order to investigate crimes committed during the authoritative rule in East Germany: the first was set up in 1992,[170] and the other in 1995.[171] Even if these two commissions were Parliamentary commissions, they could be considered to be truth commissions because they investigated crimes and violations of a former regime. Respectively in 1994 and 1998, these commissions published final reports that gave light to the abuses and violations committed and made recommendations.[172]

---

167 Art. 2, *ibid.*

168 Art. 4, *ibid.*

169 For the announcement of the release of the final report, see online: https://www.taiwanplus.com/news/taiwan-news/politics/220527030/taiwan-transitional-justice-commission-delivers-final-report.

170 Germany, Drucksache 12/2597, Enquete-Kommission, "Aufarbeitung der Geschichte und Folgen der SED-Diktatur", 13 Mai 1992.

171 Germany, Deutscher Bundestag, Drucksache 13/1535, Enquete-Kommission, "Überwindung der Folgen der SED-Diktatur im Prozeß der deutschen Einheit", 30 Mai 1995.

172 For the 1992 commission, see, for example, Deutscher Bundestag, Drucksache 12/7820, Bericht der Enquete-Kommission "Aufarbeitung von Geschichte und Folgen der SED-Diktatur in Deutschland", 31 May 1994; Materialien der Enquete-Kommission "Aufarbeitung von Geschichte und Folgen der SED-Diktatur in Deutschland" (12. Wahlperiode des Deutschen Bundestages): neun Bände in 18 Teilbänden 3, Baden-Baden: Nomos, 1995; For the 1995 commission, see Drucksache 13/11000, Deutscher Bundestag, Schlußbericht der Enquete-Kommission "Überwindung der Folgen der SED-Diktatur im Prozeß der deutschen Einheit", 10 June 1998; Materialien der Enquete-Kommission "Überwindung der Folgen der SED-Diktatur im Prozeß der Deutschen Einheit", (13. Wahlperiode des Deutschen Bundestages): acht Bände in 14 Teilbänden, Baden Baden, Nomos, 1999.

### 1.4.2 Former Yugoslavia (2001)

In the context of the armed conflict in former Yugoslavia, a short-lived truth commission was created for Serbia and Montenegro in 2001 before being dissolved.[173]

### 1.4.3 Norway (2018)

Like Canada, northern European countries, which are neither in transition nor have experienced a dictatorship or armed conflict in their recent history, have also established truth commissions to examine violations of the rights of Indigenous peoples on their territories. In Norway's Parliament, there was a push for the creation of a truth commission that began in 2016.[174] The Norway Truth and Reconciliation Commission was established in 2018 to examine the policy of Norway and injustices against the Sami, the Kven and the Norvegians Finns.[175] It issued its final report in 2023.[176]

### 1.4.4 Finland (2021)

The Government of Finland, in cooperation with the Indigenous peoples of Finland, set up the Truth and Reconciliation Commission Concerning the Sami People in 2021. The truth commission was mandated "to identify and assess historical and current discrimination, including the assimilation policy of the state and violations of rights, to find out how they affect the Sámi and their communities in the current situation and to propose ways to promote links between the Sámi and the state of Finland and among the Sámi people."[177] In

173 Serbia and Montenegro, Truth and Reconciliation Commission for Serbia and Montenegro: Presidential Decree, 30 March 2001.

174 Norway, Innst. 493 S (2016–2017), Innstilling til Stortinget fra kontroll- og konstitusjonskomiteen, Dokument 8:30 S (2016–2017).

175 Norway, Innst. 408 S (2017–2018) Innstilling til Stortinget fra Stortingets presidentskap, 12. juni 2018.

176 Norway, Sannhet og forsoning, – grunnlag for et oppgjør med fornorskingspolitikk og urett mot samer, kvener/norskfinner og skogfinner, Rapport til stortinget fra sannhets- og forsoningskommisjonen, 01. juni 2023.

177 Section 3.2, Finland, Establishing a truth and reconciliation commission concerning the Sámi people, Government of Finland in cooperation with the Sámi Parliament and the Skolt Village Assembly. Document available on the website of the truth commission, https://sdtsk.fi/en/mandate/.

2025, the commission published its final report, reporting the abuses endured by the Sámi people and making proposals.[178]

### 1.4.5 Sweden (2021)

The Government of Sweden set up a truth commission for the Sami People in 2021,[179] in order to "survey and examine the policies pursued towards the Sami" and to "analyse and shed light on [their] consequences."[180] The work of the truth commission is underway.

Thus, many truth commissions have been created in many countries. The list above presents the most known of these commissions. As well, truth commissions not identified here have been created in some of the countries presented above or in countries not listed here, for example in The Philippines and in Bangladesh.[181] In some countries, there are numerous commissions that have not been created by a national or federal state but that are labelled as "truth commission" or "truth and reconciliation commission" nonetheless. For example, some bodies with the words "truth" and "commissions" in their name have been created in the United States to deal with racial crimes or injustices. The Greensboro Truth and Reconciliation Commission is one such commission. It was set up to look at "the context, causes, sequence and consequence of the events of November 3, 1979" in Greensboro, North Carolina, during which five people were shot dead and ten others were wounded.[182] This commission was not officially created by the United States government but was a private initiative.[183] In the United States, many other "truth commissions" have been

---

178 Finland, Sámi Truth and Reconciliation Commission, '"I want a better life for my people". A summary of the proposals given by the Sámi Truth and Reconciliation Commission in Finland', Publications of the Finnish Government, 2025. See also the website, https://sdtsk.fi/en/home/.

179 See the website of the truth commission, online: https://sanningskommissionensamer.se/en/about-the-commision/.

180 See the website of the truth commission, online: https://sanningskommissionensamer.se/en/about-the-assignment/.

181 Philippines (The), OP Executive Order No. 1, S. 2010, July 30, 2010, *Creating the Philippine Truth Commission*. The commission was to investigate "graft and corruption" (see section 1 of the Executive order); Bangladesh, Commission of Inquiry on Enforced Disappearances, *Unfolding the Truth: A Structural Diagnosis of Enforced Disappearance in Bangladesh*, Final Report, vol. 1, 2026.

182 See the Mandate for the Greensboro Truth and Reconciliation Commission, available on the website of the Greensboro Truth and Reconciliation Commission: https://greensborotrc.org/mandate.php.

183 *Ibid.*

created this way and others are under consideration.[184] For example, the death of George Floyd, an African–American man murdered in Minneapolis, Minnesota, in 2020, following a violent arrest by white police, spurred action in different cities. The Iowa City Council established the Ad Hoc Truth and Reconciliation Commission for its own purposes following the murder of George Floyd, in order to examine racism in its own community. The mandate of the Commission was "to bear witness to the truth of racial injustice in Iowa City and to carry out restorative justice through the collection of testimony and public hearings, with such work to include a recommendation to the Council of a plan for dedicating and/or renaming public spaces and/or rights of way in honor of the Black Lives Matter movement."[185] But these initiatives are local initiatives and there is no official federally backed truth commission in the United States.

In Victoria, one of the states of Australia, the Yoorrook Justice Commission was established in 2021 following negotiations between First Peoples and the Victorian government, "to hear, record and address the truths about First Peoples' experiences of colonisation in Victoria since 1788 to now."[186] This commission, which considered itself a truth commission,[187] rendered a final report in 2025 that concluded that many violations, abuses and crimes, including genocide, were committed against First Peoples in Victoria.[188]

In the same vein, a province of the Democratic Republic of the Congo (DRC), Kasaï-Central, established a Provincial Truth, Justice and Reconciliation Commission in 2021 with the objective of addressing violations and abuses committed on its territory.[189]

The proliferation of these truth commissions reflects the universal success of this transitional justice mechanism. One piece of evidence of that success is the fact that today there are always propositions of creating truth commission when the means of how to end an armed conflict are discussed. Now that we

---

184 For an overview, Daniel Posthumus, Kelebogile Zvobgo, 'Democratizing Truth: An Analysis of Truth Commissions in the United States' (2021) 15(3) *International Journal of Transitional Justice* 510.

185 See City of Iowa, Ad Hoc Truth & Reconciliation Commission, available online https://www.iowa-city.org/WebLink/DocView.aspx?id=2190021&dbid=0&repo=CityofIowaCity.

186 Yoorrook Justice Commission, Interim Report, 2 June 2022. For the mandate, and other elements of this commission, see Letter Patent, 12 May 2021. The document is available in Interim Report, *Ibid*, Annex 1, 74–81.

187 *Ibid*, 4.

188 Yoorrook Justice Commission, Summary Report, 2025, 32.

189 Kasaï-Central, Edit N°006/KC/2021 portant création, organisation et fonctionnement de la commission provinciale vérité, justice et réconciliation dans la province du Kasaï Central, 15 juillet 2021.

have identified a number of truth commissions, we can take a look at the authorities who create them.

## 2 The Authorities that Create Truth Commissions

Truth commissions are "official bodies." An important criterion for identifying truth commissions and distinguishing them from other commissions is the fact that they are established by states or official authorities. With regard to the authority that establishes truth commissions, a distinction can be made between those established as a result of action by national bodies within the state – the executive, legislative or judicial branches; those resulting from a peace agreement between former belligerents; or those established at the international level.[190] However, some truth commissions are the combination of several actions from different authorities or legal instruments.

### 2.1 Executive Branch

Many truth commissions have been created by the executive branch of the state, generally the president or the prime minister. This was the case in Uganda (1974 and 1986), Bolivia, Argentina, Zimbabwe, Chad, Nigeria, Morocco, Togo, Bolivia, Argentina, Uruguay (2000), Chile, Haiti, Peru, Panama, Ecuador, Honduras, Nepal (1990), Sri Lanka, Mali, Côte d'Ivoire, Former Yugoslavia, Canada, Sweden and Finland.

Sometimes, even when the truth commission is created by the executive branch of the state, there is an intervention by Parliament, which makes the truth commission appear to be the product of a joint action by the executive and legislative branches of the state. For example, the truth commissions of Mali and Côte d'Ivoire were created by an ordinance in addition to a presidential decree. An ordinance is a legislation adopted by the executive that requires parliamentary authorisation and approval before the government can enact it. In the same way, the truth commission in Canada was established by the executive branch after a judicial process.[191]

---

190 In this section, the legal instruments establishing truth commissions that are mentioned will not be quoted. For details on the legal instruments establishing these truth commissions, see above Section 1 of this chapter.

191 See below Section 2.3 of this chapter on Judicial branch.

## 2.2 Legislative Branch

Truth commissions created by the legislative branch, or the Parliament, include those established in South Africa, Ghana, Sierra Leone, Liberia, Democratic Republic of the Congo, Kenya, Nepal, Mauritius, Tunisia, Burundi, Burkina Faso, Gambia, Central African Republic, Paraguay, Brazil, Solomon Islands, Tunisia, Taiwan, South Korea in 2005, Germany and Norway.

The adoption of a law establishing a truth commission does not always mean that this law was the first legal instrument adopted in the process of establishing a truth commission. In some post-armed conflict contexts, the legislative act may have been preceded by the adoption of peace agreements that provided for the establishment of a truth commission. This was the case, for example, in Sierra Leone, Liberia and Nepal.[192]

## 2.3 Judicial Branch

The judicial branch of a state does not generally intervene in the creation of a truth commission. However, in Canada, for the first time, the judicial branch was the body of the state that prompted the establishment of the Truth and Reconciliation Commission of Canada. Indeed, as we saw, the truth commission was the result of a judicial action that ended up with an agreement between the plaintiffs, the Canadian government, representatives of Indigenous peoples and some churches (Indian Residential Schools Settlement Agreement, 2006) in which the creation of a truth and reconciliation commission was one of the provisions. Later, the commission was established by the Canadian executive branch of power. However, this creation was initiated by the Indian Residential Schools Settlement Agreement and was to be implemented under the court's supervision.

## 2.4 Peace Agreements

Several truth commissions, in the context of post-armed conflict, were the result of a peace agreement between the government and an organised armed group. Some of these peace agreements were later followed by a law adopted by the legislative branch of the state. It was the case in Sierra Leone, Liberia and Nepal. However, in some circumstances, the peace agreement alone created the truth commission. This was the case in El Salvador, Guatemala and Colombia.

---

192 See below Section 2.4 of this chapter on Peace agreements.

### 2.5 Bilateral Agreement and Creation by an International Organisation

Some truth commissions can be considered as international truth commissions in terms of the authority that established them. These commissions were established by more than one state or by an international organisation. To date, two truth commissions fall into this category. The first was the truth commission established jointly by a bilateral agreement between Timor-Leste and Indonesia. The other was established by the UN Transitional Administration in Timor-Leste after the armed conflict.[193]

The diversity of authorities that create truth commissions is generally the result of the different contexts that govern the state's decision to establish such a commission. For example, the creation by a peace agreement is linked to the armed conflict experienced by the state. This form of creation is different from that of the executive branch, which usually faces social pressure regarding human rights violations and is obliged to create a truth commission, or which sometimes has to create a truth commission to distinguish itself from the previous political regime or to shame that previous regime. The use of Parliament, in which there are many political parties, makes the truth commission look like the sense of consensus in the country about the need to establish the truth about past abuses or violations.

## 3 The Composition of Truth Commissions

Truth commissions tend to have staff with a wide range of profiles. The staff may include nationals and foreigners, advisers, lawyers, investigators, computer specialists, managers, secretaries, drivers and so on. But the focus of the composition of truth commissions is on the commissioners, who are the members of the commission and whose characteristics are quite diverse.

### 3.1 Number of Commissioners

There is absolutely no rule on how many truth commissioner members there should be. The number of commissioners varies from one truth commission to another; for example, going from three members for the truth commissions

193 Agreement to establish a Commission of Truth and Friendship between Indonesia and Timor-Leste, 14 December 2004.

of El Salvador, Guatemala and Canada,[194] to five for the Solomon Islands,[195] to nine for Kenya[196] and to fifteen for Mali.[197]

## 3.2 Nationality of the Commissioners

In terms of their nationalities, truth commissioners may be classified into three categories: national, international and mixed. The commissioners may be nationals of the state that establishes the commission. For the most part, truth commissions have a national composition. One truth commission, the truth commission of El Salvador, was entirely composed of foreigners.[198] In recent years, there has been a growing number of truth commissions with mixed composition, a combination of commissioners of national and foreign origins. It was the case, for example, in Sierra Leone,[199] Kenya,[200] the Solomon Islands,[201] Honduras[202] Grenada[203] and South Sudan.[204] In South Africa, the

194 For El Salvador, Section 1, Peace Accords signed by representatives of the Government of El Salvador and the Frente Farabundo Martí para la Liberacíon Nacional (FLMN) in Mexico City, 27 April 1991, (UN doc. A/46/553, S/23130, 9 October 1991, Annex, IV, 16; For Guatemala, Agreement on the Establishment of the Commission to Investigate Human Rights Violations and Acts of Violence that have Caused Suffering to the Guatemalan Population, signed by the Government of Guatemala and the Unidad Revolucionaria Nacional Guatemalteca (UNRG) in Oslo, 23 June 1994, (UN doc. A/48/954, S/1994/751, 1 July 1994, Annex II; For Canada, Canada, Indian Residential Schools Settlement Agreement (8 May 2006b); see Section 5, Schedule "N" Mandate For The Truth And Reconciliation Commission.

195 Section 3(3), Solomon Islands, Truth and Reconciliation Commission Act, 2008.

196 Section 10, Kenya, Kenya Truth, justice and Reconciliation Act, 2008 (revised).

197 Art. 2, Mali, Décret No 2014 0013 P-RM portant organisation et modalités de fonctionnement de la Commission vérité, justice et réconciliation, 15 January 2014.

198 El Salvador, 'Report of the Commission on the Truth for El Salvador, From Madness to Hope. The 12-Year War in El Salvador', UN doc. S/25500, 1 April 1993, Annex, 195.

199 Part II, 3.1., Sierra Leone, Truth and Reconciliation Commission Act, 2000.

200 Section 10, Kenya, Kenya Truth, Justice and Reconciliation Act, 2008 (revised): 9 members (3 non-citizens and 6 nationals).

201 Section 3 (3), Solomon Islands, Truth and Reconciliation Commission Act, 2008: 5 members (3 nationals and 2 non-nationals).

202 Art. 3, Honduras, Decreto Ejecutivo Nùmero PCM 011-2010, 13 de abril de 2010 (3 foreigners out of 5 members).

203 Grenada, 'Truth and Reconciliation Report, Redeeming the Past. A Time for Healing', vol. 1, 2006, 11 (2 nationals and 2 foreigners).

204 Section 5.2.3.2, Signed Revitalized Agreement on the Resolution of the Conflict in South Sudan (R-ARCSS), Addis Ababa, 12 September 2018, Section 5.2 Commission of Truth, Reconciliation and Healing (CTRH): 7 members (4 nationals and 3 from other African States).

act establishing the truth commission opened the possibility of appointing two foreigners as members.[205]

### 3.3 Gender Representation

Gender representation has become a common requirement in many legal instruments that are used to establish truth commissions. Some of these require women to be included in their composition. The legal instruments with such requirements are, for example, those of Tunisia,[206] Timor,[207] Taiwan,[208] South Sudan,[209] Central African Republic,[210] Nepal,[211] Liberia[212] and Kenya.[213]

---

205 Section 7 (b), South Africa, Promotion of National Unity and Reconciliation Act, No. 34, 1995 "…Provided that not more than two persons who are not South African citizens may be appointed as commissioners."

206 Art. 19, Tunisia, Organic Law 2013-53 on the establishment of transitional justice and its organisation, 24 December 2013, Title II: "La proportion des membres de chaque sexe ne peut être inférieur au tiers." The commission was composed of 15 members.

207 Section 4.1, Regulation No. 2001/10, On the Establishment of a Commission for Reception, Truth and Reconciliation in East Timor, UN doc UNTAET/REG/2001/10, 13 July 2001: "At least thirty per cent (30%) of the National Commissioners shall be women." The commission was composed of "five to seven National Commissoners," *ibid.*

208 Art. 8, Taiwan, Act on Promoting Transitional Justice CH, Executive Yuan, 27 December 2017 (creation and Statute of the Transitional Justice Commission: "The chairperson, vice chairperson, and three other commissioners shall serve in fulltime positions, while the remaining four commissioners shall serve in part-time positions; provided, however, that among all the commissioners, members of a single political party shall not exceed three in number, and members of either gender shall not be fewer than three in number." The commission was composed of nine members, *ibid.*

209 Section 5.2.3.2, Signed Revitalized Agreement on the Resolution of the Conflict in South Sudan (R-ARCSS), Addis Ababa, 12 September 2018, Section 5.2 Commission of Truth, Reconciliation and Healing (CTRH): 7 members (at least 3 women) out of 7 members.

210 Art. 7, Central African Republic, Loi No. 20.009 portant création, organisation et fonctionnement de la commission vérité, justice, réparation et réconciliation (CVJRR), 07 avril 2020: at least 4 women out of 11 members.

211 Para. 3 (2), Nepal, The Enforced Disappearances Enquiry, Truth and Reconciliation Commission Act, 2071 (2014), Nepal Gazette 2071/01/28 (11 May 2014): at least 1 woman out of 5 members.

212 Section 7, Liberia, An Act to Establish the Truth and Reconciliation Commission (TRC) of Liberia, 2005: "not less than four (4) women" out of 9 members.

213 Section 10 (a), Kenya, Kenya Truth, justice and Reconciliation Act: at least one woman among the "non citizens" members of the Commission. In addition, regarding the citizens members of the Commission: "In nominating or appointing persons as commissioners, the National Assembly and the President shall have regard to gender equity and regional balance," see *Ibid*, First Schedule.

### 3.4 Geographical or Regional Representation of the State

Some acts creating truth commissions take into account the geographical representation or representation of regions or different parts of the country. This demand can be found in the act creating the truth commission in Sierra Leone.[214]

### 3.5 Professional Qualifications

There is no restriction on the qualifications of commissioners. Observation of the composition of truth commissions shows that there is considerable diversity in this area. One might think that because truth commissions are set up to deal with human rights violations, their members would be specialists in these areas of violations or lawyers. The composition of truth commissioners does include law specialists, including eminent university professors, lawyers, human rights activists and so on.[215] But many commissioners are not legal specialists. To give just a few examples, theologians, medical professionals and engineers, etc, can be found in the composition of truth commissions.[216]

## 4 The Mandate of Truth Commissions

The mandate of truth commissions varies greatly from one truth commission to another. It is therefore difficult to describe the mandates of the nearly fifty truth commissions that have been established around the world. However, it is possible to divide the mandate of truth commissions into three categories. First, all truth commissions have an investigative mandate. Second, the majority of truth commissions are mandated to make recommendations. Even if the mandate to make recommendations is not explicitly mentioned in the legal instrument establishing a truth commission, truth commissions make recommendations in their final reports. Third, truth commissions sometimes have

214 Sierra Leone, Sierra Leone TRC Act, Schedule – Subsection (1) of section 3), a (v).

215 For example, International Law professor William Schabas was a member of the Sierra leone truth commission and International Law professor Christian Tomuschat, was a member of the Guatemala truth commission.

216 For example, among the members of the Liberia truth commission were "a registered nurse" (Commissioner Oumu K. Syllah), "an electrical engineer" (Commissioner Ambassador Rev. Gerald Coleman), and a "Methodist prelate." See Liberia, 'Report of the Truth and Reconciliation Commission', vol. II, Monrovia, 2009, 15–18. However, these commissioners also had other professional activities, see *ibid.*

other elements in their mandate, which vary from one commission to another. Among these elements, reconciliation and sometimes peace seem to be the most common. The first and second categories include what most truth commissions have in common in terms of their mandates. The third category includes elements that do not always appear in the mandates of all truth commissions.

### 4.1 Investigations

Almost all truth commissions have an investigative mandate, and where this is not the case, investigations are always a part of their work. These investigations generally relate to violations of human rights or, in the case of armed conflicts, violations of international humanitarian law. However, the similarities between all truth commissions end there, because the content of this investigative mandate is not the same for all of them. It varies from one commission to another. So, what is important to find out is what the truth commissions are investigating. What do they have to investigate? In this area, a distinction has been made between specialised and generalist truth commissions.[217] This distinction is based on the mandate of the truth commissions as set out in the legal instruments establishing them. Specialised truth commissions are those established to investigate specific human rights violations, violations against a specific and identified group of persons, or violations committed during a specific event. Generalist commissions are those that have investigated non-specific violations or groups of persons. These investigations are usually limited to a period of time defined by the legal text establishing the truth commission or by the truth commission itself. Truth commissions use various methods to investigate.

#### 4.1.1 Specialised Truth Commissions

Specialised truth commissions can be divided into two main categories: the types of violations, crimes or abuses that are investigated, and the groups of victims of violations that are investigated.

In terms of specialisation according to crimes or abuses, the majority of the first truth commissions were specialised truth commissions. They were

217 On this categorisation, see an article in French, Emmanuel Guematcha, 'Les commissions vérité: maillon faible de la lutte contre l'impunité en Afrique ?' in Catherine Maia, Jean-François Akandji-Kombé, Jean-Baptiste Harelimana (ed), *L'apport de l'Afrique à la justice internationale pénale* (L'Harmattan, 2018).

responsible for investigating disappearances or enforced disappearances. In fact, this violation of human rights, which consisted in the abduction and "disappearance" of people often suspected of being opponents of dictatorial regimes, was very common in the countries that established the first truth commissions. Finding out the truth about these disappeared people was therefore the mandate of these first truth commissions.[218] In the 1970s and 1980s, the Ugandan (1974), Bolivian (1982) and Argentine (1983) truth commissions were mandated to investigate disappearances or enforced disappearances.[219] The focus on enforced disappearances is not, however, limited to these first commissions. The Sri Lankan truth commissions were also entrusted with investigations into disappeared persons, as was the Moroccan truth commission.[220]

The specialisation of truth commissions in terms of the violations they investigate is not limited to enforced disappearances. The Moroccan truth commission, for example, was mandated to investigate arbitrary detention in addition to enforced disappearances. The mandate of the Panamanian truth commission included the investigation of violations of the fundamental right to life, including enforced disappearances.[221] Similarly, the Mauritius truth commission was mandated to investigate slavery and forced labour.[222]

With regard to specialisation by category of persons, the specialised truth commissions, set up to investigate violations suffered by certain category of persons, have tended to be established in states that have not experienced dictatorships or armed conflicts in their recent history. These are also developed states with fewer economic problems than most transitional or post-conflict states in Latin America and Africa. The categories of persons concerned are, first and foremost, Indigenous peoples. Canada was the first country to establish a truth commission exclusively to investigate abuses committed against Indigenous peoples in the context of Indian residential schools.[223]

---

218 Mark Freeman, *Truth Commissions and Procedural Fairness* (Cambridge University Press 2006) 33.

219 See above for the legal texts creating these truth commissions.

220 *Ibid.*

221 Art. 1, Panama, Decreto Ejecutivo No. 2, 18 de enero de 2001.

222 Mauritius, Truth and Justice Commission Act 2008, para. 3.

223 Australia had established a commission to investigate violations against aboriginal children in Australia. However, it was not a so-called "truth" commission. See: Australia, 'National Inquiry into the Separation of Aboriginal and Torres Strait Islander Children from Their Families, Bringing them home: Report of the National Inquiry into the Separation of Aboriginal and Torres Strait Islander Children from Their Families', 1997.

This experience, which was widely publicised in the media, has inspired Nordic countries such as Norway, Sweden and Finland to create truth commissions to investigate abuses against Indigenous peoples.

Apart from these cases, a truth and reconciliation commission has been set up in Honduras to investigate events that took place in the context of a coup d'état.[224] In the end, few truth commissions are specialised. Most of them are generalists.

### 4.1.2 Generalist Truth Commissions

Generalist truth commissions are mandated to investigate a range of violations. Their specificity is that their mandates do not limit their investigations to, for example, one particular human rights violation. Many legal instruments that have created truth commissions have mandated them to investigate human rights violations or serious human rights violations. These commissions include those established in Brazil,[225] South Africa,[226] Chile,[227] Burundi,[228] Côte d'Ivoire,[229] South Korea (2005),[230] Ecuador (2007),[231] Gambia,[232]

224 Honduras, Decreto Ejecutivo Nùmero PCM 011-2010, 13 de abril 2010.

225 Art. 1, Brazil, Lei Nº 12.528, 18 de novembro de 2011.

226 Para. 3 (1, a), Promotion of National Unity and Reconciliation Act 34, 1995. For the definition of gross violations, see para. 1: " 'gross violation of human rights' means the violation of human rights through- (*a*) the killing, abduction, torture or severe ill-treatment of any person; or (*b*) any attempt, conspiracy, incitement, instigation, command or procurement to commit an act referred to in paragraph (*a*)."

227 Art. 1, Chile, National Commission for Truth and Reconciliation, Supreme Decree No. 355: "Serious violations are here to be understood as situations of those persons who disappeared after arrest, who were executed, or who were tortured to death, in which the moral responsibility of the state is compromised as a result of actions by its agents or persons in its service, as well as kidnappings and attempts on the life of persons committed by private citizens for political purposes."

228 Art. 6 para. 1, Burundi, Loi nº1/ 18 portant création, mandat, composition, organisation et fonctionnement de la commission vérité et réconciliation, 15 mai 2014.

229 Art. 5, Ordonnance No. 2011-167 portant création, attributions, organisation et fonctionnement de la commission dialogue, vérité et réconciliation, du 13 juillet 2011.

230 Section 1, South Korea, Framework Act on Clearing up Past Incidents for Truth and Reconciliation, Enacted by Law No. 7542, 31 May 2005.

231 Art. 1, Ecuador, Ministerial Accord No. 305 Se creó la Comisión de la Verdad "para impedir la impunidad," 3 de mayo de 2007.

232 Section 13 (a), Gambia, Truth, Reconciliation and Reparations Commission Act, 2017. For the definition, see para. 1, *ibid.*

Ghana,[233] Guatemala,[234] Haiti,[235] Solomon Islands,[236] Indonesia-Timor,[237] Kenya,[238] Liberia,[239] Mali,[240] Nepal,[241] Uganda (1986),[242] Paraguay,[243] Peru,[244] Central African Republic,[245] Democratic Republic of the Congo,[246] Sierra Leone,[247] Chad,[248] Timor[249] and Colombia.[250] In the field of human rights, the implementation of transitional justice mechanisms has been criticised for focusing exclusively on violations of civil and political rights, such as physical violence, violations of the right to life and the prohibition of torture

233 Section 3 (1, a), Ghana, The National Reconciliation Commission Act, 2002.

234 Agreement on the Establishment of the Commission to Investigate Human Rights Violations and Acts of Violence that have Caused Suffering to the Guatemalan Population, signed by the Government of Guatemala and the Unidad Revolucionaria Nacional Guatemalteca (UNRG) in Oslo on 23 June 1994, (UN Doc. A/48/954, S/1994/751, 1 July 1994, Annex II.

235 Art. 2, Haiti, Arrêtés créant la Commission nationale de vérité et justice, 17 décembre 1994/28 mars 1995.

236 Section 5 (1, b), Solomon Islands, Truth and Reconciliation Commission Act, 2008.

237 Agreement to establish a Commission of Truth and Friendship between Indonesia and Timor-Leste, 14 December 2004, para. 14 (a).

238 Section 5 (a), Kenya, Truth, Justice and Reconciliation Commission Bill, 9 May 2008.

239 Art. IV, section 4 (a), Liberia, Truth and Reconciliation Commission Act, 2005. For definitions, see art. II.

240 Art. 2, Mali, Ordonnance No. 2014-003/P-RM portant création de la commission vérité, justice et réconciliation, 15 janvier 2014.

241 Section 3, Nepal, The Enforced Disappearances Enquiry, Truth and Reconciliation Commission Act, 2071 (2014), Nepal Gazette 2071/01/28 (11 May 2014). See also Preamble of the text. For the definition, see section 2 (j).

242 Uganda, The Commission of Inquiry Act Legal Notice No. 5, 16 May 1986.

243 Art. 3, Paraguay, Ley No. 2225, Por la cual se crea la Comisión de Verdad y Justicia, 16 de octubre de 2003.

244 Art. 1, Peru, Decreto Supremo No. 065-2001-PCM, 4 de junio de 2001.

245 Art. 6, Central African Republic, Loi No. 20.009 portant création, organisation et fonctionnement de la commission vérité, justice, réparation et réconciliation (CVJRR), 07 avril 2020.

246 Art. 8 (c), DRC, Loi No. 04/018 portant organisation, attributions et fonctionnement de la commission vérité et réconciliation, 30 juillet 2004.

247 Section 6 (1) Sierra Leone, The Truth and Reconciliation Commission Act, 2000.

248 Art. 2, Chad, Décret No. 014/P.CE/CJ/90 portant création de la commission d'enquête sur les crimes et détournements commis par l'ex-Président, ses co-auteurs et/ou complices, 29 décembre 1990.

249 Regulation No. 2001/10, On the Establishment of a Commission for Reception, Truth and Reconciliation in East Timor, UN doc UNTAET/REG/2001/10, 13 July 2001, section 3.1. For the definition see section 1 (c): "'Human rights violations' means: (i) violations of international human rights standards; (ii) violations of international humanitarian law; and (iii) criminal acts."

250 Para. 5.1.1.1.2, Colombia, Final Agreement to End the Armed Conflict and Build a Stable and Lasting Peace.

and ill-treatment, as set out in treaties such as the 1966 International Covenant on Civil and Political Rights.[251] Even though many truth commissions have focused on these violations, some have interpreted their mandate as including violations of economic, social and cultural rights, notably in Sierra Leone[252] and Timor Leste.[253]

Apart from investigating human rights violations, some truth commissions were created in the context of an armed conflict and were tasked to investigate international humanitarian law violations. This was the case in Sierra Leone,[254] Colombia,[255] Liberia[256] and Burundi.[257] Some truth commissions were mandated to investigate crimes; for example, crimes against humanity for the Haiti and Nepal truth commissions,[258] economic crimes for the Liberia, Kenya and Burkina-Faso truth commissions,[259] political crimes for the DRC truth commission[260] and blood crimes for the truth commission of Burkina

251 Dustin N Sharp, 'Addressing Economic Violence in Times of Transition: Toward a Positive-Peace Paradigm for Transitional Justice' (2012) 35(3) *Fordham International Law Journal* 780, 783; Louise Arbour, 'Economic and Social Justice for Societies in Transition' (2007) 40 *New York University Journal of International Law and Politics* 1; Prosper Maguchu, *Transitional Justice and Socio-Economic Rights in Zimbabwe* (T.M.C. Asser Press 2019); William Schabas, 'War Economics, Economic Actors, and International Criminal Law' in Karen Ballentine and Heiko Nitzsshke (eds), *Profiting from Peace. Managing the Resource Dimensions of Civil War* (Lynne Rienner Publishers 2005) 435–437.

252 Sierra Leone, 'Report of the Truth and Reconciliation Commission of Sierra Leone, Witness to Truth', vol. 1, chap. 1, 37–38, para. 52.

253 Timor Leste, 'Report of the Commission of Reception, Truth and reconciliation, *Chega!*', 2005, Part 7, chap. 7. 9.

254 Section 6 (1), Sierra Leone, The Truth and Reconciliation Commission Act, 2000.

255 Para. 5.1.1.1.2, Colombia, Final Agreement to End the Armed Conflict and Build a Stable and Lasting Peace.

256 Art. IV, section 4 (a), Liberia, Truth and Reconciliation Commission Act, 2005. For definitions, see Art. II.

257 Art. 6 para. 1, Burundi, Loi n°1/ 18 du 15 mai 2014 portant création, mandat, composition, organisation et fonctionnement de la commission vérité et réconciliation.

258 Art. 3, Haiti, Arrêtés créant la Commission nationale de vérité et justice, 17 décembre 1994/28 mars 1995; Section 3, Nepal, The Enforced Disappearances Enquiry, Truth and Reconciliation Commission Act, 2071 (2014), Nepal Gazette 2071/01/28 (11 May 2014). See also the Preamble of the text.

259 Art. IV, section 4 (a), Liberia, Truth and Reconciliation Commission Act, 2005; Section 5 (a) Kenya, Truth, Justice and Reconciliation Commission Bill, 9 May 2008; Art. 4, Burkina Faso, Loi organique n°003-2015/cnt portant attributions, composition, organisation et fonctionnement de la commission de la réconciliation nationale et des réformes.

260 DRC, Art. 8 (c), Loi No. 04/018 portant organisation, attributions et fonctionnement de la commission vérité et réconciliation, 30 juillet 2004.

Faso.[261] Other expressions are used in the mandate of truth commissions to determine the object of their investigations; for example, politically motivated violence in Togo,[262] violations in Tunisia,[263] serious cases of violence in El Salvador[264] and terrorist violence in Peru.[265]

So, to summarise, most of the generalist truth commissions have been mandated to investigate human rights violations or grave human rights violations, others to investigate violations of international humanitarian law. Their mandates may sometimes also refer to other specific violations or crimes.

### 4.1.3 Period Investigated

The legal instruments that create specialised and generalist truth commissions have sometimes determined the period covered by their investigations. These periods generally depend on the country's history in relation to the violations committed, and are determined by the political authorities that create truth commissions. Consequently, they vary a lot from one commission to another. Few examples will illustrate this diversity. The truth commission of Gambia was mandated to investigate human rights violations and abuses "from 1994 to January 2017";[266] in Peru, it was from May 1980 to November 2000;[267] in the Central African Republic, from 29 March 1959 to 31 December 2019;[268] in the DRC from 30 June 1960 until the end of transition;[269] in Sierra Leone, "from the beginning of the Conflict in 1991 to the signing of the Lomé Peace Agreement";[270] in the Solomon Islands from 1 January 1998 to

261 Art. 4, Burkina Faso, Loi organique No. 003-2015/cnt portant attributions, composition, organisation et fonctionnement de la commission de la réconciliation nationale et des réformes.

262 Art. 2, Togo, Décret No. 2009/046/PR portant création de la commission vérité, justice et réconciliation, 25 février 2009.

263 Art. 39, Tunisia, Loi organique 2013-53 relative à l'instauration de la justice transitionnelle et à son organisation, 24 décembre 2013.

264 Peace Accords signed by representatives of the Government of El Salvador and the Frente Farabundo Martí para la Liberacíon Nacional (FLMN) in Mexico City on April 27, 1991, (UN Doc. A/46/553, S/23130, October 9, 1991, Annex, IV).

265 Art. 1, Peru, Decreto Supremo No. 065-2001-PCM of 4 June 2001, art. 1.

266 Section 13 (a), Gambia, Truth, Reconciliation and Reparations Commission Act, 2017.

267 Art. 1, Peru, Supreme Decree no065-2001-PCM.

268 Art. 1, Central African Republic, Loi portant création, organisation et fonctionnement de la Commission vérité, justice, réparation et réconciliation, 7 avril 2020.

269 Art. 8 (c), DRC Loi No. /04/018 portant organisation, attributions et fonctionnement de la Commission vérité et reconciliation, 30 juillet 2004.

270 Section 6.1, Sierra Leone, Truth and Reconciliation Commission Act, 2000.

23 July 2003;[271] in South Korea (2005) "from August 14, 1945 to the end of the Korean War period" for some violations, and "to the end of the authoritarian regimes" for others;[272] in South Sudan "from the date of signing of [the] Agreement to July 2005";[273] in Taiwan, from 15 August 1945 to 6 November 1992;[274] in Timor Leste, from 25 April 1974 to 25 October 1999;[275] in Togo from 1958 to 2005;[276] in Tunisia from 1 July 1955 to the adoption of the Transitional justice law;[277] in Paraguay, from May 1954 to 2003;[278] in Uganda (1986) from 9 October 1962 to 25 January 1986;[279] in Haiti, from 29 September 1991 to 15 October 1994;[280] in Kenya, from 12 December 1963 to 28 February 2008;[281] in Liberia, from 1979 to 14 October 2003;[282] in Mali, from 1960 to 2013;[283] in Mauritius from "the colonial period up to the present";[284] and in South Africa, from 1 March 1960 "to the cut-off date,"[285] which according to the *Truth and Reconciliation Commission Act* meant "the latest date allowed as the cut-off date in terms of the Constitution as set out under the heading 'national Unity and Reconciliation'."[286]

However, the legal instruments of some truth commissions do not mention the period to be covered by the investigations. This was the case, for example, in Côte d'Ivoire, Argentina and Nepal (2014). When the legal instrument establishing truth commissions fails to provide the *ratione temporis* mandate of the

---

271 Section 5 (1), Solomon Islands, Truth and Reconciliation Commission Act, 2008.

272 Art. 2, (3, 4 and 5), South Korea, Framework Act on Clearing up Past Incidents or Truth and Reconciliation, 31 May 2005.

273 Section 5.2.2.3.1 of Signed Revitalized Agreement on the Resolution of the Conflict in South Sudan (R-ARCSS), Addis Ababa, 12 September 2018.

274 Art. 3 (1), Taiwan, Act on Promoting Transitional Justice CH, Executive Yuan, 27 December 2017.

275 Section 1 (c) and section 3, Timor Leste, Regulation no. 2001/10.

276 Art. 4, Togo, Décret no. 2009-046/PR portant création de la commission vérité, justice et réconciliation, 25 février 2009.

277 Art. 17, Tunisia, Loi organique 2013-53 du 24 décembre 2013, relative à l'instauration de la justice transitionnelle et à son organisation.

278 Art. 3, Paraguay, Ley nº 2225, Por la cual se crea la Comisión de Verdad y Justicia, 16 de octubre de 2003.

279 Uganda, Commission of Inquiry Act, 1986.

280 Art. 2, Haiti, Arrêté créant la Commission Nationale de Vérité et Justice, 17 décembre 1994.

281 Section 5 (a), Kenya, Kenya Truth, Justice and reconciliation Commission Act, 2008.

282 Section 4 (a), Liberia, Liberia TRC Act, 2005.

283 Art. 3, Mali Ordonnance portant création de la Commission vérité, justice et réconciliation, 15 Janvier 2014.

284 Section 3 (1), Mauritius, Truth and Justice Commission Act, 2008.

285 Section 3 (a), South Africa Promotion of National Unity and Reconciliation Act, *op. cit.*

286 Section 2, *ibid.*

investigations, it is up to the truth commission to solve the issue or to determine the period covered by its mandate. The Côte d'Ivoire truth commission did not give a clear indication of the period to be covered by its investigation. However, in its final report, it referred to the 1960s and to post-electoral violence in the 2010s.[287] The Argentinian truth commission referred to the period between 1976 and 1982 in its summary of the atrocities committed in Argentina.[288]

It is also worth noting that in spite of the precision of the period being covered by their mandate, some truth commissions, as in Sierra Leone, went far beyond what was indicated and explicitly assumed that decision in their final report.[289]

### 4.1.4 Methods of Investigation

In order to investigate, truth commissions use many of the tools used in the judicial field to find their evidence, such as hearings that can be confidential or public, document analyses, expert works or reports and sometimes field reports.[290] Some truth commissions, such as those in South Africa and Sierra Leone, have had legal instruments that gave them powers such as issuing a subpoena, which helped them to compel people to testify before them or to produce documents.[291]

To conclude, truth commissions present the findings of their investigations in their final reports. These findings vary. Depending on the truth commission in question, the final reports may include, for example, the history of the state in relation to the violence; the violations of human rights and international humanitarian law; the crimes or other abuses committed; the context of the violence and its consequences; the identification of institutional or individual responsibility for the violations committed; and the identification of groups or categories of victims or individual victims of violations. In these final reports,

287 Côte d'Ivoire, Commission Dialogue, vérité et réconciliation, 'Rapport final', 2014, 12.

288 Argentina, 'Nunca Más (Never Again) – Report of Conadep', 1984, see Part I, general introduction.

289 Sierra Leone, 'Report of the Truth and Reconciliation Commission of Sierra Leone, Witness to Truth', vol. 1, 2004, 43, paras. 69-71.

290 See Emmanuel Guematcha, *Les Commissions vérité et les violations des droits de l'homme et du droit international humanitaire* (Pedone 2014), 103–111.

291 See, for example, South Africa, Promotion of National Unity and Reconciliation Act 34, section 13. For Sierra Leone, TRC Act of Sierra Leone, 2000, section 8 (1) (g). On that topic, see Mark Freeman, *Truth Commissions and Procedural Fairness* (Cambridge University Press 2006) 188–221.

truth commissions also make recommendations, as often required by their mandate.

## 4.2 Recommendations

Truth commissions are also mandated to make recommendations after their investigation to find the truth. The legal instruments that establish commissions generally make it clear and sometimes indicate and detail the kind of recommendations that they have to make.[292] Even if the legal instruments do not mention making recommendation in their mandate, truth commissions

292 See, for example:

Chile, Supreme Decree No. 355 of 25 April 1990, Art. 1 (c and d);

El Salvador, Peace Accords signed by representatives of the Government of El Salvador and the Frente Farabundo Martí para la Liberacíon Nacional (FLMN) in Mexico City on April 27, 1991, UN Ddoc. A/46/553, S/23130, October 9, 1991, Annex, IV (3);

Haïti, Arrêté du 17 décembre 1994 créant la Commission Nationale de Vérité et de Justice, Art. 7 and 8;

South Africa, Promotion of National Unity and Reconciliation Act, No. 34, 1995, section 4 (f, g and h);

Sierra Leone, The Truth and Reconciliation Commission Act 2000, section 15 (2);

Peru, Supreme Decree no065-2001-PCM, Art. 2 (d);

Panama, Ministerio de Gobierno y Justicia, Decreto Ejecutivo No. 2 de 18 de enero de 2001, Art. 2 (c);

Timor Leste, Regulation No. 2001/10 on the Establishment of a Commission for Reception, Truth and Reconciliation in East Timor, UN doc. UNTAET/REG/2001/10, 13 July 2001, section 3.2 (c);

Ghana, The National Reconciliation Commission Act, Act 611, 11 January 2002, section 3 (b);

Paraguay, Ley No. 2225, Por la cual se crea la Comisión de Verdad y Justicia, 16 de octubre de 2003, Art. 2 (h and i);

Democratic Republic of the Congo, Loi No. 04/018 portant organisation, attributions et fonctionnement de la commission vérité et réconciliation, 30 juillet 2004, Art. 8 (l);

Indonesia/ Timor Leste, Agreement to establish a Commission of Truth and Friendship between Indonesia and Timor-Leste, 14 December 2004, section 14, (c);

Liberia, An Act to Establish Truth and Reconciliation Commission of Liberia, 12 May 2005, section 4 (e);

South Korea, Framework Act on Clearing up Past Incidents or Truth and Reconciliation, Law No. 7542, 31 May 2005, Art. 32 (4);

Ecuador, Ministerial Accord No. 305, 3 de mayo de 2007, Se creó la Comisión de la Verdad "para impedir la impunidad", Art. 2 (d);

Kenya, Truth, Justice and Reconciliation Commission Bill, 9 May 2008, section 6 (k, l);

Solomon Islands, Truth and Reconciliation Commission Act, 2008, section, section 16 (2);

Togo, Togo, Décret No. 2009-046/PR portant création de la commission vérité, justice et réconciliation, 25 février 2009, Art. 2;

do make recommendations in their final reports, and generally call on states to respect and implement these recommendations.[293] These recommendations vary a lot from one truth commission legal instrument to another. *Inter alia* and depending on the truth commission, these recommendations cover individual or collective reparations such as restitution, financial compensation, satisfaction measures like apologies;[294] propositions of prosecutions and/or amnesties,[295] of administrative sanctions,[296] of institutional reforms,[297] and of bodies in charge of following up and the implementation of the recommendations;[298] and measures to restore a lasting peace and/or reconciliation.[299] Thus, the observation of the types of recommendations that a truth commission can make shows that there is a link between a truth commissions and other mechanisms of transitional justice such as prosecutions, reparations and guarantees of non-repetition such as institutional

---

Côte d'Ivoire, Ordonnance No. 2011-167 du 13 juillet 2011 portant création, attributions, organisation et fonctionnement de la commission dialogue, vérité et réconciliation, 13 juillet 2011, Art. 5;

Tunisia, Loi organique 2013-53 relative à l'instauration de la justice transitionnelle et à son organisation, 24 décembre 2013, Art. 43 and 44;

Nepal, The Enforced Disappearances Enquiry, Truth and Reconciliation Commission Act, 2071 (2014), section 13 (d, e);

Mali, Ordonnance No. 2014-003/P-RM portant création de la commission vérité, justice et réconciliation, 15 janvier 2014, Art. 2;

Burkina Faso, Loi organique No. 003-2015/CNT portant attributions, composition, organisation et fonctionnement de la commission de la réconciliation nationale et des réformes, 23 January 2015, Art. 4;

Gambia, Truth, Reconciliation and Reparations Commission Act, 2017, section 13 (a, iv);

Central African Republic, Loi No. 20.009 du 07 avril 2020, portant création, organisation et fonctionnement de la commission vérité, justice, réparation et réconciliation (CVJRR), Art. 65.

293 See above, the final reports of truth commissions.

294 See below Chapter 7, Section 3, for details on reparation and truth commissions.

295 See, for example, the final report of the truth commission of Liberia, 'Report of the Truth and Reconciliation Commission, Consolidated Final Report', vol. II, 2009, see 349–353 on prosecutions, and 403 on amnesty.

296 See, for example, Liberia, *ibid*, 353.

297 See, for example, Kenya, 'Report of the Truth, Justice and Reconciliation Commission', vol. 4, 2013, 31 on police reform.

298 See, for example, the report of the truth commission of Sierra Leone, Sierra Leone TRC final Report, 'Witness to Truth' vol. 2, chap. 4, 266, para. 211.

299 See, for example, the final report of the truth commission of Colombia, Colombia, 'Hay futuro si hay verdad, Informe Final, Hallazgos y recomendaciones de la Comisión de la Verdad de Colombia', 2022, 841–890; and Kenya, 'Report of the Truth, Justice and Reconciliation Commission', vol. 4, 2013, 62.

reforms.[300] Through their recommendations, truth commissions can trigger other actions that can be taken and other mechanisms of transitional justice that can be implemented.

### 4.3 Contributing to Reconciliation and Peace

Not all truth commissions have reconciliation included in their mandate. For example, the Chadian truth commission, established in 1990, did not have a reconciliation mandate. However, contributing to reconciliation is central to the mandate of many truth commissions. This part of the mandate is so important that truth commissions are sometimes referred to as "truth and reconciliation commissions." This is certainly the result of the influence that the South African Truth and Reconciliation Commission has had, thanks to its international reputation. Truth commissions with the word "reconciliation" in their name are mandated to contribute to reconciliation. This was the case, for example, with the South African Truth and Reconciliation Commission, the Ghanaian National Reconciliation Commission, the Gambian Truth, Reconciliation and Reparations Commission, the Kenyan Truth, Justice and Reconciliation Commission, the Solomon Islands Truth and Reconciliation Commission, and the Truth and Reconciliation Commission of Canada. However, even if some truth commissions did not have the word "reconciliation" in their name, the legal instruments establishing them mandated some of them to contribute to reconciliation. This was the case, for example, of the law establishing the Peruvian truth commission, which emphasised the role of the truth commission in relation to "national reconciliation,"[301] and of the legal instrument creating the truth commission of Brazil.[302]

The inclusion of peace in mandates of truth commissions is proposed in the context of an armed conflict and the signing of peace agreements. Peace agreements provided for the creation of the truth commissions in Liberia, Sierra Leone and Colombia, and, these truth commissions were to contribute to the establishment of a lasting peace, as were some international criminal tribunals created by the UN Security Council. This suggests that truth commissions and judicial proceedings may share common goals in the field of transitional justice.

---

300 For details on some these links, see below Section 5 of this chapter, and Chapter 7, Section 3.1.2.

301 Art. 1, Peru, Decreto Supremo No. 065-2001-PCM, Crean Comisión de la Verdad, 2 Junio 2001.

302 Art. 1, Brazil, Lei No. 12.528, de 18 de Novembro de 2011.

## 5 Links between Truth Commissions and Judicial Proceedings

Apart from their recommendations that can be linked to other mechanisms of transitional justice such as reparations or institutional reforms, truth commissions often share links with judicial proceedings. During periods of transition or following an armed conflict, when states face difficulties in engaging in prosecutions, truth commissions have often been considered as an alternative to criminal justice. However, they are now generally seen as complementary to criminal prosecutions following a dictatorship or an armed conflict. The work of truth commissions and the reports they produce have sometimes led to prosecutions in states in transition.[303] In some cases, criminal proceedings were initiated while these commissions were working. This was the case, for example, in Colombia, Sierra Leone and Timor-Leste.[304] Similarly, several truth commissions have recommended prosecutions against perpetrators of crimes or violations in, for instance, Kenya[305] and Chad.[306]

A more relevant illustration of the connection between truth commissions and prosecutions is the use of their final reports in judicial proceedings, both nationally and internationally. As discussed earlier in this book, the work of the Sierra Leonean truth commission was used in the trial of Charles Taylor, Liberia's former head of state, for crimes committed in Sierra Leone during an armed conflict.[307] The same is true for the work of the Chadian truth commission in the judicial proceedings against Hissein Habré, the former president of

303 See Alison Bisset, *Truth Commissions and Criminal Courts* (Cambridge University Press 2012), 9–43.

304 For analysis of these cases in Colombia, see Line Jespersgaard Jakobsen, 'Colombia as the 'Laboratory' for Transitional Justice: Consolidation and Innovation of Global Formulas' (2024) 18(3) *International Journal of Transitional Justice* 422; in Sierra Leone, see William Schabas, 'The Relationships between Truth Commissions and International Courts: The Case of Sierra Leone' (2003) 25(4) *Human Rights Quarterly*1035; and in Timor-Leste, see Suranjan Weeraratne, 'Assessing the Many Faces of Transitional Justice in Timor-Leste' in Ajlina Karamehić-Muratović, Laura Kromják (eds), *Remembrance and Forgiveness. Global and Interdisciplinary Perspectives on Genocide and Mass Violence* (Routledge 2020).

305 Kenya, 'Report of the Truth, Justice and Reconciliation Commission', 2013, vol. 4, 161 ff.

306 Chad, 'Commission d'enquête sur les crimes et détournements commis par l'ex-Président, ses co-auteurs et/ou complices' (L'Harmattan 1992) 98.

307 SCSL, Trial Chamber II, *The Prosecutor v. Charles Ghankay Taylor*, No. 2003-01-T, Judgement, 18 may 2012, para. 18, note 58.

Chad, before the Extraordinary African Chambers,[308] and for the report of the Salvadoran truth commission in civil proceedings against former military leaders accused of crimes committed in El Salvador during the country's civil war.[309] In the Gambia, as seen earlier in this book, a Special Accountability Mechanism has been established and a Special Prosecutor's Office is responsible for investigating and prosecuting crimes and violations described and reported by the Gambian truth commission.[310]

However, some truth commissions have had the power to exonerate perpetrators from prosecution under certain conditions. The South African truth commission, for example, could grant amnesty to individuals who revealed the truth about politically motivated crimes they had committed.[311] Some truth commissions, such as those of Liberia,[312] Gambia[313] and Timor/Indonesia,[314] recognised the possibility of recommending amnesties for those who disclosed the full truth about the crimes or abuses they had committed. Nevertheless, under the Liberia truth commission Act, amnesty could not cover crimes against humanity and international humanitarian law violations,[315] and under the Gambia truth commission Act, crimes against humanity were excluded from the scope of amnesty.[316]

In the field of the relationships between truth commissions and judicial bodies, the possibility of using truth commissions and their activities as sub-

308 Chambres africaines extraordinaires-Extraordinary African Chambers (Chambre d'instruction), Ordonnance de non renvoi partiel, de mise en accusation et de renvoi devant la chambre africaine extraordinaire d'assises, 15 février 2015, 21.

309 See, for example, US District Court Southern District of Florida, *Romagoza c. Garcia, Plaintiff's Pocket Memorandum of Law in Support of the Admissibility of the United Nations Truth Commission Report*, 17 may 2002. For comments, Beth Van Schaack, 'Command Responsibility: The Anatomy of Proof in *Ramagoza v. Garcia*' (2003) 36(3) *University of California Davis Law Review* 1213.

310 Special Prosecutor's Office Act, 2024, an Act to establish an independent and autonomous Special Prosecutor's Office as the first phase in establishing the Special Accountability Mechanism for the investigation, prosecution and adjudication of cases of serious human rights violations and international crimes and domestic crimes specified in or related to acts and omissions described in the report of the Truth, Reconciliation, and Reparations Commission (TRRC), which occurred between July 1994 and January 2017.

311 Section 4, c, South Africa, Promotion of National Unity and Reconciliation Act, No. 34, 1995.

312 Art. VII, section 26 (g), Liberia, TRC Act, 2005.

313 Section 19 (1), Gambia, Truth, Reconciliation and Reparations Commission Act, 2017.

314 Section 14, c (i) of Terms of Reference for the Commission of Truth and Friendship Established by The Republic of Indonesia and The Democratic Republic of Timor-Leste, 5 August 2006.

315 Art. VII, section 26 (g), Liberia, TRC Act, 2005.

316 Section 19 (3), Gambia, Truth, Reconciliation and Reparations Commission Act, 2017.

stitutes for judicial proceedings has been ruled out by some international human rights bodies, such as the Inter-American Court of Human Rights.[317] In the same vein, the creation and activities of truth commissions in transitional states in order to establish peace and reconciliation, the adoption of amnesty or conditional amnesty and negotiations between opposed parties in the context of armed conflict have been considered challenges when criminal proceedings of the ICC are implemented. In these cases, the possibility of stopping or avoiding investigations or prosecutions in the name of the "interests of justice" provided in Article 53 of the ICC Statute has been questioned. Article 53 of the ICC Statute provides that:

> 1. The Prosecutor shall, having evaluated the information made available to him or her, initiate an investigation unless he or she determines that there is no reasonable basis to proceed under this Statute. In deciding whether to initiate an investigation, the Prosecutor shall consider whether:
>
> [...]
>
> (c) The information available to the Prosecutor provides a reasonable basis to believe that a crime within the jurisdiction of the Court has been or is being committed; The case is or would be admissible under article 17; and Taking into account the gravity of the crime and the interests of victims, there are nonetheless substantial reasons to believe that an investigation would not serve the interests of justice.
>
> [...]
>
> 2. If, upon investigation, the Prosecutor concludes that there is not a sufficient basis for a prosecution because:
>
> [...]
>
> (c) A prosecution is not in the interests of justice, taking into account all the circumstances, including the gravity of the crime, the interests of victims and the age or infirmity of the alleged perpetrator, and his or her role in the alleged crime; the Prosecutor shall inform the Pre-Trial Chamber and the State making a referral under article 14 or the Security Council in a case under article 13, paragraph (b), of his or her conclusion and the reasons for the conclusion. [...].

Even if it has recognised the complementarity between the truth commissions and international criminal proceedings, the Office of the Prosecutor of the ICC has not, to date, stopped investigations or prosecutions because a

---

317 See Part 3, Chapter 8 (2) of this book.

truth commission has been created in order to establish a lasting peace.[318] It has insisted on meeting the objective of the ICC, which is to fight against the impunity of perpetrators of international crimes such as genocide, crimes against humanity and war crimes, holding that "that there is a difference between the concepts of the interests of justice and the interests of peace and that the latter falls within the mandate of institutions other than the Office of the Prosecutor."[319] The ICC Office of the Prosecutor has pursued investigations and prosecutions, for example, in Mali and Côte d'Ivoire despite the creation of truth commissions in these states.

Finaly, truth commissions and judicial procedures are both considered mechanisms that contribute to the construction of the collective memory of a state in transition. Even if their work in this field is often considered insufficient, their accounts of human rights violations, international humanitarian law violations and international crimes contribute to knowing the truth about these violations and crimes, recognising that they were perpetrated and, thus, helping to remember what happened in order, notably, to prevent the grave mistakes of the past from occurring again.[320]

Thus, truth commissions are one of the main mechanisms of transitional justice today, along with judicial procedures. As we have seen, truth commissions are characterised by great diversity and there is no international standard in this field. Their creation and their operations depend greatly on many factors, such as the context of the state that creates them. Their work can be linked to judicial proceedings because, even if they are non-judicial bodies, they can be the first step towards criminal accountability. Consequently, because they deal with violations of some international legal norms, truth commissions also contribute to the emergence of international transitional justice law.

318 On the interpretation of the "interests of justice" by the Office of the Prosecutor, see ICC (Office of the prosecutor), 'Policy Paper on the Interests of Justice', September 2007. See also, ICC (Office of the Prosecutor), 'Policy paper on case selection and prioritization', 2016, 12.

319 'Policy Paper on the Interests of Justice', *ibid*, 1.

320 On contributions of truth commissions and judicial bodies to transitional justice mechanisms, and their limits, see Elizabeth S Bird and Fraser M Ottanelli (eds), *The Performance of Memory as Transitional Justice* (Series on Transitional Justice, Intersentia 2014).

## 6 Truth Commissions and International Transitional Justice Law

While truth commissions are typically national institutions, they also have links to international law and have contributed to the development of international transitional justice law. First, like judicial proceedings, they are a response to violations of international law, that is, violations of international human rights and humanitarian laws, and international crimes. As seen in this chapter, the establishment of many truth commissions is explicitly linked to their mandate to address violations of human rights and international humanitarian law or international crimes. It is noteworthy that a significant number of texts establishing truth commissions use a lexicon centred on human rights and international law.

Second, the majority of truth commissions utilise international law as the legal framework that guides their investigations and operations. International human rights law forms part of the legal framework of a significant number of truth commissions.[321] It is notable that a number of truth commissions, typically those established in the aftermath of an armed conflict, have also incorporated international humanitarian law into their legal framework.[322] Some

321 See, for example, South Africa, 'Truth and Reconciliation Commission of South Africa Report', 1998, vol. 1, 66, para. 64; Liberia, 'Report of the Truth and Reconciliation Report, Consolidated Final Report', 2009, vol. 2, 50–56; El Salvador, 'Report of the Commission on the Truth for El Salvador, From Madness to Hope, The 12-year war in El Salvador', 1993, 20–22; Guatemala, 'CEH report, Memoria del silencio', T. I, 1998, 44–45 and T. II, 305–308; Sierra Leone, 'Report of the Truth and Reconciliation Commission of Sierra Leone, Witness to Truth', vol. 1, 2004, 36–38; Brazil, Comissão nacional da verdade, 'Relatório', vol. 1, 2014, 34–39; Chile, 'Informe de la Comisión Nacional de Verdad y Reconciliación', tomo 1, (reedition 1996), 15–16; Ecuador, 'Informe de la comisión de la verdad, Sin verdad, no hay justicia', T. 1, 2010, 34–39; Morocco, Commission nationale pour la vérité, l'équité et la réconciliation, 'Synthèse du rapport final (résumé)', 2006, 18, and Instance équité et réconciliation, 'Rapport final', Publications du Conseil Consultatif des Droits de l'Homme, vol. 1, 2010, 54–55; Paraguay, Comisión de verdad y justicia, Informe Final, Anive haguã oiko, T. II, 2008, 18–25, and 154–161 ; Peru, Comisión de la Verdad y Reconciliación, 'Informe Final', T. 1, 2003, 198–201.

322 See, for example, South Africa, 'Truth and Reconciliation Commission of South Africa Report', 1998, vol. 1, 73–76, paras. 91-102; Liberia, 'Report of the Truth and Reconciliation Report, Consolidated Final Report', vol. 2, 51–53 and 55–56; El Salvador, 'Report of the Commission on the Truth for El Salvador, From Madness to Hope, The 12-year war in El Salvador', 1993, 21–22; Guatemala, 'CEH report, Memoria del silencio', T. I, 1998, 45–47 and T. II, 308–312; Sierra Leone, 'Report of the Truth and Reconciliation Commission of Sierra Leone, Witness to Truth', vol. 1, 2004, 38–41; Chile, 'Informe de la Comisión Nacional de Verdad y Reconciliación', T. 1, (reedition 1996), 16–17; Morocco, Commission nationale pour la vérité, l'équité et la réconciliation, 'Synthèse du rapport final (résumé)',

truth commissions have also referred to international criminal law, incorporating international rules concerning international crimes, such as genocide, crimes against humanity and war crimes, into their legal framework,[323] and they have also interpreted "gross human rights violations" to encompass international crimes, including crimes against humanity.[324] Since international law is a part of the legal framework used in their work, the final reports of many truth commissions use international law to legally qualify reprehensible acts as violations of human rights and international humanitarian law, as genocide or crimes against humanity, and so on. At the same time, because they generally use international law, truth commissions must also comply with international standards, especially those of international human rights law, when investigating violations and crimes. For example, even if they are more flexible than judicial bodies in implementing legal procedural rules, truth commissions must respect the rights of the accused and the rights of victims. Thus, truth commissions make use of international law and must comply with the standards of international law.

Third, truth commissions have also recommended transitional states to ratify and/or comply with international law. Indeed, many truth commissions proposed that states ratify some International human rights law (IHRL) treaties as part of measures to avoid the recurrence of human rights violations. For example, because the mandate of the truth commission of El Salvador provided that the commission was to make recommendations in order to avoid the repetition of acts of violence, the commission recommended that El Salvador should ratify some IHRL treaties as part of the measures to ensure the non-repetition of acts of violence and establishment of the rule of law.[325] These IHRL treaties included the "Optional Protocol to the International Covenant on Civil and Political Rights, [the] Optional Protocol to the American Convention on Human Rights (Protocol of San Salvador), [...], [the] United Nations Convention against Torture and Other Cruel, Inhuman or Degrading Treatment or Punishment and the Inter-American Convention to Prevent and

2006, 18, and Instance équité et réconciliation, 'Rapport final', Publications du Conseil Consultatif des Droits de l'Homme, vol. 1, 2010, 55; Peru, Comisión de la Verdad y Reconciliación, 'Informe Final', T 1, 2003, 201–205; Colombia, 'Hay futuro si hay verdad, Informe Final, Hallazgos y recomendaciones de la Comisión de la Verdad de Colombia', 2022, 133.

323 ICL, Guatemala, CEH report, *Memoria del silencio,* T. I, 1998, 45 and T. II, 314–315 (reference to the 1998 Genocide Convention); Peru, Comisión de la Verdad y Reconciliación. 'Informe Final', T. 1, 2003, 206 and 209–211.

324 See, for example, Liberia, 'Report of the Truth and Reconciliation Report, Consolidated Final Report', vol. 2, 2009, 55.

325 El Salvador, 'Report of the Commission on the Truth for El Salvador, From Madness to Hope. The 12-Year War in El Salvador', UN doc. S/25500, 1 April 1993, Annex, 184.

Punish Torture."[326] The Kenyan truth commission, after relating many human rights violations committed by the Kenyan state, recommended that the state ratify many treaties, including the International Convention for the Protection of All Persons from Enforced Disappearance,[327] the ILO Convention 169, the Convention on the Prevention and Punishment of the Crime of Genocide, Convention on the Protection of the Rights of All Migrant Workers and Members of Their Families,[328] and the African Union Convention for the Protection and Assistance of Internally Displaced Persons.[329] For its part, the Chilean truth commission strongly recommended that Chile ratify human rights treaties, stating:

> This Commission first recommends that the Chilean government ratify all international agreements that may be adopted or have been adopted in the area of human rights and to which Chile is not yet a signatory. It is often argued that such treaties or conventions are repetitive and simply pile up, and that hence there is no need to ratify all of them. The Commission believes that even if such is the case, it would be a good idea to ratify treaties and conventions, since such a move would be a step toward strengthening international law. Such a strengthening is absolutely necessary for preventing human rights violations in Chile and around the world.[330]

Some truth commissions have recommended similar legal actions in their final reports.[331] While the recommendations of truth commissions are often not subsequently implemented by states,[332] the focus on the ratification of international law conventions in the recommendations of truth commissions is important. It recalls that avoiding the repetition of past wrongs also depends on the recognition of the international legal framework that enshrines individual and collective rights and prohibits international crimes. It also affirms that

---

326 *Ibid.*

327 Kenya, Report of the Truth, Justice and Reconciliation Commission, vol. 4, 2013, 64.

328 *Ibid*, 66.

329 *Ibid*, 68.

330 Chile, 'Informe de la Comisión Nacional de Verdad y Reconciliación, tomo 2, (Reedition, 1996)', 840. English translation in Report of the Chilean National Commission on Truth and Reconciliation (University of Notre Dame Press 1993), vol. I/II, 1078.

331 Liberia, Final report of the truth commission of Liberia, Consolidated Final Report, vol. 2, p. 385; Report of the CEH, Memoria del silencio, Conclusiones y Recomendaciones, 70, para. 39.

332 In 2025, Kenya, for example, has not still ratified the International Convention for the Protection of All Persons from Enforced Disappearance as recommended.

international law has a central place in the legal measures that transitional and post-conflict states must take to prevent further mass violations and crimes. This reinforces the importance of the construction of the international transitional justice law through the work of truth commissions. Some other transitional justice mechanisms are also a part of this construction.

CHAPTER 7

# The Other Mechanisms of Transitional Justice

The other mechanisms of transitional justice do not have the same international audience as judicial bodies and truth commissions. However, they are also the tools that states have used, sometimes in combination with judicial bodies and truth commissions, to address human rights violations, violations of international humanitarian law and international crimes. There are three other mechanisms of transitional justice: traditional mechanisms, which are generally institutions that existed in some states before colonisation and have been reinvented to deal with the past in times of transition or after armed conflict (discussed in section 1); public administrative procedures against alleged perpetrators, which include vetting, lustration and other processes that have been used to reform institutions or remove certain individuals from public service or the military to ensure that large-scale abuses do not recur (discussed in section 2); and reparations, which are either closely linked to other transitional justice mechanisms or are independent from them (discussed in section 3). All these other mechanisms have influenced the growing of international trannsitional justice law (discussed in section 4).

## 1 Traditional Mechanisms

In the field of traditional justice, Africa has been the main focus of transitional justice scholars and practitioners. In Africa, traditional mechanisms have been used as a part of transitional justice in many states. These mechanisms are forms of justice that differ from the usual formalities of judicial rituals. These procedures generally predate the colonisation of the transitional or post-conflict state in question. The colonisation of these states by Western European countries introduced a new form of justice. Consequently, in most African countries, these old procedures began to coexist with the new justice implanted by the coloniser.

Traditional mechanisms are therefore quite different from the justice system introduced by Western Europeans in colonised countries that later faced armed conflicts, dictatorships and challenges of transition. These traditional mechanisms vary from one country to another. However, it can be said that, in general, traditional mechanisms are far removed from the rigidity of civil or criminal procedures introduced in many African countries during and

HTTPS://DOI.ORG/10.1163/9789004766655-012

after colonisation. In traditional mechanisms, communities generally play an important role in the process. The sanctions used in this form of justice are often different from those used in the modern Western justice system.

In this chapter, we have identified some countries that, first, experienced international humanitarian law violations, human rights violations and international crimes, and second, that used traditional mechanisms as part of their transitional justice. These countries, discussed below, include Rwanda, Burundi and Uganda. Traditional mechanisms have also been envisaged in Liberia and used in Timor-Leste and Sierra Leone as part of the work of truth commissions. These traditional mechanisms also exist in countries such as Mali and the Democratic Republic of the Congo (land disputes and ethnic conflicts).[1] But these two countries will not be examined here because it is difficult to know whether or not they used these mechanisms in the field of transitional justice.

## 1.1 Rwanda: Gacaca

### 1.1.1 Origins and Meaning

In Rwanda, Gacaca are traditional courts that existed before Western colonisation. Bert Ingelaere explains the origins and purpose of the Gacaca in Rwanda:

> It has become common wisdom that the word "gacaca" means "justice on the grass." In fact, the name Gacaca is derived from the word "umugaca," the Kinyarwandan word referring to a plant that is so soft to sit on that people preferred to gather on it. These gatherings were meant to restore order and harmony. The primary aim of the settlement was the restoration of social harmony, and to a lesser extent the establishment of the truth about what had happened, the punishment of the perpetrator, or even compensation through a gift. Although the latter elements could be part of the resolution, they were

1 Some studies have been conducted on these matters. See, for DRC, Janvier Koko, Julien Moriceau, Trevor Krayer, Anne Claire 'Rendering justice without a court? Experiences of community justice in Ituri (in French, Rendre justice sans tribunal? Expériences de justice communautaire en Ituri)', ASF Report, 2023; and for Mali, Diana Goff Madina Diallo Anca-Elena Ursu, 'Under the Microscope: Customary Justice Systems in Northern Mali' CRU Report, 2017.

> subsidiary to the return to harmony between the lineages and a purification of the social order.[2]

These courts began to coexist with the Western legal system that was introduced during colonisation by Germany and then Belgium. After Rwanda became independent in 1962, the two systems continued to coexist. However, with Rwanda's independence, the Gacaca courts underwent a transformation. From then on, these courts played a "filter" role. Cases were generally examined by these courts beforehand. When necessary, cases were referred to the ordinary courts. As Ingelaere put it, "Gacaca represented both the justice of proximity and a handy mechanism to relieve the pressure on the ordinary court system."[3]

### 1.1.2 The Reactivation of Gacaca Courts after the Genocide

In the aftermath of the Rwandan genocide and the bloody conflict between the government and the armed opposition group Front Patriotique Rwandais (FPR), the FPR armed forces won and came to power. They expressed a desire to bring to justice those who had committed crimes, including genocide, during this period of turmoil. As the Rwandan justice system was not fully operational due to a lack of human and material resources in the aftermath of the genocide, many in Rwanda felt that the Gacaca courts should be used to deal with the perpetrators of the genocide.[4] The United Nations High Commissioner for Human Rights, in collaboration with the Rwandan Ministers of Justice and Higher Education, organised a research project on these institutions.[5] The project reflected the view of many Rwandese and several factors contributed to the transformation of the Gacaca courts into genuine transitional justice mechanisms that would deal with the accountability of perpetrators of crimes in the post-conflict Rwandan state. First, several crimes related to the Rwandan genocide or its aftermath were already within the jurisdiction of the Gacaca. These crimes included theft, domestic disputes, land disputes and so on. Second, the Rwandan courts were unable to try all those accused of geno-

2 Bert Ingelaere, 'The Gacaca courts in Rwanda' in Luc Huyse and Mark Salter (eds), *Traditional Justice and Reconciliation after Violent Conflict. Learning from African Experiences* (IDEA 2008) 33.

3 *Ibid*, p. 34.

4 Haut-Commissaire aux droits de l'homme (opération sur le terrain au Rwanda), 'Gacaca le droit coutumier au Rwanda. Rapport final de la première phase d'enquête sur le terrain' 1996, 5.

5 *Ibid.*

cide or crimes against humanity. There were more than 100,000 people who should have been tried for genocide or other crimes. In order to give the Gacaca courts jurisdiction over the genocide and crimes against humanity, Rwanda adopted several laws:

- Organic Law No. 40/2000 of 26 January 2001 Setting up "Gacaca Jurisdictions" and Organising Prosecutions of Offences Constituting the Crime of Genocide or Crimes Against Humanity, Committed Between 1 October 1990 and 31 December 1994.
- Organic Law No. 33/2001 of 22/6/2001 Modifying and Completing Organic Law No. 40/2000 of 26 January 2001, Setting Up "Gacaca Jurisdictions" and Organising Prosecutions for Offences Constituting the Crime of Genocide or Crimes Against Humanity, Committed Between 1 October 1990 and 31 December 1994.
- Organic Law No. 16/2004 of 19/6/2004 on the Organisation, Jurisdiction and Operation of the Gacaca Courts Responsible for Prosecuting and Trying Offences Constituting the Crime of Genocide and Other Crimes Against Humanity Committed Between 1 October 1990 and 31 December 1994.
- Organic Law No. 28/2006 of 2006 Modifying and Complementing Organic Law No. 16/2004 of 19/06/2004 Establishing the Organisation, Competence and Functioning of Gacaca Courts Charged with Prosecuting and Trying the Perpetrators of the Crime of Genocide and Other Crimes Against Humanity, Committed Between 1 October 1990 and 31 December 1994.
- Organic Law No. 13/2008 of 19 May 2008 Amending and Supplementing Organic Law No. 16/2004 of 19 June 2004 on the Organisation, Jurisdiction and Operation of the Gacaca Courts Responsible for Prosecuting and Trying Offences Constituting the Crime of Genocide and Other Crimes Against Humanity Committed Between 1 October 1990 and 31 December 1994.

These laws were adopted to establish the Gacaca courts and gradually improve their implementation and functioning. Thus, the implementation and functioning of the Gacaca courts have been modified and changed in a number of aspects over time, making it sometimes difficult to summarise and present their main characteristics. However, it is possible to present their jurisdiction ratione temporis, ratione logi and ratione materiae and their overall functioning.

### 1.1.3 Jurisdiction

The *ratione temporis* jurisdiction of the Gacaca courts is indicated in the title of the laws adopted and did not change over the time. The Gacaca courts examined crimes committed "between 1 October 1990 and 31 December 1994."

This "temporal space" covered the period of the genocide in Rwanda, that is, 1994. But it went beyond that, because the period taken into account began in 1990, three years before the crimes were actually committed. This was certainly done because the date of 1 October 1990 marked the beginning of the civil war in Rwanda between the rebels and the Rwandan government, which was accused of planning and committing the genocide. The *ratione materia* jurisdiction covered two main crimes: crimes against humanity and genocide. With regard to the *ratione logi* jurisdiction of the Gacaca courts, each Gacaca was competent of trying crimes committed within the area it covered.[6]

### 1.1.4 Organisation and Functioning of the Gacaca

The organisation of the Gacaca courts was particular. In the Organic Law of June 2001, Gacaca courts were created within many administrative levels of Rwanda, that is, "in each Cell, Sector, District and Province of the Republic of Rwanda."[7] Each Gacaca court was composed of three organs: the General Assembly, the Seat and the Coordinating Committee,[8] which themselves encompassed persons designated through a complex system of selection. According to the Organic Law of 2001: "'Members of the Seats for the Cells' 'Gacaca Jurisdictions' and of the general assemblies for 'Sectors', 'Districts' and 'Provinces' 'Gacaca Jurisdictions' are honest Rwandans elected by general assemblies for the Cells in which they are residing."[9] That law also defined what it meant by "honest Rwandans," holding that they were persons who fulfilled several conditions: "a) to have good behaviour and morals; b) to always say the truth; c) to be trustworthy; d) to be characterised by a spirit of sharing speech; e) not to have been sentenced by a trial emanating from the tried case to a penalty of at least six months' imprisonment; f) not to have participated in perpetrating offences constituting the crime of genocide or crimes against humanity; and g) to be free from the spirit of sectarianism and discrimination."

---

6 See Section II, Rationae Loci, Rwanda, Organic Law No.16/2004 Establishing the Organisation, Competence and Functioning of Gacaca Courts Charged with Prosecuting and Trying the Perpetrators of the Crime of Genocide and other Crimes against Humanity, Committed between 1 October 1990 and 31 December 1994, 19 June 2004.

7 Art. 3, Rwanda, Organic Law No. 33/2001 Modifying and Completing Organic Law No. 40/2000 of 26 January 2001 Setting up "Gacaca Jurisdictions" and Organising Prosecutions for Offences Constituting the Crime of Genocide or Crimes against Humanity, Committed between 1 October 1990 and 31 December 1994, 22 June 2001.

8 Art. 5, *ibid.*

9 Art. 10, *ibid.*

The 2004 Organic Law changed the organisation of the Gacaca courts, with the establishment of "the Gacaca Court of the Cell in each Cell, the Gacaca Court of the Sector and the Gacaca Court of Appeal in each Sector of the Republic of Rwanda."[10] The organs of the Gacaca courts were still the General Assembly, the Seat and the Coordinating Committee. Article 14 of the 2004 Organic Law provided that "[m]embers of organs for Gacaca Courts are Rwandans of integrity elected by General Assemblies for their Cells of residence." Persons of integrity were those who fulfilled certain conditions: "1° not to have participated in genocide; 2° to be free from the spirit of sectarianism; 3° not to have been sentenced to a penalty of at least six (6) months of imprisonment; 4° to be of high morals and conduct; 5° to be truthful; 6° to be honest; and 7° to be characterised by a spirit of speech sharing."

The people who sat on the Gacaca courts were not traditional judges found in the Rwanda judicial system, and the Gacaca courts were to introduce restorative justice.[11] The accused were encouraged to tell the victims the truth. They could be sentenced (some of the prison sentences handed down were usually commuted to suspended sentences or community service) or not sentenced at all, particularly for property offences. The aim was to reconcile grievances while punishing those guilty of crimes against humanity and genocide. Those perpetrators found guilty could appeal the decision to another Gacaca court. Nearly 2 million people were tried by the Gacaca courts, which completed their work on the Rwandan genocide in May 2012.[12]

### 1.2 Burundi: The Bashingantahe

In Burundi, there is a traditional justice mechanism called *Bashingantahe*. The expression refers to wise elders, "to men of integrity who are responsible for settling conflicts at all levels, from the top of the hill to the courts of kings."[13]

---

10 Art. 3, Rwanda Organic Law No. 16/2004 on the organisation, jurisdiction and operation of the Gacaca courts responsible for prosecuting and trying offences constituting the crime of genocide and other crimes against humanity committed between 1 October 1990 and 31 December 1994, 19 June 2004.

11 Sylvère Hategekimina, *La justice pénale restaurative : essai de sa mise en œuvre dans les juridictions Gacaca au Rwanda*, Phd Dissertation, University of Nantes, 2009.

12 Human Rights Council, 'National report submitted in accordance with paragraph 5 of the annex to Human Rights Council resolution 16/21', Rwanda, UN doc. A/HRC/WG.6/23/RWA/1, 27 October 2015, para. 38.

13 Assumpta Naniwe-Kaburahe, 'The Institution of Bashingantahe in Burundi' in Luc Huyse and Mark Salter (eds), *Traditional Justice and Reconciliation after Violent Conflict. Learning from African Experiences* (IDEA 2008) 145. On this traditional justice mechanism, see also Dominik Kohlhagen, 'Le bushingantahe au Burundi: Transformations et réminis-

The Bashingantahe have existed for centuries. During colonisation, they coexisted with the colonial courts. They survived colonisation and coexisted with the modern justice system after Burundi's independence, and they continued to play a role in disputes between individuals over land, theft, inheritance, descent and so on.

For ten years (1993–2003), Burundi was torn apart by violent conflict and experienced regular cycles of violence between the Hutus and the Tutsis. Traditional justice courts in Burundi played an essential role in this context, protecting victims and persecuted people, and acting as mediators and conciliators. During and after the conflict, these courts reorganised themselves and played a role in reconciling communities that had been at loggerheads during the conflict.[14] The Bashingantahe were mobilised in this context of conflict resolution. As one scholar put it: "They demonstrated their influence particularly during the massacres of October 1993, when they intervened, interposing themselves as a barrier between the warring parties and attempting to save many lives. In areas where a strong and operational body of *bashingantahe* existed, the damage in terms of loss of human lives was relatively limited and the Bahutu and Batutsi remained united thanks to these elders."[15]

There were efforts to build a lasting peace. In order to put an end to this continuous cycle of violence, the Government of Burundi and many political parties and groups concluded a peace agreement in Arusha in 2000.[16] Article 1 of the Arusha agreement acknowledged that during precolonial times, the existence of the Bashingantahe, made up of elders "who were judges and counsellors at all levels of power," was one of the factors of cohesion in Burundi. Describing the Burundi's judiciary, the peace agreement also included traditional court institutions as part of it, mentioning that they seated at the *colline* level and would render justice with a spirit of conciliation.[17] The parties to the agreement all agreed on the use of traditional justice mechanisms at the local level for local issues.[18]

---

cences d'un concept judiciaire ancien' in Laboratoire d'anthropologie juridique de paris, Cahiers d'Anthropologie du droit 2009, *Dire le droit, rendre la justice* (Karthala 2010).

14 Philippe Ntahombaye and *al., Traditional Institutions of Peaceful Resolution of Conflicts. Testimonies of Bashingantahe During the 1993 Crisis in Burundi,* University of Burundi, 2003.

15 Assumpta Naniwe-Kaburahe, *ibid*, 153–154.

16 Accord d'Arusha pour la paix et la réconciliation au Burundi, 28 août 2000.

17 Art. 9, para. 8, *ibid.*

18 Accord d'Arusha pour la paix et la réconciliation au Burundi, 28 August 2000, 172 (Commentary of article 9, para. 8 of this Agreement).

In spite of some criticisms related to accusations of corruption because of the link between official authorities and the Bushingantahe, traditional justice mechanisms did play a role in settling many disputes and had the confidence of local populations.[19] However, these Burundian Bashingantahe did not enjoy the same status as the Gacaca courts in Rwanda.

### 1.3 Uganda: The *Mato Oput*

The practice of the *Mato Oput* "means 'drinking oput', a bitter root common to Acholi, which must be drunk by both sides to a dispute (usually, in cases of intentional murder or accidental killing) as a symbol that they are willing to swallow and wash away the bitterness that once existed between them."[20] It comes from the Acholi people of northern Uganda, where it is a ritual of reconciliation and forgiveness.[21] The practice could not be considered an "institution" but it could be considered a traditional justice mechanism. Originally, it was a reconciliation rite performed after a murder.[22] It included the payment of "blood money" by the clan of the killer, the ostracisation of the individual responsible for the crime, the sacrifice of animals and the drink of a mixture of "the pounded extract from the roots of the oput tree with an alcoholic drink."[23] The Mato Oput is based on accepting the responsibility and asking forgiveness. This ritual was "predicated on full acceptance of one's responsibility for the crime that has been committed or the breaking of a taboo. In its practice, redemption is possible, but only through this voluntary admission of wrongdoing, the acceptance of responsibility and the seeking of forgiveness, which then opens the way for healing."[24]

The proposition to use this traditional justice mechanism in the scope of transitional justice in Uganda came in the context of an armed confrontation between the Ugandan government and the rebels of the Lord's Resistance Army (LRA), and the perpetration of crimes against humanity and human

---

19 Alexander J Buszka, 'When Alternative Dispute Resolution Works: Lessons Learned from the Bashingantahe' (2019) 67 *Buffalo Law Review* 165, 191.

20 'Report of the High Commissioner for Human Rights and follow-up to the World Conference on Human Rights Addendum', UN doc. A/HRC/4/49/Add.2, 12 February 2007, 18, note 12.

21 See Dinah Senkungu Walusimbi, *Mato Oput: The Drinking of a Bitter Potion Made from the "Oput" Tree* (AuthorHouse 2012).

22 See James Ojera Latigo, 'Northern Uganda: Tradition-based Practices in the Acholi Region' in Luc Huyse and Mark Salter (eds), *Traditional Justice and Reconciliation after Violent Conflict. Learning from African Experiences, Stockholm* (IDEA 2008), 103.

23 See the description of the ceremony in James Ojera Latigo, *ibid*, 104–105.

24 *Ibid*, 107–108.

rights violations. The government requested the intervention of the ICC in 2003 because of crimes committed by rebels of the LRA, and the ICC issued its first arrest warrants. Later, peace talks began between the government and the rebels. They led to the signing of an agreement on the cessation of hostilities between the government and the LRA on 26 January 2006.[25] Both parties also engaged in negotiations for a more comprehensive peace agreement.[26] In these negotiations, the LRA rebels demanded the withdrawal of the ICC arrest warrants as a condition for continuing the peace process, and the Ugandan government referred to the use of the Mato Oput to deal with violations and crimes committed.[27]

In 2007, both parties signed an Agreement on Accountability and Reconciliation.[28] This agreement indicated that the Mato Oput "refers to the traditional rituals performed by the Acholi to reconcile parties formerly in conflict, after full accountability."[29] It also cited the Mato Oput among the traditional mechanisms that "shall be promoted, with necessary modifications, as a central part of the framework for accountability and reconciliation."[30] It is reported that some Mato Oput rituals were held in Uganda.[31] However, the efficiency of this traditional justice mechanism in reaching reconciliation or achieving accountability following crimes against humanity or war crimes has been questioned.[32]

---

25 Agreement on Cessation of Hostilities between the Government of the Republic of Uganda and the Lord's Resistance Army/Movement (LRA/M), 26 August 2006.

26 UN Security Council Report, 'Update Report, Uganda', No. 2, 14 November 2006.

27 *Ibid*, 2. The ICC did not withdraw the arrest warrants.

28 Agreement on Accountability and Reconciliation between the Government of the Republic of Uganda and the Lord's Resistance Army/Movement, Juba, Sudan, 29 June 2007. See UN doc. S/2007/435, 17 July 2007.

29 Para. 1, *ibid.*

30 Para. 3.1, *ibid.*

31 'Report of the Secretary-General on Women and Peace and Security, UN doc. S/2007/567, 12 September 2007, para. 31.

32 See on that matter, 'Report of the High Commissioner for Human Rights and follow-up to the World Conference on Human Rights', Addendum, UN doc. A/HRC/4/49/Add.2 12 February 2007, para. 62; James Ojera Latigo, "Northern Uganda: Tradition-based Practices in the Acholi Region" in Luc Huyse and Mark Salter (eds), *Traditional Justice and Reconciliation after Violent Conflict. Learning from African Experiences, Stockholm,* (IDEA 2008) 113–114; Amos Deogratius Mwaka and Willy Obol Olango, 'Reconciliation Among the Central Luo of Northern Uganda: The Ingredients and Process of Mato Oput' (2023) 9(1) *Cogent Social Sciences* 1, 21–24.

### 1.4 Use of Traditional Justice Mechanisms in the Course of Truth Commissions' Activities

Sometimes, traditional justice can be an integral part of truth commissions. Indeed, some truth commissions have relied on existing forms of traditional justice to better integrate local populations into the reconciliation process at the heart of their activities. Following are two such examples.

In East Timor, in order to achieve reconciliation, the truth commission had a "main reconciliation initiative at the grassroots level [which] was its Community Reconciliation Process (CRP) programme."[33] The CRP was set up to deal with "less serious crimes."[34] It had to decide whether abuses fell into that category. For example, theft, minor assault, arson, the killing of livestock or the destruction of crops were included into that category.[35] The CRP relied on the traditional mechanisms of the *lisan* and *nahe biti boot* ceremonies for its work. The truth commission's final report defined the traditional mechanism of *lisan* as "a combination of beliefs, customs and traditions of East Timorese people."[36] It added that it "varies from community to community and is generally an important aspect of community life, especially in rural areas."[37] The CRP relied on *lisan* procedures during its hearings, whose "primary aim [was] to assist [in] reconciliation between perpetrators, victims and their community."[38] The work of the CRP in which the *lisan* was used involved truth-telling by the perpetrators, questions by victims and reconciliation. The truth commission gave a clear description of the hearings that included a reconciliation ceremony. According to the truth commission:

> Hearings were presided over by a panel of between three and five local leaders, including a Regional Commissioner of the CAVR who would act as chair. At the hearing the perpetrator was required to make a formal public admission, and could be asked questions by victims and community members. Traditional *lisan* procedures and the participation of spiritual leaders were incorporated into the process in accordance with local custom. After hearing from all parties the panel would decide what appropriate "acts of reconciliation" the perpetrator should perform in order to be accepted back into the community. These acts

---

33 Part 9, 2, para. 2, Timor Leste, '*Chega,* The Report of the Reception, Truth, and Reconciliation Timor Leste', 5 vol., 2005.

34 Part 9, 11, para. 34, *ibid.*

35 Part 9, 11-12, para. 36, *ibid.*

36 Part 9, 3 (see the note), *ibid.*

37 *Ibid.*

38 Part 9, 17, *ibid.*

> might include community service, an apology or the payment of reparations. If the perpetrator accepted the panel's decision, an agreement would be drafted in simple terms. It would then be forwarded to the appropriate District Court, where it would be formalised as an Order of the Court. On completion of all required "acts of reconciliation" the perpetrator was automatically entitled to civil and criminal immunity for all actions covered in the agreement.[39]

The East Timor truth commission also referred to the *nahe biti boot* ceremony and wrote that this "ceremony usually takes place with the parties seated on a mat (*biti* in Tetum), hence the term *nahe biti boot* (lit: 'spreading the large mat') to describe the traditional procedure for resolving disputes. The opening of the mat marks the opening of the process of seeking a resolution. Normally, the mat should not be rolled up again until a resolution has been reached."[40] The truth commission reported that "the ceremony of *nahe biti boot* was a part of most of the CRP hearings."[41] Thus, the role of these traditional mechanisms was to foster reconciliation among the Timorese by using mechanisms that were familiar to them.

In Liberia, the truth commission, faced with a large number of potential criminals, recommended the use of the traditional justice mechanism called *Palava hut*, which "derives legitimacy from a host of cultural influences [...] and has the greatest legitimacy and viability in rural areas."[42] According to the truth commission, this recommended mechanism could "foster national healing and reconciliation at the community and grass root levels creating the opportunity for dialogue and peace building."[43] The Palava hut could examine less serious crimes such as "assaults, destruction of property, forced displacement, looting, robbery and extortion," and could pronounce public sanctions against perpetrators, but these perpetrators could seek pardon before them.[44] The truth commission provided a list of more than 7,000 people that it recommended to be brought before the Palava hut, but held that its list was not exhaustive.[45]

Thus, traditional justice mechanisms have become important tools of transitional justice. They are the expression of the appropriation of transitional

---

39 Part 9, 10, *ibid.*

40 Part 9, 5, para. 20, *ibid.*

41 Part 9, 23, para. 87, *ibid.*

42 Liberia, 'Report of the Truth and Reconciliation Commission', vol. 2, 365.

43 *Ibid.*

44 *Ibid.*

45 *Ibid*, vol. 3, Appendices, Title XII: Towards National Reconciliation and Dialogues: The Palava Hut or Peace Forums, 4–142.

justice not only at the national level but also at the rural and community levels within post-conflict or transitional states. This appropriation, even if generally sponsored by the state, is crucial in turning the page. It is often within these rural areas and communities that serious crimes have been committed during armed conflicts or dictatorships. These local communities are therefore often seriously impacted by these crimes. Traditional justice mechanisms, which are at the centre of local transitional justice, offer communities the possibility to stigmatise abuses of the past, to play a role in the field of accountability for abuses, international crimes, violations of human rights and international humanitarian law, to promote reconciliation and re-establish harmony and peace within their communities in order to prevent future atrocities. The public administrative procedures follow the same path.

## 2 Public Administrative Procedures against Alleged Perpetrators: Lustration and Vetting

In the field of transitional justice, administrative measures are the processes that are put in place in transitional or post-conflict states to remove people from their public service positions or to prevent them from occupying public service position because of their implication in crimes and violations of human rights and international humanitarian law. Several public services such as the police, the army and security forces, but also part of the bureaucracy and political elites, may be targeted by these measures. During transition or after an armed conflict, these administrative measures are a core element of institutional reforms and guarantees of non-recurrence, one of the pillars of transitional justice. They may vary from one country to another and several expressions or phrases are used to designate them. Depending on the case, administrative measures may be referred to, for example, as purges, lustration and vetting.

The phrase "purges" was used for a long time. As we have seen in Part 1 of this book, some scholars wrote about purges in their presentation of the history of transitional justice when they referred to the disqualification of individuals from public office after regime changes, in United Kingdom, for example. After the Second World War, "purges" was used to designate the removal of Nazi collaborators from their public service positions in several European countries, whether or not these removals were preceded by trials before special courts.[46] The term was also used during the Cold War when some countries, after experiencing dictatorships, decided to ban some individuals from public office. Greece, for example, adopted "purges" after the colonels' dictatorship in the 1970s.[47]

The phrase "lustration" comes from the Latin word *lustratio* that means "purifying by sacrifice."[48] Lustration actually originated in Antiquity, when it referred to "sacrifices or ceremonies by which the ancient purified their cities, fields, armies or people, defiled by any crime or impurity."[49] In the field of transitional justice, it started to be used in the context of decommunisation of many Central and Eastern European countries at the end of the Cold War. These countries, in order to hold individuals who worked for the previous public administration accountable for serious human rights violations, decided to adopt lustration laws to remove them from the public administration of the post-communist regime. Thus, lustration, in connection with the experiences of Eastern European countries, is "the disqualification and, where in office, the removal of certain categories of office-holders under the prior regime from certain public or private offices under the new regime."[50] In legal doctrine, lustration is often seen as a collective measure applied to the public administration or to some part of the public administration, with some insisting that the generalised nature of the disqualification can sometimes target thousands of people without specifying what they are personally and individually accused of. For example, Cherif Bassiouni, referring to lustration laws in Eastern and Central Europe, wrote that "modern lustration consists of widespread disqualification from governmental positions of those individuals associated with the previous regime."[51] This collective characteristic of lustration is generally criticised and has led to distinguishing it from "vetting."

---

46 See, for example the French case: Denis Salas, 'Introduction. La transition démocratique française après la Seconde Guerre mondiale' in AFHJ, *La justice de l'épuration à la fin de la Seconde Guerre mondiale* (La documentation française, 2008).

47 Harry J Psomiades, 'Greece: From the Colonels' Rule to Democracy' in Neil J Kritz (ed), *Transitional Justice*, vol. II, (United States Peace Institute 1995).

48 Alexandra Barahona de Brito, Carmen González-Enríquez and Paloma Aguilar, 'Introduction' in Alexandra Barahona de Brito, Carmen González-Enríquez and Paloma Aguilar (eds), *The Politics of Memory. Transitional Justice in Democratizing Societies* (Oxford University Press 2001), 6.

49 *Encyclopœdia Britannica: Or, a Dictionary of Arts, Sciences, and miscellaneous, Literature*, 6th Edn, vol. 12, 1823, 266.

50 Hermann Schwartz, 'Lustration in Eastern Europe' in Neil J Kritz (ed), *Transitional Justice*, vol. II, (United States Peace Institute 1995) 461.

51 Cherif Bassiouni, 'Perspectives on International Criminal Justice' (2010) 50(2) *Virginia Journal of International Law* 269, 315.

"Vetting" is different from "lustration" in that it is a process that targets specific individuals to determine whether they are suitable to carry out specific functions and, as a consequence, possibly refusing them access to certain positions on the basis of their past actions. Indeed, in the field of transitional justice and regarding the removal of some people from public office, the United Nations prefers using the phrase "vetting" and defines it "as assessing integrity to determine suitability for public employment."[52] It aims "at excluding from public service persons with serious integrity deficits in order to (re-) establish civic trust and (re-)legitimize public institutions."[53] Vetting, then, is an individualised process.

Many transitional states around the world have experienced lustration or vetting processes in the course of institutional reforms after a dictatorship, an armed conflict or large-scale serious human rights violations. It is not always easy to have access to the original versions of lustration laws or national vetting processes used in these situations. However, several scholars have studied the transitional justice processes in countries that have applied them. They have studied the laws or decrees that were adopted for the most part in the 1990s or later, analysed their implementation or non-implementation, and examined their shortcomings. Regarding implementation of lustration laws in Europe, the states that have been studied include Albania (1991, 1993 and 1995),[54] the former Czechoslovakia (1991 and 1992) with the Czech Republic having continued to apply these laws after the split of that state,[55] Bulgaria (1992),[56] Hungary (1994),[57] Lithuania (1991),[58] Estonia

52 OHCHR, 'Rule of law tools in post-conflict societies. Vetting: An Operational Framework', New York and Geneva, United Nations, 2006, 4.

53 *Ibid.*

54 Valbona Ndrepepaj, 'Lustration laws dealing with state administration in Albania' in Transitional Justice in Albania, Papers compiled by OSCE Presence in Albania and Konrad-Adenauer-Stiftung, 2020, 78–79.

55 Veronika Bílková, 'Lustration: the Experience of Czechoslovakia/The Czech Republic', Conference paper, *Past and Present-Day Lustration: Similarities, Differences, Applicable Standards*", Hosted by the Ministry of Foreign Affairs of the Czech Republic, Prague, Czech Republic, 7 September 2015.

56 Mark S Ellis, 'Purging the Past: The Current State of Lustration Laws in the Former Communist Bloc' (1996) 59(6) *Law and Contemporary Problems* 181, 187–188.

57 *Ibid*, 183–184.

58 Decree Banning KGB Employees and Informers from Government Positions. No. 418, October 1991; Mark S. Ellis, *Ibid.*, 190.

(1992, 1995),[59] Latvia (1993, 1995),[60] Poland (1997),[61] Serbia[62] and Romania (2012).[63] Germany also experienced and implemented administrative measures aimed at dismissing certain persons and excluding some people from holding any public office or position in the future. After the fall of the Berlin Wall, the Unification Treaty "provided the means for extraordinary dismissal when the employee had 'violated the principles of humanity or the rule of law' or had worked for the MfS, and for this reason 'a continuation of the employment contract appear[ed] unacceptable."[64]

Many other countries, often states transitioning from post-armed conflict, have also experienced administrative measures in a vetting process. For example, in Bosnia and Liberia, vetting efforts of law enforcement took place with the help of the United Nations Mission in Bosnia-Herzegovina and the United Nations Mission in Liberia after the armed conflicts.[65] El Salvador experienced the same type of process,[66] as well as Iraq where the efficiency of collective dismissal of public administration employees in preventing new armed clashes and serious violations of human rights has been questioned.[67]

The main role of lustration or vetting during the transitional process is to prevent future violations of human rights by expelling some people from the public administration. This process also has a punitive aspect.[68] For example,

59 Mark S Ellis, *ibid.*, 191–192.

60 *Ibid*, 190–191.

61 *Ibid*, 192–193.

62 Accountability for Human Rights Violations Act ("Official Gazette of the RS" No. 58/2003), translated by the Legal Translation Unit OSCE Mission to Serbia and Montenegro. This has reportedly never been implemented; see Marija Ristic, Serbia's Unused Lustration Law Set to Expire, 27 May 2013, online: https://balkaninsight.com/2013/05/27/serbia-may-be-left-without-lustration/.

63 Mark S Ellis, 'Purging the Past: The Current State of Lustration Laws in the Former Communist Bloc' (1996) 59(6) *Law and Contemporary Problems* 181, 194.

64 See Sanya Romeike, 'Transitional Justice in Germany after 1945 and after 1990', International Nuremberg Principles Academy, Occasional Paper No. 1, 50.

65 'Report of the Special Rapporteur on the promotion of truth, justice, reparation and guarantees of non-recurrence', UN doc. A/70/438, 21 October 2015, paras. 31-32.

66 Alexander Mayer-Rieckh, 'Vetting' in Carsten Stahn and Jens Iverson (eds), *Just Peace After Conflict* (Oxford University Press 2020) 284–297.

67 Al-Dabbagh Harith, 'Débaathification en Irak: Justice Transitionnelle ou Simple Vengeance' (2014) 27 *Revue Québécoise de Droit International* 31; Miranda Sissons and Abdulrazzaq Al-Saiedi, 'A Bitter Legacy: Lessons of De-Baathification in Iraq', International Center for Transitional Justice, 2013; Cherish M. Zinn, 'Consequences of Iraqi De-Baathification' (2016) 9(2) *Cornell International Affairs Review* 80.

68 On vetting, see 'Report of the independent expert appointed to update the Set of Principles to combat impunity', Ms Diane Orentlicher, UN doc, E/CN.4/2005/102, 18 February 2005, para. 68.

"vetting can also play a part in addressing the 'impunity gap' between the number of individuals who actively participated in past abuses and the capacity of any justice system – national or international – to prosecute all those who may be criminally responsible."[69] This means that in places where it is impossible to try all the individuals who are accused of seriously violating human rights, which is generally the case, vetting may be a way to hold individuals accountable for their past actions. Along these lines, vetting processes can also encourage the telling of truth about past human rights violations. By screening individuals, vetting procedures delve into the history of the state. In some cases, the opening up of archives and access to the truth about the state history and human rights violations can lead to the removal from public office those individuals who have participated "bureaucratically" or otherwise in the commission of human rights violations.

## 3 Reparations

In law, reparations are sometimes defined as "[t]he act of making amends for a wrong" or "[c]ompensation for an injury or wrong."[70] At the heart of reparations, there is the idea that redress of wrong or harm is necessary, and that victims of violations of the law, individually or collectively, are entitled to something that is aimed at redressing the harm that they have endured. Therefore, because of the violations and abuses that are committed in states that have engaged in transitional justice, the issue of the reparations to be awarded to victims is always at the heart of transitional justice. However, the identification of the measures of reparations and the forms of reparations to be awarded to victims can be a challenge when assessing international crimes and violations of human rights and international humanitarian law. Fortunately, there is an emerging body of case law, especially in the field of international human rights law and recently in the field of international criminal law. International human rights bodies such as the European Court of Human Rights and the Inter-American Court of Human Rights, the Inter-American Commission on Human Rights, the African Court on Human and Peoples' Rights and the African Commission on Human and Peoples' Rights, have examined cases of violations of international human rights treaties in states in transition and have concluded that these states have to award reparations

69 *Ibid.*
70 Brian A Garner, *Black's Law Dictionary* (10th edn, Thomson Reuters, 2015) 1087.

to victims of these violations.[71] In the case law, forms of reparations like financial compensation and restitution, or collective forms of reparation, especially in the case law of the Inter-American Court of Human Rights, are identifiable. In the same vein, the statutes of some international and hybrid criminal courts provide for the possibility of these tribunals to order reparations, and there is currently a growing case law from these tribunals in this field.

However, one of the most important developments on reparations comes from the United Nations, where efforts by the United Nations General Assembly have led to the adoption of the *Basic Principles and Guidelines on the Right to a Remedy and Reparation for Victims of Gross Violations of International Human Rights Law and Serious Violations of International Humanitarian Law* in 2005.[72] Even if this legal instrument is not a treaty that imposes legal international obligations on states, it is the more developed international legal instrument in the field of reparations. It includes all the forms of reparations that have been identified in international law, but also provides much more detail. As such, this UN legal instrument is a great help in the identification of what can be considered measures or forms of reparations in the field of transitional justice. According to the legal instrument, "restitution, compensation, rehabilitation, satisfaction and guarantees of non-repetition" are forms of reparation.[73] The following principles detail the significance and the components of these five forms of reparation:

> 19. Restitution should, whenever possible, restore the victim to the original situation before the gross violations of international human rights law or serious violations of international humanitarian law occurred. Restitution includes, as appropriate: restoration of liberty, enjoyment of human rights, identity, family life and citizenship, return to one's place of residence, restoration of employment and return of property.
>
> 20. Compensation should be provided for any economically assessable damage, as appropriate and proportional to the gravity of the violation and the circumstances of each case, resulting from gross violations of international human rights law and serious violations of international humanitarian law, such as: (a) Physical or mental harm; (b) Lost opportunities, including employment, education and social benefits; (c) Material damages and loss of earnings,

---

71 See Part 3 of this book for more details on this case law and other international law developments.

72 Basic Principles and Guidelines on the Right to a Remedy and Reparation for Victims of Gross Violations of International Human Rights Law and Serious Violations of International Humanitarian Law, UN doc. A/RES/60/147, 16 December 2005.

73 Para. 18, *ibid.*

including loss of earning potential; (d) Moral damage; (e) Costs required for legal or expert assistance, medicine and medical services, and psychological and social services.

21. Rehabilitation should include medical and psychological care as well as legal and social services.

22. Satisfaction should include, where applicable, any or all of the following: (a) Effective measures aimed at the cessation of continuing violations; (b) Verification of the facts and full and public disclosure of the truth to the extent that such disclosure does not cause further harm or threaten the safety and interests of the victim, the victim's relatives, witnesses, or persons who have intervened to assist the victim or prevent the occurrence of further violations; (c) The search for the whereabouts of the disappeared, for the identities of the children abducted, and for the bodies of those killed, and assistance in the recovery, identification and reburial of the bodies in accordance with the expressed or presumed wish of the victims, or the cultural practices of the families and communities; (d) An official declaration or a judicial decision restoring the dignity, the reputation and the rights of the victim and of persons closely connected with the victim; (e) Public apology, including acknowledgement of the facts and acceptance of responsibility; (f) Judicial and administrative sanctions against persons liable for the violations; (g) Commemorations and tributes to the victims; (h) Inclusion of an accurate account of the violations that occurred in international human rights law and international humanitarian law training and in educational material at all levels.

23. Guarantees of non-repetition should include, where applicable, any or all of the following measures, which will also contribute to prevention: (a) Ensuring effective civilian control of military and security forces; (b) Ensuring that all civilian and military proceedings abide by international standards of due process, fairness and impartiality; (c) Strengthening the independence of the judiciary; (d) Protecting persons in the legal, medical and health-care professions, the media and other related professions, and human rights defenders; (e) Providing, on a priority and continued basis, human rights and international humanitarian law education to all sectors of society and training for law enforcement officials as well as military and security forces; (f) Promoting the observance of codes of conduct and ethical norms, in particular international standards, by public servants, including law enforcement, correctional, media, medical, psychological, social service and military personnel, as well as by economic enterprises; (g) Promoting mechanisms for preventing and monitoring social conflicts and their resolution; (h) Reviewing and reforming laws contributing to or allowing gross violations of international human rights law and serious violations of international humanitarian law.

This very detailed text covers both individual and collective reparations, as well as material and symbolic reparations. Individual reparations, such as restitution, compensation or rehabilitation, are those awarded to a specific individual, while collective reparations, such as commemoration, which is a satisfaction measure, are awarded to groups or communities. Compensation and restitution are considered to be material reparations, while satisfaction measures such as apologies and memorialisation through, for example, "commemorations and tributes to the victims" are considered to be a symbolic form of reparation.

If we consider the provisions outlined in the 2005 *Basic Principles and Guidelines* quoted above, reparations can be seen as a holistic mechanism of transitional justice that has closed links with other mechanisms of transitional justice. First, the other transitional justice mechanisms may all be seen as reparative measures. Indeed, a judicial decision outlining violations of law can be seen as a reparative measure. Judicial decisions or sanctions are included in "satisfaction," which is a form of reparation. Final reports of truth commissions that have researched and published the truth about violations do so along the same lines because, indeed, "[v]erification of the facts and full and public disclosure of the truth" are among the elements of "satisfaction." Overall, judicial procedures, truth commissions that have sought and published the truth about violations, public administrative procedures such as vetting, and traditional justice mechanisms aiming to bring some accountability to the violations committed during an authoritarian regime or an armed conflict, can all be considered "guarantees of non-repetition," which is a form of reparations. Second, many other mechanisms of transitional justice contribute to the implementation of reparations. Tribunals may award reparations to victims. Truth commissions generally make recommendations of reparations.

However, this important overlap between reparations and other mechanisms of transitional justice does not mean that reparations, as a transitional justice mechanism, cannot be engaged independently. States in transition have sometimes designed reparations programmes that have not been linked to other transitional justice mechanisms.

## 3.1 The Contribution of Other Mechanisms of Transitional Justice to Reparations: Links between Reparations, Judicial Bodies and Truth Commissions

The two main mechanisms of transitional justice, judicial proceedings and truth commissions, have contributed much to reparations in the field of transitional justice.

### 3.1.1 Judicial Proceedings

With regard to international and hybrid criminal tribunals, the statutes of the Nuremberg and Tokyo International Military Tribunals did not contain provisions on reparations. However, despite their differences, many other statutes of international or hybrid criminal tribunals used in post-conflict transitions include provisions on reparations. The statutes of the international criminal tribunals for the former Yugoslavia and for Rwanda each contained a provision on restitution, and both tribunals could order them.[74] This was also the case with the Special Court for Sierra Leone.[75] The statute of the ICC, which was a revolution in the field of reparations in international criminal law when it was adopted in 1998, provides that the court can order reparations to victims, including "restitution, compensation and rehabilitation," and it also provides for the establishment of a Trust Fund for the victims.[76] The statute of the Extraordinary African Chambers did the same.[77] The statute of the hybrid court for Timor provided for the creation of a Trust Fund for victims and the possibility for the court to order that "money and other property collected through fines, forfeiture, foreign donors or other means to be transferred to the Trust Fund."[78] In the same vein, the Rules of Procedure and Evidence of the Special Court for the Central African Republic provided the court the possibility of awarding reparations to victims following a criminal judgment against a perpetrator.[79] These reparations could be individual or collective, and could include financial compensation and rehabilitation measures.[80]

A review of the jurisprudence of these international and hybrid tribunals shows that the ICC has recently provided significant developments on the issue of reparations due to victims of international crimes committed in the context of armed conflicts or in the aftermath of authoritarian regimes. The ICC has ordered reparations for a large number of victims in several of the cases it has examined, following international crimes committed mainly in the context of armed conflicts in Mali and the Democratic Republic of the

74 Art. 24, para. 3 of the ICTY Statute and Art. 23, para. 3 of the ICTR Statute.
75 Art. 19, para. 3 of the SCSL Statute.
76 Art. 75 of the ICC Statute.
77 Art. 27, paras. 1 and 2 of the EAC Statute.
78 Section 25, Regulation No. 2000/15 on the Establishment of Panels with Exclusive Jurisdiction over Serious Criminal Offences, UNTAET Doc. UNTAET/REG/2000/15, 6 June 2000.
79 Article 129, Central African Republic, Loi No. 18.010 portant règlement de procédure et de preuve devant la cour pénale spéciale de la République centrafricaine, 02 juillet 2018.
80 Article 129 (A and B), *ibid.*

Congo.[81] Some hybrid courts have also ruled on reparations and awarded them. This was the case of the Extraordinary African Chambers in the landmark trial of Hissein Habré that awarded compensation to victims,[82] and the case of the Special Court of the Central African Republic that did the same.[83] Some national courts have also awarded reparations to victims of authoritarian regime or after an armed conflict. For example, a Chadian criminal court awarded individual financial reparations and collective reparations to the victims of the authoritarian regime of Hissein Habré.[84] In the same vein, the participation of some traditional justice mechanisms that had quasi-judicial aspects, such as the Rwanda Gacaca, awarded reparations to victims, including restitution and financial compensation.[85]

### 3.1.2 Truth Commissions

Surely, truth commissions are the mechanism of transitional justice that have a closer link to reparations. The act establishing several truth commissions explicitly mandated them to make recommendations in the field of reparations.[86] In the particular case of Gambia, apart from the fact that the Gambian

---

81 See, for example, ICC, *The Prosecutor* v. *Thomas Lubanga Dyilo*, No. ICC-01/04-01/06, 7 August 2012, Decision establishing the principles and procedures to be applied to reparations; ICC, *The Prosecutor* v. *Ahmad Al Faqi Al Mahdi*, No. ICC-01/12-01/15, 17 August 2017, Reparations Order; ICC, *The Prosecutor* v. *Germain Katanga*, No. ICC-01/04-01/07, 27 March 2017, Order for Reparations pursuant to Article 75 of the Statute, 27 March 2017; see also the Annuals Trust Fund for Victims Reports which detailed different measures of reparations for victims after the rulings of the ICC.

82 EAC (Extraordinary African Assize Chamber), *Ministère public* v. *Hissein Habré*, 29 July 2016, Décision sur les intérêts civils; EAC (Extraordinary African Assize Appeals Chamber), *Le Procureur général* v. *Hissein Habré*, 27 April 2017, Arrêt, 132 ff. See also the Trust Fund for Victims created by the African Union that has started to implement a reparation agenda for the victims of the authoritarian regime of Hissein Habré, African Union, *Statute of a Trust Fund for the benefit of victims of the crimes of Hissène Habré*, doc. EX.CL/1040(XXXI) Annex, 2018.

83 Cour pénale spéciale, Chambre d'appel, Arrêt no. 13 relatif à l'appel interjeté contre le jugement n 0001-2023 du 16 juin 2023 de la Première Section d'Assises, 23 octobre 2023.

84 Chad, Cour d'appel de N'Djamena, *Ministère Public et Ismael Hachim et autres c. Saleh Younous Ali, Waroun Fadoul ali et autres*, Répertoire n°01/15, 25 March 2015.

85 See, for example, the account of Bert Ingelaere on this matter: Bert Ingelaere, 'Reparation in Rwanda's Gacaca Courts' (2019) *Témoigner. Entre histoire et mémoire* 84.

86 See, for example, Art. 1 (c), Chile, Supreme Decree No. 355 of 25 April 1990; section 3 (3, c) and section 4 (f), South Africa, Promotion of National Unity and Reconciliation Act, No. 34, 1995; Art.2 (d), Peru, Supreme Decree no0065-2001-PCM; Art. 2 (c), Panama, Ministerio de Gobierno y Justicia, Decreto Ejecutivo No. 2 de 18 de enero de 2001; section 20 (2, h), Ghana, The National Reconciliation Commission Act, Act 611, 11 January 2002;

truth commission "may make regulations for the granting of reparations,"[87] it was directly mandated to "grant reparations to victims in appropriate cases."[88] Even if all the acts establishing truth commissions have not always included a clear reference to the need to recommend reparations, the majority of truth commissions have recommended reparations for victims in their final reports.[89] These recommendations on reparations vary from one commission

---

Art. 2 (i), Paraguay, Ley No. 2225, Por la cual se crea la Comisión de Verdad y Justicia, 16 de octubre de 2003; Art. 25, Democratic Republic of the Congo, Loi No. 04/018 portant organisation, attributions et fonctionnement de la commission vérité et réconciliation, 30 juillet 2004; section 26, j (i), Liberia, An Act to Establish Truth and Reconciliation Commission of Liberia, 12 May 2005; Art. 2 (c), Ecuador, Ministerial Accord No. 305, 3 de mayo de 2007; section 6, k (i), Kenya, Truth, Justice and Reconciliation Commission Bill, 9 May 2008; Art. 2, Togo, Togo, Décret No. 2009-046/PR portant création de la commission vérité, justice et réconciliation, 25 février 2009; Art. 3 (VI), Brazil, Lei N° 12.528, 18 De Novembro De 2011; section 13 (d) and section 23, Nepal, The Enforced Disappearances Enquiry, Truth and Reconciliation Commission Act, 2071 (2014; Art. 2, Mali, Ordonnance No. 2014-003/P-RM portant création de la commission vérité, justice et réconciliation, 15 janvier 2014; Art. 65, Central African Republic, Loi No. 20.009 du 07 avril 2020, portant création, organisation et fonctionnement de la commission vérité, justice, réparation et réconciliation (CVJRR); Titre II, Art. 39, Tunisia, Loi organique 2013-53 relative à l'instauration de la justice transitionnelle et à son organisation, 24 décembre 2013.

87 Section 20 (2), Gambia, Truth, Reconciliation and Reparations Commission Act, 2017.

88 Section 13 (d), *ibid.* See also section 20 (1) *ibid.*

89 See, for example, reparations recommended in the following truth commissions final reports: South Africa, 'Truth and Reconciliation Commission of South Africa Report',- vol. 5, 1998, 170–195; Morocco, Commission nationale pour la vérité, l'équité et la réconciliation, Synthèse du rapport final (résumé), 2006, 18, et Instance équité et réconciliation, 'Rapport final', Publications du Conseil Consultatif des Droits de l'Homme, vol. 3, 2010; Kenya, 'Report of the Truth, Justice and Reconciliation Commission', vol. IV, 2013, 97–124; Mauritius, Report of the Truth and Justice Commission, vol. I, 2011, 394–396; Liberia, 'Report of the Truth and Reconciliation Commission, Consolidated Final Report', vol. II, 2009, 377–381; Nigeria, Human Rights Violations Investigations Commissi-on: Aka Oputa Panel Report, vol. 6, 2002, 46–52 and vol. 7, 2002, 55; Sierra Leone, 'Report of the Truth and Reconciliation Commission of Sierra Leone', vol. 2, 2004, chap. 4; Chad, Commission d'enquête sur les crimes et détournements commis par l'ex-Président, ses co-auteurs et/ou complices, 'Rapport de la Commission nationale d'enquête du ministère tchadien de la Justice', (L'Harmattant 1992) 98; Togo, 'Rapport final de la Commission vérité, justice et réconciliation' 2012, 213–260; Uganda (1986), 'The Report of the Commission of Inquiry into Violations of Human Rights', 1994, chap. 13, 590 and 627–628; Côte d'Ivoire, Commission Dialogue, vérité et réconciliation, 'Rapport final', 2014, 88–90; Guatemala, Memoria del silencio, T. V, 1998, 62–71; El Salvador, 'Report of the Commission on the Truth for El Salvador, From Madness to Hope, The 12-year war in El Salvador', 1993, 186; Brazil, Comissão nacional da verdade, 'Relatório', vol. 1, 2014, 972; Canada, Truth and Reconciliation Commission of Canada, 'Calls to Action', 2015; Chile, 'Informe de la Comisión Nacional de Verdad y Reconciliación', T. 2, (reedition 1996), 823–836; Colombia, Hay futuro si hay verdad,' Informe Final, Hallazgos y recomenda-

to another. They generally include individual and/or collective reparations and mention forms of reparations recognised in international law and in the UN's 2005 *Basic Principles and Guidelines*, including restitution, compensation, rehabilitation, satisfaction and guarantees of non-repetition. They sometimes design reparations programmes, identify the beneficiaries of reparations and propose bodies to implement the reparations. Some reparations have been implemented. For example, El Salvador awarded some reparations to victims and a president of El Salvador later apologised;[90] Guatemala adopted some reparations measures that included compensation and an apology;[91] Sierra Leone implemented rehabilitation measures such as treatment for victims of sexual violence, as well as symbolic reparations such as a remembrance commemoration;[92] Chile awarded compensation to many victims and a president of Chile issued an official apology to victims;[93] Ghana implemented compensation and restitution;[94] South Africa awarded compensation to victims.[95] However, in spite of these efforts, there are many reports on the fact that the

ciones de la Comisión de la Verdad de Colombia', 2022, 791–807; Ecuador, 'Informe de la comisión de la verdad, Sin verdad, no hay justicia, T. 5, 2010, 439–462; Haiti, Commission nationale de Justice et de Vérité, 'Si m pa rele', 29 septembre 1991–14 octobre 1994, Institute of Haïtian Studies, University of Kansas, 1998, 196–198; Paraguay, Comisión de verdad y justicia, 'Informe Final, Anive haguã oiko', T. I, 2008, 102–118; Peru, Comisión de la Verdad y Reconciliación. 'Informe Final', T. 9, 2003, 139–205; Solomon Islands Truth and Reconciliation Commission, 'Confronting the Truth for a better Solomon Islands, Final Report', vol. 3, 2012, 752–761.

90 Alexander Segovia, 'The Reparations Proposals of the Truth Commissions in El Salvador and Haiti: A History of Noncompliance' in Pablo De Greiff, *The Handbook of Reparations* (Oxford University Press 2006) 170–171; 'Report of the Working Group on the Universal Periodic Review. El Salvador', UN doc. A/HRC/14/5, 18 March 2010, para. 20.

91 Human Rights Committee, 'Third Periodic Report of Guatemala to the Human Rights Committee', UN doc. CCPR/C/GTM/3, submitted on 20 October 2009, paras. 36-43.

92 Human Rights Council, 'Assistance to Sierra Leone in the field of human rights. Report of the United Nations High Commissioner for Human Rights', UN doc. A/HRC/13/28, 12 February 2010, para. 44.

93 See for comments on the implementation on reparation, Elisabeth Lira, 'The Reparations Policy for Human Rights Violations in Chile" in Pablo De Greiff (ed), *The Handbook of Reparations* (Oxford University Press 2006) 55–101.

94 Human Rights Council, 'National report submitted in accordance with paragraph 5 of the annex to Human Rights Council resolution 16/21, Ghana', UN doc. A/HRC/WG.6/14/GHA/1, 10 August 2012, para. 108.

95 Human Rights Council, 'Universal Periodic Review, Report of the Working Group on the Universal Periodic Review, South Africa', UN doc. A/HRC/8/32, 23 May 2008, para. 30.

implementation of reparations after the work of truth commissions is either insufficient or ineffective.[96]

### 3.2 The Independent Design of Reparations Programmes by States in Transition

In some cases, transitional or post-conflict states have adopted reparations programmes or awarded reparations that were not directly linked to truth commissions or judicial proceedings. In Brazil, for example, laws were passed in 1995 and in 2002 in order to financially compensate victims of the country's dictatorship.[97] Such laws establishing reparations procedures have also been adopted in transitional states such as Paraguay, as well as Morocco, Malawi and Brazil.[98] Before the creation of the truth commission in 2004, Morocco established an Independent Arbitration Commission in 1999, which awarded compensation to victims of human rights violations.[99]

## 4 Other Transitional Justice Mechanisms and International Transitional Justice Law

Traditional mechanisms are an original response to violations of international law, far removed from the more commonly used institutions. When it comes to dealing with violations and crimes of the past, they are evidence of the capacity of states to reinvent the way justice is delivered in times of transition.

96 See, for example, the inefficient implementation of reparations in Sierra Leone, HRC, Concluding observations on the initial report of Sierra Leone, UN doc. CCPR/C/SLE/CO/1, 17 April 2014, para. 8, mentioning that many victims did not receive reparation; also in South Africa, see 'South African Coalition for Transitional Justice, Comments on the Draft Regulations Published by the Department of Justice Dealing with Reparations for Apartheid Era Victims', 8 June 2011. In Chad, for example, no reparation programme was adopted after the final report of the Chadian truth commission.

97 See, for example, Lei nº 9.140, de 04 de Dezembro de 1995; Lei nº 10.536, de 14 de Agosto de 2002. For comments on these laws, Glenda Mezarobba, 'Between Reparations, Half Truths and Impunity: The Difficult Break with the Legacy of the Dictatorship in Brazil' (2010) 7(13) *International Journal on Human Rights* 7; Ignacio Cano and Patrícia Salvão Ferreira, 'The Reparations Program in Brazil' in Pablo de Greiff (ed), *The Handbook of Reparations* (Oxford University Press 2006).

98 See OHCHR, 'Rule-of-Law Tools for Post-conflict States, Reparations Programmes', 2006, 12.

99 On that commission, see Morocco, Instance Equité et Réconciliation, Commission nationale pour la vérité, l'équité et la réconciliation, Synthèse du rapport final, 2006, 5 and 19–20.

They are also an evidence of the potential existence of mechanisms at the local level in transitional or post-conflict states that can be mobilised to implement transitional justice and respond to violations of human rights, international humanitarian law and international crimes. However, even if they are original responses to violations and crimes in times of transition and can help to bring justice to affected communities, they cannot depart from international human rights standards, for example, with regard to victims and defence rights. In Rwanda, for example, Gacaca faced criticism for not always respecting the rights of the accused – the right to a defence – and the Rwandan authorities have had to reorganise Gacaca to bring them into line with international human rights standards. There have been debates on, for example, whether these traditional mechanisms can be used to respond to serious crimes such as sexual violence committed during armed conflict. Obviously, these traditional mechanisms should not be used for these serious crimes if they are not capable of ensuring that the victims' right to protection and their right to justice are guaranteed. If, for example, the conditions are not met to avoid retraumatisation of the victims, they must not be used for these types of crimes. In short, like truth commissions, they are used to respond to international violations and must respect the human rights of both the accused and the victims.

Of course, the lustration and vetting procedures implemented in transitional states are responses to violations of international law, in particular violations of international human rights law and, in the case of armed conflict, violations of international humanitarian law. However, these national procedures, just as truth commissions and traditional justice mechanisms, must comply with international human rights standards, such as due process and respect for the rights of the accused.[100]

When it comes to reparations, they are rooted in international law. In the field of transitional justice, the contribution of judicial bodies and truth commissions to reparations and the design of reparations programmes by transitional states are clear indications that reparations have a strong place in responses to violations of international law, in particular international crimes and violations of human rights and international humanitarian law. Far from classical reparations between states for violations of international law, these practices of implementing or proposing reparations in times of transition and after armed conflict show that reparations are now part of the growing international transitional justice law.

100 See Part 3 of this book, especially the jurisprudence of the European Court of Human Rights.

# Conclusion of Part 2

The extensive implementation of various mechanisms of transitional justice is a vital sign that transitional justice has become a relevant part of how to deal with international crimes and violations of human rights and international humanitarian law. As we saw with the reparation programmes, truth commissions and judicial bodies, the mechanisms of transitional justice have become complementary and some transitional states have used several mechanisms, simultaneously or consecutively. Practices of states and the international community, materialised by these mechanisms, have become so important and widely diffused that there seems to be no way today to deal with large-scale crimes or violations without referring to transitional justice. Unavoidably, these mechanisms and the practices in the field have been influencing the growing of an international transitional justice law in which international obligations of transitional states are progressively defined.

# PART 3

# The Identification of States' International Obligations in the Field of International Transitional Justice Law

# Introduction to Part 3

Since the 1990s, many scholars and organisations have explored the link between international law and transitional justice in general, or between international law and some mechanisms of transitional justice in particular.[1] In 2004, immediately after defining transitional justice in its report entitled *Rule of Law and Transitional Justice*, the UN Secretary-General connected the work of the UN in that field with international law. He wrote that "[t]he normative foundation for work in advancing the rule of law is the Charter of the United Nations itself, together with the four pillars of the modern international legal system: international human rights law; international humanitarian law; international criminal law; and international refugee law."[2] Later, he held that "[t]ransitional justice has strong foundations in international law, particularly international humanitarian law and international human rights law."[3] In the same vein, the UN Special Rapporteur on the promotion of truth, justice, reparation and guarantees of non-recurrence has examined "the inter-

---

1 See, for example, Kai Ambos, 'The Legal Framework of Transitional Justice: A Systematic Study with a Special Focus on the Role of the ICC' in Kai Ambos, Judith Large and Marieke Wierda (eds), *Building a Future on Peace and Justice: Studies on Transitional Justice, Peace and Development* (Springer 2009); Christine Bell, 'The New Law of Transitional Justice' in Kai Ambos et al. (eds), *Building a Future on Peace and Justice: Studies on Transitional* (Springer 2009); Gerhard Werle and Moritz Vormbaum, *Transitional Justice: The Legal Framework*, (Springer 2022); Valeria Vázquez Guevara, *Truth Commissions and International Law: Jurisdiction, Representation, Authority* (Cambridge University Press 2026); William Schabas, 'Transitional Justice and the Norms of International Law', Presentation to the Annual meeting of the Japanese Society of International Law, Kwansei Gakuin University, 8 October 2011; Helène Tigroudja, *Conflits armés et droit international des droits de l'homme*, Recueil des cours de l'Académie de droit international de La Haye, vol. 444, 2025, in this book, see the section intitled IHRL (International human rights law) and the pillars of transitional justice/In French, DIDH (droit international des droits de l'homme) et piliers de la justice transitionnelle), 365; Noémie Turgis, *La justice transitionnelle en droit international* (Bruylant 2014); Koumba Bories-Dembele, *Le droit à la justice transitionnelle en droit international* (Doctoral thesis, University of Loraine 2024); On some elements regarding transitional justice and international law presented in this Introduction and Part 3, see also Emmanuel Guematcha, 'Human Rights and International Obligations of Post-conflict States', Conference Paper, Association of Human Rights Institutes Annual Conference, University of Postdam, 7 September 2019.

2 'The Rule of Law and Transitional Justice in Conflict and Post-conflict Societies', Report of the Secretary-General, UN doc. S/2004/616, 23 August 2004, para. 9.

3 Guidance Note of the Secretary-General, 'Transitional Justice: A Strategic Tool for People, Prevention and Peace', 2023, 5.

 | HTTPS://DOI.ORG/10.1163/9789004766655-014

national legal standards underpinning the pillars of transitional justice" and refers to international human rights law and international humanitarian law.[4]

However, even if they have attempted to fill the void in that field, the identification of the international obligations of states in transition remains open. The existence of an international transitional justice law depends on the identification of a set of international rules that are aimed at applying to states in transitions, after a dictatorship or after an armed conflict, and are aimed at defining their international obligations. The identification of these obligations is worthy because the times of transition or post-armed conflict are times of constraints and challenges for states that have experienced violations, breaches and crimes, and it is important for the states to know what international law expects them to do in response to these violations, breaches and crimes.

Despite the problems that transitional states may face, international law does not provide that these states are free of international obligations. As seen in the second part of this book, many transitional justice mechanisms rely on the provisions of international law to operate in the field of accountability because the violations, the breaches and crimes that are dealt with during transition or after armed conflicts have themselves a close link with international law. International law here appears as a set of rules in which certain rights are recognised, and in which certain breaches and crimes are defined. Consequently, dealing with the violations of these rights, and with these breaches or crimes can be implemented using international law. In the same vein, dealing with these violations, breaches and crimes cannot be pursued without interrogating the international obligations of states in transition or post-conflict states which are submitted to international law. This is why identifying the international obligations of transitional and post-conflict states and the potential limits of international law in this field is an important part of the step in determining what international transitional justice law contains. To do so, international law sources have to be explored.

In public international law, it is generally accepted that the sources of international law are those listed in Article 38, paragraph 1 of the Statute of the International Court of Justice. This article provides that:

4 'International Legal Standards Underpinning the Pillars of Transitional Justice', Report of the Special Rapporteur on the promotion of truth, justice, reparation and guarantees of non-recurrence, Fabián Salvioli, UN doc. A/HRC/54/24 (2023). See the references to these branches of international law throughout the report.

1. The Court, whose function is to decide in accordance with international law such disputes as are submitted to it, shall apply:
   a. international conventions, whether general or particular, establishing rules expressly recognized by the contesting states;
   b. international custom, as evidence of a general practice accepted as law;
   c. the general principles of law recognized by civilized nations;
   d. subject to the provisions of Article 59, judicial decisions and the teachings of the most highly qualified publicists of the various nations, as subsidiary means for the determination of rules of law.

According to this provision, the sources of international law are international conventions (treaties), international custom, general principles of law recognised by "civilised nations", judicial decisions and doctrine. The identification of international obligations of transitional states within the international transitional justice law has to be done by examining these sources of international law.

In transitional justice, however, there are many non-binding international rules, that are not included in Article 38 of the ICJ Statute and that belong to soft law, that is, a set of rules that are not binding on states but are considered to provide guidance to states in their conduct and to assist in the interpretation of their international obligations. At the international level, through the production of norms by international organisations and others, soft law is an important element to be considered in determining the international rules when it comes to what transitional or post-conflict states should do in the area of accountability for past violations and abuses when implementing transitional justice. Because of the importance of soft law in transitional justice, it is crucial to examine how it provides guidance on the conduct that transitional states should adopt with respect to past serious violations and crimes. In transitional justice, this soft law is generally not opposed to the hard law contained in the sources of international law. Rather, it generally complements the sources of international law that contain international obligations for transitional states and sometimes helps to casuistically clarify these international obligations.

Identifying the international obligations of transitional states through sources of international and the conduct expected from them through soft law is challenging. The main reason for this is that there is currently no explicit set of international rules adopted by states that is solely and explicitly dedicated to transitional justice. This means that an autonomous international transitional justice law does not exist, although the growing number of rules applicable to transitional states may lead to such an autonomy in the future. Rather, international transitional justice law is based on and dependent upon other branches of international law. Indeed, the observation of transitional justice mechanisms presented in Part 2 of this book shows that they make use of several branches of international law that recognise rights of individuals and groups, define international crimes and contain obligations of states. These branches are mainly international human rights law (IHRL), international humanitarian law (IHL) and international criminal law (ICL). For example, international criminal tribunals rely on their statutes, which are part of the development of ICL. Truth commissions use IHRL, IHL and, although rarely, ICL. Reparations for violations and abuses are based on a progressive interpretation of international law and are now an important part of the jurisprudence of the International Criminal Court and some hybrid criminal tribunals. In this context, the international obligations of states and the conduct expected from them in the field of transitional justice have to be drawn from different branches of international law.

So, relying on different branches of international law, this part of the book examines the sources of international law and soft law when it comes to international transitional justice law. Chapter 7 examines the international obligations of transitional states from the sources of international law. Chapter 8 examines the contribution of soft law in the identification and development of international obligations of transitional states.

CHAPTER 8

# The Sources of International Transitional Justice Law and States' Obligations

In order to identify the international obligations of transitional or post-conflict states, this chapter examines the sources of international law listed in Article 38 of the ICJ Statute: treaties or conventions, international custom, general principles of law, judicial decisions and legal doctrine. Against the background of general international law, which provides rules for all branches of international law, the examination of IHL, IHRL and ICL shows that the main sources of international obligations of states in the field of transitional justice are treaties and judicial decisions. The determination of international legal obligations in other sources of international law – international custom, general principles of law and the teachings of eminent publicists (doctrine) – remains controversial as it lacks legal authority in the field of transitional justice. In what follows, Section 1 deals with treaties and transitional justice, Section 2 with decisions of judicial decisions, and Section 3 with the limited importance of other sources of international law in the field of transitional justice.

## 1 Treaties and Transitional Justice

In the contemporary era, treaties represent the primary source of international law. Once a state has consented to be a party to a treaty, whether through ratification or adherence, it is bound by the obligation to respect and implement the provisions of that treaty in accordance with the general rule of public international law, known as the *Pacta Sunt Servanda* rule: "Every treaty in force is binding upon the parties to it and must be performed by them in good faith."[1] Despite the recent exponential development of transitional justice, there is currently no treaty on the subject. This is not to say that there are no treaties that provide international obligations for states in transition. Since transitional states are most often confronted with serious human rights violations, especially violations of the right to life and physical and mental integrity,

1 Article 26 of the Vienna Convention on the Law of Treaties, 23 May 1969. Entered into force on 27 January 1980. United Nations, Treaty Series, vol. 1155, 331.

the international obligations of transitional states are mainly found in international human rights treaties. International humanitarian law and international criminal law also provide some international obligations for transitional states faced with armed conflict and international crimes.

## 1.1 IHRL Treaties and Transitional Justice

Many human rights treaties have been adopted since the end of the Second World War. An examination of these treaties leads to the conclusion that some of their provisions are of good interest to transitional states, both in the field of prevention of human rights violations and in the field of dealing with past human rights violations.

### 1.1.1 Identification of Applicable IHRL Treaties

Although international human rights law has roots that can be traced back several centuries, the birth of modern international human rights law through the adoption of declarations and then treaties is intrinsically and naturally linked to transitional or post-conflict periods. Indeed, modern international human rights law was developed in the context of the end of an armed conflict, the Second World War, which was a period of transition from armed conflict to peace.[2]

In this context, the UN Charter of 1945 made many references to human rights, even though it was not a treaty dedicated to the subject. The UN Charter includes "respect for human rights" among the purposes of the new global organisation (Article 1). The Charter also refers to human rights in the functions of some UN organs, such as the General Assembly (Article 17, paragraph 1, b) and the Economic and Social Council (Article 62, paragraph 2). Thus, in the post–Second World War context, human rights became one of the most important elements of international law. States also began to consider and negotiate a legal instrument devoted exclusively to human rights. Their efforts initially resulted in declarations. The International Conference of American States adopted the American Declaration of the Rights and Duties of Man in April 1948, and the UN General Assembly adopted the Universal Declaration of Human Rights in December 1948. These declarations recognised the

2 On this topic, see, for example, Ellen L Lutz, 'Understanding Human Rights Violations in Armed Conflict' in Julie Mertus and Jeffrey W Helsing (eds), *Human Rights and Conflict. Exploring the Links between Rights, Law, and Peacebuilding* (United States Peace Institute 2006) 24.

rights of individuals without distinction. They were not treaties and therefore did not bind states or create international legal obligations.

However, states did consider adopting human rights treaties to recognise human rights and establish international obligations for states. They began to adopt human rights treaties in the 1950s, and this post–Second World War movement went well beyond that immediate period. A look at the history of the adoption of these treaties shows that between the 1950s and the 2000s, states had concluded at least one core human rights treaty in every decade since the end of the Second World War. In the 1950s, the Council of Europe adopted the European Convention on Human Rights. In the 1960s, the United Nations adopted three human rights conventions (the International Convention on the Elimination of All Forms of Racial Discrimination of 1965, the International Covenant on Civil and Political Rights of 1966 and the International Covenant on Social, Economic and Cultural Rights of 1966). The Organisation of American States adopted the American Convention on Human Rights in 1969. In the 1970s, the United Nations adopted the Convention on the Elimination of All Forms of Violence against Women (1979). In the 1980s, it adopted the Convention against Torture and other Cruel, Inhuman or Degrading Treatment or Punishment (1984) and the Convention on the Rights of the Child (1989). The Organisation of African Unity adopted the African Charter on Human and Peoples' Rights in 1981.

In the 1990s, the United Nations adopted the International Convention on the Protection of the Rights of All Migrant Workers and Members of Their Families in 1990. The League of Arab States adopted the Arab Charter for Human Rights in 1994 (revised in 2004). Following into the next decade, the European Union adopted the Charter of Fundamental Rights in 2000, and the United Nations adopted the International Convention for the Protection of All Persons from Enforced Disappearance and the International Convention on the Rights of Persons with Disabilities in 2006.

Thus, the United Nations has adopted nine core human rights conventions, three regions (Europe, the Americas and Africa) have adopted at least one core or principal human rights treaty, and an organisation that includes African and Asian states has adopted a human rights treaty. Many other human rights treaties have been adopted by regional organisations in Europe, Africa and the Americas. These treaties deal with other rights such as social rights (for instance, European Social Charter of 1961, revised in 1996) or the prohibition of torture (European Convention for the Prevention of Torture and Inhuman or Degrading Treatment or Punishment of 1987), but also with the special protection of categories of persons such as children (for example, Inter-American Convention on the International Return of Children of 1989 and African Charter on the Rights and Welfare of the Child of 1990) or persons with disabilities (Protocol to the African Charter on Human and Peoples' Rights on the Rights of Persons with Disabilities in Africa of 2018).

Thus, in a global movement that began after the Second World War, states adopted international human rights treaties. These treaties apply to the new period of peace after the war. They were designed to apply to a transitional or post-conflict period and to avoid a repetition of what happened during the war. Therefore, from the outset, the IHRL treaties recognised human rights and imposed an inherent obligation on transitional or post-conflict states to prevent violations of these rights.

### 1.1.2 IHRL treaties as a Tool for Non-repetition and Prevention of Human Rights Violations

The idea behind the adoption of international human rights treaties, particularly those adopted in the 1950s and 1960s was that the recognition of human rights and the obligations of states in this field would prevent the recurrence of the atrocities of the Second World War. During the discussions and negotiations that led to the adoption of the first treaty in the field of human rights, the 1950 European Convention on Human Rights, many insisted on the need to recognise the human rights of individuals in order to avoid a repetition of what happened during the war.[3] The preamble of the European Convention on Human rights refers to the fact that "fundamental freedoms [...] are the foundation of justice and peace in the world." The same rationale is found in the United Nations where states adopted several human rights treaties from the 1960s onwards. For example, the preambles of the 1966 ICCPR and ICESCR both state that "recognition of the inherent dignity and of the equal and inalienable rights of all members of the human family is the foundation of freedom, justice and peace in the world." This means that, from the outset, the adoption of human rights treaties and the recognition of individual rights was a way of guaranteeing peace and thus preventing atrocities. State action to prevent human rights violations under this international human rights treaty rationale falls under the guarantees of non-repetition that are at the heart of transitional justice. In international human rights treaties, there is an inherent international obligation for states to ensure the non-repetition of human rights violations in the future, that is, to prevent future violations of the rights

3 See, for example, Collected Edition of the "Travaux Préparatoires" of the European Convention on Human Rights: Preparatory Commission of the Council of Europe, Committee of Ministers, Consultative Assembly, 11 May-8 September 1949, vol. 1, Martinus Nijhoff, 1975, 112.

enshrined in the treaty. And once these treaties have been adopted, states parties also have an obligation to address violations of the rights enshrined.

### 1.1.3 IHRL Treaties and the Dealing with Past Human Rights Violations

With regard to dealing with the past, there are a number of questions that need to be answered: Does IHRL treaties provide legal actions in the case of violations of the human rights they enshrine? Are IHRL treaties applicable to past human rights violations committed during dictatorships or armed conflicts? Does IHRL provide obligations for states with regard to human rights violations committed during authoritarian regimes or armed conflicts? The answers to these questions are logically affirmative, particularly if the state on whose territory these violations were committed was a state party to the IHRL treaties at the time these violations occurred. First, and this is common sense, it would be inconsistent for a treaty to provide for human rights while, in the event of violations of those rights, there are no obligations on states and no legal consequences for those who have committed those violations. This means that states, including transitional states, must always legally respond to human rights violations and address them. Second, as will be explained in this section, IHRL treaties sometimes explicitly indicate what states must do, including in the area of universal jurisdiction, which sometimes allows foreign states to deal with human rights violations committed outside their territory. In this area, there is a clear distinction between, on the one hand, IHRL treaties that deal with specific human rights, such as torture or enforced disappearance, or categories of persons such as women, and, on the other hand, general IHRL treaties.

#### 1.1.3.1 Obligations of Transitional States in IHRL Treaties That Deal with Specific Violations or Categories of Persons

Many IHRL treaties dealing with specific human rights violations or concerning certain categories of individuals contain provisions on how to deal with perpetrators and victims of past human rights violations.

With regard to perpetrators, some of these treaties provide that states have an international obligation to prosecute or extradite, and sometimes to punish, those who have violated the rights they enshrine. This is the case for Article 7 of the 1984 Convention against Torture and Other Cruel, Inhuman or Degrading Treatment or Punishment, which refers to the obligation to prosecute or extradite the perpetrator; Article I(b) of the 1994 Inter-American Convention on Enforced Disappearances, which refers to the obligation to punish, and its Article VI, which refers to the obligation to extradite or prosecute; Article 3 of the 2006 International Convention for the Protection of All Persons from Enforced Disappearance, which insists on the obligation to investigate cases of enforced disappearance and to "bring to justice those responsible," and Article 11 paragraph 1 of the same Convention which leaves open the possibility to extradite the alleged perpetrator; and Article 16, paragraph 5 of the 2006 UN Convention on the Rights of Persons with Disabilities, which imposes obligations on states "to ensure that instances of exploitation, violence and abuse against persons with disabilities are identified, investigated and, where appropriate, prosecuted."

With regard to victims, some of these treaties recognise that they have rights in the event of violations, which logically leads to positive obligations for states parties to ensure that these rights are respected in the aftermath of dictatorships and/or armed conflicts. In general, the rights recognised are essentially the right to have their case investigated, and the right to obtain reparations. Article 24, paragraph 2 of the 2006 International Convention for the Protection of All Persons from Enforced Disappearance provides that victims have "the right to know the truth regarding the circumstances of the enforced disappearance, the progress and results of the investigation and the fate of the disappeared person." The same article provides that state parties have the obligation to "take all appropriate measures to search for, locate and release disappeared persons and, in the event of death, to locate, respect and return their remains" (paragraph 3). Victims have "the right to obtain reparation and prompt, fair and adequate compensation (paragraph 5), and states have the obligation "to ensure" that their "legal system" protects that right. In the same vein, Article 14 of the 1984 Convention against Torture provides that victims are entitled to "an enforceable right to fair and adequate compensation, including the means for as full rehabilitation as possible." It insists on the obligation of states to ensure that victims can obtain redress under their legal system. According to Article 13 of the 1984 Convention, victims have "the right to complain [...] and to have [their] case promptly and impartially examined," and states have the obligation to provide for that right. Article 6 of the 1965 UN Convention for the Elimination of Racial Discrimination provides for the right of "effective protection and remedies" but also insists on "the right to seek [...] reparation or satisfaction." It states that "States Parties shall assure to everyone within their jurisdiction effective protection and remedies, through the competent national tribunals and other State institutions, against any acts of racial discrimination which violate his human rights and fundamental freedoms contrary to this Convention, as well as the right to seek from such tribunals just and adequate reparation or satisfaction for any damage suffered as a result of such discrimination." Thus, victims have the right to the truth, the right to complain and have their case heard, and the right to redress and reparation. Accordingly, when the protected human rights are violated, transitional or post-conflict states parties to these treaties have an obligation to provide victims with the truth, to ensure that their case is heard, and to provide them with redress and reparation.

#### 1.1.3.2 Obligations of Transitional States by General IHRL Treaties

Unlike these IHRL treaties which are dedicated to specific rights or categories of persons, general IHRL treaties do not generally provide equally clear and specific obligations when it comes to how transitional states must deal with violations committed during armed conflicts and authoritarian regimes. Of course, the majority of general IHRL treaties provide for a right to an effective remedy for victims, meaning that states must ensure that there is a response from a state authority when the rights enshrined are violated. Article 13 of the ECHR, Article 47 of the CFREU, Article 2, paragraph 3 of the ICCPR and Article 25 of the ACHR all provide for a right to a remedy before a national court or authority in the event of violations of the human rights enshrined in these treaties. But these provisions do not provide clear guidance on what states must do in order to ensure effective remedies. It is the dynamic interpretation of these and other provisions by some international human rights bodies, as we will see, that specifically defines the international obligations of states.[4]

However, some of these general IHRL treaties provide a right to reparation for specific human rights violations. For example, in the case of a miscarriage of justice, victims have a right to compensation under Article 10 of the ACHR and Article 14, paragraph 6 of the ICCPR; in the case of unlawful arrest, under Article 5, paragraph 6 of the ECHR and Article 3 of Protocol No. 7 to the ECHR; in the case of unlawful detention, under Article 9, paragraph 5 of the ICCPR. So, when these violations are committed, states, including transitional states, have to award reparations to victims. These general IHRL treaties also provide for the possibility for the bodies established by them to monitor respect for human rights by states to award reparation to victims of human rights violations that they have examined. Article 63, paragraph 1 of the ACHR, Article 41 of the ECHR and Article 27, paragraph 1 of the Protocol to the ACHPR establishing the African Court on Human and Peoples' Rights provide for this possibility. If these courts decide to award reparations to victims, states have an

4 See *infra* on judicial decisions and on decisions of UN human rights bodies.

obligation to implement their decisions and to actually award these reparations to the victims.

Meanwhile, perpetrators and accused persons also have rights, and transitional or post-conflict states have an obligation to respect them. These rights, which come under the general heading of the right to a fair trial, the presumption of innocence and the rights of the accused, are recognised in many general international human rights treaties, such as Article 6 of the ECHR, Article 8 of the ACHR, Article 14 of the ICCPR, Article 7 of the ACHPR and Article 13 of the ArCHR.

In summary, depending on the human right or category of persons covered by some IHRL treaties, states have international obligations to investigate certain human rights violations, to prosecute, extradite or punish perpetrators, and to ensure that victims' rights are respected. Under general IHRL treaties, states also have an international obligation to ensure that victims have a remedy when their rights have been violated and to respect the rights of those accused of human rights violations. Transitional states are bound by these international obligations when dealing with past human rights violations.

However, as seen earlier in the introduction of Part 3, transitional states generally face political, economic and social difficulties. These difficulties may have the potential to reduce or prevent their ability to comply with their international obligations. The question may then arise as to whether, in such difficult times, transitional or post-conflict states are permitted to derogate from certain rights and not comply with their international obligations under IHRL treaties.

In the field of the possibility of derogating certain human rights, the African Charter on Human and Peoples' Rights (ACHPR) does not include a list of non-derogable rights, literally leaving African states with no choice but to accept the fact that they cannot derogate from any of the recognised rights. However, many IHRL treaties are not silent. Some of these treaties refer to unusual situations in which a state may be confronted with the impossibility of complying with all international human rights rules. Article 15 of the European Convention on Human Rights (ECHR) refers to "time of emergency"; Article 27 of the American Convention on Human Rights (ACHR) to "time of war, public danger, or other emergency that threatens the independence or security of a State"; Article 4 of the International Covenant on Civil and Political Rights (ICCPR) and Article 4 of the Arab Charter on Human Rights (ArCHR) to "time of public emergency which threatens the life of the nation."[5]

5 See also Art. F of the European Revised Social Charter that refers to "time of war or other public emergency threatening the life of the nation."

In each of these situations, states parties, including transitional states, are allowed to derogate from some, but not all, human rights.[6] The list of human rights that are not subject to derogation varies from one instrument to another. In the ECHR, four human rights are listed: the right to life (except in respect of deaths resulting from lawful acts of war); the prohibition of torture and inhuman or degrading treatment or punishment; the prohibition of slavery and servitude; and the right not to be subject to retroactive application of criminal laws.[7] Three protocols to the ECHR also prohibit derogations from their provisions: Protocol 6 on the abolition of the death penalty in peacetime and the limitation of the death penalty in time of war;[8] Protocol 7 on the principle of *ne bis in idem*;[9] and Protocol 13 on the complete abolition of the death penalty.[10] In the ICCPR, many rights are enumerated: the right to life (except in respect of deaths resulting from lawful acts of war); the prohibition of torture and cruel, inhuman or degrading treatment or punishment; the prohibition of slavery and servitude; the prohibition of imprisonment solely on the ground of inability to fulfil a contractual obligation; the prohibition of lawless punishment; the right to recognition everywhere as a person before the law; and the right to freedom of thought, conscience and religion.[11] In the ACHR, the list is longer and includes: the right to legal personality; the right to life; the right to humane treatment; the freedom from slavery; the freedom from ex post facto laws; the freedom of conscience and religion; family rights; the right to a name; the rights of the child; the right to a nationality; the right to participate in government; as well as the judicial guarantees essential for the protection of the enumerated rights.[12] The ArCHR goes on the same vein by stating that there is "no derogation" from its Articles 5 (right to life), 8 (prohibition of "to physical or mental torture or to cruel, inhuman or degrading treatment or punishment"), 9 (prohibition of medical or scientific experimentation without free and informed consent), 10 (prohibition of slavery, forced labour and human trafficking), 13 (right to a fair trial), 14 (right to liberty and security), 15 (the non-retroactivity of criminal law), 18 (prohibition to be imprisoned for debt or civil obligation), 19 (*ne bis in idem* principle), 20 (rights to persons convicted or accused detained), 22 (right to be recognized as a person by the law), 27 (rights related to the freedom to live in his country), 28 (right to political asylum) and

6 Art. 15(1) and (2) ECHR, Art. 27(1) and (2) ACHR and Art. 4(1) and (2) ICCPR.
7 Art. 15(2) of the ECHR.
8 Art. 3 of Protocol 6 to the ECHR, 28.IV.1983.
9 Art. 4(3) of Protocol 7 to the ECHR, 22.XI.1984.
10 Art. 2 of Protocol 13 to the ECHR, 3.V.2002.
11 Art. 4(2) of the ICCPR.
12 Art. 27(2) of the ACHR.

29 (right to nationality).[13] The provisions of these treaties also insist on a procedure that states parties have to follow when they decide to use these derogation rules, and on an obligation to inform other states parties or a specifically designated body.[14]

Thus, the rationale of these provisions is that even if states facing emergencies, wars or serious difficulties, including transitional states, decide to invoke these provisions, they must still ensure respect for certain rights. This also means that states will have to respect all the international obligations attached to these rights, including, for example, the obligation to ensure the right to an effective remedy for victims in the event of violations. For example, states will still have to respect the right to life and, if this right is (or has been) violated, they will still have to provide an effective remedy for victims. The same reasoning can be extended to the prohibition of torture and inhuman and degrading treatment and other non-derogable rights.

In addition to the three core human rights treaties, some conventions on specific human rights prohibit derogations, which means that transitional states cannot rely on them to restraint the scope of their international obligations in case of violations. Article X of the Inter-American Convention against Enforced Disappearances states: "In no case may exceptional circumstances such as a state of war, the threat of war, internal political instability, or any other public emergency be invoked to justify the forced disappearance of persons. In such cases, the right to expeditious and effective judicial procedures and recourse shall be retained as a means of determining the whereabouts or state of health of a person who has been deprived of freedom, or of identifying the official who ordered or carried out such deprivation of freedom." The International Convention for the Protection of All Persons from Enforced Disappearance goes in the same direction in its Article 1, stating: "No exceptional circumstances whatsoever, whether a state of war or a threat of war, internal political instability or any other public emergency, may be invoked as a justification for enforced disappearance."

For states in transition, the existence of non-derogable rights means that even if they choose to invoke and apply these non-derogable provisions because of the challenges they face, they still have international obligations with respect to the non-derogable rights, most of which, especially the right to life and the prohibition of torture and cruel, inhuman and degrading treatment, are often violated during dictatorships and armed conflicts.

13 Art. 4 (2) of the Arab Charter on Human Rights.

14 Art. 15(3) of the ECHR, Art. 27(3) of the ACHR, Art. 4(3) of the ICCPR and Art. 4 (3) of the ArCHR.

States in transition, therefore, have international obligations under international human rights treaties following human rights violations, whether these obligations relate to some human rights and categories of persons, all human rights, or only non-derogable human rights. The difficulties they may face during transition do not allow them to derogate from all human rights. They cannot stop complying with their obligations under IHRL treaties, which are part of international transitional justice law. International humanitarian law treaties follow the same logic.

### 1.2 International Humanitarian Law Treaties and Transitional Justice

International humanitarian law (IHL) is a branch of international law that provides rules to be respected by the parties engaged in an armed conflict. For a long time, this branch of international law was governed by custom. Beginning in the nineteenth century, however, states began to adopt treaties in this area, as discussed in Part 1 of this book, beginning with the 1864 Geneva Convention for the Amelioration of the Condition of Military Wounded in Armies in the Field. Since then, states have adopted several treaties in the field of armed conflict that have consolidated international humanitarian law, leading to two main categories known as "the law of The Hague" and "the Law of Geneva." These treaties include, in particular, Hague Conventions,[15] which generally contain rules on the conduct of combat, and the four Geneva Conventions and their three protocols,[16] which generally insist on the need to protect the victims at war.

15 See, for example, Hague Convention (II) with Respect to the Laws and Customs of War on Land and its annex: Regulations concerning the Laws and Customs of War on Land, 29 July 1899; Hague Convention (III) relative to the Opening of Hostilities, 18 October 1907; Hague Convention (IV) respecting the Laws and Customs of War on Land and its annex: Regulations concerning the Laws and Customs of War on Land, 18 October 1907; Hague Convention (V) respecting the Rights and Duties of Neutral Powers and Persons in Case of War on Land, 18 October 1907; Hague Convention (VI) relating to the Status of Enemy Merchant Ships at the Outbreak of Hostilities, 18 October 1907; Hague Convention (VII) relating to the Conversion of Merchant Ships into War-Ships, 18 October 1907; Hague Convention (VIII) relative to the Laying of Automatic Submarine Contact Mines, 18 October 1907; Hague Convention (IX) concerning Bombardment by Naval Forces in Time of War, 18 October 1907; Convention (XI) relative to certain Restrictions with regard to the Exercise of the Right of Capture in Naval War, 18 October 1907; Convention (XIII) concerning the Rights and Duties of Neutral Powers in Naval War, 18 October 1907.

16 Geneva Convention (I) for the Amelioration of the Condition of the Wounded and Sick in Armed Forces in the Field, 12 August 1949; Geneva Convention (II) for the Amelioration of the Condition of Wounded, Sick and Shipwrecked Members of Armed Forces at

Today, these international humanitarian law treaties, in particular the Geneva Conventions of 1949, contain rules that must be respected not only by states but also by other belligerents, such as armed opposition groups or rebellions. In this context, the question arises as to the existence of international obligations with regard to violations of IHL committed during armed conflicts. Does international humanitarian law provide transitional justice with international obligations to be implemented by post-conflict states? Are there rules of IHL relating to violations of IHL committed during the armed conflict, and if so, are they still applicable after the end of the armed conflict? First, there are certainly rules of IHL applicable to violations of IHL committed during international armed conflicts and, logically, states have international obligations with respect to these violations. Second, the applicability of these rules to non-international armed conflict may be controversial, but it is consistent.

### 1.2.1 International Obligations of States Concerning Accountability for the Violations of International Humanitarian Law in International Armed Conflicts

There is a certitude about the existence of states' international obligations in cases of "grave breaches" of the IHL committed during an international armed conflict. As discussed in Part 1 of this book, before the Second World War, some treaties and other legal instruments have dealt with the need of prosecutions of those who violated the law during armed conflicts. After the Second World War, states decided to negotiate the adoption of treaties in the field of humanitarian law. This led to the adoption in 1949 of the four Geneva Conventions and, later, of three protocols to these conventions. These conventions, which have been ratified by almost all states, are now the main legal instruments of international humanitarian law, alongside the Hague Treaties adopted before the Second World War and international custom. In the field of transitional justice, therefore, in order to determine the international obligations of post-conflict states with regard to violations committed during an

Sea, 12 August 1949; the Geneva Convention (III) Relative to the Treatment of Prisoners of War, 12 August 1949; Geneva Convention (IV) Relative to the Protection of Civilian Persons in Time of War, 12 August 1949; Protocol Additional to the Geneva Conventions of 12 August 1949, and relating to the Protection of Victims of International Armed Conflicts (Protocol I), 8 June 1977; Protocol Additional to the Geneva Conventions of 12 August 1949, and relating to the Protection of Victims of Non-international Armed Conflicts (Protocol II), 8 June 1977; Protocol additional to the Geneva Conventions of 12 August 1949, and relating to the Adoption of an Additional Distinctive Emblem (Protocol III), 8 December 2005.

armed conflict, it is necessary to go through these main universal conventions.

Strangely enough, a reading of these conventions is somewhat disappointing. There are not many rules devoted to accountability for violations of all the rules contained in the 1949 Geneva Conventions. Rather, in the area of accountability, there are only rules dedicated to what the four conventions call "grave breaches," which impose some international obligations on the states parties. Geneva Conventions I, II and III of 1949 contain a list of these "grave breaches." According to these conventions, these breaches are "any of the following acts, if committed against persons or property protected by the Convention: wilful killing, torture or inhuman treatment, including biological experiments, wilfully causing great suffering or serious injury to body or health, and extensive destruction and appropriation of property, not justified by military necessity and carried out unlawfully and wantonly."[17] Geneva Convention IV of 1949 also has a similar provision, but more detailed. It provides that these grave breaches are "any of the following acts, if committed against persons or property protected by the present Convention: wilful killing, torture or inhuman treatment, including biological experiments, wilfully causing great suffering or serious injury to body or health, unlawful deportation or transfer or unlawful confinement of a protected person, compelling a protected person to serve in the forces of a hostile Power, or wilfully depriving a protected person of the rights of fair and regular trial prescribed in the present Convention, taking of hostages and extensive destruction and appropriation of property, not justified by military necessity and carried out unlawfully and wantonly."[18]

The conventions provide that when these "grave breaches" are committed, states parties have the obligation to take actions in order to identify the perpetrators, prosecute or extradite them, and to respect the rights of persons accused:

> The High Contracting Parties undertake to enact any legislation necessary to provide effective penal sanctions for persons committing, or ordering to be

---

17 See: Art. 50 of the Geneva Convention (I) for the Amelioration of the Condition of the Wounded and Sick in Armed Forces in the Field, 12 August 1949; Art. 51 of Geneva Convention (II) for the Amelioration of the Condition of Wounded, Sick and Shipwrecked Members of Armed Forces at Sea, 12 August 1949; Art. 130 of the Geneva Convention Relative to the Treatment of Prisoners of War (III), 12 August 1949.

18 Art. 147 of the Geneva Convention (IV) Relative to the Protection of Civilian Persons in Time of War, 12 August 1949.

> committed, any of the grave breaches of the present Convention defined in the following Article.
>
> Each High Contracting Party shall be under the obligation to search for persons alleged to have committed, or to have ordered to be committed, such grave breaches, and shall bring such persons, regardless of their nationality, before its own courts. It may also, if it prefers, and in accordance with the provisions of its own legislation, hand such persons over for trial to another High Contracting Party concerned, provided such High Contracting Party has made out a prima facie case.
>
> Each High Contracting Party shall take measures necessary for the suppression of all acts contrary to the provisions of the present Convention other than the grave breaches defined in the following Article.
>
> In all circumstances, the accused persons shall benefit by safeguards of proper trial and defence, which shall not be less favourable than those provided by Article 105 and those following of the Geneva Convention relative to the Treatment of Prisoners of War of August 12, 1949.[19]

These provisions are only applicable in the strict sense and in accordance with common Article 2 of the Geneva Conventions to international armed conflicts. In fact, only common Article 3 of the Geneva Conventions is dedicated to non-international armed conflicts and, even if it contains rules to be respected, it does not provide for any obligation of accountability in case of violation of these rules. Since the Second World War, and particularly since the 1990s, many post-conflict states have experienced non-international armed conflicts. The question therefore arises as to whether states parties to IHL have international obligations with respect to the violations listed in grave breaches but committed during non-international armed conflicts.

### 1.2.2 International Obligations Regarding the Accountability for Grave Breaches Committed during Non-international Conflict?

Unfortunately, there is no IHL treaty today that explicitly provides for accountability, for obligations to investigate, prosecute or punish perpetrators

19 Art. 49 of the Geneva Convention (I) for the Amelioration of the Condition of the Wounded and Sick in Armed Forces in the Field, 12 August 1949. See in the same vein, Art. 50 of Geneva Convention (II) for the Amelioration of the Condition of Wounded, Sick and Shipwrecked Members of Armed Forces at Sea, 12 August 1949; Art. 129 of the Geneva Convention (III) Relative to the Treatment of Prisoners of War, 12 August 1949; Art. 146 of the Geneva Convention (IV) Relative to the Protection of Civilian Persons in Time of War, 12 August 1949.

of "grave breaches" that would have been committed during a non-international armed conflict. It is possible, however, to interpret the 1949 Geneva Conventions broadly and to hold that their provisions on sanctions, prosecutions and/or extradition, and that the respect of the rights of the accused in case of "grave breaches" apply to non-international armed conflicts. Legal experts have proposed this interpretation, based on the objective of IHL to protect humanity from "grave breaches" committed during wars.[20] Indeed, when it comes to the protection of human beings, it would be inconsistent to recognise that certain acts are prohibited, as provided for in common Article 3 of the Geneva Conventions, and at the same time accept that violations of this provision do not require any legal consequences for the perpetrators. The fact that the same conventions contain rules on accountability for "grave breaches" is a clear indication that when IHL in general is seriously violated, states have an obligation to investigate, prosecute and punish the perpetrators, while respecting their rights. This interpretation is also consistent with the fact that violations of common Article 3 are considered war crimes under international criminal law.[21]

However, another legal development in the field of international humanitarian law is the possibility for states to provide amnesty following non-international armed conflicts, a possibility that legal scholar William Schabas has labelled "a bone that sticks in the throats of those who insist upon the illegality of amnesty."[22] Indeed, Article 6, paragraph 5 of the Protocol Additional to the Geneva Conventions of 12 August 1949, which relates to the Protection of Victims of Non-International Armed Conflicts, states that:

> At the end of hostilities, the authorities in power shall endeavour to grant the broadest possible amnesty to persons who have participated in the armed conflict, or those deprived of their liberty for reasons related to the armed conflict, whether they are interned or detained.

---

20 Chile Eboe-Osuji, ' 'Grave Breaches' as War Crimes: Much Ado About ... 'Serious Violations'? ' 9 *International Criminal Court*, online: https://www.icc-cpi.int/sites/default/files/NR/rdonlyres/827EE9EC-5095-48C0-AB04-E38686EE9A80/283279/GRAVEBREACHESMUCHADOABOUTSERIOUSVIOLATIONS.pdf.

21 See art. 8 para. 2 (c) of the ICC Statute.

22 William Schabas, 'Transitional Justice and the Norms of International Law', Presentation to the Annual meeting of the Japanese Society of International Law, Kwansei Gakuin University, 8 October 2011, at 18, online: www.jsil.jp/annual_documents/2011/fall/schabas_trans_just911.pdf.

Even if arguments have been exposed, claiming that it is not applicable to international crimes such as war crimes,[23] this provision clearly leaves open the possibility for states to provide amnesty at the end of a non-international conflict and does not contain any exceptions. However, amnesties have been considered contrary to the international obligations of post-conflict states by some international human rights bodies and courts,[24] and have sometimes been rejected, for example, in the case of international crimes such as torture.[25]

### 1.3 International Criminal Law Treaties and Transitional Justice

International criminal law, the body of international law that provides rules for international crimes, has always been at the heart of transitional justice. As seen in the first part of this book, the birth of modern transitional justice can be traced to the creation of the International Military Tribunals after the Second World War. In order to respond to international crimes – mainly crimes against peace, aggression, genocide, crimes against humanity and war crimes – generally committed in the context of armed conflict and/or dictatorship, several international criminal tribunals and hybrid tribunals have been created since the 1990s. One of these tribunals, the International Criminal Court, is permanent. Despite this momentum in the creation of international and hybrid tribunals to deal with international crimes, and despite these responses by international organisations and states to international crimes, the question remains as to the existence of international obligations for transitional or post-conflict states when international crimes are committed. Today, it is generally admitted that there are three main international crimes when it comes to individuals and groups: genocide, crimes against

23 See below this chapter, Section 3.1, on international customary law and the position of the International Committee of the Red Cross (ICRC).

24 See below Section 2 and Chapter 9, for details on the jurisprudence of international courts and human rights bodies.

25 For example, ICTY, *The Prosecutor v. Anto Furundzija*, Case No. IT-95-17/1-T, Judgement, 10 December 1998, para. 155. According to the tribunal which was examining crimes committed during the former Yugoslavia armed conflict: "The fact that torture is prohibited by a peremptory norm of international law has other effects at the inter-state and individual levels. At the inter-state level, it serves to internationally de-legitimise any legislative, administrative or judicial act authorising torture. It would be senseless to argue, on the one hand, that on account of the jus cogens value of the prohibition against torture, treaties or customary rules providing for torture would be null and void ab initio, and then be unmindful of a State say, taking national measures authorising or condoning torture or absolving its perpetrators through an amnesty law."

humanity and war crimes. However, there are only a few treaties that deal with these core international crimes and explicitly set international obligations for states.

### 1.3.1 The Crime of Genocide

After the Second World War, states adopted the Convention on the Prevention and Punishment of the Crime of Genocide on 9 December 1948. The convention defines genocide as "any of the following acts committed with intent to destroy, in whole or in part, a national, ethnical, racial or religious group, as such: (a) Killing members of the group; (b) Causing serious bodily or mental harm to members of the group; (c) Deliberately inflicting on the group conditions of life calculated to bring about its physical destruction in whole or in part; (d) Imposing measures intended to prevent births within the group; (e) Forcibly transferring children of the group to another group."[26] The convention explicitly states that genocide is punishable whether it is committed "in time of peace or in time of war."[27] This clearly means that the convention is an instrument applicable to transitional states and that the obligations it provides are also applicable to transitional states parties.

There are many obligations in that treaty. The states parties to the treaty engage to prevent and punish genocide.[28] They are also obliged to provide legislation in their legal system that gives effect to the convention.[29] In particular, the convention provides that persons charged with the crime shall be tried either by territorial states or by an international penal tribunal if state parties have accepted the jurisdiction of that tribunal.[30] This clearly means that states have to prosecute and try persons accused of genocide, and that an international tribunal can also pursue that goal. In order to make the trial effective, the convention also insists on extradition and provides that genocide "shall not be considered as political crimes for the purpose of extradition," and that in such case, states have to proceed to extradition.[31] For transitional states, all these provisions mean that they have to prosecute and try, and in

26 Art. 2 of the Convention on the Prevention and Punishment of the Crime of Genocide on 9 December 1948.

27 Preamble of the Convention on the Prevention and Punishment of the Crime of Genocide on 9 December 1948.

28 Art. I, Convention, *ibid.*

29 Art. V, *ibid.*

30 Art. VI, *ibid.*

31 Art. VII, *ibid.*

the case of conviction, to punish those who have committed genocide. They also have to prevent genocidal acts from being repeated.

### 1.3.2 War Crimes

There is no equivalent to the 1948 Genocide Convention in ICL when it comes to war crimes. However, "grave breaches" of IHL as defined in the 1949 Geneva Conventions are considered to be war crimes, although these crimes are not limited to these "grave breaches." The 1998 Rome Statute establishing the ICC, which is a treaty, provides for the prosecution of war crimes by the ICC and gives a broad definition of these crimes, including not only "grave breaches" but also other violations of international humanitarian law, such as violations of the provisions of common Article 3 of the Geneva Conventions applicable to non-international armed conflicts. Nevertheless, as we shall see, the interpretation of the Rome Statute as a treaty that imposes international obligations on states parties to prosecute recognised international crimes – that is, war crimes but also crimes against humanity, genocide and aggression – remains open.

### 1.3.3 Crimes against Humanity

Draft articles on the Prevention and Punishment of Crimes against Humanity have been adopted by the UN International Law Commission, and is under consideration by UN states.[32] It defines crime against humanity as "any of the following acts when committed as part of a widespread or systematic attack directed against any civilian population, with knowledge of the attack: (a) murder; (b) extermination; (c) enslavement; (d) deportation or forcible transfer of population; (e) imprisonment or other severe deprivation of physical liberty in violation of fundamental rules of international law; (f) torture; (g) rape, sexual slavery, enforced prostitution, forced pregnancy, enforced sterilization, or any other form of sexual violence of comparable gravity; (h) persecution against any identifiable group or collectivity on political, racial, national, ethnic, cultural, religious, gender, or other grounds that are universally recognized as impermissible under international law, in connection with any act referred to in this paragraph; (i) enforced disappearance of persons; (j) the crime of apartheid; (k) other inhumane acts of a similar character intentionally causing great suffering, or serious injury to body or to mental or physical health."[33] The

32 Draft articles on Prevention and Punishment of Crimes against Humanity 2019, 'Yearbook of the International Law Commission', 2019, vol. II, Part Two.

33 Art. 1 para. 1, *ibid.*

analysis of this "treaty on crimes against humanity" shows that states, including transitional states, will have some international obligations in cases where crimes against humanity have been perpetrated. According to the draft article, just as in the 1948 genocide convention, states will have the obligation to prevent and punish crimes against humanity, whenever they are perpetrated, in peace time or during an armed conflict.[34] They will have to take national measures and legislation in order to prevent these crimes and ensure that they do not go unpunished.[35] States will also have the obligation to respect the rights of the individuals accused, and to respect the rights of victims and witnesses.[36] Just as for war crimes, crimes against humanity are provided in the Rome Statute, which is treaty.[37] This, as in the case of war crimes within the same statute, raises the question of the existence of international obligations for transitional states in this treaty.

### 1.3.4 International Cooperation to Investigate and Prosecute International Crimes

Adopted in 2023, the Ljubljana Convention – the Hague Convention on International Cooperation in the Investigation and Prosecution of the Crime of Genocide, Crimes against Humanity, War Crimes and other International Crimes – emphasises cooperation between states to combat impunity in cases involving the perpetration of international crimes.[38] The Ljubljana Convention is relevant to transitional justice as it aims "to facilitate international cooperation in criminal matters between States Parties with a view to strengthening the fight against impunity for the crime of genocide, crimes against humanity, war crimes, and, where applicable, other international crimes."[39] This international legal instrument would, therefore, be useful in investigating certain international crimes perpetrated during authoritarian rule or armed conflict, and in prosecuting accused individuals, matters that are often at the core of transitional justice.

---

34 Art. 3, *ibid.*

35 Art. 4, and 6–10, *ibid.*

36 Art. 11 and 12, *ibid.*

37 Art. 7 of the Rome Statute establishing the International Criminal Court, 17 July 1998.

38 The Hague Convention on International Cooperation in the Investigation and Prosecution of the Crime of Genocide, Crimes against Humanity, War Crimes and other International Crimes, adopted in Ljubljana, Slovenia, 26 May 2023.

39 Art. 1, *ibid.*

### 1.3.5 ICC Rome Statute: Any International Obligations for Transitional States?

In the 1998 Rome Statute, the crime of aggression, war crimes, crimes against humanity and genocide are included in the *ratione materiae* jurisdiction of the International Criminal Court. The question, however, is whether the Rome Statute imposes obligations on states. In fact, one could consider that the Rome Statute does not, *stricto sensu*, impose international obligations on states. Even though it is a treaty, that treaty is a statute of a court. Its main objective is to provide the "jurisdiction and functioning of the Court" as stated in its Article 1.

However, the preamble of the Rome Statute deals with some issues that can be seen as implying that states parties must prosecute the perpetrators of the international crimes defined in the treaty. It provides that the ICC is complementary to national courts and affirms that states must combat impunity for international crimes, carry out prosecutions and prevent these crimes. Although in international law preambles to treaties are not considered to be binding on states, they underline principles of international law that are important for the interpretation of treaties. Here, the reaffirmation of the importance of combating impunity for international crimes such as genocide, crimes against humanity and war crimes is part of the evidence that transitional states are now under pressure to take action and prosecute those accused of committing international crimes.

Similarly, some provisions of the Rome Statute implicitly or explicitly impose international obligations on states. First, Article 17 provides that the ICC may declare cases inadmissible if they are being investigated or prosecuted by states, unless it is demonstrated that the state is unwilling or unable to do so. This implicitly recognises that states have an important role to play in the investigation and prosecution of international crimes, and that the ICC may decide not to intervene where states are investigating and prosecuting international crimes. This also means that the ICC can intervene, investigate and prosecute when states parties, including post-conflict and transitional states, are not willing to do so or are not able to do so. All of this is a strong indication that states, including post-conflict states, must act to investigate or prosecute international crimes.

Second, there are explicit international obligations for states parties in the implementation of the ICC's activities, which are to prosecute and punish the perpetrators of international crimes provided for in its statute. In the area of cooperation with the court, Article 86 of the Rome Statute provides that "States Parties shall, in accordance with the provisions of this Statute, cooperate fully with the Court in its investigation and prosecution of crimes within the jurisdiction of the Court."[40] In the same vein, Article 88 of the statute requires states parties to "ensure that there are procedures available under their national law for all of the forms of cooperation which are specified" in the part of the statute dealing with cooperation. Article 89 continues by stating that states must "comply with requests for arrest and surrender" that the Court issues. Article 93 also lists many forms of cooperation that states parties shall provide to the court. The obligation of states parties to cooperate with the ICC in order to achieve its objective is very important in transitional processes because the most part of crimes examined by the ICC are generally committed in the context of armed conflict or authoritarian rule regimes. By cooperating with the ICC, transitional or post-conflict states participate in establishing criminal accountability for perpetrators of crimes committed on their territory. Under the statute, this obligation to cooperate is therefore one of the international obligations of post-conflict or transitional states when the ICC investigates international crimes committed on their territory.

### 1.3.6 Bilateral Agreements Establishing Hybrid Criminal Tribunals

Another argument for the growing need to investigate, prosecute and punish international crimes is the fact that, as discussed in Part 2 of this book, some states have concluded bilateral treaties with international organisations to establish hybrid criminal tribunals to prosecute international crimes committed in certain countries. These treaties establish statutes and rules for these courts. They do not contain international obligations for post-conflict states such as those found in multilateral treaties such as the 1948 Genocide Convention. However, the creation of hybrid criminal tribunals through bilateral treaties is one of the elements showing that there is now a tendency for many post-conflict states to express their desire to achieve criminal accountability for the crimes committed.

## 1.4 Complementary of IHRL, IHL and ICL Treaties in the Field of International Transitional Justice Law

Although it is important to distinguish between the provisions of treaties adopted in IHL, IHRL and ICL, which are not similar and may establish differ-

---

40 Even if they were not treaties, the Statutes of the ICTY (Article 29) and of the ICTR (Article 27) mentioned the obligation for states to cooperate with these international criminal tribunals.

ent types of international obligations for transitional and post-conflict states, the close relationship between these branches of international law leads to the assertion that they are complementary in practice when it comes to international transitional justice law. An act of torture, for example, may at the same time be a violation of IHRL, IHL and ICL. Thus, the repression of that act under IHRL international obligations may also serve the need for repression under IHL and ICL, even if that repression was not pursued by the transitional state on the basis of IHL and ICL. For example, there is a link between torture as a human rights violation and torture as a violation of IHL and ICL. A post-conflict state may prosecute torture in order to fulfil its international obligations under IHL treaties. At the same time, however, it may also play an indirect role in the repression of torture as a violation of IHL in the context of armed conflict and "grave breaches," or as a violation of ICL, since torture constitutes an act of crimes against humanity, depending on the context in which it is committed. Because of the close links between IHL, IHRL and ICL, a post-conflict state may be fulfilling its international obligations under these three branches of international law at the same time.

As an illustration of that complementarity, the Inter-American Court of Human Rights has sometimes claimed the right to conclude that some violations of the ACHR are similar to violations of international humanitarian law, even though it does not have jurisdiction over violations of international humanitarian law. For example, in a case involving Guatemala, a post-conflict state, it wrote that although it "lacks competence to declare that a State is internationally responsible for the violation of international treaties that do not grant it such competence, it can observe that certain acts or omissions that violate human rights, pursuant to the treaties that they do have competence to apply, also violate other international instruments for the protection of the individual, such as the 1949 Geneva Conventions and, in particular, common Article 3."[41] In the context of armed conflict, for example, in relation to civilians, it is very difficult to distinguish between violations that are categorised as IHL violations, ICL violations and violations that are categorised as IHRL violations. This may lead to the conclusion that for those violations that fall into these categories, states have obligations to investigate, prosecute, punish perpetrators and provide reparations to victims. This conclusion is consistent because even if violations of IHL during non-international armed conflicts cannot be brought to justice under the umbrella of IHL because of the shortcomings of that branch of international law, they can still

41 IACtHR, *Bámaca Velásquez v. Guatemala*, Judgment, (Merits), 25 November 2000, para. 208.

be brought to justice under the umbrella of IHRL or ICL. Thus, in post-conflict contexts, international transitional justice law allows post-conflict states to fulfil many of their international obligations under IHRL, IHL and ICL simultaneously when dealing with past violations and international crimes. In so doing, it allows for the permeability between IHL and IHRL, and also ICL, when it comes to accountability for serious violations.

To conclude on treaties and transitional justice, it is certain that treaties are central to defining the international obligations of transitional or post-conflict states. They impose many obligations on states in the area of dealing with past violations. Depending on the treaty under consideration, states have various international obligations: an obligation to investigate and prosecute violations of human rights, violations of international humanitarian law and international crimes; an obligation to respect the rights of the accused; an obligation to respect the rights of victims, including their right to the truth and to reparation; and an obligation to prevent the recurrence of such violations or crimes.

However, treaties alone are not enough to determine the international obligations of states when it comes to responding to serious violations and crimes of the past. Treaties are not always clear about what states must do. For example, the general IHRL treaties do not provide clear guidance on what states must do, even when they refer to the right to an effective remedy. Most treaty provisions need interpretation through case law in order to determine the specific international obligations of transitional or post-conflict states. That is why decisions of judicial bodies play a key role when it comes to these international obligations.

## 2 Decisions of Judicial Bodies

Decisions of judicial bodies are not considered to be a primary source of international law. Article 38, paragraph 1(d) of the ICJ Statute provides that there are "subsidiary means for the determination of rules of law." This means that there are means that are used when other sources of international law do not provide sufficient information on the rules to be applied. Contrary to the subsidiary status of judicial decisions in Article 38, in international transitional justice law, these decisions are one of the main sources. In the absence of a treaty dealing with transitional justice, international courts have been playing an important role in defining the international obligations of transitional or post-conflict states, generally through the interpretation of treaty provisions or other developments in international law. These courts, which interpret and provide insight into international obligations relating to transitional justice, are generally found within IHRL. Two international human rights bodies, the Inter-American Court of Human Rights and the European Court of Human Rights, have made significant contributions to the definition of the international obligations of transitional or post-conflict states through their case law on transitional or post-conflict states. Other courts, such as the African Court on Human and Peoples' Rights and the Economic Community of West African States (ECOWAS) Court of justice, have also contributed to providing guidance on what transitional states need to do in the area of accountability for past violations. Apart from the IHRL courts, even if its contribution is limited, the International Court of Justice has defined some international obligations of states by interpreting some treaties that deal with human rights or international crimes.

### 2.1 The Inter-American Court of Human Rights

Twenty American states have recognised the jurisdiction of the Inter-American Court of Human Rights, which is in charge of monitoring the respect of human rights on the American continent: Argentina, Barbados, Bolivia, Brazil, Chile, Colombia, Costa Rica, Dominican Republic, Ecuador, El Salvador, Guatemala, Haiti, Honduras, Mexico, Nicaragua, Panama, Paraguay, Peru, Suriname and Uruguay.

Generally in the context of the Cold War between the West and the East after the 1940s, most of these South and Central American countries experienced either authoritarian rule or armed conflict, or both, especially between the 1960s and the 1990s, and sometimes beyond. Argentina, Bolivia, Brazil, Chile, Colombia, Ecuador, El Salvador, Guatemala, Haiti, Honduras, Nicaragua, Panama, Paraguay, Peru, Suriname and Uruguay experienced serious difficulties and political repression in the context of the political and social opposition between the right and the left, often respectively supported by the West, the United States, or the East, the former Soviet Union and Cuba. In these contexts, many human rights were violated. Victims have complained about these violations nationally and internationally, and some states have used or created transitional justice mechanisms to deal with them, as discussed in Part 2 of this book. Unsatisfied with the responses of these states to the violations they experienced, many victims have taken their cases of human rights violations to the Inter-American Commission on Human Rights, which later referred them to the Inter-American Court of Human Rights. Some developments in transitional justice in South and Central American states have also been implemented after rulings by the court that pushed transitional and post-conflict states to take action on past human rights violations.

The court has examined numerous cases of human rights violations in many of these transitional states after they decided to become parties to the American Convention of Human Rights (ACHR). These violations include those that occurred after these states became parties to the ACHR, as well as some violations that occurred prior to this event but were "continuing" – such as enforced disappearances – and had effects after transitional states became parties to the ACHR. The court has interpreted the ACHR and clarified international obligations of transitional and post-conflict states in the field of dealing with past human rights violations committed during authoritarian rule and/or armed conflict.

The international obligations of transitional states are generally based on a broad interpretation of some articles of the ACHR, in particular Article 25, which deals with the right to judicial protection or the right to an effective remedy. Article 25 is usually combined with some other articles, such as Article 1, paragraph 1 of the ACHR which deals with general obligations of states, to establish two main international obligations for transitional or post-conflict states: the obligation to investigate human rights violations and establish truth about them, and the obligation to prosecute perpetrators and punish them. In many of these cases, the Inter-American Court of Human Rights has also pushed transitional states to award material and symbolic reparations to victims.

### 2.1.1 The Obligation to Investigate and Establish Judicial Truth about Human Rights Violations

In a number of cases of human rights violations in transitional states, the Inter-American Court of Human Rights has ruled that these states have an obligation to establish the truth about human rights violations through judicial proceedings, and that victim of human rights violations have a right to the truth that transitional states must guarantee. For example, in the case of *Bámaca-Velásquez*, a rebel leader who was the victim of enforced disappearance during the armed conflict, the court ruled that Guatemala failed to "adequately investigate" the case and punish the persons responsible for this violation.[42] It referred to the right for victims to the truth, relying on Article 8 (right to a fair trial) and Article 25 (right to judicial protection) of the ACHR,

42 *Ibid.*, para. 18.

stating that "the right to the truth is subsumed in the right of the victim or his next of kin to obtain clarification of the facts relating to the violations and the corresponding responsibilities from the competent State organs."[43] Using Article 1, paragraph 1 of the ACHR that deals with the obligation of states parties to the ACHR to respect the rights and freedoms recognised by it without discrimination, the court held that Guatemala had "the obligation to investigate" and that Guatemala had violated this article "in relation to" Article 4 (right to life), Article 5 (right to humane treatment), and Article 7 (right to personal liberty), along with Article 8 and Article 25 of the ACHR.[44]

The Inter-American Court of Human Rights took the same line in a case involving El Salvador, which also concerned violations committed in the context of an armed conflict. In the *Case of Massacres of El Mozote and Neighboring Villages v. El Salvador*, concerning massacres perpetrated in El Salvador during the armed conflict, the court clearly stated that "[t]he obligation to investigate human rights violations is one of the positive measures that States must adopt to guarantee the rights recognized in the Convention."[45] This statement relied on Article 8, paragraph 1, Article 25 and Article 1 paragraph 1 of the ACHR.[46] The court also strongly stated that El Salvador had a duty to investigate and that this "duty to investigate is an obligation of means and not of results that must be assumed by the State as its inherent legal duty and not as a simple formality preordained to be ineffective, or merely as a measure taken by private interests that depends on the procedural initiative of the victims, their next of kin, or the private submission of evidence."[47] What is very interesting about this case is that prior to the court's ruling, El Salvador had established a truth commission, which had produced a final report exposing the human rights violations committed during the Salvadoran Civil War. The court held that the final report of the truth commission could not be used to argue that El Salvador had fulfilled its obligation to investigate. The court found that the establishment of the truth through judicial processes was mandatory, writing that it "considers it pertinent to reiterate, as it has in other cases, that, in compliance with its obligation to guarantee the right to know the truth, States may establish truth commissions, which contribute to the creation and preservation of the historical memory, the elucidation of the

43 *Ibid.*, para. 201.

44 *Ibid.*, paras. 212–214.

45 IACtHR, *Case of Massacres of El Mozote and neighboring villages v. El Salvador*, Judgment, (Merits, Reparations and Costs), 25 October 2012, para. 243.

46 *Ibid.*, para. 242.

47 *Ibid.*, para. 248.

facts, and the determination of the institutional, social and political responsibilities during certain historical periods of a society. Nevertheless, this does not complete or substitute for the State's obligation to establish the truth through judicial proceedings; hence, the State had the obligation to open and expedite criminal investigations to determine the corresponding responsibilities."[48] Other rulings by the Inter-American Court of Human Rights have followed the same line regarding El Salvador's obligation to investigate human rights violations committed during the civil war.[49]

In spite of the establishing of a truth commission in Bolivia in the 1980s, the Inter-American Court of Human Rights stated that Bolivia, a state that experienced dictatorship and enforced disappearances, still had an "obligation to establish the truth and investigate crimes through judicial proceedings."[50] In a case involving Brazil, a state that at the time was envisaging the creation of a national truth commission after enduring a dictatorship marked by several serious and large-scale human rights violations, the court stated that creating a truth commission was a good idea, but that it did not "substitute the obligation of the State to establish the truth and ensure the legal determination of individual responsibility by means of criminal legal procedures."[51] In a case involving Ecuador, another state that has established a truth commission, it insisted on the obligation to investigate human rights violations through judicial bodies.[52]

In the context of the obligation to investigate, the Inter-American Court of Human Rights has demonstrated an appreciation for the contributions of non-judicial bodies of transitional justice, such as truth commissions, in this domain. However, it has stated that the work of truth commissions is not sufficient and that, in addition to the truth established by these bodies, the state must also give effect to the right to truth through judicial proceedings. This means that even if a collective and historical truth has been established by non-judicial bodies, an individual truth, linked to individual cases, must also be estab-

48 *Ibid.*, para. 298.

49 See, for example, IACtHR, *Case of Contreras et al. v. El Salvador*, Judgment, (Merits, Reparations and Costs), 31 August 2011, para. 135.

50 IACtHR, *Case of Ibsen Cárdenas and Ibsen Peña v. Bolivia*, Judgment, (Merits, Reparation, and Costs), 1st September 2010, para. 158.

51 IACtHR, *Case of Gomes Lund et al. ("Guerrilha Do Araguaia") v. Brazil*, Judgment, (Preliminary Objections, Merits, Reparations, and Costs), 24 November 2010, para. 297.

52 IACtHR, *Case of Zambrano Vélez et al v. Ecuador*, Judgment, (Merits, Reparations and Costs), 4 July 2007, para 128.

lished by the transitional state. In other words, according to the court, the truth established by truth commissions is only complementary to the truth that must be established through judicial procedures. Based on the specific jurisprudence of the court, it can be concluded that this human rights body requires transitional or post-conflict states that are parties to the ACHR to judicially investigate serious human rights violations committed in the past and to establish an individual truth for each case of these violations. In the rulings of the court, this obligation is generally included in reparations measures, just like the subsequent obligation to prosecute and punish perpetrators of violations.

#### 2.1.2 The Obligation to Prosecute Perpetrators and Punish Them and the Obligation Not to Adopt Amnesties

The jurisprudence of the Inter-American Court of Human Rights is replete with examples of transitional states being called upon to prosecute human rights violations and punish perpetrators. These cases include countries such as El Salvador and Guatemala that have faced bloody armed conflicts,[53] and such as Peru,[54] Chile,[55] Bolivia,[56] Ecuador[57] and Uruguay[58] that dealt with

53 For El Salvador, IACtHR, *Serrano-Cruz Sisters v. El Salvador*, Judgment, (Merits, Reparations and Costs), 1st March 2005, para. 175; IACtHR, *Contreras et al. v. El Salvador*, Judgment, (Merits, Reparations and Costs), 31 August 2011 para. 185; IACtHR, *Case of Rochac Hernández et al. v. El Salvador*, Judgment, (Merits, Reparations and Costs), 14 October 2014, para. 188; For Guatemala, IACtHR, *The "Las Dos Erres" Massacre v. Guatemala*, Judgment (Preliminary Objection, Merits, Reparations and Costs), 24 November 2009, paras. 232–233; IACtHR, *Plan de Sánchez Massacre v. Guatemala*, Judgment (Reparations and Costs), 19 November 2004, paras. 95–99; IACtHR, *Myrna Mack Chang v. Guatemala*, Judgment, (Merits, Reparations and Costs), 25 November 2003, paras. 217–218; IACtHR, *Maritza Urrutia v. Guatemala*, Judgment, (Merits, Reparations and Costs), 27 November 2003, paras. 126 and 130.

54 IACtHR, *Anzualdo-Castro v. Peru*, Judgment, (Preliminary Objection, Merits, Reparations and Costs), 22 September 2009, para. 180; IACtHR, *La Cantuta v. Peru*, Judgment, (Merits, Reparations and Costs), 29 November 2006, para. 224.

55 IACtHR, *Almonacid-Arellano et al. v. Chile*, Judgment, (Preliminary Objections, Merits, Reparations and Costs), 26 September 2006, para. 150.

56 IACtHR, *Ibsen-Cárdenas and Ibsen-Peña v. Bolivia*, Judgment, (Merits, Reparations and Costs), 1st September 2010, para. 158.

57 IACtHR, *Zambrano-Vélez et al. v. Ecuador*, Judgment, (Merits, Reparations and Costs), 4 July 2007, paras. 128–129.

58 IACtHR, *Case of Gelman v. Uruguay*, Judgment, (Merits and Reparations), 24 February 2011, para. 252.

authoritarian regimes. In general, inter-American bodies have relied on Article 8, paragraph 1 (right to a fair trial) and Article 25 (right to judicial protection), combined with Article 1 paragraph 1 (obligations to respect rights) of the ACHR to find an obligation to prosecute and punish the perpetrators of serious human rights violations.[59]

This opinion of the Inter-American Court of Human Rights is also marked by the rejection of amnesty laws and other laws preventing investigations and prosecutions of cases in many Central and South American countries that have experienced authoritarian regimes and/or armed conflicts. Generally, using Article 8, Article 25, Article 1 paragraph 1, and Article 2 (domestic legal effects) of the ACHR, the court has opposed amnesties laws in many rulings against states that went through dictatorships or armed conflict like El Salvador,[60] Guatemala,[61] Peru,[62] Chile[63] and Brazil.[64] Thus, according to the court, transitional and post-conflict states have an obligation to prosecute and punish perpetrators, and an obligation not to adopt amnesty laws or other laws to prevent prosecution and punishment. These measures are generally included in the reparation measures to be implemented by states, which also include other forms of reparation recognised under international law.

---

59 IACtHR, *Serrano-Cruz Sisters v. El Salvador*, Judgment, (Merits, Reparations and Costs), 1st March 2005, para. 175; IACtHR, *Contreras et al. v. El Salvador*, Judgment, (Merits, Reparations and Costs), 31 August 2011, para. 185; IACtHR, *Case of Rochac Hernández et al. v. El Salvador*, Judgment, (Merits, Reparations and Costs), 14 October 2014), para. 188; IACtHR, *The "Las Dos Erres" Massacre v. Guatemala*, Judgment, (Preliminary Objection, Merits, Reparations and Costs), 24 November 2009, paras. 232–233; IACtHR, *Plan de Sánchez Massacre v. Guatemala*, Judgment, (Reparations and Costs), 19 November 2004), paras. 95–99; IACtHR, *Myrna Mack Chang v. Guatemala*, Judgment, (Merits, Reparations and Costs), 25 November 2003, paras. 217–218; IACtHR, *Maritza Urrutia v. Guatemala*, Judgment, (Merits, Reparations and Costs), 27 November 2003, paras. 126 and 130.

60 IACtHR, *Serrano-Cruz Sisters v. El Salvador*, Judgment, (Merits, Reparations and Costs) 1st March 2005, para. 172.

61 IACtHR, *The "Las Dos Erres" Massacre v. Guatemala*, Judgment, (Preliminary Objection, Merits, Reparations and Costs), 29 November 2009, para. 131; IACtHR, *Chitay-Nech et al. v. Guatemala*, Judgment, (Preliminary Objections, Merits, Reparations and Costs), 25 May 2010, para. 235 (b); IACtHR, *Myrna Mack-Chang v. Guatemala*, Judgment, (Merits, Reparations and Costs), 25 November 2003, para. 276.

62 IACtHR, *Case of Barrios Altos v. Peru*, Judgment, (Merits), 14 March 2001, paras. 41–44; IACtHR, *La Cantuta v. Peru*, Merits, Judgment, (Reparations and Costs), 29 November 2006, para. 189.

63 IACtHR, *Almonacid-Arellano et al. v. Chile*, Judgment, (Preliminary Objections, Merits, Reparations and Costs), 26 September 2006, paras. 126–128.

64 IACtHR, *Case of Gomes Lund et al. ("Guerrilha Do Araguaia") v. Brazil*, Judgment, (Preliminary Objections, Merits, Reparations, and Costs), 24 November 2010, para. 180.

### 2.1.3 The Insistence on the Necessity to Award Reparations to Victims and the Affirmation of the Obligation to Repair

There is not, in the strict sense, a general right to reparation for victims in the ACHR with a corresponding obligation for states to award these reparations. Article 63, paragraph 1 of the ACHR provides that the Inter-American Court of Human Rights may rule on compensation: "If the Court finds that there has been a violation of a right or freedom protected by this Convention, the Court shall rule that the injured party be ensured the enjoyment of his right or freedom that was violated. It shall also rule, if appropriate, that the consequences of the measure or situation that constituted the breach of such right or freedom be remedied and that fair compensation be paid to the injured party." However, interpreting that article in many cases, including in a case that involved a post-conflict state, Guatemala, the court has been holding that Article 63, paragraph 1 "contains a customary norm that constitutes one of the basic principles of contemporary international law on State responsibility. When an unlawful act occurs, which can be attributed to a State, this gives rise immediately to its international responsibility for violating the international norm, with the consequent obligation to cause the consequences of the violation to cease and to repair the damage caused."[65] Thus, in a human rights case pitting individuals against the state, the court interpreted this provision in the line of state-to-state disputes, holding that the state, in this case a post-conflict state, has an obligation to repair as a consequence of a violation of international law.

In cases involving serious violations of human rights in dictatorships and armed conflicts contexts, the court has ruled on reparations to be awarded to victims by states. It has built through its jurisprudence one of the most advanced contributions to obligations to repair, as per the court, after serious and large-scale violations of human rights. These reparations that transitional states have to award to victims according to the court include forms of reparation like financial compensation,[66] rehabilitation medical measures,[67] and

---

65 IACtHR, *Plan de Sánchez Massacre v. Guatemala*, Judgment, (Reparations and Costs), 19 November 2004, para. 52.

66 See, for example, IACtHR, *Serrano-Cruz Sisters v. El Salvador*, Judgment, (Merits, Reparations and Costs), 1st March 2005, paras. 152 and 160; IACtHR, *Plan de Sánchez Massacre v. Guatemala*, Judgment, (Reparations and Costs), 19 November 2004), paras. 74–76.

67 See, for example, IACtHR, *Plan de Sánchez Massacre v. Guatemala*, Judgment, (Reparations and Costs), 19 November 2004, para. 107: "the State shall provide, free of charge, through its specialized health institutions, the medical treatment that the victims require, including, inter alia, any necessary medication"; IACtHR, *Case of Gomes Lund*

satisfaction measures, including memorialisation.[68] Consequently, the awarding of reparations to be implemented by transitional and post-conflict states creates a sense of the existence of an obligation for states to repair in case of serious violations of human rights. The field of reparations is the main field in which the Inter-American Court of Human Rights has been developing its jurisprudence on the international obligations of states which have endured dictatorships and armed conflicts. The European Court of Human Rights takes a different approach.

## 2.2 The European Court of Human Rights

Europe, the continent most affected by the First and Second World Wars, adopted the European Convention on Human Rights in 1950. Today, 46 countries are parties to this treaty, which established the European Court of Human Rights (ECtHR) in order to examine allegations of human rights violations by contracting states. Apart from the two world wars, in which many European states were involved, armed conflicts and/or authoritarian regimes have mainly affected countries in Southern, Central and Eastern Europe, some between the 1950s and 1990s, the communist countries during the Cold War, Spain between the 1940s and mid-1970s, the Balkans in the 1990s, Turkey and Greece in the 1970s, and Turkey against the Kurdistan Workers' Party (PKK) since the 1980s. Northern Ireland also saw a bloody armed confrontation between the 1970s and the 1990s. Since 2014, an armed conflict between Russia and Ukraine has once again plunged Europe into a storm of wars.

---

*et al.* (*"Guerrilha Do Araguaia"*) *v. Brazil*, Judgment, (Preliminary Objections, Merits, Reparations, and Costs), 24 November 2010, para. 267: the State must "provide the victims, per their requests, free of charge and immediately, appropriately, and effectively, with the medical and psychological or psychiatric care by means of public health institutions."

68 See, for example, IACtHR, *Plan de Sánchez Massacre v. Guatemala*, Judgment, (Reparations and Costs), 19 November 2004, para. 101, ("honor publicly the memory of those executed," para. 101; "implement a housing program to provide adequate housing, para. 105; etc.); IACtHR, *'Street Children' (Villagrán-Morales et al.) v. Guatemala*, Judgment, (Reparations and Costs), 26 May 2001, para. 123 (giving the name of victims to an educative center); IACtHR, *Case of Myrna Mack-Chang v. Guatemala*, Judgment, (Merits, Reparations and Costs), 25 November 2003, para. 301 (11) (creating a scholarship that has the name of the victim); IACtHR, *Almonacid-Arellano et al. v. Chile*, Judgment, (Preliminary Objections, Merits, Reparations and Costs), 26 September 2006, para. 162, "the State shall publish the chapter on proven facts and the operative part of this Judgment, for a single time and without footnotes, in the Official Gazette and in another newspaper of wide national circulation."

Because of human rights violations committed on the territory of many European states, including during the Second World War, and because of the limited legal responses of these states to these violations, both victims of human rights violations and individuals accused of having committed human rights violations have brought their cases to the European Court of Human Rights. The ECtHR generally rules that it has jurisdiction only over human rights violations committed after the entry into force of the ECHR for the state accused of committing human rights violations.[69] With regard to human rights violations committed after the entry into force of the ECHR for states concerned, the ECtHR has examined many cases that can be used to draw conclusions about the international obligations of transitional and post-conflict states with regard to past human rights violations. These obligations concern investigations, prosecutions, prohibition of amnesty laws, the respect of the rights of persons accused and restitution.

### 2.2.1 Obligations to Consider the Procedural Aspects of the Human Rights Recognized by the ECHR: Articles 2 and 3 of the ECHR

An examination of the large body of case law of the ECHR shows that transitional or post-conflict states are obliged to take into account the procedural aspects of some of the human rights enshrined in the ECHR, in particular the rights contained in Article 2 (right to life) and Article 3 (prohibition of torture and inhuman or degrading treatment or punishment). Although the ECtHR's jurisprudence in this area has generally been developed outside the exclusive context of transitional states, some of its judgments do concern them. Obligations of transitional states are derived from these procedural aspects. It is the case for the obligation to investigate human rights violations, and the obligation to prosecute and punish perpetrators of human rights violations. These obligations are also sometimes derived from Article 13 of the ECHR, which recognises the right to an effective remedy.

The ECtHR has ruled that states in transition and post-conflict states have an obligation to investigate cases of violations of the right to life and to prosecute and punish those responsible for such violations. For example, in some cases involving Turkey, in relation to its armed confrontation against the PKK and the violations that have occurred, the ECtHR has used Article 2 (right to life) to consider that the Turkish authorities' investigations into violations of

69 See, for example, the analysis of the Court on the massacre of Katyn that occurred during the Second World War, ECtHR [GC], *Janowiec and Others v. Russia*, No. 55508/07 29520/09, 21 October 2013.

the right to life were inadequate,[70] and Article 13 (right to effective remedy) to insist on the need for "a thorough and effective investigation capable of leading to the identification and punishment of those responsible for the deprivation of life."[71] In *Ukraine v. Russia*, in the context of the armed conflict between the two countries, the ECtHR also found that Russia had violated Article 2 by failing to investigate cases of alleged enforced disappearances.[72]

In the case of *Georgia v. Russia*, two European states at odds in an armed conflict followed by Russia's occupation of part of Georgia's territory, the ECtHR ruled that in difficult times or under conditions of armed conflict, states (in this case, Russia) are still obliged to investigate violations of the right to life.[73] It held that "the investigations carried out by the Russian authorities were neither prompt nor effective nor independent, and accordingly did not satisfy the requirements of Article 2 of the Convention," and concluded that Russia, which has effective control on part of the territory of Georgia, had violated Article 2 in its procedural aspect.[74] The particularity of this case, which is of great interest to post-conflict states generally facing political, economic and social challenges, is that the ECtHR did not ignore the fact that difficulties such as those encountered during an armed conflict may impede investigations. Citing another case, the ECtHR wrote that in some circumstances "the procedural duty under Article 2 must be applied realistically, to take account of specific problems faced by investigators."[75]

This orientation of the ECtHR raises a question. In terms of realistic problems that may face states in post-conflict contexts, it is questionable how far these states need to go in terms of investigations and trials to prove their good faith in promptly and effectively investigating violations of the right to life. The response appears to be based on a case-by-case ruling. It is within the purview of the ECtHR to assess whether a post-conflict state has conducted sufficient investigations when examining a case. In a decision concerning Bosnia and Herzegovina, a post-conflict state, the ECtHR found that the state had made great efforts to clarify a case of disappearance that occurred during the

---

70 ECtHR, *Mahmut Kaya c. Turkey*, No. 22535/93, 28 March 2000), paras. 102–109; see also ECtHR [GC], *Salman v. Turkey*, No. 21986/93, 27 June 2000, para. 109; ECtHR, *Wolf-Sorg v. Turkey*, No. 6458/03, 8 June 2010, paras. 82–83; ECtHR, *Gülbahar Özer and others v. Turkey*, No. 44125/06, 2 July 2013, paras. 75–76.

71 ECtHR, *Mahmut Kaya c. Turkey*, *ibid.*, para. 124; see also *Salman v. Turkey*, *ibid.*, para. 123.

72 ECtHR [GC], *Ukraine v. Russia* (*Re Crimea*), No. 20958/14 38334/18, 25 June 2024, paras. 973–974.

73 ECtHR [GC], *Georgia v. Russia* (II), No. 38263/08, 21 January 2021, paras. 326–337.

74 *Ibid.*, paras. 336–337.

75 *Ibid.*, para. 327.

armed conflict.[76] The ECtHR emphasised that Bosnia was a post-conflict state and, in view of the challenges it faced, concluded that Bosnia had done its best to elucidate the case.[77] It explicitly wrote that it took "into account the complex situation in Bosnia and Herzegovina, notably in the first ten years following the war. In such a post-conflict situation, what amounts to an impossible and/or disproportionate burden must be measured by the very particular facts and context. In this connection, the Court notes that more than 100,000 people were killed, almost 30,000 people went missing and more than two million people were displaced during the war in Bosnia and Herzegovina. Inevitably choices had to be made in terms of post-war priorities and resources. Furthermore, after a long and brutal war, Bosnia and Herzegovina underwent fundamental overhaul of its internal structure and political system [...]."[78] The ECtHR, "taking into account the special circumstances prevailing in Bosnia and Herzegovina up until 2005 and indeed the particular circumstances of" the case, did not find a violation of the right to life.[79] This jurisprudence suggests that the ECtHR may be able to assess the efforts of the post-conflict state to fulfil its international obligation to investigate. It also suggests that for post-conflict states, as does the Inter-American Court of Human Rights,[80] there is an "obligation of means" and not an "obligation of results" when regarding investigations of complex cases related to human rights violations in an armed conflict.

In another case concerning Romania, a state under authoritarian rule prior to the 1990s, the ECtHR decided to examine alleged human rights violations (the death of one person and the ill-treatment of another) that took place in the context of protests against the authoritarian regime prior to the entry into force of the ECHR for Romania in 1994.[81] The ECtHR admitted the case because the complaints about these violations were related "to the criminal investigation conducted [...] after the entry into force of the Convention in respect of Romania."[82] The ECtHR decided that one complainant "did not have the benefit of an effective investigation as required by Article 2 of the Convention," and that another "was also deprived of an effective investigation

76 ECtHR, *Palić v. Bosnia-Herzégovina*, No. 4704/04, 15 February 2011, para. 70.

77 *Ibid.*, para. 70.

78 *Ibid.*

79 *Ibid.*, para. 71.

80 See IACtHR, *Case of Massacres of El Mozote and neighboring villages v. El Salvador*, Judgment, (Merits, Reparations and Costs), 25 October 2012, para. 248.

81 ECtHR [GC], *Mocanu and Others v. Romania*, No. 10865/09, 45886/07, 32431/08, (Merits and Just Satisfaction), 17 September 2014.

82 *Ibid.*, para. 211.

for the purposes of Article 3."[83] In this case, the ECtHR strongly "held that the procedural obligation under Articles 2 and 3 continues to apply in difficult security conditions, including in a context of armed conflict. Even where the events leading to the duty to investigate occur in a context of generalised violence and investigators are confronted with obstacles and constraints which compel the use of less effective measures of investigation or cause an investigation to be delayed, the fact remains that Articles 2 and 3 entail that all reasonable steps must be taken to ensure that an effective and independent investigation is conducted."[84] This statement leads to the conclusion that a transitional or post-conflict state still has an obligation to investigate violations of the right to life and violations of the prohibition of torture and inhuman and degrading treatment and punishment, even if it faces difficulties during a transition or a post-conflict context.

This insistence of the ECtHR on the international obligation to investigate has, ineluctably, a consequence on the need of prosecutions and, after conviction, punishment, when the investigations identify the perpetrators. Although the ECtHR does not always establish a clear and explicit obligation for post-conflict or transitional states to prosecute, its tendency to put pressure on the state to always respect the procedural aspects of certain rights is a strong indication that these states must act to bring to justice perpetrators of human rights violations, especially those related to violations of the right to life and the prohibition of torture and inhuman and degrading treatment and punishment. This evidence is also supported by the ECtHR's view on amnesty laws that prevent prosecution for past human rights violations.[85]

### 2.2.2 Obligation Not to Award Amnesty in Case of Serious Human Rights Violations?

When considering the possibility of amnesties in European transitional states, the European Court of Human Rights has insisted on the need to bring perpetrators to justice. In the *Marguš* case involving Croatia, a post-conflict state, the ECtHR highlighted the tendency in international law to consider amnesty as being incompatible with the universal obligation to prosecute and punish the

83 *Ibid.*, para. 352.

84 *Ibid.*, para. 319.

85 For more details, see: Anja Seibert-Fohr, *Prosecuting Serious Human Rights Violations* (Oxford University Press 2009); Monica Pinto, 'Awakening the Leviathan through Human Rights Law – How Human Rights Bodies Trigger the Application of Criminal Law' (2018) 34 *Utrecht Journal of International and European Law* 161.

perpetrators of serious human rights violations.[86] However, in that case, the ECtHR took a position that raised questions. It stated:

> In the present case the applicant was granted amnesty for acts which amounted to grave breaches of fundamental human rights such as the intentional killing of civilians and inflicting grave bodily injury on a child, and the County Court's reasoning referred to the applicant's merits as a military officer. A growing tendency in international law is to see such amnesties as unacceptable because they are incompatible with the unanimously recognized obligation of states to prosecute and punish grave breaches of fundamental human rights. *Even if it were to be accepted that amnesties are possible where there are some particular circumstances, such as a reconciliation process and/or a form of compensation to the victims, the amnesty granted to the applicant in the instant case would still not be acceptable since there is nothing to indicate that there were any such circumstances.*[87]

The last sentence of this quote questions how the ECtHR would react if mechanisms such as truth commissions were set up in "special circumstances" and if amnesties were adopted as part of the work of a truth commission. For example, how would the ECtHR react to a process such as that in South Africa, where perpetrators could be granted amnesty if they confessed and revealed to the Truth and Reconciliation Commission the full truth about the gross human rights violations committed during the apartheid regime?[88] There is no clear answer in the judgment of the ECtHR. However, the ECtHR has suggested that the adoption of an amnesty law that would prevent the investigation and prosecution of human rights violations would be generally contrary to the ECtHR.

### 2.2.3 Obligations to Respect Due Process and the Rights of the Accused

Persons accused of violating or contributing to violations of human rights during authoritarian regimes have the right to a fair trial and due process. As discussed in Part 2 of this book, lustration laws were adopted in a number of European countries in the context of decommunisation. These laws made it

86 ECtHR, *Marguš c. Croatie*, No. 4455/10, 27 May 2014, para. 139.
87 *Ibid.*, Emphasis added.
88 See on the South African Truth Commission in relation to international law, John Dugard, 'Is the Truth and Reconciliation Process Compatible with International Law? An Unanswered Question' (1997) 13 *South African Journal on Human Rights* 258.

possible to exclude, generally from public office, people accused of involvement in human rights violations during the former authoritarian regimes, mainly in Eastern Europe. Some of the excluded persons have taken their case to the ECtHR, arguing that their rights have been violated, generally the right to a fair trial as enshrined in Article 6 of the ECHR, and in particular Article 6, paragraph 1, which recognises the right to an independent and impartial tribunal. Thus, the ECtHR has had occasion to determine the international obligations of transitional states when it comes to lustration laws or vetting procedures. In general, the Council of Europe has expressed its rejection of collective lustration measures, insisting on the need to individualise the process, and the ECtHR has followed in that vein and held states responsible when they have failed to respect the rights of accused persons in the lustration or vetting process.[89]

Indeed, given the seriousness of the decision to remove a person from the public service, the ECtHR considers that the guarantees provided for in criminal proceedings are applicable. Several European states that are parties to the ECtHR have been found responsible of violating the rights of people subject to vetting.[90] For example, in *Turek v. Slovakia*, the applicant had been removed from his position following a "security clearance" based on a lustration law.[91] The ECtHR ruled that "if a State is to adopt lustration measures, it must ensure that the persons affected thereby enjoy all procedural guarantees under the Convention in respect of any proceedings relating to the application of such measures."[92] In that case, the applicant had challenged the decision to remove him from his public position without success, and claimed that the process took too much time and also violated his right to respect for his private and family life. The ECtHR found a violation of Article 6, paragraph 1 noting that

89 See Para. 12, CE Resolution 1096 (1996) Measures to dismantle the legacy of former totalitarian communist systems, adopted by the Council of Europe that insists on the respect of individual rights in the process and rejects collective measures put in place by lustration laws. This resolution has been used by the European Court of Human Rights to insist on individualisation of measures and respect for due process. See, for example, ECtHR, *Turek v. Slovakia*, No. 57986/00, 14 February 2006, para. 78; ECtHR, *Matyjek v. Poland*, No. 38184/03, 24 April 2007, para. 39; ECtHR, *Ivanovski v. the former Yugoslav Republic of Macedonia*, No. 29908/11, 21 January 2016, para. 106.

90 See, for example, Cynthia M Home, 'International Legal Rulings on Lustration Policies in Central and Eastern Europe: Rule of Law in Historical Context' (2009) 34(3) *Law & Social Inquiry* 713; ECtHR, *Ivanovski v. The Former Yugoslav Republic of Macedonia*, No. 29908/11, 21 January 2016 (case of a judge accused of collaboration with the former regime).

91 ECtHR, *Turek v. Slovakia*, No. 57986/00, 14 February 2006.

92 *Ibid*, para. 115.

"the length of the proceedings at issue was excessive and did not satisfy the requirement of a 'reasonable time.'"[93] It also held that there was violation of Article 8 that protected the right to respect for his private and family life.[94]

The ECtHR took the same line in *Matyjek v. Poland*, a case in which the complainant was "prevented from being a candidate in elections and from holding other public functions for a period of 10 years."[95] The ECtHR reaffirmed that "if a State is to adopt lustration measures, it must ensure that the persons affected thereby enjoy all procedural guarantees under the Convention in respect of any proceedings relating to the application of such measures."[96] In this case, the ECtHR found that the confidentiality of certain documents was not such as to enable the applicant to defend himself and was contrary to the principle of equality of arms, and that the applicant had no effective remedy. The ECtHR therefore found a violation of Article 6, paragraph 1 in conjunction with Article 6, paragraph 3 of the ECHR.[97]

In *Ivanovski v. The former Yugoslav Republic of Macedonia*, which concerned the case of a judge accused of collaborating with the former regime and removed from office, the ECtHR found that the entire procedure against the former judge was unfair and lacked impartiality and independence, in particular because of the involvement of the prime minister who had published a letter denouncing the former judge while the lustration procedure was pending. The ECtHR concluded that Article 6, paragraph 1 had been violated.[98] In *Korbely v. Hungary*, the ECtHR examined the case of a person accused of committing crimes against humanity, for crimes that, according to the ECHR, did not fall into that category "in the light of relevant international standards at the time."[99] The ECtHR held that Hungary had violated Article 7 of the ECHR that guarantees the non-retroactivity of criminal law.[100]

From all of this jurisprudence, therefore, it can be concluded that the transitional state has an obligation to respect the rights of the person subject to lustration or vetting processes, including their rights that do not fall into the category of the right to a fair trial, such as the rights to the non-retroactivity of

93 *Ibid.*, para. 99. On the duration of the proceedings, it began "on 25 May 1992 and ended on 26 October 1999."

94 *Ibid.*, para. 116.

95 ECtHR, *Matyjek v. Poland*, No. 38184/03, 24 April 2007), para. 26.

96 *Ibid.*, para. 62.

97 *Ibid.*, paras. 63–65.

98 ECtHR, *Ivanovski v. The Former Yugoslav Republic of Macedonia*, No. 29908/11, 21 January 2016, paras. 146–151.

99 ECtHR [GC], *Korbely v. Hungary*, No. 9174/02, (Merits and Just Satisfaction), 19 September 2008, para. 94.

100 *Ibid.*, paras. 94–95.

criminal law and to respect for their private and family life. Accordingly, in transitional justice, the investigation of past violations in a transitional or post-conflict context and the need for prosecution and punishment cannot be an occasion for the violation of human rights, even of those accused of serious crimes.

### 2.2.4 Obligations in the Field of Restitution and the Right to Property

According to Article 1 of Protocol 1 to the ECHR:

> Every natural or legal person is entitled to the peaceful enjoyment of his possessions. No one shall be deprived of his possessions except in the public interest and subject to the conditions provided for by law and by the general principles of international law.
>
> The preceding provisions shall not, however, in any way impair the right of a State to enforce such laws as it deems necessary to control the use of property in accordance with the general interest or to secure the payment of taxes or other contributions or penalties.

This provision, which enshrines the right to property, also implicitly deals with reparations, since, in international law, restitution is a form of reparation, which leads to the view that restitution of confiscated property is a form of reparation for the victim. A case of confiscation of property in the public interest may also lead states to award financial compensation to victims, which is another form of reparation. As a consequence, the ECtHR has been applying this provision in cases pertaining to restitution, the right to property and compensation in the event of the confiscation of property.

As a result of armed conflicts in Europe, including the Second World War, and the authoritarian rule of communist regimes, many people were dispossessed of their property, often in the context of nationalisation. Many of these dispossessions generally took place long before the accused state became a party to Protocol 1 to the ECHR. For that reason, the ECtHR has declared that it does not have jurisdiction *ratione temporis* when applicants who have been dispossessed of their property bring their case before it, arguing that transitional states have violated Article 1 of Protocol 1 to the ECHR and are obliged to order the restitution of these properties to them. For example, in *Malhous v. Czech Republic* in 2000, the ECtHR wrote:

> [T]he Court first recalls that it can examine applications only to the extent that they relate to events which occurred after the Convention entered into force

> with respect to the relevant Contracting Party. In the present case, the property of the applicant's father was expropriated in June 1949 and assigned to other natural persons in 1957, that is long before 18 March 1992, the date of the entry into force of the Convention with regard to the Czech Republic [...]. Therefore, the Court is not competent *ratione temporis* to examine the circumstances of the expropriation or the continuing effects produced by it up to the present date.[101]

However, the ECtHR has reacted differently when, after the fall of communist regimes, European countries adopted new restitution laws with the aim of returning property to owners who had been dispossessed by the former regime. In this situation, claimants relied on the new law to argue that the transitional state had violated their right to property. The claims have been made by people who acquired property in good faith after nationalisation and were forced to return it to the dispossessed owner, or by people who were dispossessed after an armed conflict or by the former authoritarian regime and were entitled to compensation under the new national law.

With regard to the first category, the problem was that in some European authoritarian states, many of those who owned property after the previous owners had been dispossessed had themselves acquired that property "legally." The transitional states asked them to return their property to the original owners and offered them some compensation. This compensation was generally considered insufficient, leading some of these "faithful owners" to take their case to the ECtHR, arguing that the states had violated Article 1 of Protocol 1. Most of the claims in the European transitional contexts were not *stricto sensu* about an obligation to give back a property to the owner that had been deprived; rather, the claims were to ensure that the "faithful owners" were not submitted to restitution without a fair or sufficient compensation. The ECtHR ruled in favour of these owners in a case that involved the Czech Republic legal reform pertaining to restitution[102] stating:

> The Court accepts that the general objective of the restitution laws, namely to attenuate the consequences of certain infringements of property rights caused by the communist regime, is a legitimate aim and a means of safeguarding the lawfulness of legal transactions and protecting the country's socio-economic development. However, it considers it necessary to ensure that the attenuation of those old injuries does not create disproportionate new wrongs. To that end,

101 ECtHR [GC], *Malhous v. Czech Republic*, No. 33071/96, 13 December 2000.

102 ECtHR, *Pincová and Pinc v. The Czech Republic*, No. 36548/97, 5 November 2002.

> the legislation should make it possible to take into account the particular circumstances of each case, so that persons who acquired their possessions in good faith are not made to bear the burden of responsibility which is rightfully that of the State which once confiscated those possessions.[103]

In another case, even if the ECtHR considered that states had a margin of appreciation in reforming their laws in the field of restitution, it held that a control of proportionality of measures was appropriate, and summarised the three elements to be considered: "i) whether or not the applicants had acquired the property from the State in good faith and without being able to influence the terms of the transaction [...]; (ii) the amount of the compensation paid compared to the value of the property [...]; and (iii) 'social' factors, such as whether the property at issue was the applicants' only housing available and their chances to purchase another dwelling."[104]

In examining these cases on restitution, the ECtHR did not ignore the difficulty faced by transitional states engaged in restitution in the context of the fall of communist regimes, stating, for example, that it is "mindful of the exceptional nature of the Restitution Law and accepts that in the difficult conditions of transition from a totalitarian regime to a democratic society its aims could not be realised without affecting third parties in certain circumstances."[105] In this kind of difficult transition to democracy, the ECtHR held that "a certain 'threshold of hardship' must have been crossed for the Court to find a breach of the applicants' Article 1 Protocol No. 1 rights."[106] However, despite these difficulties, in many cases examined, the ECtHR found that the state in transition had violated Article 1 of Protocol 1.[107] This clearly means that in times of transition or after an armed conflict, the state has to respect the right of property, and in the event of the restitution of legally acquired property, it has to act fairly and sufficiently compensate those who acquired their properties in a good faith during authoritarian regimes.

With regard to the second category, persons dispossessed after an armed conflict or by a former authoritarian regime who claim restitution or compensation under new national restitution laws, the ECtHR has relied on new legis-

103 *Ibid.*, para. 58.

104 ECtHR, *Velikovi and Others v. Bulgaria*, No. 43278/98 45437/99 48380/99, 15 March 2007, paras. 180–181.

105 *Ibid.*, para. 246.

106 *Ibid.*, para. 192.

107 See *Ibid.*, para. 249; ECtHR, *Pincová and Pinc v. The Czech Republic*, No. 36548/97, 5 November 2002, para. 64; ECtHR, *Tunaitis v. Lithuania*, No. 42927/08, 24 November 2015, para. 43.

lation adopted by states after the entry into force of Protocol 1 for these states. For example, in *Broniowski v. Poland*, the ECtHR found that Poland had violated Article 1 of Protocol 1 because despite the adoption of a legislation that was aimed to implement "the right to credit" (a form of compensation) for persons who had lost their properties and lands in the aftermath of the Second World War, they had been "successive limitations on the applicant's right to credit, [...] practices that made it unenforceable and unusable in practice, rendered that right illusory and destroyed its very essence."[108] In this case, the ECtHR used the now well-known "pilot judgment" technique, holding that because many individuals (80,000) were in the same situation as the applicant, it was a systemic problem that Poland had to resolve.[109]

It is notable that while the Inter-American Court of Human Rights and the European Court of Human Rights do not always align on matters of international obligations pertaining to transitional and post-conflict states, there is a shared recognition of the necessity to investigate serious violations of human rights and a general opposition to amnesty laws. Their input into identifying the international obligations of transitional states is substantial and distinct from that of the African Court on Human and Peoples' Rights.

### 2.3 African Court on Human and Peoples' Rights: The Obligation to Respect the Rights of Arrested Members of the Former Regime

Africa is one of the areas where transitional justice has been implemented. Armed conflicts and authoritarian rule regimes have affected several African states. In Africa, since the Second World War and colonisation, almost all of the 54 or 55 states have been subjected to either authoritarian political regimes or armed conflicts, or both. This situation has naturally led to many violations of human rights. Several transitional justice mechanisms have investigated these violations as discussed in Part 2 of this book. Curiously, despite this favourable terrain for the implementation of transitional justice, the African Court on Human and Peoples' Rights (African Court), which was established in 1998 to examine, inter alia, violations of human rights enshrined in the African Charter on Human and Peoples' Rights (ACHPR), has not examined many cases of serious human rights violations committed during authoritarian regimes and/or during armed conflicts in Africa. This is certainly due to the fact that it is a very young human rights court, but also due to the weaknesses of the African human rights system itself. For example, only a few

108 ECtHR, *Broniowski v. Poland*, No. 31443/96, 22 June 2004, paras. 185–187.
109 *Ibid.*, paras. 193–194.

countries have accepted the jurisdiction of the African Court to hear individual complaints. This has certainly prevented thousands of people who have suffered violations from bringing their cases to the court.

Nevertheless, the African Court has examined a case in which an international transitional justice obligation was invoked, the obligation to respect the rights of former regime figures arrested and detained. The case concerned the aftermath of the fall of the authoritarian regime of Moammar Gaddafi in Libya in 2011 when a transitional government, the National Transitional Council, was set up and called for transitional justice for the human rights violations committed by that regime. Saif Al-Islam Gaddafi, the former Libyan leader's son and one of the most important figures of the former regime, was arrested, held incommunicado and without charge or trial. He complained to the African Commission on Human and Peoples' Rights (African Commission) that his rights protected by the ACHPR had been violated. The African Commission referred the case to the African Court. The African Court was asked to review the respect of the rights of a prominent individual from the previous regime, making the case interesting in the field of transitional justice. The African Court ordered provisional measures in 2013, requiring Libya to respect the rights of the accused, in particular access to a lawyer, while it examined the case.[110]

Libya did not comply. Instead, Saif Al-Islam Gaddafi was sentenced to death in absentia in 2015. In its judgments on the merits in 2016, the African Court found that the new Libyan authorities had violated Articles 6 and 7 of the ACHPR, which guarantee the right to liberty and security and the right to a fair trial, including the rights of the accused.[111] The African Court held that Libya, despite the political transition it was undergoing, had to respect the rights of the accused. This led to the conclusion that in times of transition, new authorities must respect the rights of the accused when they decide to try former authorities, even when they are accused of having participated in the perpetration of the most serious human rights violations. This conclusion was also the one reached by the Economic Community of West African States Court of Justice.

110 ACtHPR, *African Commission on Human and Peoples' Rights v. Libya*, No. 004/2011, (Provisional Measures), 25 March 2011.

111 ACtHPR, *African Commission on Human and Peoples' Rights v Libya*, (Merits), 3 June 2016, 1 *AfCLR* 153.

## 2.4 Economic Community of West African States (ECOWAS) Court of Justice

The ECOWAS Court of Justice (ECOWAS Court) is a sub-regional court in West Africa whose role includes monitoring respect for human rights by West African states. It has been called upon to examine cases of violations in the context of transitional justice and has posed some obligations for states. The first case was that of Hissein Habré, the former head of state of Chad. When he lost power in 1990, he went into exile in Senegal. Many individuals claimed that his former regime had seriously violated their rights. They sought to have him prosecuted in Senegal under universal jurisdiction. Shortly after the start of the proceedings against Habré, Senegal's highest court (Cour de Cassation) ruled that he could not be tried in Senegal because he enjoyed immunity as a former head of state.[112] But thanks to NGOs and international pressure, Senegal began to consider bringing Habré to trial. Faced with the prospect of a "new" trial, Habré decided to refer his case to the ECOWAS Court, claiming that his human rights, the principle of *res judicata* and the principle of non-retroactivity of criminal law had been violated.[113]

The ECOWAS Court ruled that Senegal had to respect the rights of the defendant, Hissein Habré, and that a new trial by Senegalese courts would violate his rights. Therefore, according to the ECOWAS Court in this case, in the field of implementation of transitional justice based on universal jurisdiction, the third state concerned had to respect the rights of persons accused of committing serious human rights violations. However, the ECOWAS Court left open the possibility that Habré could be tried under what it called an "*ad hoc* procedure as practiced in international law."[114] So, in the event of a legal obstacle, it would be preferable for the state to engage in an international criminal procedure in which the rights of the accused would not be violated. This is what happened in the case of Habré, who was finally tried by a hybrid court, the Extraordinary African Chambers, following a bilateral agreement between Senegal and the African Union.[115]

---

112 Cour de cassation (Sénégal), *Souleymane Guengueng et autres c. Hissène Habré*, Arrêt No. 14 du 20-3-2001 Pénal.

113 See ECOWAS Court of justice. *Hissein Habré v. République du Sénégal*, Doc. No. ECW/CCJ/APP/07/08 ARRET NO: ECW/CCJ/JUD/06/10, 18 November 2010.

114 *Ibid.*, para. 61.

115 Agreement between the Government of the Republic of Senegal and the African Union on the Establishment of the Extraordinary African Chambers within the courts of Senegal, 22 August 2012.

A second case was filed on behalf of victims of a massacre that had been committed in Liberia in 1990, during the civil war.[116] The complainants asked the ECOWAS Court to rule that Liberia had an obligation to investigate the case, prosecute the perpetrators of the massacre and provide reparations to the victims. If the ECOWAS Court had decided to investigate and rule on the merits of the case, it would have certainly helped to determine Liberia's international obligations as a post-conflict state and would have been an important contribution to determining the international obligations of states in the field of transitional justice with regard to accountability. However, the ECOWAS Court ruled that it lacked *ratione temporis* jurisdiction to examine the case concerning violations of human rights committed in 1990, because it was created in 1991 and its jurisdiction concerning violations of human rights was established by a supplementary protocol in 2005.[117]

This short review of the role of the African Court and ECOWAS Court in the field of human rights reveals that only a limited number of cases have been examined, and that their contribution to the identification of international obligations in the field of transitional justice is constrained. The International Court of Justice has also defined some international obligations in the field of transitional justice.

## 2.5 The International Court of Justice

The International Court of Justice (ICJ) is an international court that settles disputes between states and provides advisory opinions. It is not an institution that examines disputes between individuals and states. The question, then, is whether its jurisprudence provides guidance on the international obligations of states facing transitional justice for violations of international law committed during dictatorship and/or armed conflict. The answer is in the affirmative. The ICJ examines disputes that are often based on treaties that states have ratified and that provide for the possibility of its jurisdiction in case of questions concerning their interpretation or application. For this reason, the ICJ has examined cases involving the interpretation or implementation of international obligations contained in treaties that enshrine rights violated or crimes committed during dictatorship and/or armed conflict. In addition to finding that states have violated international law, the ICJ has also held, in

116 *The Global Justice & Research Project and al. v. The Republic of Liberia*, Complaint to ECOWAS Court of Justice, 29 September 2022.

117 ECOWAS Court of justice, *The Global Justice & Research Project & 3 ORS v. The Republic of Liberia*, Application No: ECW/CCJ/APP/48/22, Ruling No: ECW/CCJ/RUL/04/24, 17 October 2024.

cases involving transitional states and crimes committed in the past, that states must respect the provisions of treaties establishing international obligations in the case of violations of human rights and international humanitarian law and in the case of international crimes.

### 2.5.1 The 1948 Genocide Convention and the Obligation to Prevent Genocide and to Punish Perpetrators of Genocide after an Armed Conflict

In the context of the post-conflict situation in the Balkans, the case on the application of the Convention on the Prevention and Punishment of the Crime of Genocide (*Bosnia and Herzegovina v. Serbia and Montenegro*) led the ICJ to clarify the international obligations of states with regard to genocide.[118] In this case, Bosnia accused Serbia of violating Article 1 of the 1948 Genocide Convention, which stated that states were to "undertake to prevent and to punish" genocide. The ICJ found that Serbia had violated the 1948 Genocide Convention by failing to prevent the genocide in Srebrenica. It ruled that Serbia had the means to prevent this genocide but had failed to do so, thus violating Article 1 of the Convention.[119] However, with regard to what a state such as Serbia had to do in a post-conflict situation such as this, the ICJ ruled that Serbia had an obligation to punish the perpetrators of this genocide, and in this regard it gave a particular interpretation of Article VI of the 1948 Genocide Convention, which provides that the perpetrators of this genocide "shall be tried by a competent tribunal of the State in the territory of which the act was committed, or by such international penal tribunal [...]." The ICJ particularly held that "Article VI must at least cover all international criminal courts created after the adoption of the Convention (at which date no such court existed) of potentially universal scope, and competent to try the perpetrators of genocide or any of the other acts enumerated in Article III. The nature of the legal instrument by which such a court is established is without importance in this respect."[120] The ICTY, as discussed in Part 2 of this book, was an international criminal tribunal in charge of examining the violations of international humanitarian law committed in the former Yugoslavia. According to the ICJ, the ICTY fell into the category of "international criminal court"

118 Application of the Convention on the Prevention and Punishment of the Crime of Genocide (*Bosnia and Herzegovina v. Serbia and Montenegro*), Judgment, I.C.J. Reports 2007, 43.

119 *Ibid.*, para. 438.

120 *Ibid.*, para. 445.

and, by refusing to co-operate with the tribunal to bring to justice those accused of genocide, Serbia had violated its duty to punish the perpetrators of that genocide.[121]

In this case, the ICJ gave a clear interpretation of what Serbia should have done in a post-conflict context to deal with the genocide committed. Serbia should have cooperated with the ICTY to fulfil its international obligation to punish the perpetrators of genocide, as required by the 1948 Genocide Convention. Even if this ruling applied to the case of Serbia, it could be argued that it contributed to clarifying the international obligations of post-conflict states when it came to the criminal accountability of perpetrators of certain international crimes.

### 2.5.2 The 1984 Convention against Torture and the Obligation to Initiate an Inquiry and to Prosecute or Extradite Perpetrators of Torture after a Dictatorship

In another case concerning transitional justice for the crimes committed in Chad during its dictatorship, Belgium referred a case to the ICJ against Senegal, after an unsuccessful request of extradition. Belgium claimed Senegal had violated the 1984 Convention against Torture because it did not prosecute or extradite the former Chadian head of state, Hissein Habré, who had taken refuge in that country after losing power in 1990 and who faced accusations of torture and crimes against humanity committed when he was president of Chad.[122] The ICJ ruled that in that case, Senegal had violated Article 6, paragraph 2 and Article 7 of the 1984 Convention against Torture because it did not "immediately initiate a preliminary inquiry as soon as they had reason to suspect Mr. Habré, who was in their territory, of being responsible for acts of torture"[123] and because it failed to prosecute or extradite the accused.[124] The ICJ held that Senegal had the obligation to prosecute Habré or extradite him.[125] Here, again, the ICJ reminded states of their international obligations in the field of transitional justice when it came to the search for accountability for violations that had been committed, which was torture in this case. These

---

121 *Ibid.*, paras. 448–450.

122 ICJ, Application Instituting Proceedings, Questions Relating to the Obligation to Prosecute or Extradite (*Belgium V. Senegal*), filed in the Registry of the Court on February19, 2009.

123 Questions relating to the Obligation to Prosecute or Extradite (*Belgium v. Senegal*), Judgment, I.C.J. Reports 2012, para. 88.

124 *Ibid.*, paras. 92–117.

125 *Ibid.*, para. 122 (6).

obligations, which included the launch of an inquiry, prosecutions and the option of extradition, applied in the context of universal jurisdiction provided by the 1984 Convention against Torture.

In this case, as requested by Belgium, the ICJ could have given more elements on the legal basis of these rules by examining the existence of the customary international obligations to launch legal proceedings in cases of crimes against humanity, war crimes and genocide.[126] This could have helped more precisely define the general obligations of states, including post-conflict states, to investigate certain international crimes and prosecute their alleged perpetrators. However, the ICJ refused to do so, concluding "that, at the time of the filing of the Application, the dispute between the Parties did not relate to breaches of obligations under customary international law and that it thus has no jurisdiction."[127]

### 2.5.3 Individual Reparations for Individual Victims in Cases of Serious Human Rights Violations or International Crimes

In general public international law, a state that is the victim of a breach of international law may be awarded reparations as a result of that breach attributed to another state. This is part of state responsibility for wrongful acts, which has been well established since the *Chorzow* case heard by the Permanent Court of International Justice,[128] and more recently by the UN International Law Commission.[129] This has an implication in transitional justice. Post-conflict states may be awarded reparations by the ICJ after it has ruled that a state has breached international law. For example, in the genocide case of Bosnia against Serbia, the ICJ ruled that Bosnia was entitled to reparations in the form of satisfaction, declaring that Serbia was "indeed in breach of Article VI of the Convention" of 1948, and holding that that declaration was "one appropriate form of satisfaction."[130]

126 *Ibid.*, para. 53.

127 *Ibid.*, para. 55.

128 Factory at Chorzow (*Germany v. Poland*), 1928 P.C.I.J. (ser. A, No. 17). The Court held that: "It is a principle of international law that the breach of an engagement involves an obligation to make reparation in an adequate form."

129 Art. 31 and Art. 34-37 of the ICL Project articles for the Responsibility of States for Internationally Wrongful Acts, General Assembly resolution 56/83 of 12 December 2001, UN doc. A/56/83, Annex.

130 Application of the Convention on the Prevention and Punishment of the Crime of Genocide (*Bosnia and Herzegovina v. Serbia and Montenegro*), Judgment, I.C.J. Reports 2007, para. 464.

However, when it comes to granting reparations to individuals, the situation is not so clear and explicit. Of course, a state can protect one of its nationals through diplomatic protection. But in that case, it is defending its own rights, which have been violated. Even if a case of reparation for individuals could be invoked in a diplomatic protection procedure against a state, this would not be a recognition of a direct right to reparation for individuals and a corresponding obligation for states to grant reparation to individuals. In a case involving Germany and Italy that concerned some acts related to the Second World War, the question of reparations for individual victims after an armed conflict was discussed. But the ICJ did not examine the topic, holding that it needed "not rule on whether, as Italy contend[ed], international law confers upon the individual victim of a violation of the law of armed conflict a directly enforceable right to claim compensation."[131] At present, therefore, there is no clear indication in the case law of the ICJ that states have an obligation to compensate victims of serious violations of human rights or international humanitarian law after an armed conflict or during a transitional period.

To conclude, international judicial bodies have contributed to the identification of the international obligations of transitional or post-conflict states with regard to violations of human rights and international humanitarian law and international crimes. In reviewing the compliance of transitional states with international law, they have interpreted many treaties as requiring state action in the area of accountability. These international obligations are established in the field of investigations, prosecutions, punishment, reparations, respect of the rights of victims and respect of the rights of persons accused. In addressing the difficulties and challenges faced by states in transition or post-conflict states, international judicial bodies such as the Inter-American Court of Human Rights and the European Court of Human Rights do not disregard these issues. Such considerations are even occasionally explicitly referenced. In some instances, they even make a point of mentioning them explicitly. Even if they hold that post-conflict and transitional states may only have an obligation of means in the field of investigations because of these challenges and difficulties, they examine the efforts made by these states to investigate cases. Furthermore, the existence of these challenges and difficulties does not serve as a basis for asserting that post-conflict or transitional states are exempt from their international obligations regarding violations and crimes committed.

---

131 Jurisdictional Immunities of the State (*Germany v. Italy*: Greece intervening), Judgment, I.C.J. Reports 2012, para. 108.

However, this contribution is limited in scope as the judgments of these judicial bodies are typically addressed to the state in question and on a case-by-case basis. It is not typical for judicial bodies to impose general obligations on states, and even the establishment of the international responsibility of a particular transitional state does not mean that it would comply with the judicial decision and, for instance, conduct investigations, engage in prosecutions and award reparations to victims. However, their case law provides a general indication of what is generally expected from states in the area of accountability for violations and crimes committed during authoritarian rule and armed conflict. An examination of these sources of international law, treaties and decisions of judicial bodies, shows that there are indeed international rules in the field of transitional justice. In contrast, the legal development of other sources of international law is less clear and decisive than that of treaties and judicial bodies' decisions.

## 3 Limited Importance of Other Sources of International Law

It is difficult to determine the international obligations of transitional and post-conflict states with certainty using the other sources of international law, namely, international custom, general principles and legal doctrine.

### 3.1 Incertitude of International Custom

In international law, two cumulative conditions are required for a custom to exist: a general practice and the *opinio juris*, the fact that states consider that practice to be an international obligation. Are there international customs that make it mandatory for post-conflict states or transitional states to implement transitional justice, that create international obligations for them, for instance to investigate serious violations of human rights and IHL, or international crimes, to prosecute perpetrators and punish them, and to award reparations to victims? The answer is not obvious because there is no set of established customary rules. Instead, and without an undisputed answer to this question, there are many doctrinal debates on whether or not there is a customary law obligation to investigate serious violations and international crimes, to prosecute perpetrators or to provide reparations to victims.[132] In

132 See, for example, on these debates and different opinions on that matter: Louise Mallinder, 'Can Amnesties and International Justice Be Reconciled ?' (2007) 1 *International Journal of Transitional Justice* 208, 214; Miles M Jackson, 'The Customary International

addition, the lack of general practice, with many states failing to engage in accountability proceedings following the commission of violations and crimes, casts doubt on the existence of an authoritative customary law requiring transitional states to take measures to investigate, prosecute, sanction or provide reparations in case of serious violations and crimes.

However, in international humanitarian law, the International Committee of the Red Cross (ICRC) has stated that there are customary rules in the field of accountability for IHL violations, and this is relevant for transitional justice. According to its published study *Customary International Humanitarian Law*: "States must investigate war crimes allegedly committed by their nationals or armed forces, or on their territory, and, if appropriate, prosecute the suspects. They must also investigate other war crimes over which they have jurisdiction and, if appropriate, prosecute the suspects."[133] This customary law, according to the ICRC, provides the prohibition of amnesties in case of war crimes. According to Rule 159 in the study: "At the end of hostilities, the authorities in power must endeavour to grant the broadest possible amnesty to persons who have participated in a non-international armed conflict, or those deprived of their liberty for reasons related to the armed conflict, with the exception of persons suspected of, accused of or sentenced for war crimes."[134] In the field of reparation, Rule 150 provides: "A State responsible for violations of international humanitarian law is required to make full reparation for the loss or injury caused."[135] The comments about Rule 150 mention "an increasing trend in favour of enabling individual victims of violations of international humanitarian law to seek reparation directly from the responsible State."[136] So according to the ICRC study, there are international customary

Law Duty to Prosecute Crimes against Humanity: A New framework' (2007–2008) 16(1) *Tulane Journal of International and Comparative Law* 117, 132; William Schabas, 'La place de la coutume dans les travaux des Commissions vérité, justice et réconciliation: Le cas de la Sierra Leone' in Paul Tavernier and Jean-Marie Henckaerts (eds), *Droit international coutumier: Enjeux et défis contemporains*, (Bruylant 2008) 158; John Dugard, 'Possible Conflicts of Jurisdiction with Truth Commissions' in Antonio Cassese, Paola Gaeta and John R. W. D. Jones (eds), *The Rome Statute of the International Criminal Court: A Commentary*, (Oxford University Press 2002) 698; Robert Cryer, Håkan Friman, Darryl Robinson and Elisabeth Wilmshurst, *An Introduction to International Criminal Law and Procedure*, (Cambridge University Press 2007) 59; Naomi Roht-Arriaza, 'State Responsibility to Investigate and Prosecute Grave Human Rights Violations in International Law' (1990) 78 *California Law Review* 449, 489.

133 Jean-Marie Henckaerts and Louise Doswald-Beck, *Customary International Humanitarian Law*, Vol. I: Rules, (Cambridge University Press 2005), Rule 158, 607.

134 *Ibid.*, Rule 159, 611.

135 *Ibid.*, Rule 150, 537.

136 *Ibid.*, 441.

rules that oblige states to investigate war crimes, prosecute perpetrators of war crimes and award reparations.

In addition, in the area of customary law, it is impossible to ignore the growing practice of transitional justice, with many states either investigating or prosecuting, punishing and awarding reparations, as discussed in Part 2 of this book. At the same time, recent legal developments, including those of the judicial mechanisms examined in the Part 2 of this book, as well as resolutions and soft law developments in the field of transitional justice,[137] are a sign that there is an *opinio juris* on the obligation to investigate, prosecute, punish and award reparation in cases of international crimes and serious violations of human rights and international humanitarian law. This cumulative growing practice, albeit limited, and the *opinio juris* on the obligation to implement transitional justice indicate that there is at least an emerging customary law in international transitional justice law that obliges transitional states to investigate, prosecute, punish and provide reparation in the case of the commission of serious violations and crimes. A customary law is emerging, even if it can be argued that it presents a high level of uncertainty, just as the general principles of international law.

### 3.2 The Relative Relevance of the General Principles of International Law

This source of international law contains principles that are found and shared in most national legal systems. It is common knowledge among international law academics and experts that this source of international law is controversial. There are no authoritative legal documents that list the general principles of international law. Moreover, even if they are identified, the relevance of the use of these principles is questioned, as they are often found in treaties. Many of these principles are identified by international judicial bodies which, when considering a case and looking at the national legal systems, may decide that a principle belongs to these general principles of international law. This means that identifying general principles of international law often requires looking at the decisions of international judicial bodies, which is another source of international law. For example, reparation, which is part of transitional justice, is considered a general principle of international law. In the landmark *Chorzow Factory* case, the Permanent Court of International Justice ruled: "It is a principle of international law that the breach of an engagement involves

137 See below Chapter 9.

an obligation to make reparation in an adequate form."[138] The same can be said of the right to defence and, more generally, of the need to respect and protect human rights, which are found in many legal systems. However, the uncertainty of this source of international law suggests that it does not currently appear to be a decisive source of international obligations for transitional states, nor does legal doctrine.

### 3.3 Limited Impact of Legal Doctrinal Developments

There are, of course, numerous legal writings, articles and books on transitional justice that express different views on transitional justice, as demonstrated throughout this volume. The work of some scholars and legal experts has attempted to establish rules and principles in the field of accountability following the commission of violations and crimes. Even if they lack legal authority and cannot impose any international obligations to transitional states, these works are important because they seek to establish rules and principles that transitional or post-conflict states should apply to violations committed in the past, thus contributing to the understanding of legal doctrine opinion on the international obligations of these states. Because they are the product of the collaboration of numerous scholars, some results of scholarship initiatives can be mentioned in this respect.

In 2002, several legal scholars, gathered at a conference in Brussels, adopted the Brussels Principles against Impunity and for International Justice, which, they wrote, were "based on international law."[139] They added that "when in some cases they depart from it, they are formulated according to the optative or conditional mode." Among the 24 principles adopted by these legal scholars, some dealt with the obligations of states in the field of accountability. For example, principle 1 (paragraph 3) provides: "The obligation to repress serious crimes constitutes a peremptory norm (jus cogens) of international law." This makes it clear that states have to make sure that the perpetrators of these crimes are prosecuted, at the international or national level. In the same vein, insisting on the rights of victims to "know the truth about serious crimes" and "to obtain justice," principle 2 implicitly holds that states have a role to play in the implementation of these rights. The cooperation between states is also highlighted (principle 4), as well as rules of international law

138 Case Concerning the Factory at Chorzow (Claim for Indemnity) (Jurisdiction), Publications of the Permanent Court of International Justice. Series A. – No. 9, July 26th, 1927, 21.

139 These principles are available online https://www.legal-tools.org/doc/7205b9/pdf/. See also a copy in Carreras Montserrat (ed), *Lutter contre l'impunité, Actes du Colloque du 11 au 13 mars 2002*, (Bruylant 2002), 115–130.

regarding the imprescriptibly of genocide, crimes against humanity and war crimes (principles 7). Principle 14 deals with the obligation of the state to exercise universal jurisdiction when the perpetrator of a "serious crime" is in its territory. Taken as a whole, these principles give an importance to the need of accountability as a response to international crimes.

The other legal doctrinal developments are in the field of *post bellum* and post-conflict justice. Some scholars, aware of the absence of a clear set of international humanitarian law rules applicable to states after an armed conflict, have tried to fill that void and there is now a well-established debate on the identification of a category of rules that academics have termed *jus post bellum* and defined as "the laws and norms of justice that apply to the process of ending war and building peace."[140] According to those who propose the new concept, these "laws and norms" apply to states in post-conflict situations.[141] This *jus post bellum* includes transitional justice proceedings, and seems to be larger than these proceedings that generally only deal with responses to serious violations and ways to prevent them. In spite of the current momentum regarding *jus post bellum*, the identification of *jus post bellum* rules does not seem easy in international law as there are no international rules or treaties devoted to *jus post bellum*. Consequently, there is a general question whether the rules of *jus post bellum* should be found in existing rules of international law, especially international humanitarian law, or whether they are new rules that are emerging or should emerge.[142] There is no authoritative legal answer to this question at the moment.

Regarding legal doctrine development on post-conflict justice, a research project conducted by Cherif Bassiouni and several researchers has proposed seven principles, referred to as the Chicago Principles, which post-conflict states must or should respect.[143] These seven principles are:

---

140 Jennifer S Easterday, Jens Iverson and Stahn Carsten, 'Exploring the Normative Foundations of Jus Post Bellum: An Introduction' in Jennifer S Easterday, Jens Iverson, and Stahn Carsten (eds), *Jus post bellum: Mapping the normative foundations* (Oxford University Press 2014) 1.

141 See, for example, Jennifer S Easterday, Jens Iverson et Carsten Stahn, *ibid.;* Stahn Carsten and Jann K Kleffner (eds), *Jus Post Bellum. Towards a Law of Transition from Conflict to Peace* (T.M.C. Asser Press 2008).

142 See 'Dossier: Le jus post bellum – nouveau cheval de Troie du droit des conflits armés ?' (2011) *Revue Belge de Droit International.*

143 See Cherif Bassiouni *et al.* (eds), *The Chicago Principles on Post-conflict Justice* (IHRL Institute 2007) 16–17. Available online: https://law.depaul.edu/about/centers-and-institutes/international-human-rights-law-institute/projects/Documents/chicago_principles.pdf (last visited May 19, 2024).

1. States shall prosecute alleged perpetrators of gross violations of human rights and humanitarian law.
2. States shall respect the right to truth and encourage formal investigations of past violations by truth commissions or other bodies.
3. States shall acknowledge the special status of victims, ensure access to justice, and develop remedies and reparations.
4. States should implement vetting policies, sanctions, and administrative measures.
5. States should support official programs and popular initiatives to memorialize victims, educate society regarding past political violence, and preserve historical memory.
6. States should support and respect traditional, indigenous, and religious approaches regarding past violations.
7. States shall engage in institutional reform to support the rule of law, restore public trust, promote fundamental rights, and support good governance.[144]

According to Bassiouni and colleagues, they use "the term 'shall' to indicate an established obligation under international law and the term 'should' to reference a suggested action based on international norms."[145] This leads to the conclusion that investigations, prosecutions, remedies, sanctions and reparations are, according to these scholars, the areas in which post-conflict states have international obligations. This is consistent with what has been explored in the area of treaty and judicial jurisprudence. Investigations, prosecutions, remedies and reparations are at the core of what is required of the state when it comes to transitional justice obligations under international law. Nevertheless, this legal doctrine and these writings are very limited as a source of international law. It is no exaggeration to say that they do not have a decisive and authoritative impact on the identification of international obligations in the field of transitional justice.

Despite the uncertainty and lack of authoritative and decisive effect, this accumulation of legal developments in international customs, general principles of international law and legal doctrine, as well as in treaties and decisions of judicial bodies, is evidence of an existing and a growing body of international transitional justice law. In the same vein, in addition to these recognised sources of international law, soft law contributes significantly to the construction and development of this growing legal field.

144 *Ibid.*
145 *Ibid.*, 3.

CHAPTER 9

# Soft Law Sources and Transitional Justice

Certainly, it is in the area of soft law, of non-binding law, that international legal aspects of transitional justice issues have been well developed. Many non-binding legal instruments and much of the jurisprudence of non-judicial human rights bodies have been adopted, especially within several international organisations. Even though these instruments and the jurisprudence are not binding, they provide guidance on what is expected from states in transition or post-conflict states with regard to serious violations or crimes of the past. Some of these international soft law elements were presented in Part 1 of this book because they are part of the evolution and dissemination of transitional justice. In this chapter, the focus is on the definition of the international obligations of states as proposed by soft law within international organisations. It is therefore important to examine the contribution of soft law to the construction of international transitional justice law within the United Nations, the European Union, the Council of Europe, the Organisation of American States and the African Union. When it comes to the legal developments of transitional justice in these international organisations, we find non-binding legal instruments on the one hand (discussed in section 1) and the jurisprudence of quasi-judicial human rights bodies on the other (discussed in section 2).

## 1 Non-binding Legal Instruments: Resolutions and Others

### 1.1 United Nations

Since the creation of the United Nations, many of its organs have been interested in the question of what states have to do to deal with human rights violations in the aftermath of armed conflicts or authoritarian regimes. In order to describe the role of the United Nations, it is convenient to examine certain of its organs that have been playing a significant role in determining some international legal aspects of transitional justice. These organs are the UN General Assembly, the UN Security Council and the UN Human Rights bodies.

 | HTTPS://DOI.ORG/10.1163/9789004766655-016

### 1.1.1 UN General Assembly

From the outset, the UN General Assembly has been interested in the human rights obligations of transitional and post-conflict states. The adoption of the Universal Declaration of Human Rights (UDHR) by a 1948 resolution was part of this interest. The preamble to the UDHR recognises the idea that "disregard and contempt for human rights have resulted in barbarous acts which have outraged the conscience of mankind," and that "the advent of a world in which human beings shall enjoy freedom of speech and belief and freedom from fear and want has been proclaimed as the highest aspiration of the common people."[1] It also emphasises the need for states to promote and respect human rights. The preamble implicitly states that because of the atrocities committed in the past, it is necessary to move forward, to recognise human rights and freedom for all and to avoid repeating the past. This idea is at the heart of transitional justice today. This idea did not stop at the General Assembly in 1948. Since 1948, the General Assembly has assisted in passing many resolutions on the need to respect human rights.

Initially, the General Assembly's resolutions focused mainly on states experiencing dictatorship and armed conflict, where human rights were being violated. In 1949, for example, it condemned the Soviet Union's measures to prevent women from leaving their country of origin with a spouse of a different nationality, and it used the UDHR as one of its instruments.[2] The same year, it denounced "the suppression of human rights and fundamental freedoms in" Bulgaria and Hungary.[3] The General Assembly insisted on the "observance of human rights" by UN member states in 1952.[4] In the 1960s, it denounced the policies of apartheid in South Africa,[5] and, in the 1970s and

1 UN General Assembly, Resolution 217 (III), International Bill of Human Rights, A Universal Declaration of Human Rights, UN doc. A/RES/217(III), 10 December 1948.

2 UN General Assembly, Resolution 285 (III), Violation by the Union of Soviet Socialist Republics of fundamental human rights, traditional diplomatic practices and other principles of the Charter, UN doc. A/RES/285(III), 25 April 1949.

3 UN General Assembly, Resolution 272 (III), Observance in Bulgaria and Hungary of human rights and fundamental freedoms, A/RES/272(III), 30 April 1949.

4 UN General Assembly, Resolution 540 (VI), Observance of human rights, UN doc. A/RES/540(IV), 4 February 1952.

5 See among others resolution on that topic, UN General Assembly, Resolution 1598 (XV). Question of race conflict in South Africa resulting from the policies of apartheid of the Government of the Union of South Africa, UN doc. A/RES/1598(XV), 13 April 1961.

1980s, the violations of human rights in Chile,[6] and in El Salvador and Guatemala.[7]

In the 1970s, the General Assembly began to pay attention to human rights in states that had just undergone a regime change (including from democracy to dictatorship) and/or were trying to cope with armed conflict. For example, it urged Chile, which was experiencing a regime change when the democratic regime failed following a coup d'état and the accession to power of General Pinochet, not only to cease human rights violations but also to "prosecute and punish those responsible for [...] torture and other forms of inhuman and degrading treatment [...], to investigate and clarify the fate of" persons who have disappeared, and to respect the human rights of people living in Chile.[8] In the context of growing practices of "enforced or involuntary disappearances" in dictatorial political regimes, the General Assembly called on governments "to devote appropriate resources to searching for such persons and to undertake speedy and impartial investigations."[9]

In the 1980s, the UN General Assembly again called on Chile to put an end to human rights violations, including enforced disappearances, and to investigate, prosecute and punish those responsible for, inter alia, enforced disappearances, unexplained deaths and torture.[10] Calls for investigations in cases of enforced disappearances and other violations, and sometimes for punishment of those responsible, were also addressed to countries experiencing dictatorship and/or armed conflicts that included Guatemala[11] and El Salvador,[12] two countries that were facing civil wars opposing governments and armed rebels groups.

---

6 UN General Assembly, Resolution 32/118, Protection of human rights in Chile, UN doc. A/RES/32/118, 16 December 1977.

7 UN General Assembly, Resolution 38/101, Situation of human rights and fundamental freedoms in El Salvador, UN doc. A/RES/38/101, 16 December 1983; Resolution 38/100. Situation of human rights and fundamental freedoms in Guatemala, UN doc. A/RES/38/100, 16 December 1983.

8 UN General Assembly, Resolution 33/175, Protection of human rights in Chile, A/RES/33/175, 20 December 1978.

9 UN General Assembly, Resolution 33/173, Disappeared persons, UN doc. A/RES/33/173, 20 December 1978.

10 UN General Assembly, Resolution 36/157, Protection of human rights in Chile, UN doc. A/RES/36/157, 16 December 1981.

11 UN General Assembly, Resolution 38/100, Situation of human rights and fundamental freedoms in Guatemala, UN doc. A/RES/38/100, 16 December 1983.

12 UN General Assembly, Resolution 38/101. Situation of human rights and fundamental freedoms in El Salvador, UN doc. A/RES/38/101, 16 December 1983.

These demands on many countries under authoritarian rule or in armed conflict expanded in the 1990s. Since the 1990s, the General Assembly has adopted resolutions calling on several states in situations of armed conflict, authoritarian rule, transition or post-conflict to investigate and/or prosecute perpetrators of human rights violations, including enforced disappearances and killings.[13] Some of these resolutions calling for the investigation, prosecution or punishment of perpetrators of human rights violations were addressed to countries in transition, such as El Salvador.[14] Some also referred to the need for transitional justice in some states. For example, a General Assembly resolution called on Afghanistan "[t]o develop a human rights-based strategy addressing, in particular, issues of accountability, transitional justice [...]."[15]

In addition to these resolutions relating to specific states, the General Assembly has also adopted a resolution on the principles of reparations, as discussed in Part 2 of this book, a resolution that insists on the need for reparations in cases of serious violations of human rights and international humanitarian law.[16] Influenced by the former Human Rights Commission and the Human Rights Council, the General Assembly also adopted a Reso-

13 See, for example, the UN General Assembly resolutions in these UN documents: UN doc. A/RES/45/174, 18 December 1990 (Afghanistan); UN doc. A/RES/46/133, 17 December 1991 (El Salvador); UN doc. A/RES/47/142, 18 December 1992 (Sudan); UN doc. A/RES/47/147, 18 December 1992 (Former Yugoslavia); UN doc. A/RES/153, 20 December 1993 (Former Yugoslavia); UN doc. A/RES/49/206, 20 December 1994 (Rwanda); UN doc. A/RES/50/200, 22 December 1995 (Rwanda); UN doc. A/RES/51/108, 12 December 1994 (Afghanistan); UN doc. A/RES/52/138, 12 December 1997 (Haiti); UN doc. A/RES/53/163, 9 December 1998 (Bosnia and Herzegovina); UN doc. A/RES/54/187, 17 December 1999 (Haiti); UN doc. A/RES/54/116, 4 December 2000 (Sudan); UN doc. A/RES/56/231, 24 December 2001 (Myanmar); UN doc. A/RES/57/234, 18 December 2002 (Afghanistan); UN doc. A/RES/58/191, 22 December 2003 (Cambodia); UN doc. A/RES/59/207, 20 December 2004 (DRC); UN doc. A/RES/60/170, 16 December 2005 (DRC); UN doc. A/RES/61/176, 19 December 2006 (Iran); UN doc. A/RES/62/169, 18 December 2007 (Belarus); UN doc. A/RES/63/245, 24 December 2008 (Myanmar); UN doc. A/RES/64/175, 18 December 2009 (North Korea); UN doc. A/RES/65/241, 24 December 2010 (Myanmar); UN doc. A/RES/66/175, 19 December 2011 (Iran); UN doc. A/RES/66/253 B, 3 August 2012 (Syria); UN doc. A/RES/68/182, 18 December 2013 (Syria); UN doc. A/RES/69/190, 18 December 2014 (Iran); UN doc. A/RES/70/77, 9 December 2015 (Afghanistan); UN doc. A/RES/71/205, 19 December 2016 (Ukraine-Russia); UN doc. A/RES/72/190, 19 December 2017 (Ukraine-Russia); UN doc. A/RES/73/182, 17 December 2018 (Syria); UN doc. A/RES/74/246, 27 December 2019 (Myanmar); UN doc. A/RES/75/192, 16 December 2020 (Ukraine-Russia); UN doc. A/RES/76/228, 24 December 2021 (Syria); UN doc. A/RES/77/227, 15 December 2022 (Myanmar); UN doc. A/RES/78/221, 19 December 2023 (Ukraine-Russia).

14 UN doc. A/RES/46/133, 17 December 1991 (El Salvador).

15 UN doc. A/RES/57/234, 18 December 2002 (Afghanistan).

16 UN General Assembly, Resolution 60/147, Basic Principles and Guidelines on the Right to a Remedy and Reparation for Victims of Gross Violations of International Human Rights

lution on the Right to the Truth in 2013.[17] This resolution recognised the importance of the right to the truth for victims and encouraged states in transition to take certain measures "to disseminate, implement and monitor the implementation of the recommendations of non-judicial mechanisms,"[18] to establish "specific judicial mechanisms and, where appropriate, truth and reconciliation commissions to complement the justice system to investigate and address gross violations of human rights and serious violations of international humanitarian law."[19] It called for cooperation and assistance in the field of the right to the truth.[20] States should "acknowledge the important role of civil society in monitoring the implementation of recommendations of truth commissions,"[21] sign, ratify or adhere to the International Convention for the Protection of All Persons from Enforced Disappearance,[22] "establish a national archival policy" in other inter alia to preserve "the archives pertaining to human rights."[23] The General Assembly also adopted a resolution on peacebuilding and established the Peacebuilding Commission, an instrument that the UN has used to provide assistance to many countries confronted by armed conflict or transition.[24] Even if the resolution did not address what needs to be done in transitional states, it stressed that peacebuilding has many facets that need to be addressed in a comprehensive approach to states in conflict.

Taken together, these resolutions on transitional justice require states to investigate human rights violations during dictatorships, armed conflicts or in their aftermath, and/or to prosecute and punish the perpetrators of these violations. Victims' rights, such as the right to truth and the right to reparations, and the role that states should play to make them effective, are also central in these resolutions. What is also striking about many of these resolutions is the fact that they do not only address the obligations related to human rights violations but also refer to the same obligations in the case of violations of international humanitarian law, in the case of international crimes such as

---

Law and Serious Violations of International Humanitarian Law, UN doc. A/RES/60/147, 16 December 2005.

17 UN General Assembly, Resolution 68/165, Right to the truth, UN doc. A/RES/68/165, 18 December 2013.

18 *Ibid.*, para. 3.

19 *Ibid.*, para 4.

20 *Ibid.*, para. 5.

21 *Ibid.*, para. 6.

22 *Ibid.*, para. 7.

23 *Ibid.*, para. 10.

24 UN General Assembly, Resolution 70/262, Review of the United Nations peacebuilding architecture, UN doc. A/RES/70/262, 27 April 2016.

war crimes, crimes against humanity and also genocide. The Security Council follows the same line.

### 1.1.2 UN Security Council

Indeed, the UN Security Council has also acted in the same vein over the years, insisting on the need for states in transition to address human rights violations, including by investigating, prosecuting and punishing perpetrators.[25] Its resolutions are often general, that is, they are not addressed to a particular state, and are not based on Chapter VII of the United Nations Charter, which gives the Security Council the power to adopt resolutions that are binding on states in the event of threats to international peace and security.[26] However, some of these Security Council resolutions are not soft law because they are based on this Chapter VII and are addressed to specific states, especially in transitional contexts.[27]

---

25 See the UN Security Council resolutions in these documents: UN doc. S/RES/1265 (1999), 17 September 1999; UN doc. S/RES/1318 (2000) 7 September 2000; UN doc. S/RES/1379 (2001), 20 November 2001; UN doc. S/RES/1484 (2003), 30 May 2003; UN doc. S/RES/1529 (2004), 29 February 2004; S/RES/1602 (2005), 31 May 2005; UN doc. S/RES/1721 (2006), 1st November 2006; UN doc. S/RES/1826 (2008), 29 July 2008; UN doc. S/RES/1906 (2009), 23 December 2009; UN doc. S/RES/1959 (2010), 16 December 2010; UN doc. S/RES/1998 (2011), 12 July 2011; S/RES/2062 (2012), 26 July 2012.

26 For example, UN Security Council, Resolution 1265, UN doc. S/RES/1265 (1999), 17 September 1999 emphasising "the responsibility of States to end impunity and to prosecute those responsible for genocide, crimes against humanity and serious violations of international humanitarian law," para. 6; UN Security Council, Resolution 1318, UN doc. S/RES/1318 (2000), 7 September 2000, stressing that "that the perpetrators of crimes against humanity, crimes of genocide, war crimes, and other serious violations of international humanitarian law should be brought to justice," para. VI of the resolution deals in particular with Africa; UN Security Council, Resolution 1379, UN doc. S/RES/1379 (2001), 20 November 2001, urging states, regarding the protection of children, to "Put an end to impunity, prosecute those responsible for genocide, crimes against humanity, war crimes, and other egregious crimes perpetrated against children and exclude, where feasible, these crimes from amnesty provisions and relevant legislation, and ensure that post-conflict truth-and-reconciliation processes address serious abuses involving children" para. 9 (a); In the same vein, UN Security Council, Resolution 1998, UN doc. S/RES/1998 (2011), 12 July 2011, para. 11.

27 UN Security Council, Resolution 1484, UN doc. S/RES/1484 (2003), 30 May 2003 (DRC) condemning "the deliberate killing of unarmed MONUC personnel and staff of humanitarian organizations in Ituri and demand[ing] that the perpetrators be brought to justice," para. 6; UN Security Council, Resolution 1529, UN doc. S/RES/1529 (2004), 29 February 2004 (Haiti) stating that "there will be individual accountability and no impunity for violators," para. 7; UN Security Council, Resolution 1602, UN doc. S/RES/1602 (2005), 31 May 2005 (Burundi) urging "troop-contributing countries to take appropriate prevent-

### 1.1.3 UN Human Rights Commission and UN Human Rights Council Resolutions

The Human Rights Council, which took over from the Human Rights Commission in 2006, has made some commitments to transitional justice by specifying what states have to do. Indeed, the work of Louis Joinet and Diane Orentlicher who developed the principles of the fight against impunity under the Commission on Human Rights have become the pillars of transitional justice.[28] The Human Rights Council has also expressed interest in transitional justice issues. In this area, it has considered what transitional states need to do and has adopted several resolutions.

One of the most important developments in the field of transitional justice is the adoption, first by the Human Rights Commission and then by the Human Rights Council, of resolutions on the right to truth,[29] a right which, at the time, was becoming central for victims in many states struggling with a dark past. In these resolutions, the Commission, and then the Council, recognised the importance of this right in the field of ending impunity, the importance of the role of judicial mechanisms and truth commissions in contributing to the realisation of this right in cases of violations of human rights and international humanitarian law. These resolutions have also encouraged states to take action in many areas. For example, in the 2012 resolution on the right to truth, the Human Rights Council encouraged the implementation of the recommendations of truth commissions, the importance for states to demonstrate that they comply with judicial decisions, the establishment of complementary judicial mechanisms and truth commissions, the accession to, or ratification of, the Convention for the Protection of All Persons from Enforced

---

ive and disciplinary action to ensure that such acts are properly investigated and punished in cases involving their personnel," para. 6; UN Security Council, Resolution 1721, UN doc. S/RES/1721 (2006), 1st November 2006 (Côte d'Ivoire), urging Cote d'Ivoire authorities to investigate violations of human rights and international humanitarian law these "without delay in order to put an end to impunity," para. 30; UN Security Council, Resolution 1906, UN doc. S/RES/1906 (2009), 23 December 2009 (DRC), urging the government of DRC to investigate human rights violations "and that all those responsible be brought to justice through a robust and independent process," para. 11.

28 See above the introduction of Part 2 of this book.

29 For the Human Rights Commission, see Resolution 2005/66, UN doc. E/CN.4/RES/2005/66, 20 April 2005; For Human Rights Council, see Resolution 9/11, Right to the truth, UN doc. A/HRC/RES/9/11, 18 September 2008; Resolution 12/12, Right to the truth, A/HRC/RES/12/12, 1 October 2009 and Resolution 21/7, Right to the truth, UN doc. A/HRC/RES/21/7, 27 September 2012.

Disappearance, and the cooperation of states and assistance in the implementation of the right to truth.[30] These activities on the right to truth were instrumental in the adoption of a resolution on the right to truth by the UN General Assembly in 2013.[31]

Recognising the work of the United Nations on transitional justice, the Human Rights Council adopted a resolution on Transitional Justice and Human Rights in 2008.[32] The resolution did not specifically address the issue of international obligations of states in relation to transitional justice. However, it insisted on what is important in the context of transitional justice, including the need for a comprehensive approach that takes into account all transitional justice mechanisms. It also insisted on taking into account the needs of victims and respecting the rights of the accused.

### 1.2 The African Union and the African Commission on Human and Peoples' Rights Resolutions

As seen in Part 1 of this book, the African Union has adopted a policy document on transitional justice. This document contains some indications for states in transition. For example, it provides that states "shall have the primary responsibility with respect to pursuing TJ [transitional justice] processes."[33] And further, that states "should establish institutions and media space and create conditions that promote educational programmes which reinforce equality and dignity and emphasize people's common humanity,"[34] and should also create "social institutions" to promote forgiveness and reconciliation.[35]

However, it is the African Commission on Human and Peoples' Rights (African Commission), which along with the African Court on Human and Peoples' Rights, is one of the main bodies responsible for monitoring respect for human and peoples' rights in Africa, that has adopted a number of resolutions proposing international obligations for African states in transition. Referring to serious violations of international humanitarian law and human rights, crimes against humanity, genocide and war crimes committed in Africa, the African Commission adopted a resolution stressing the fight against impunity

30 HRC Resolution 21/7, *ibid.*

31 See above, General Assembly Resolutions.

32 Human Rights Council Resolution 9/10, Human rights and transitional justice, UN doc. A/HRC/RES/9/10, 2008.

33 AU, *Transitional Justice Policy*, 2019, 25.

34 *Ibid.*

35 *Ibid.*, 26.

in Africa.[36] In this resolution, the African Commission refers to three main elements that can be considered as soft law in transitional justice. It urges the African states to "[c]omply with their obligations to investigate serious human rights violations, and hold perpetrators accountable in accordance with applicable regional and international human rights standards," to "[t]ake the necessary legislative and other measures to put an end to impunity and ensure that all the perpetrators of serious human rights violations are prosecuted," and to "[a]dopt the necessary laws, policies and mechanisms to guarantee the rights to justice, truth and reparation for victims of serious human rights violations and international crimes." In short, African transitional states must investigate violations and crimes, prosecute and punish perpetrators, and fulfil victims' rights to justice, truth and reparation.

In 2013, the African Commission also adopted its first resolution on transitional justice and appointed a commissioner to conduct a study on the issue, with a focus on Africa.[37] This resolution, and another one adopted to appoint a new commissioner for the same task,[38] led to a study that the African Commission carried out in 2018,[39] publishing its findings in 2019.[40] The study contains a segment entitled "Review of Continental Legislative Framework Relevant to Transitional Justice."[41] This segment shows that at the continental level, there are many legally binding instruments applicable to transitional justice processes in Africa and identifies some international obligations for African states in transition. It indicates that the legislative framework of transitional justice consists of the African Charter on Human and Peoples' Rights, the Maputo Protocol, the African Charter on the Rights and Welfare of the Child, the Constitutive Act of the African Union and other African Union instruments,[42] and the Kampala Convention.[43] The study details these treaties and holds that they all contain elements that can be used in transitional just-

36 AcomHPR, Resolution on the fight against impunity in Africa, doc. ACHPR/Res. 344 (LVIII) (2016).

37 AcomHPR, Resolution on Transitional Justice in Africa, doc. ACHPR/Res.235(LIII)2013, 23 April 2013.

38 AcomHPR, Resolution on the Appointment of a New Commissioner for the Transitional Justice Study in Africa, doc. ACHPR/Res.326(LVII)2015, 28 November 2015.

39 See AcomHPR, '44th Activity Report of the AcomHPR, (period of 10 May to 13 November 2018),' 18.

40 AComHPR, 'Study on Transitional Justice and Human and Peoples' Rights in Africa,' 28 April 2019.

41 *Ibid.*, 28.

42 *Ibid.*

43 *Ibid.*, 39.

ice processes in Africa, and refers to rights that are protected in these instruments and that states must respect in transitional processes.

Regarding the African Charter on Human and Peoples' Rights (African Charter), the study acts as a reminder that the treaty recognises civil and political rights; economic, social and cultural rights; Peoples' rights; and holds that African states must take into account all these rights in transitional justice processes.[44]

Looking at the Maputo Protocol, which recognises the rights of women in Africa, the study stresses that this treaty provides protection for women against violence in conflict situations, emphasises the role of women in peace processes and the need for rehabilitation, which is a form of reparation, when their rights are violated.[45] The study also identifies the African Charter on the Rights and Welfare of the Child as protecting children in times of armed conflict.[46]

Examining several provisions of the Constitutive Act of the African Union, the Protocol establishing the Peace and Security Council of the African Union and subsidiary instruments, the study highlights the role of the African Union in the field of peace, linking it to the right to peace provided in Article 23 of the ACHPR.[47] Finally, examining the Kampala Convention, a treaty that deals with the rights of displaced persons, the study refers to the importance for states to fight against arbitrary displacement during armed conflict.[48]

In summary, this study on transitional justice in Africa takes a comprehensive approach. First, it insists on the obligation of states to respect all human rights enshrined in the African system. Second, it highlights the role that states, the African Union and women can play in transitional processes.

In addition to the resolutions that led to this study on transitional justice in Africa, the African Commission adopted specific resolutions dedicated to specific African states in transition or post-conflict situations, recommending that these states take specific actions. For example, the African Commission has adopted several resolutions on South Sudan,[49] a country where a peace agreement provides the adoption of transitional justice institutions. In a 2022

44 *Ibid.*, 28–35.
45 *Ibid.*, 36.
46 *Ibid.*, 37.
47 *Ibid.*, 37–38.
48 *Ibid.*, 39.
49 AcomHPR, Resolution on the human rights situation in the Republic of South Sudan, doc. ACHPR/Res.428(LXV)2019, 10 November 2019; AcomHPR, Resolution on the Situation of Human Rights in the Republic of South Sudan, doc. ACHPR/Res.542 (LXXIII) 2022, 9 November 2022.

resolution, the African Commission called "for the institution of measures, including through empowering and guaranteeing the effective functioning of the South Sudan Human Rights Commission, for the monitoring, reporting, investigation, prosecution and reforms to address these acts of violations affecting the civilian population, particularly women and vulnerable groups," and urged the government to take "urgent measures to ensure that security institutions halt harassment and intimidation of, and attacks against, human rights defenders, members of civil society organisations, journalists and humanitarian workers, violations committed against civilians, including sexual and conflict-related sexual violence, and undue restrictions to the freedoms of opinion and expression online and offline, peaceful assembly and association."[50]

Concerning Egypt, a state that at the time was experiencing a political transition, the African Commission called the transitional government of that country to respect human rights, "to conduct impartial and transparent investigations into all cases of death, torture, degrading treatment and harassment of peaceful protestors, and ensure that the perpetrators are brought to justice," and "to expedite actions to return the country to democratic rule."[51] In the same vein, the African Commission urged Mali to respect human rights and "to take the necessary measures to put an end to impunity, including by ensuring that the perpetrators and accomplices of these acts of violence are brought to justice,"[52] and called on the DRC government "to bring to justice the perpetrators of crimes committed in Congolese territory."[53] It also called on the transitional authorities in Liberia, the Council of State of the Liberian Transitional Government, to respect human rights and "to take all necessary measures to fight against impunity and ensure that all perpetrators of crimes against the Liberian people are brought to justice."[54]

In some of its general resolutions, which did not target a specific state, the African Commission addressed transitional justice. For example, in a resolution dedicated to victims of torture, it insisted on the need of reparations, explicitly encouraging "State Parties which are undergoing transitional justice

50 *Ibid.*, Resolution of 2022, paras. 2–3.

51 AcomHPR, Resolution on the Human rights Situation in the Arab Republic of Egypt, doc. ACHPR/Res.240(EXT.OS/XIV)2013, 24 July 2013.

52 AcomHPR, Resolution on the Political Situation in the Republic of Mali, doc. ACHPR/Res.238(EXT.OS/XIV)2013, 24 July 2013.

53 AcomHPR, Resolution on the Situation in the Democratic Republic of Congo, doc. ACHPR/Res.90(XXXVIII)05, 5 December 2005.

54 AcomHPR, Resolution on Liberia, doc. ACHPR/Res.20(XIX)96, 4 April 1996.

processes to include explicit provisions on the rehabilitation of victims of torture."[55]

### 1.3 European Parliament Resolutions

Within the European Union, the European Parliament has played a dynamic role in adopting resolutions that insist on the conduct that post-conflict states should adopt in the field of human rights and transitional justice, in highlighting the external action of the European Union (EU) on these issues and calling on the EU and some of its institutions to support transitional justice. In many resolutions, it has referred to transitional or post-conflict states and to the importance in several states of combating impunity and implementing transitional justice in cases of human rights violations, including, for example, the initiation of prosecutions or the establishment of truth commissions. These states include Zimbabwe,[56] Egypt,[57] Mali,[58] South Sudan,[59] Syria,[60] Iraq[61] and Afghanistan.[62]

The European Parliament has sometimes adopted a regional approach when it comes to the cooperation of the EU with transitional states. For example, it has called on the Arab world to set up transitional mechanisms to combat

55 AcomHPR, Resolution on the Right to Rehabilitation for Victims of Torture, doc. ACHPR/Res.303(LVI)2015, 7 May 2015.

56 European Parliament Resolution, Situation in Zimbabwe, P6_TA(2008)0364, 10 July 2008, para. 10.

57 European Parliament Resolution, Situation in Egypt (2013/2542(RSP), P7_TA(2013)0095, 14 March 2013, para. 8.

58 European Parliament Resolution, Reconstruction and democratisation of Mali (2013/2587(RSP)), P7_TA(2013)0281, 13 June 2013, para. 21.

59 European Parliament Resolution, Humanitarian situation in South Sudan, (2014/2922 (RSP)), P8_TA(2014)0053, 13 November 2014, para. 15.

60 European Parliament Resolution, Situation in Syria European (2016/2933(RSP)), P8_TA (2016)0449, 24 November 2016, para. 17.

61 European Parliament Non-legislative Resolution, EU–Iraq Partnership and Cooperation Agreement, Resolution of on the draft Council decision on the conclusion of a Partnership and Cooperation Agreement between the European Union and its Member States, of the one part, and the Republic of Iraq, of the other part (10209/1/2012 – C8-0038/2018 – 2010/0310M(NLE)), P8_TA(2018)0286, 4 July 2018, para. 20.

62 European Parliament Non-legislative Resolution, EU–Afghanistan Cooperation Agreement on Partnership and Development, Resolution on the draft Council decision on the conclusion, on behalf of the Union, of the Cooperation Agreement on Partnership and Development between the European Union and Its Member States, of the one part, and the Islamic Republic of Afghanistan, of the other part (15093/2016 – C8-0107/2018 – 2015/0302M(NLE)), P8_TA(2019)0170, 13 March 2019, para. 19.

impunity,[63] and it has urged the ASEAN states "to support initiatives for transitional justice, reconciliation and the fight against impunity across the region."[64]

The European Parliament has also adopted general resolutions that are not dedicated to a particular state or a region, and has called for action in the implementation of transitional justice mechanisms and the support of the EU in cases of human rights violations. It called the EU institutions, the European Council and the European Commission, "to encourage" the promotion of transitional justice so that justice is served for victims of human rights violations.[65] It has also insisted on the need of institutional reform and criminal accountability in the implementation of transitional justice, stressing the role that the EU should play in this field.[66]

In the field of accountability and the combat against impunity, the European Parliament has particularly emphasised the application of principles of universal jurisdiction domestically, urging "the Commission to develop an ambitious programme to build the capacity of Member States and third countries" in that field.[67] On this matter, and concerning Syria, the European Parliament reaffirmed "that the persons responsible for core international crimes must be duly prosecuted, including by EU Member States, in the absence of other international or national processes of transitional justice."[68]

On a more global scale, in 2022, the European Parliament made a strong statement on transitional justice, writing that the European Parliament "[c]alls for the promotion of transitional justice processes that empower civil society, victims, marginalised and vulnerable populations, women, children, young people, and rural and urban residents alike; encourages the creation of links between permanent structures such as national justice systems and

63 European Parliament Resolution, EU Strategy for Reform in the Arab World: What Strategy Should the European Union Adopt? (2006/2172(INI)), P6_TA(2007)0179, 10 May 2007, para. 6.

64 European Parliament Resolution, EU political relations with ASEAN (2017/2026(INI)), P8_TA(2017)0367, 3 October 2017, para. 25.

65 European Parliament Resolution, Human rights in the world 2006 and the EU's policy on the matter, (2007/2020(INI)), P6_TA(2007)0165, 26 April 2007, para. 37.

66 European Parliament Resolution, Human rights in the world 2012 and EU policy on the matter, (2013/2152(INI)), P7_TA(2013)0575, 11 December 2013, para. 60; See also European Parliament Resolution, Building EU capacity on conflict prevention and mediation (2018/2159(INI)), P8_TA(2019)0158, 12 March 2019, para. 10.

67 European Parliament Resolution, Implementation of the common foreign and security policy – annual report 2022, (2022/2048(INI)), P9_TA(2023)0009, 18 January 2023, para. 59.

68 European Parliament Resolution, The Syrian conflict – 10 years after the uprising (2021/2576(RSP)), P9_TA(2021)0088, 11 March, para. 17.

national institutions and atrocity prevention networks and transitional justice initiatives; stresses the need to provide the victims and the communities affected with tools, space and access to information."[69]

In summary, the work of the European Parliament insists on the obligation to implement transitional justice when serious violations or crimes have been committed, and on the obligation of the EU to contribute to the implementation of transitional justice. This insistence on the need to implement transitional justice in states struggling with a dark past is also supported by the dynamic jurisprudence and monitoring activities of non-judicial international human rights bodies.

## 2 Jurisprudence and Other Monitoring Activities of Non-judicial International Human Rights Bodies: Interpretation of Human Rights Treaties as Imposing International Obligations to Transitional and Post-conflict States

Through litigation and other monitoring activities, such as reviewing states' reports on human rights, many international human rights bodies, which are not courts but are responsible for monitoring states' respect for human rights, have addressed the behaviour of transitional states with regard to accountability for past violations. Even though they are not courts, these bodies interpret human rights treaties and indicate to post-conflict or transitional states what their international obligations are under the considered treaty. Although their comments, observations and recommendations to states are not binding in the strictest sense, they have proposed legal action to be taken by these states in case of human rights violations. These bodies include several UN committees in the field of human rights, the African Commission on Human and Peoples' Rights and the Inter-American Commission on Human Rights.

### 2.1 UN Human Rights Committee

The UN Human Rights Committee (HRC), the UN body responsible for monitoring compliance with the 1966 International Covenant on Civil and Political Rights (ICCPR), has examined human rights violations in several transitional

69 European Parliament Resolution, Human rights and democracy in the world and the European Union's policy on the matter – annual report 2021 (2021/2181(INI)), P9_TA (2022)0041, 17 February 2022, para. 96.

states that are parties to the ICCPR and its first Optional Protocol, which allows the HRC to consider individual complaints when violations occur. It has done so both through its conclusions on cases brought against these states and through its examination of reports from transitional states on compliance with the ICCPR in their territories. In many of its concluding observations and recommendations, the HRC has generally taken the view that these states have an obligation to take legal action, particularly in the area of remedy and reparation.

In terms of litigation, Uruguay is a good example of a country in transition that has come under the scrutiny of the HRC because of serious human rights violations committed on its territory during the dictatorship that it experienced. Uruguay became a state party to ICCPR in 1970 and was one of the first to accede to the ICCPR and its Optional Protocol. Some individuals who complained that their rights had been violated during the country's authoritarian rule brought their cases to the HRC. In a series of decisions, the HRC found that Uruguay had violated human rights and considered that it had to provide effective remedies, including compensation, to those individuals.

Indeed, in the context of authoritarian rule in Uruguay, the HRC ruled that Uruguay had violated the rights of a Uruguayan citizen who had been arrested in 1976, illegally detained, allegedly ill-treated and not compensated after his release.[70] In this and other cases, the HRC found that Uruguay had failed to investigate allegations of human rights violations – generally illegal arrest and detention followed by ill-treatment – and to provide effective remedies, including compensation, to the victims.[71] When Uruguay returned to democracy in the mid-1980s, the HRC insisted that Uruguay had the obligation "to take effective measures to remedy the violations which" individuals had endured under the authoritarian rule, and to provide "adequate compensation" to

70 HRC, *Edgardo Dante Santullo Valcada v. Uruguay*, Communication No. R.2/9, see General Assembly Official Records: Thirty-Fifth Session Supplement No. 40 (A/35/40), 1980, 107–110.

71 *Ibid.*, 110, para. 13. For other cases concerning Uruguay, *Ana María García Lanza de Netto on behalf of her aunt Beatriz Weismann Lanza and her uncle Alcides Lanza Perdomo who later joined as submitting parties v. Uruguay*, Communication No. R.2/8, *ibid.*, 119, para. 17; *William Torres Ramírez v. Uruguay*, Communication No. R.l/4, *ibid.*, 126, para. 19; *Miguel Angel Millan Sequeira v. Uruguay*, Communication No. R.l/6, *ibid.*, 131, para. 17; *Alberto Grille Motta on his own behalf as well as on behalf of other persons v. Uruguay*, Communication No. R.2/ll, *ibid.*, 137, para. 18; *Luciano Weinberger Weisz v. Uruguay*, Communication No. R.7/28. See General Assembly Official Records: Thirty-Sixth Session. Supplement No. 40 (A/36/40), 119, para. 17.

them.[72] In a 1994 decision, the HRC even held explicitly that it did not agree with Uruguay's argument that Uruguay had no obligation to investigate human rights violations, including acts of torture, committed by the prior authoritarian regime.[73]

The HRC has also showed its oppositions to the granting of an amnesty that prevented the prosecution of perpetrators of human rights violations. For example, concerning Uruguay, the HRC expressed its opposition to amnesty law when it came to "gross violations of human rights," writing that such law was "incompatible with the obligations of the State party under the Covenant, that the amnesty law adopted in Uruguay (*Ley de Caducidad de la Pretension Punitiva del Estado*) was preventing investigations for past abuses and effective remedies for victims," and was contributing "to an atmosphere of impunity in the new democratic Uruguay."[74] Insisting on the need for effective remedies, the HRC listed the actions to be taken, urging Uruguay "to take effective measures (a) to carry out an official investigation into the author's allegations of torture, in order to identify the persons responsible for torture and ill-treatment and to enable the author to seek civil redress; (b) to grant appropriate compensation to [the victim], and (c) to ensure that similar violations do not occur in the future."[75] This list offers an example of what is expected from transitional states.

In the area of litigation, the HRC considered cases concerning vetting and lustration laws, which allowed some transitional states to exclude from public office persons accused of having participated in human rights violations during the previous political regime. In a case involving Slovakia, the HRC stated that it was not opposed to such measures. However, it insisted that the procedure must respect the rights of the accused, in particular the right to non-discrimination and due process.[76] The HRC's statement in this regard was very instructive for transitional states wishing to engage in vetting or lustration processes: "States Parties are not prevented under article 26 [right to equality before the law and the prohibition of discrimination] from vetting or remov-

72 See, for example, HRC, *Gilboa de Reverdito v. Uruguay*, UN doc. CCPR/C/26/D/147/1983, 1 November 1985, para. 15.1; HRC, *Ornar Berterretche Acosta v. Uruguay*, Communication No. *162/1983*, 25 October 1988, para. 12.

73 HRC, *Rodriguez v. Uruguay*, UN doc. CCPR/C/51/D/322/1988, 19 July 1994, para. 12.3.

74 *Ibid.*, para. 12.4.

75 *Ibid.*, para. 14.

76 HRC, *M.K., V.G., M.T. and J.Z. v. Slovakia*, No. 2062/2011, UN doc. CCPR/C/116/D/2062/2011, 23 March 2016, para. 9.3.

ing civil servants who collaborated with prior regimes and who, due to their positions, may pose a significant danger to human rights or democracy. However, in order for these vettings or removals to be compatible with the Covenant, they should comply with the non-discrimination principle, due process guarantees and other rights protected by the Covenant."[77]

Other important developments on the international obligations of transitional or post-conflict states can be found in the concluding observations of the HRC following its review of national reports on the implementation of the ICCPR by states. In many of these observations, the HRC analyses the fight against impunity and dealing with past human rights violations. For example, in 1996, the HRC called on Guatemala, then in transition after a bloody armed conflict that ended with the signing of peace accords, to take many measures related to human rights violations committed during the armed conflict, including investigation of violations, prosecution of perpetrators, administrative sanctions, reparations, and so on:

> 25. The Committee urges the Guatemalan Government to continue working in the process of national reconciliation which may bring lasting peace to Guatemalan society. The Guatemalan Government should take all pertinent measures to avoid cases of impunity and, especially, to allow the victims of human rights violations to find out the truth about those acts, to know who the perpetrators of such acts are and to obtain appropriate compensation.
>
> 26. The Committee recommends that the State party endeavour to bring to justice perpetrators of human rights abuses, notwithstanding the positions they may have held, in accordance with the Covenant. It urges the State party to investigate allegations of human rights violations, past and present, to act on the findings of its investigations, to bring to justice those suspected, to punish the perpetrators and to compensate the victims of such acts. Persons found guilty of having committed human rights violations should be expelled from the armed or security forces and punished accordingly.[78] .

The HRC has regularly made such comments to many states in transition or states experiencing armed conflict or dictatorship, urging them to take action to address human rights violations. For example, in 2023, the HRC expressed concerns regarding the non-implementation of the recommendations of the

77 *Ibid.*, para. 9.3.

78 HRC, Concluding observations of the Human Rights Committee, Guatemala, UN doc. CCPR/C/79/Add.63, 3 April 1996, para. 25.

Brazil truth commission, the lack of "adequate redress for victims," the absence of accountability for perpetrators of human rights, and the absence of investigations of crimes committed against Indigenous peoples during the dictatorship.[79] It recommended that Brazil investigate the human rights violations committed between 1946 and 1988, prosecute perpetrators, take sanctions and ensure remedies for victims.[80]

Generally, the HRC addresses past human rights violations and expresses, *inter alia*, concern about the absence or inadequacy of investigations into human rights violations committed during dictatorships and/or armed conflicts, the lack of prosecution of many perpetrators, the fact that transitional or post-conflict states have not provided reparations to many victims and have not implemented guarantees of non-repetition. The HRC recommends transitional states, *inter alia*, to investigate violations of human rights, prosecute and, where appropriate, punish perpetrators, provide reparations to victims, and sometimes provide measures of non-repetition and preservation of memory.

States with a recent history of dictatorship and/or armed conflict, to which the HRC made such statements and recommendations, include Peru,[81] Croatia,[82] Suriname,[83] Chile,[84] Indonesia,[85] Serbia,[86] Colombia,[87] Panama,[88]

79 HRC, Concluding observations on the third periodic report of Brazil, UN doc. CCPR/C/BRA/CO/3, 20 July 2023, para. 12.

80 *Ibid.*, para. 13.

81 HRC, Concluding observations on the sixth periodic report of Peru, UN doc. CCPR/C/PER/CO/6, 20 March 2023, paras. 10–11.

82 HRC, Concluding observations on the fourth periodic report of Croatia, UN doc. CCPR/C/HRV/CO/4, 18 July 2024, paras. 11–14.

83 HRC, Concluding observations on the fourth periodic report of Suriname, UN doc. CCPR/C/SUR/CO/4, 22 July 2024, paras. 11–12.

84 HRC, Concluding observations on the seventh periodic report of Chile, UN doc. CCPR/C/CHL/CO/7, 22 March 2024, paras. 7-8.

85 HRC, Concluding observations on the second periodic report of Indonesia, UN doc. CCPR/C/IDN/CO/2, 26 March 2024, paras. 10–11.

86 HRC, Concluding observations on the fourth periodic report of Serbia, UN doc. CCPR/C/SRB/CO/4, 26 March 2024, paras. 24–25.

87 HRC, Concluding observations on the eighth periodic report of Colombia, UN doc. CCPR/C/COL/CO/8, 4 September 2023 paras. 8-9.

88 HRC, Concluding observations on the fourth periodic report of Panama, UN doc. CCPR/C/PAN/CO/4, 21 March 2023, paras. 9-10.

Ireland,[89] Uruguay,[90] Iraq,[91] Cambodia,[92] Togo,[93] Central African Republic,[94] Tunisia,[95] Paraguay,[96] Gambia,[97] Liberia,[98] El Salvador,[99] DRC,[100] Burkina Faso,[101] Ecuador,[102] Argentina,[103] Rwanda,[104] South Africa,[105] Spain,[106] Cro-

89 HRC, Concluding observations on the fifth periodic report of Ireland, UN doc. CCPR/C/IRL/CO/5, 22 July 2022, paras. 11–12.

90 HRC, Concluding observations on the sixth periodic report of Uruguay, UN doc. CCPR/C/URY/CO/6, 20 July 2022, paras. 26–27.

91 HRC, Concluding observations on the sixth periodic report of Iraq, UN doc. CCPR/C/IRQ/CO/6, 23 March 2022, paras. 8-9.

92 HRC, Concluding observations on the third periodic report of Cambodia, UN doc. CCPR/C/KHM/CO/3, 22–23 March 2022, paras. 12–13.

93 HRC, Concluding observations on the fifth periodic report of Togo, UN doc. CCPR/C/TGO/CO/5, 23 July 2021, paras. 13–14.

94 HRC, Concluding observations on the third periodic report of the Central African Republic, CCPR/C/CAF/CO/3, 27 March 2020, paras. 9-10.

95 HRC, Concluding observations on the sixth periodic report of Tunisia, UN doc. CCPR/C/TUN/CO/6, 27 March 2020, para. 11.

96 HRC, Concluding observations on the fourth periodic report of Paraguay, UN doc. CCPR/C/PRY/CO/4, 22 July 2019, paras. 12–13.

97 HRC, Concluding observations on the Gambia in the absence of its second periodic report, UN doc. CCPR/C/GMB/CO/2, 19 July 2018, paras. 23–26.

98 HRC, Concluding observations on the initial report of Liberia, UN doc. CCPR/C/LBR/CO/1, 23 July 2018, paras. 10–11.

99 HRC, Concluding observations on the seventh periodic report of El Salvador, CCPR/C/SLV/CO/7, 28–29 March 2017, paras. 17–20.

100 HRC, Concluding observations on the fourth periodic report of the Democratic Republic of the Congo, UN doc. CCPR/C/COD/CO/4, 6 November 2017, paras. 11–12.

101 HRC, Concluding observations on the initial report of Burkina Faso, UN doc. CCPR/C/BFA/CO/1, 11 July 2016, paras. 9-10.

102 HRC, Concluding observations on the sixth periodic report of Ecuador, UN doc. CCPR/C/ECU/CO/6, 27–28 June 2016, paras. 19–10.

103 HRC, Concluding observations on the fifth periodic report of Argentina, UN doc. CCPR/C/ARG/CO/5, 11 July 2016, paras. 27–28.

104 HRC, Concluding observations on the fourth periodic report of Rwanda, UN doc. CCPR/C/RWA/CO/4, 24 March 2016, paras; 23–24.

105 HRC, Concluding observations on the initial report of South Africa, UN doc. CCPR/C/ZAF/CO/1, 23 March 2016, paras; 12–13.

106 HRC, Concluding observations on the sixth periodic report of Spain, UN doc. CCPR/C/ESP/CO/6, 20 July 2015, para. 21.

atia,[107] Côte d'Ivoire,[108] Haiti,[109] Montenegro[110] and Bolivia.[111] What is very interesting about the HRC's comments on these states' reports is that they follow the UN's language on transitional justice. Indeed, in relation to past human rights violations committed during dictatorship and/or armed conflict, these comments refer to the importance of state action to implement investigations, prosecutions, reparations, guarantees of non-recurrence and memory, which are at the heart of transitional justice. In many cases where transitional justice is implemented, the HRC welcomes the establishment and implementation of transitional justice mechanisms.[112] In some post-conflict states where prosecutions and investigations have already been carried out, the HRC has highlighted shortcomings in the implementation of transitional justice and has held that full reparations should be made to victims.[113] In some cases, it has explicitly called for the establishment of transitional justice mechanisms,[114] encouraged the implementation of vetting procedures and the exclusion from public administration or law enforcement of individuals responsible

107 HRC, Concluding observations on the third periodic report of Croatia, UN doc. CCPR/C/HRV/CO/3, 31 March 2015.

108 HRC, Concluding observations on the initial report of Côte d'Ivoire, UN doc. CCPR/C/CIV/CO/1, 31 March 2015, para. 7.

109 HRC, Concluding observations on the initial report of Haiti, CCPR/C/HTI/CO/1, 27 October 2014, para. 7.

110 HRC, Concluding observations on the initial report of Montenegro, UN doc. CCPR/C/MNE/CO/1, 28 October 2014.

111 HRC, Concluding observations on the third periodic report of the Plurinational State of Bolivia, UN doc. CCPR/C/BOL/CO/3, 29 October 2013, para. 12.

112 See, for example, HRC, Concluding observations on the third periodic report of the Central African Republic, UN doc. CCPR/C/CAF/CO/3, 27 March 2020, para. 10; HRC, Concluding observations on the sixth periodic report of Tunisia, para. 11; HRC, Concluding observations on the Gambia in the absence of its second periodic report, UN doc. CCPR/C/GMB/CO/2, 19 July 2018, para. 23.

113 See the case of Sierra Leone: HRC, Concluding observations on the initial report of Sierra Leone, UN doc. CCPR/C/SLE/CO/1, 25 March 2014.

114 For example, see HRC, Concluding observations on the fifth periodic report of Ireland, UN doc. CCPR/C/IRL/CO/5, 22 July 2022, paras. 11–12. Here, the HRC recommended to "establish a transitional justice mechanism to fight impunity and guarantee the right to truth for all victims" of some institutions that violated the rights of women and children in the past, para. 12 (a). Also HRC, Concluding observations on the fourth periodic report of the Democratic Republic of the Congo, UN doc. CCPR/C/COD/CO/4, 6 November 2017, para. 12. The HRC calls for the establishing of a transitional justice system with investigation, prosecutions and reparations.

for human rights violations,[115] and called for the implementation of truth commission recommendations.[116]

In addition to jurisprudence and observations on state reports, the HRC has adopted general comments addressed to all states parties and, of course, to transitional states. In this area, it has consistently reminded states of the obligation to investigate certain human rights violations and to bring perpetrators to justice, for example, in its General Comment 36 on the right to life and, in particular, in its General Comment 31 on the nature of state obligations.[117]

All these developments on transitional justice in the activities of the HRC with regard to transitional or post-conflict states strongly suggest the emergence of an international "obligation" under international soft law to implement transitional justice after a dictatorship or an armed conflict, with implementation including, *inter alia*, investigations, prosecutions, reparations, guarantees of non-repetition, that is, prevention, and respect for the rights to remedy for victims, respect for the rights of the accused for alleged perpetrators. The "obligation" also includes the implementation of the recommendations of state transitional mechanisms, such as truth commissions' recommendations. This tendency to insist on the implementation of transitional justice mechanisms after dictatorship and/or armed conflict and serious human rights violations is also common in the legal developments of other UN human rights committees and bodies.

### 2.2 UN Committee against Torture

In its monitoring of the implementation of the 1984 UN Convention against Torture, the UN Committee against Torture (CAT) has addressed the issue of transitional justice, detailing what states in transition from armed conflict or authoritarian rule should do in cases of allegations of torture and enforced disappearances committed in the past. In the Hissein Habré case, concerning

115 See, for example, HRC, Concluding observations on the third periodic report of the Central African Republic, UN doc. CCPR/C/CAF/CO/3, 27 March 2020. The Committee recommend the Central African Republic to "Strengthen vetting processes to prevent those accused of Covenant violations from holding public office or being promoted," para. 10 (e).

116 For example, HRC, Concluding observations on the initial report of Liberia, UN doc. CCPR/C/LBR/CO/1, 23 July 2018, para. 11; HRC, Concluding observations on the second periodic report of Honduras, UN doc. CCPR/C/HND/CO/2, 24 July 2017, para. 9.

117 HRC, General Comment No. 36, Article 6 of the International Covenant on Civil and Political Rights, on the right to life, UN doc. CCPR/C/GC/36, 30 October 2018, para. 67; HRC, General Comment No. 31, The nature of the general legal obligation imposed on States parties to the Covenant, UN doc. CCPR/C/21/Rev.1/Add.13, 26 May 2004, para. 18.

the prosecution of the former head of state of Chad for torture, the CAT ruled that Senegal, where the former head of state resided, had an obligation under the 1984 Convention against Torture to prosecute or extradite him.[118]

In some concluding observations following the examination of states' reports, the CAT has welcomed steps taken by some states in the field of transitional justice to address allegations of torture, but the CAT has also expressed concerns about the absence or inadequacy of investigations, prosecutions of perpetrators and reparations for victims, including compensation, restitution and rehabilitation, and has urged states to investigate, prosecute and provide reparations. As in the case of the HRC, the states targeted by these statements and recommendations are numerous. They include Ethiopia,[119] Burundi,[120] Spain,[121] Colombia,[122] El Salvador,[123] South Africa,[124] Peru,[125] Timor Leste[126] and Ecuador.[127]

With regards to allegations of torture and other related crimes, the CAT has, in certain cases, called for the implementation of truth commissions' recommendations regarding investigations and prosecutions and sometimes redress,

118 CAT, *Suleymane Guengueng et al. v. Senegal*, UN doc. CAT/C/36/D/181/2001, 17 May 2006, para. 10.

119 CAT, Concluding observations on the second periodic report of Ethiopia, UN doc. CAT/C/ETH/CO/2, 10 May 2023, paras. 18–19.

120 CAT, Concluding observations on the third periodic report of Burundi, UN doc. CAT/C/BDI/CO/3, 12 November 2023, paras. 37–38.

121 CAT, Concluding observations on the seventh periodic report of Spain, UN doc. CAT/C/ESP/CO/7, 27 July 2023, paras. 35–36. The Committee particularly pushed for the repeal of the 1977 Spain Law, para. 36.

122 CAT, Concluding observations on the sixth periodic report of Colombia, UN doc. CAT/C/COL/CO/6, 8 May 2023, paras. 20–21. Interestingly, a section of the Concluding observations dedicated to these concerns and recommendations is entitled "Transitional Justice."

123 CAT, Concluding observations on the third periodic report of El Salvador, UN doc. CAT/C/SLV/CO/3, 23 November 2022, paras. 12–13.

124 CAT, Concluding observations on the second periodic report of South Africa, UN doc. CAT/C/ZAF/CO/2, 14 May 2019, paras. 28–29 and paras. 38–39.

125 CAT, Concluding observations on the seventh periodic report of Peru, UN doc. CAT/C/PER/CO/7, 29 November 2018, paras. 32–35.

126 CAT, Concluding observations on the initial report of Timor-Leste, UN doc. CAT/C/TLS/CO/1, 4 December 2017, paras. 8-11.

127 CAT, Concluding observations on the seventh periodic report of Ecuador, UN doc. CAT/C/ECU/CO/7, 28 November 2016, paras. 23–24, and 41–42.

as it did in the cases of Kenya,[128] South Africa,[129] Timor Leste[130] and Paraguay.[131] The CAT has also called for the implementation of transitional justice mechanisms. In Maldives, for example, it recommended the creation of "an impartial and effective transitional justice mechanism" to investigate "allegations of torture and cruel, inhuman and degrading treatment or punishment."[132]

### 2.3 UN Committee against Enforced Disappearances

The UN Committee against Enforced Disappearances (CED) is responsible for monitoring states' compliance with the 2006 Convention for the Protection of All Persons from Enforced Disappearance. Enforced disappearances is a very common practice in many states that have faced authoritarian rule and/or armed conflict. This practice is a human rights violation that has the particularity of often being a "continuous" violation in transitional or post-conflict states; that is, in many cases, even when the enforced disappearance happened in the past, the violation is often still ongoing because the state has not located the disappeared person, has not provided information about his/her fate or investigated the case.

In many of its "Concluding Observations," the CED has reminded transitional states of their obligation under the 2006 Convention to investigate cases of enforced disappearance, to prosecute perpetrators and to provide reparation to victims. Cases of enforced disappearance, including those that occurred before the adoption of the Convention and have not been resolved, are also covered. For example, with regard to cases of enforced disappearances in Uruguay during the dictatorship between 1968 and 1985, the CED called on Uruguay to investigate the cases, prosecute and punish the perpetrators, continue the search for the disappeared and provide reparations to the victims.[133]

128 CAT, Concluding observations on the third periodic report of Kenya, UN doc. CAT/C/KEN/CO/3, 11 May 2022, para. 24 (a).

129 CAT, Concluding observations on the second periodic report of South Africa, UN doc. CAT/C/ZAF/CO/2, 14 May 2019, para. 29.

130 CAT, Concluding observations on the initial report of Timor-Leste, UN doc. 4 December 2017, para. 9.

131 CAT, Concluding observations on the seventh periodic report of Paraguay, UN doc. CAT/C/PRY/CO/7, 8 August 2017, paras. 38–39.

132 CAT, Concluding observations on the initial report of Maldives, UN doc. CAT/C/MDV/CO/1, 6 December 2018, para. 8 (a).

133 CED, Concluding observations on the additional information submitted by Uruguay under article 29 (4) of the Convention, UN doc. CED/C/URY/OAI/1, 23 September 2022, paras. 16–21.

It particularly stressed that investigations, prosecutions and punishment should be carried out "irrespective of the time that has elapsed since the commencement of the criminal conduct."[134] In the same vein, concerning Mali, a state that has been struggling to overcome an armed conflict for several years, the CED used transitional justice language when it recommended that Mali "increase its efforts to guarantee the right of all victims of enforced disappearance to justice, truth and reparation."[135] The CED made the same recommendation for Spain when it dealt with cases of enforced disappearances that occurred during the Franco dictatorship and that have not been resolved, and called for the repeal of the 1977 Spanish amnesty law that prevents investigations.[136] Regarding Brazil, the CED insisted that enforced disappearances committed between 1964 and 1985 during the authoritarian rule that have not been resolved should be investigated, recommending that Brazil prosecute and punish perpetrators, award reparations to victims and repeal the amnesty law that constitutes a legal obstacle to legal actions.[137]

With regards to enforced disappearances committed in the past of transitional or post-conflict states, the CED recommended investigations, prosecutions, punishments and reparations in Colombia,[138] Iraq,[139] Honduras,[140]

134 *Ibid.*, para. 16.

135 CED, Concluding observations on the report submitted by Mali under article 29 (1) of the Convention, UN doc. CED/C/MLI/CO/1, 22 September 2022, para. 29.

136 CED, Concluding observations on the additional information submitted by Spain under article 29 (4) of the Convention, UN doc. CED/C/ESP/OAI/1, 22 September 2021, para. 19.

137 CED, Concluding observations on the report submitted by Brazil under article 29 (1) of the Convention, UN doc. CED/C/BRA/CO/1, 23 September 2021, paras. 22–23.

138 CED, Concluding observations on the additional information submitted by Colombia under article 29 (4) of the Convention, UN doc. CED/C/COL/OAI/1, 12 April-7 May 2021, para. 19 and paras. 32–33.

139 CED, Concluding observations on the additional information submitted by Iraq under article 29 (4) of the Convention, UN doc. CED/C/IRQ/OAI/1, 7 September–25 November 2020, paras. 14–15.

140 CED, Concluding observations on the report submitted by Honduras under article 29 (1) of the Convention, UN doc. CED/C/HND/CO/1, 31 May 2018, paras. 24–25, and para. 36–37.

Albania,[141] Ecuador,[142] Tunisia,[143] Montenegro[144] and, Japan for enforced disappearances of "comfort-women during the Second World War."[145] This means that, according to the CED, when cases of enforced disappearance have not been resolved, states must respond and take legal action to ensure accountability, regardless of the period during which the crime was committed and the time that has elapsed.

### 2.4 UN Committee on the Elimination of Discrimination against Women

In its "Concluding Observations" on the implementation by states of the 1979 Convention on the Elimination of All Forms of Discrimination against Women, the UN Committee on the Elimination of Discrimination against Women (CEDAW) tends to focus on two main elements of what transitional states need to do with regard to human rights violations. First, it highlights the experiences of women and girls during dictatorships and armed conflicts and the measures that transitional states need to take in this regard, and second, it insists that states should increase the role of women in the peace process and transitional justice mechanisms.

With regards to the women's experiences and the measures that transitional states should take, the CEDAW has pointed out that transitional states have to protect women during transitions.[146] It has recommended that they ensure accountability for human rights violations, particularly sexual violence, experienced by women and girls, and take into account the gender dimension of human rights violations. In this area, it has stressed, *inter alia*, the need for

141 CED, Concluding observations on the report submitted by Albania under article 29 (1) of the Convention, UN doc. CED/C/ALB/CO/1, 31 May 2018, paras. 36–37.

142 CED, Concluding observations on the report submitted by Ecuador under article 29 (1) of the Convention, UN doc. CED/C/ECU/CO/1, 15 March 2017, paras. 9-10.

143 CED, Concluding observations on the report submitted by Tunisia under article 29 (1) of the Convention, UN doc. CED/C/TUN/CO/1, 15 March 2016, paras. 23–24.

144 CED, Concluding observations on the report submitted by Montenegro under article 29 (1) of the Convention, UN doc. CED/C/MNE/CO/1, 16 September 2015, para. 17 and paras. 30–31.

145 CED, Concluding observations on the report submitted by Japan under article 29 (1) of the Convention, UN doc. CED/C/JPN/CO/1, 14 November 2018, paras. 25–26.

146 CEDAW, Concluding observations on the fourth periodic report of Timor-Leste, UN doc. CEDAW/C/TLS/CO/4, 9 May 2023, para. 28 (b and c).

investigations,[147] for reparations including rehabilitation measures,[148] prosecutions and punishment.[149] Sometimes, the CEDAW has insisted that all these elements should be implemented in transitional states.[150] CEDAW has opposed amnesties in post-conflict contexts for international crimes and sexual violence. In its "Concluding Observations" on Côte d'Ivoire and the crimes committed in that state and the adoption of an amnesty law in 2018, it recommended that Côte d'Ivoire, a state that has undergone a violent political transition and an armed conflict, ensured that "amnesty does not apply to persons suspected, accused or convicted of war crimes, crimes against humanity or gross violations of human rights, including conflict-related sexual violence, recalling that amnesties are impermissible if they interfere with victims' right to an effective remedy, including reparation, or if they restrict victims' and societies' right to know the truth about violations of international human rights law and international humanitarian law."[151] In some cases, CEDAW has called for the allocation of resources to truth commissions and the removal of legal obstacles so that they can function properly,[152] and, when a truth commission has produced a final report, it has called for the implemen-

---

147 CEDAW, Concluding observations on the fourth periodic report of Côte d'Ivoire, UN doc. CEDAW/C/CIV/CO/4, 30 July 2019, para. 10 (a).

148 CEDAW, Concluding observations on the fourth periodic report of Timor-Leste, UN doc. CEDAW/C/TLS/CO/4, 9 May 2023, paras. 27–28; Concluding observations on the ninth periodic report of Peru, UN doc. CEDAW/C/PER/CO/9, 1 March 2022, para. 26 (b); CEDAW, Concluding observations on the fourth periodic report of Côte d'Ivoire, UN doc. CEDAW/C/CIV/CO/4, 30 July 2019, para. 10 (e); Concluding observations on the sixth periodic report of Nepal, UN doc. CEDAW/C/NPL/CO/6, 14 November 2018, para. 23 (c); .

149 CEDAW, Concluding observations on the ninth periodic report of Peru, UN doc. CEDAW/C/PER/CO/9, 1 March 2022, paras. 25–26; CEDAW, Concluding observations on the fourth periodic report of Côte d'Ivoire, UN doc. CEDAW/C/CIV/CO/4, 30 July 2019, para. 9 and para. 10 (a).

150 CEDAW, Concluding observations on the combined sixth and seventh periodic reports of Ireland, UN doc. CEDAW/C/IRL/CO/6-7, 9 March 2017, para. 15 (on the Magdalen Laundries, Mother and Baby Homes); CEDAW, Concluding observations on the eighth periodic report of the Republic of Korea, UN doc. CEDAW/C/KOR/CO/8, 14 March 2018, para. 27 (b) (on "comfort-women"); CEDAW, Concluding observations on the combined seventh and eighth periodic reports of Japan, UN doc. CEDAW/C/JPN/CO/7-8, 10 March 2016, para. 27 (on comfort-women").

151 CEDAW, Concluding observations on the fourth periodic report of Côte d'Ivoire, UN doc. CEDAW/C/CIV/CO/4, 30 July 2019, para. 10 (b).

152 CEDAW, Concluding observations on the sixth periodic report of Nepal, UN doc. CEDAW/C/NPL/CO/6, 14 November 2018, para. 22 and para. 23 (a and b);.

tation of its recommendations that insist on the need to protect and promote women's rights.[153]

With regard to the role of women in transitional justice, the CEDAW recommends that women be involved in transition processes, that states reserve a place for women and emphasise the role they can play during transition and after armed conflict in peace processes, peace-building and reconstruction, including within transitional justice mechanisms.[154]

## 2.5 UN Committee on the Elimination of Racial Discrimination

The UN Committee on the Elimination of Racial Discrimination (CERD) has been concerned with human rights violations based on racial discrimination committed against groups, peoples and/or individuals during dictatorships and armed conflicts. In some of its "Concluding Observations," following the examination of states' reports on the implementation of the 1965 International Convention on the Elimination of All Forms of Racial Discrimination, it has noted or welcomed the achievements of some states in the field of transitional justice, highlighted the shortcomings and recommended transitional and post-conflict states to investigate cases of violations of the Convention, prosecute – and sometimes punish – the perpetrators and provide reparations to the victims. These transitional states include many states where racial discrimination has been at the root of human rights violations. With regard to some human rights violations committed during the apartheid era, the CERD recommended that South Africa investigate, prosecute and provide repar-

153 CEDAW, Concluding observations on the sixth periodic report of the Gambia, UN doc. CEDAW/C/GMB/CO/6, 1 November 2022 para. 12 (a), specifically on "sexual and gender-based violence"; Concluding observations on the eighth periodic report of Kenya, UN doc. CEDAW/C/KEN/CO/8, 2 November 2017, para. 13 (d).

154 CEDAW, Concluding observations on the seventh periodic report of Iraq, UN doc. CEDAW/C/IRQ/CO/7, 12 November 2019, para. 11 and para. 12 (c); CEDAW, Concluding observations on the fourth periodic report of Côte d'Ivoire, UN doc. CEDAW/C/CIV/CO/4, 30 July 2019, paras. 11–12; Concluding observations on the eighth periodic report of the United Kingdom of Great Britain and Northern Ireland, UN doc. CEDAW/C/GBR/CO/8, 14 March 2019, para. 40; Concluding observations on the eighth periodic report of Sri Lanka, UN doc. CEDAW/C/LKA/CO/8, 9 March 2017, para. 17 (a); Concluding observations on the combined sixth and seventh periodic reports of Mali, UN doc. CEDAW/C/MLI/CO/6-7, 15 July 2015, para. 10.

ations.[155] With regard to Uruguay and the cases of forced evictions suffered by some people of African descent during the dictatorship, it recommended that the state provide reparations to the victims.[156] There are similar recommendations for states that have experienced authoritarian rule or armed conflict, such as Zimbabwe,[157] Togo,[158] Croatia[159] and Iraq.[160]

Following recent developments in transitional justice, which tends to be used to address historical and colonial injustices based on racial discrimination, the CERD assessed transitional justice initiatives in some states, expressed concerns about the legacies of these injustices, and recommended that these states address these injustices through the use of transitional justice mechanisms, such as reparations and/or memorialisation initiatives. For example, the CERD made such recommendations to the United States, which has not faced authoritarian rule or armed conflict in its recent past, regarding the injustices suffered by African Americans and Native Americans.[161] The CERD also called for the implementation of the recommendations of truth commissions to address issues of racial discrimination in Mauritius,[162] and in Canada, particularly with regard to Indigenous peoples.[163]

### 2.6 UN Committee on Economic, Social and Cultural Rights

In reviewing state reports on the implementation of the 1966 International Covenant on Economic, Social and Cultural Rights (ESCR), the Committee on Economic, Social and Cultural Rights (CESCR) has been interested in some of the transitional initiatives taken by developed states to establish

155 CERD, Concluding observations on the combined ninth to eleventh periodic reports of South Africa, UN doc. CERD/C/ZAF/CO/9-11, 6 December 2023, paras. 10–11.

156 CERD, Concluding observations on the combined twenty-fourth to twenty-sixth periodic reports of Uruguay, UN doc. CERD/C/URY/CO/24–26, 24 August 2023, paras. 27–28.

157 CERD, Concluding observations on the combined fifth to eleventh periodic reports of Zimbabwe, UN doc. CERD/C/ZWE/CO/5-11, 26 August 2022, paras. 17–18.

158 CERD, Concluding observations on the combined eighteenth and nineteenth periodic reports of Togo, UN doc. CERD/C/TGO/CO/18–19, 6 December 2016, paras. 17–18.

159 CERD, Concluding observations on the combined ninth to fourteenth periodic reports of Croatia, UN doc. CERD/C/HRV/CO/9-14, 23 August 2023, paras. 23–24.

160 CERD, Concluding observations on the combined twenty-second to twenty-fifth periodic reports of Iraq, UN doc. CERD/C/IRQ/CO/22–25, 10–11 December 2018, para. 18.

161 CERD, Concluding observations on the combined tenth to twelfth reports of the United States of America, UN doc. CERD/C/USA/CO/10–12, 24 August 2022, paras. 55–56.

162 CERD, Concluding observations on the combined twentieth to twenty-third periodic reports of Mauritius, UN doc. CERD/C/MUS/CO/20–23, 24 August 2018, paras. 16–17.

163 CERD, Concluding observations on the combined twenty-first to twenty-third periodic reports of Canada, UN doc. CERD/C/CAN/CO/21–23, 23–24 August 2017, paras. 17–18.

transitional justice to address injustices suffered by Indigenous peoples. For example, it recommended that Sweden, which has established a truth commission to deal with violations against the Indigenous Sámi people, "[s]upport the work of the Truth Commission for the Sámi People, ensuring it has access to all necessary information and resources to conduct its investigations thoroughly, while guaranteeing that its findings and recommendations are fully considered and implemented, where appropriate, to address historical injustices and promote reconciliation."[164] The CESCR has recommended that post-conflict states, such as Yemen, prevent violations of ESCR, but also investigate cases of violations of these rights, prosecute and punish those who have violated them, ensure remedies and reparations, and undertake the reconstruction of infrastructure essential to the realisation of certain ESCR.[165] Where transitional justice efforts are underway in some post-conflict states, the CESCR recommended that they take ESCR into account and ensure their implementation.[166]

### 2.7 UN Committee on the Rights of Persons with Disabilities

The UN Committee on the Rights of Persons with Disabilities (CRPD), which is responsible for monitoring compliance with the 2006 Convention on the Rights of Persons with Disabilities, has rarely addressed transitional justice. However, it has expressed concern at the lack of specific attention to victims with disabilities in the peace process in Colombia, particularly in the area of reparations.[167] For example, it has recommended that these rights be considered[168] and has recommended that Colombia "[i]nvestigate and initiate proceedings in civilian courts to determine the criminal liability of the military and self-defence groups in cases of sexual violence against women and

164 CESCR, Concluding observations on the seventh periodic report of Sweden, UN doc. E/C.12/SWE/CO/7, 1 March 2024, para. 15 (b).

165 CESCR, Concluding observations on the third periodic report of Yemen, UN doc. E/C.12/YEM/CO/3, 3 March 2023, para. 8.

166 CESCR, Concluding observations on the sixth periodic report of the Democratic Republic of the Congo, UN doc. E/C.12/COD/CO/6, 4 March 2022, para. 7; CESCR, Concluding observations on the initial report of Mali, UN doc. E/C.12/MLI/CO/1, 12 October 2018, para. 5; CESCR, Concluding observations concerning the initial report of the Central African Republic, UN doc. E/C.12/CAF/CO/1, 29 March 2018, para. 10; CESCR, Concluding observations on the fifth periodic report of Sri Lanka, UN doc. E/C.12/LKA/CO/5, 23 June 2017, para. 72.

167 CRPD, Concluding observations on the initial report of Colombia, UN doc. CRPD/C/COL/CO/1, 31 August 2016, para. 25.

168 *Ibid.*, para. 29 and para. 65.

girls with disabilities during the armed conflict and in the period of transition towards peace."[169]

## 2.8 UN Committee on the Rights of the Child

The UN Committee on the Rights of the Child (CRC), which is responsible for monitoring compliance with the 1989 Convention on the Rights of the Child, has recommended that post-conflict states take children into account in the implementation of transitional justice, including, as appropriate, investigations, prosecutions and reparations for crimes against children committed during armed conflict.[170] It has also insisted on the implementation of the recommendations of the Truth Commission of Canada that has acknowledged violations "concerning physical and sexual violence, abuse and neglect of Indigenous children in residential boarding schools that lasted for decades."[171]

## 2.9 African Commission on Human and Peoples' Rights

The African Commission on Human and Peoples' Rights (African Commission) has considered a number of cases that raised issues relating to investigations of human rights violations and the prosecution of perpetrators by post-conflict states. In the case of Chad, a post-conflict state which was accused of human rights violations, the African Commission stated: "The African Charter, unlike other human rights instruments, does not allow for state parties to derogate from their treaty obligations during emergency situations. Thus, even a civil war in Chad cannot be used as an excuse by the state violating or permitting violations of rights in the African Charter."[172] The African Commission found that Chad had a responsibility "to conduct investigations into murders"[173] and had violated several human rights enshrined in the ACHPR.[174]

169 *Ibid.*, para. 45 (b).

170 CRC, Concluding observations on the combined fifth and sixth periodic reports of El Salvador, UN doc. CRC/C/SLV/CO/5-6, 5 October 2018, para. 55; CRC, Concluding observations on the combined fifth and sixth periodic reports of Sri Lanka, UN doc. CRC/C/LKA/CO/5-6, 2 February 2018, para. 48 (specifically investigations and prosecutions); CRC, Concluding observations on the combined third to fifth periodic reports of Nepal, UN doc. CRC/C/NPL/CO/3-5, 3 June 2016, para. 29 (b).

171 CRD, Concluding observations on the combined fifth and sixth periodic reports of Canada, UN doc. CRC/C/CAN/CO/5-6, 3 June 20222, para. 18 (e).

172 AComHPR, Communication No. 74/92, *Commission nationale des droits de l'homme et des libertés v. Chad*, October 1995, para. 21.

173 *Ibid.*

174 *Ibid.*, para. 23.

In this case, the African Commission was not very explicit about the obligation to prosecute, although it could be assumed that murder investigations could lead to prosecutions.

In the case of Sudan, another post-conflict state, the African Commission was clearer. In this case, which concerned a number of violations committed in the region of Darfur, in the context of an internal armed conflict, the African Commission reminded "[p]arties to the African Charter to respect human and peoples' rights at all times including in times of armed conflict."[175] It found that there were no effective remedies in that country[176] and concluded that Sudan should "take steps to prosecute those responsible for the human rights violations, including murder, rape, arson and destruction of property."[177]

In an *obiter dictum* in the case of *Thomas Kwoyelo v Uganda*, the African Commission dealt with blanket amnesties.[178] Although, it opposed blanket and unconditional amnesties for serious human rights violations, it left open the possibility of conditional amnesties and insisted that, when they were adopted, victims should always be taken into account, the right to truth and reparation for victims should be respected and reconciliation should be sought with perpetrators who acknowledge their responsibility, without excluding the participation of communities and victims. The African Commission explicitly wrote:

> It is, therefore, the considered view of the Commission that blanket or unconditional amnesties that prevent investigations (particularly of those acts amounting to most serious crimes referred to in Article 4(h) of the AU Constitutive Act) are not consistent with the provisions of the African Charter.
>
> [...] African states in transition from conflict to peace should at all times and under any circumstances desist from taking policy, legal or executive/administrative measures that in fact or in effect grant blanket amnesties, as that would be a flagrant violation of international law. When they resort to amnesties as necessary measures for ending violence and continuing violations and achieving peace and justice, they should respect and honor their international and regional obligations. Most particularly, they should ensure that such amnesties comply with both procedural and substantive conditions. In procedural terms,

175 AComHPR, *Sudan Human Rights Organisation v. Sudan and Centre on Housing Rights and Evictions v. Sudan*, communications 279/03 and 296/05, May 2009, para. 165.

176 *Ibid.*, para. 102.

177 *Ibid.*, para. 229 (3).

178 AComHPR, *Thomas Kwoyelo v. Uganda*, communication n°431/12, February 2018, paras. 283–293.

> conditional amnesties should be formulated with the participation of affected communities including victim groups. Substantively speaking, amnesties should not totally exclude the right of victims for remedy, particularly remedies taking the form of getting the truth and reparations. They should also facilitate a measure of reconciliation with perpetrators acknowledging responsibility and victims getting a hearing about and receiving acknowledgment for the violations they suffered.[179]

This *obiter dictum* is particularly important for African states engaged in reconciliation and transitional justice following serious human rights violations. It underlines the prohibition of blanket and unconditional amnesties and addresses the complexity of some transitional situations where negotiations are necessary and imperative to end violence. The insistence on the participation of affected communities and victims, on respect for the right to a remedy, especially in the area of truth and reparation, seems like a barrier to prevent abuses by the state when it adopts amnesties. But the *obiter dictum* of the African Commission on the possibility of conditional amnesties in the field of transitional justice raises many questions: Questions about the sincerity of the perpetrators who accept responsibility and the sincerity of the authorities who engage in such a conditional amnesty process; questions about the timing of the implementation of truth and reparation for victims and whether they should be implemented before or after the adoption of the conditional amnesty; questions about the means by which the affected communities express their acceptance of the conditional amnesty; questions about who in these communities expresses this acceptance and whether it is the acceptance of every member of the community and the groups of victims; and questions about what happens if an individual victim refuses to agree to the conditional amnesty process. Even though transitional and post-conflict contexts are generally challenging when it comes to accountability of perpetrators, all these questions lead to being very cautious about the willingness of transitional states to adopt any amnesty laws, including conditional amnesties, because they could be adopted to mislead victims and actually cover up serious human rights violations.

### 2.10 Inter-American Commission on Human Rights

The Inter-American Commission on Human Rights (IACHR) published a document in 2023 that summarises its view of the obligations of transitional just-

179 *Ibid.*, para. 293.

ice states. Entitled *Compendium of the Inter-American Commission on Human Rights on Truth, Memory, Justice and Reparation in Transitional Contexts*, the document includes "a review of the documents and reports approved and published by the IACHR," including "thematic and country reports," "decisions on individual cases" and many other published reports and some press releases.[180]

The document is a "the systematization of inter-American standards on transitional justice."[181] It "seeks to systematize the standards developed by the IACHR, in the framework of its various mandates, on truth, justice and reparations for serious human rights violations in contexts of transition from dictatorships to democracy and in processes of search for and consolidation of peace, also addressing the guarantees of non-repetition of such violations."[182] It stresses that transitional states must take action against serious human rights violations which, according to the IACHR "include violations to life and personal integrity such as extrajudicial executions, forced disappearances and torture, gender and sexual violence as an aggravated violation faced in a systematic and differential way by women and girls in the aforementioned contexts."[183]

In order to highlight these actions and to help, *inter alia*, countries in transition to know what the IACHR believes it needs to do, the document identifies the "Inter-American standards" in the transitional justice field. It determines and examines three standards: Justice Standards, Truth Standards and Reparations Standards.[184] These standards set out the obligations of transitional states, and they include, in particular, key obligations in the areas of investigating and truth-telling about serious human rights violations, prosecuting and punishing the perpetrators of these violations and providing reparations to the victims of these violations. Indeed, with regard to the Truth Standards, the IACHR underlines the role that states have to play in order to fulfil the right to truth of victims, a right that, according to the IACHR "entails the obligation of States to clarify, investigate, prosecute, and punish those responsible for cases of serious human rights violations, as well as, depending on the circumstances of each case, to guarantee access to information on serious human rights violations held in State facilities and arch-

180 IACHR, Compendium of the Inter-American Commission on Human Rights on Truth, Memory, Justice and Reparation in Transitional Contexts, OEA/Ser.L/V/II., Doc. 121, 12 April 2021, 19.

181 *Ibid.*, 9.

182 *Ibid.*, 14.

183 *Ibid.*, 9.

184 *Ibid.*, see the three chapters of the document.

ives."[185] With regard to the Justice Standards, the IACHR insists on the right to justice for victims of serious human rights violations, stating that, in the case of such violations, "States have an obligation to investigate them criminally ex officio, identify those responsible, submit them to trial and impose the corresponding sanctions."[186] Logically, when it comes to these serious violations, the IACHR opposes amnesties, statutes of limitations and any legal obstacles that prevent the satisfaction of victims' right to justice, and even encourages cooperation between states through extradition or universal jurisdiction to ensure that perpetrators are held accountable.[187] With regard to Reparations Standards, the IACHR underlines the existence of a "right of victims to obtain appropriate reparation" in international human rights law in case of an "unlawful act." It also summarises its position on reparations, clearly stating that "any violation of an international obligation that has caused damages entails the duty to make adequate reparation to each victim."[188]

Soft law is therefore very rich in the field of transitional justice. It is the evidence of the growing and exponential legal developments on transitional justice. The non-binding nature of soft law could lead one to believe that international transitional justice law is fragile. But often, this soft law development is either a repetition of what is in the recognised sources of international law – for example, regarding investigations, prosecutions and reparations for serious violations and crimes – or a practice that is evidence of the existence or at least an emergence of customary law – for example, regarding the obligation to implement transitional justice after serious violations and crimes. The importance of soft law in international transitional justice law can also be explained by the fact that the decisive developments in this branch of international law are recent. There is also a lack of systematisation of the legal developments of this branch of law. The growth of this soft law opens the possibility to transform some of these legal developments into hard law, for example, by drafting a treaty on transitional justice. This work could be done within the United Nations International Law Commission.

185 *Ibid.*, 74–75.
186 *Ibid.*, 23.
187 *Ibid.*, see chapter 1.
188 *Ibid.*, 109.

# Conclusion of Part 3

Thus, a body of international transitional justice law has been growing over the years. It imposes international obligations on transitional and post-conflict states with respect to serious violations of human rights and international humanitarian law, as well as international crimes. Three main conclusions can be drawn from this branch of international law regarding the international obligations of states. First, investigation, prosecution, reparation and respect for the rights of both the accused and the victims are at the core of the international obligations of transitional or post-conflict states. Second, it is possible to take into account the challenges of transitional states in implementing these obligations, especially regarding investigation, prosecutions and reparations. International jurisprudence sometimes takes these challenges into account. It is therefore impossible to anticipate, on a case-by-case basis, what the position of, for example, a human rights court might be when the transitional state faces difficult problems. Here, the obligation of means plays a role in analysing the efforts of the state.

The third conclusion is that the prevention of violations and crimes is at the heart of the international obligations of transitional states. In principle, engaging in transitional justice mechanisms to deal with the past violations and crimes is intrinsically part of that prevention. But in order to prevent violations and crimes, these states must also take action to recognise the rights of all their people and ensure that these rights are effectively respected in the future. The implementation of transitional justice reactivates the values of the rule of law, which are mobilised to avoid the repetition of the terrible mistakes of the past.

# Conclusion

Transitional justice emerged in the 1990s as a concept designed to address large-scale crimes and violations. It has since expanded and been implemented around the world in various contexts, including post-authoritarian and post-conflict situations, as well as efforts to end dictatorships and armed conflicts. Recently, it has been adopted by established democracies. The implementation of transitional justice has involved many judicial and non-judicial mechanisms, such as international, hybrid, and national criminal tribunals; various truth commissions; reparations in multiple forms, including memorialisation; traditional justice; and guarantees of non-repetition and institutional reforms. These mechanisms respond to international crimes and violations of rights and rules established in international law. In doing so, they have contributed to acknowledging that these crimes and violations were contrary to international law, and have contributed to the emergence of international transitional justice law. They have been feeding the responses to violations of international law through practices at international, national and community levels. The inventiveness in establishing and designing transitional justice mechanisms to respond to violations of international law seems limitless, and often depends on international or national contexts. It would not be surprising if new mechanisms were to emerge in countries wishing to respond to large-scale violations and crimes, as demonstrated by the use of traditional, local and indigenous justice systems in transitional justice. The justice systems of local communities can indeed be relied upon to deliver justice in times of transition, provided they comply with human rights standards and, importantly, take into account the needs of victims – a factor that should always be at the heart of the establishment and design of transitional justice mechanisms.

While the mechanisms of transitional justice contributed to the emergence of international transitional justice law in response to large-scale violations of international law, international rules have also been developed in this field, progressively establishing the international obligations of post-conflict and transitional states. Even though there is no treaty solely dedicated to transitional justice, some treaties or treaty provisions are relevant to determining the international obligations of transitional and post-conflict states. These treaties provide guidance on how states should respond when confronted with international crimes, human rights violations and breaches of international humanitarian law – the very issues that transitional justice addresses. Similarly, international bodies and courts, primarily international human

 | HTTPS://DOI.ORG/10.1163/9789004766655-018

rights courts and bodies, have played a significant role in determining these obligations on a case-by-case basis through jurisprudence because they have examined numerous cases of violations committed during dictatorships and/or armed conflicts. Many of these courts and bodies have linked international law to the practices of states in transition when responding to violations of international law. They have assessed whether these responses comply with treaties and have examined the actions required of states when facing challenges and difficulties during or after an armed conflict. The jurisprudence of these courts and bodies, along with many soft law developments in international organisations and the activities of international human rights bodies promoting human rights in states that have experienced armed conflicts and authoritarian rule, or are recovering from them, all point towards the idea that states cannot escape their international obligations when it comes to past violations and crimes.

Since the 1990s, a body of international rules dedicated to transitional justice has been emerging, primarily at the intersection of international human rights law, international humanitarian law and international criminal law. As argued in this book, this has led to the development of international transitional justice law, a branch of international law. Although international transitional justice law depends on other branches of international law, such as international human rights law, international humanitarian law and international criminal law, in order to exist, it has grown constantly since the 1990s. The fact that international transitional justice law is not yet autonomous does not diminish its importance. Rather, it is a sign that the different branches of international law are interested in addressing past violations and large-scale crimes and that this trend will continue to inform international transitional justice law. According to this branch of international law, states in transition and post-conflict states must respond to violations of international law and respect their international obligations.

As discussed earlier in this book, there is no treaty dedicated solely to transitional justice. It is too soon to predict whether states will negotiate and adopt one. Even if they do not always reject international law, many states may feel that adopting a treaty would impose too many international constraints on transitional justice, an area in which flexibility and adaptation to context should prevail when tackling the dilemmas and difficulties of transitions and post-conflict situations. However, if a treaty were to be negotiated and adopted in this area, it would address at least three key issues. First, it would take into account the existing international legal obligations of states relating to transitional justice in different branches of international law. Second, it would address the question of flexibility in the implementation of transitional justice and emphasise the efforts states must make to deliver justice in times of transition or after an armed conflict. Third, it would clarify the role of local or community models of justice in implementing transitional justice and set minimum standards for their alignment with international law, beyond the familiar reminder that traditional and local justice systems must respect minimum standards of international human rights law. One of the current challenges in transitional justice research is studying all community-level and traditional justice systems. These systems are generally close to victims of atroci ties and exist in various forms in many countries. Despite the international and national institutionalisation of transitional justice, its implementation should never ignore these traditional mechanisms or the needs of victims and communities affected by violations, abuses and crimes.

Of course, international law does not provide all the answers in times of transition or after armed conflicts. International transitional justice law is certainly not the panacea that can solve all problems in the field of transitional justice. However, the values of justice and peace set out in international law, and also in the growing body of international transitional justice law, over the last few decades should always serve as a reminder that individuals and groups have rights. When these rights are violated on a large scale, as in authoritarian regimes or during armed conflicts, states and/or the international community must respond by holding the perpetrators accountable, restoring the victims' dignity, and preventing future violations.

In a world constantly shaken by mass and large-scale human rights violations, protecting human beings should always be a priority – and this has been said and written numerous times since the Second World War and the advent of the concept of transitional justice. Nevertheless, it is worth reminding ourselves of this because our world has not yet fully learnt from the past. The constant presence of armed conflicts and authoritarian rule in many states reminds us that there is always a risk of repeating a dark past, which poses a threat to respecting the rights of individuals and groups. During transitions or after armed conflicts, the healing of victims and the prevention of future violations, abuses, crimes and atrocities must always be prioritised. In this area, continuing the development and improvement of international transitional justice law will contribute to affirm or reaffirm that crimes and violations committed by authoritarian regimes and/or in the context of armed conflicts are wrong and that the world would be a better place without them. At a time when attacks on the rule of law are becoming increasingly common, even in established democracies, building lasting peace, reinforcing the rule of law, protecting and promoting respect for human rights remain challenging. International transitional justice law can help address these challenges.

# Selected Bibliography

## 1 Books

Alexion Elizabeth Marie, *"The Judge Will Be Your Neighbor": Transitional Justice in Ancient Athens and Post-genocide Rwanda*, Dissertation (Wesleyan University 2016).

Arendt Hannah, *Eichmann in Jerusalem: A Report on the Banality of Evil* (Viking Press 1963).

Bassiouni Cherif (ed), *Post-conflict Justice* (International and Comparative Criminal Law Series, Transnational Publishers 2002).

Bird Elizabeth and Fraser M Ottanelli (eds), *The Performance of Memory as Transitional Justice* (Series on Transitional Justice, Intersentia 2014).

Bisset Alison, *Truth Commissions and Criminal Courts* (Cambridge University Press 2012).

Boraine Alex, *A Country Unmasked: Inside South Africa's Truth and Reconciliation Commission* (Oxford University Press 2000).

Boraine Alex, Janet Levy and Ronel Scheffer (eds), *Dealing with the Past: Truth and Reconciliation in South Africa* (2nd edn, Institute for Democracy in South Africa 1997).

Brudholm Thomas and Thomas Cushman (eds), *The Religious in Responses to Mass Atrocity Interdisciplinary Perspectives* (Cambridge University Press 2009).

Bubenzer Ole, *Post-TRC Prosecutions in South Africa: Accountability for Political Crimes After the Truth and Reconciliation Commission's Amnesty Process* (Brill 2009).

Buckley-Zistel Susanne, Teresa Koloma Beck, Christian Braun and Friederike Mieth (eds), *Transitional Justice Theories* (Routledge 2013).

Carsten Stahn and Jann K. Kleffner (eds), *Jus Post Bellum. Towards a Law of Transition from Conflict to Peace* (T.M.C. Asser Press 2008).

Collins Cath, *Post transitional Justice: Human Rights Trial in Chile and El Salvador* (Pennsylvania State University Press 2010).

Commission nationale consultative des droits de l'homme et Commission internationale des juristes, *L'impunité des auteurs de violations graves des droits de l'homme* Rencontres internationales, 2–5 novembre 1992 (Dijon-Chenôve, 1993).

Corradetti Claudio, Nir Eisikovitts Suffolk and Jack Volpe Rotondi (eds), *Theorizing Transitional Justice* (Ashgate-Routledge 2015).

Crowe M David, *War Crimes, Genocide, and Justice. A Global History* (Palgrave Macmillan 2014).

Davis Laura, *EU Foreign Policy, Transitional Justice and Mediation: Principle, Policy, Practice* (Routledge 2014).

Destrooper Tine, Line Engbo Gissel and Kerstin Bree Carlson (eds), *Transitional Justice in Aparadigmatic Contexts: Accountability, Recognition, and Disruption* (Routledge 2023).

De Greiff Pablo, *The Handbook of Reparations* (Oxford University Press 2006).

Domenico Roy Palmer, *Italian Fascists on Trial, 1943–1948* (University of North Carolina Press 1991).

Drumbl A Mark, *Atrocity, Punishment, and International Law* (Cambridge University Press 2007).

Elster Jon, *Closing the Books: Transitional Justice in Historical Perspective* (Cambridge University Press 2004).

Fineman Albertson Martha and Estelle Zinsstag (eds), *Feminist Perspectives on Transitional Justice: From International and Criminal to Alternative Forms of Justice* (Series on Transitional Justice, Intersentia 2013).

Fisk Milton, *The State and Justice: An Essay in Political Theory* (Cambridge University Press 1989).

Freeman Mark, *Truth Commissions and Procedural Fairness* (Cambridge University Press 2006).

Gallen James, *Transitional Justice and the Historical Abuses of Church and State* (Cambridge University Press 2023).

Garapon Antoine, *Des crimes que l'on ne peut ni punir ni pardonner* (Ed. Odile Jacob 2002).

Georg Schwarzenberger, *International Law as Applied by International Courts and Tribunals: The Law of Armed Conflict*, vol. II (Steven and Sons Limited 1968).

Glasius Marlies, *The International Criminal Court: A Global Civil Society Achievement* (Routledge 2006).

Golsan J Richard, *Justice in Lyon: Klaus Barbie and France's First Trial for Crimes against Humanity* (University of Toronto Press 2022).

Gready Paul and Simon Robins (eds), *From Transitional to Transformative Justice* (Cambridge University Press 2019).

Guematcha Emmanuel, *Les Commissions vérité et les violations des droits de l'homme et du droit international humanitaire* (Pedone 2014).

Guzman Bouvard Marguerite, *Revolutionizing Motherhood: The Mothers of the Plaza de Mayo* (SR Books-Rowman & Littlefield Publishers 2002).

Henckaerts Jean-Marie and Louise Doswald-Beck, *Customary International Humanitarian Law*, Vol. I: Rules (Cambridge University Press 2005).

Herf Jeffrey, *Divided Memory: the Nazi Past in the Two Germanys* (Harvard University Press 1997).

Herz H. John (ed), *From Dictatorship to Democracy: Coping with the Legacies of Authoritarianism and Totalitarianism* (Greenwood, 1982).

Huntington P Samuel, *The Third Wave. Democratization in the Late Twentieth Century* (Adarsh Books 1991).

Israël Liora and Guillaume Mouralis (eds), *Dealing with Wars and Dictatorships – Legal Concepts and Categories in Action* (T.M.C. Asser Press-Springer 2013).
Karamehić-Muratović Ajlina and Laura Kromják (eds), *Remembrance and Forgiveness. Global and Interdisciplinary Perspectives on Genocide and Mass Violence* (Routledge 2020).
Kerr Rachel and Eirin Mobekk, *Peace and Justice. Seeking Accountability after War* (Policy Press 2007).
Kritz J Neil (ed), *Transitional Justice, How Emerging Democracies Reckon with Former Regimes*, 3 vol. (United States Peace Institute 1995).
Lawther Cheryl and Luke Moffett (eds), *Research Handbook on Transitional Justice* (Edward Elgard Publishing 2017) and (2nd edn, Edward Elgar Publishing 2023).
Lessa Francesca, *Memory and Transitional Justice in Argentina and Uruguay: Against Impunity* (Palgrave Macmillan 2013).
Lévy Bernard-Henri, *Archives d'un procès: Klaus Barbie* (Librairie générale française 1986).
Lutz L. Ellen and Caitlin Reiger (eds), *Prosecuting Head of States* (Cambridge University Press 2009).
Maguchu Prosper, *Transitional Justice and Socio-Economic Rights in Zimbabwe* (T.M.C. Asser Press 2019).
Marcos Zunino, *Justice Framed: A Genealogy of Transitional Justice* (Cambridge University Press 2019).
McAdams A James, *Transitional Justice and the Rule of Law in New Democracies* (University of Notre Dame Press 1997).
McEvoy Kieran and Lorna McGregor (eds), *Transitional Justice from Below: Grassroots Activism and the Struggle for Change* (Hart Publishing 2008).
Montserrat Carreras (ed), *Lutter contre l'impunité, Actes du Colloque du 11 au 13 mars 2002* (Bruylant 2002).
Morten Bergsmo, Wolfgang Kaleck and Kyaw Yin Hlaing (eds), *Colonial Wrongs and Access to International Law* (Torkel Opsahl Academic EPublisher 2020).
Moynier Gustave Moynier, *Etude sur la Convention de Genève pour l'amélioration du sort des militaires blessés dans les armées en campagne (1864–1868)* (Librairie de Joël Cherbuliez 1870).
Mubiala Mutoy, *La justice transitionnelle en Afrique. 30 ans de pratique et de réflexion* (Presses universitaires juridiques de Poitiers 2026).
Mullin Claud, *The Leipzig Trials-An Account of the War Criminals' Trials and a Study of German Mentality* (Witherby 1921).
Murphy Colleen, *The Conceptual Foundations of Transitional Justice* (Cambridge University Press 2017).
Novick Peter, *L'épuration française. 1944–1949* (Balland 1985).

O'Donnell Guillermo and Philippe C Schmitter, *Transitions from Authoritarian Rule. Tentative Conclusions about Uncertain Democracies* (The Johns Hopkins University Press 1986).

O'Donnell Guillermo, Philippe C Schmitter and Laurence Whitehead (eds), *Transitions from Authoritarian Rule: Southern Europe* (The Johns Hopkins University Press 1986).

O'Donnell Guillermo, Philippe C Schmitter and Laurence Whitehead (eds), *Transitions from Authoritarian Rule: Latin America* (The Johns Hopkins University Press 1986).

O'Donnell Guillermo, Philippe C Schmitter and Laurence Whitehead (eds), *Transitions from Authoritarian Rule: Comparative Perspectives* (The Johns Hopkins University Press 1986).

Ostwald Martin, *From Popular Sovereignty to the Sovereignty of Law: Law, Society, and Politics in Fifth-Century Athens* (University of California Press 1986).

Ostwald Martin, *Nomos and the Beginnings of the Athenian Democracy* (Oxford University Press 1969).

Palmer Nicola, Phil Clark and Danielle Granville, *Critical Perspectives in Transitional Justice* (Series on Transitional Justice, Intersentia 2012).

Rojas Hugo and Miriam Shaftoe, *Human Rights and Transitional Justice in Chile. Memory Politics and Transitional Justice* (Palgrave Macmillan 2022).

Root K Rebecca, *Transitional Justice in Peru* (Palgrave Macmillan 2012).

Rotberg I Robert and Dennis Thompson (eds), *Truth v. Justice. The Morality of Truth Commissions* (Princeton University Press 2000).

Rothenberg Daniel, *Memory of Silence. The Guatemalan Truth Commission* (Palgrave Macmillan 2012).

Rouquet François and Fabrice Virgili, *Les Françaises, les Françaises et l'Épuration. De 1940 à nos jours* (Folio 2018).

Santamaría Julián (Compilación de), *Transición a la democracia en el sur de Europa y América Latina* (Centro de Investigaciones Sociológicas 1982).

Schabas A William, *The Trial of the Kaiser* (Oxford University Press 2018).

Schabas William, *An Introduction to the International Criminal Court* (6th edn, Cambridge University Press 2020).

Schabas William, *An Introduction to International Criminal Court* (4th edn, Cambridge University Press 2011).

Seibert-Fohr Anja, *Prosecuting Serious Human Rights Violations* (Oxford University Press 2009).

Sérant Paul, *Les vaincus de la libération. L'épuration en Europe occidentale à la fin de la Seconde Guerre mondiale* (Robert Laffont 1964).

Sikkink Kathryn, *The Justice Cascade: How Human Rights Prosecutions Are Changing World Politics* (W. W. Norton & Company 2010).

Simić Olivera and Zala Volčič (eds), *Transitional Justice and Civil Society in the Balkans* (Springer 2013).

Skaar Elin, *Judicial Independence and Human Rights in Latin America* (Palgrave Macmillan 2011).

Simić Olivera (ed), *An Introduction to Transitional Justice* (2nd edn, Routledge 2021)

*State Crimes: Punishment or Pardon* (The Aspen Institute, 1989).

Teitel G Ruti, *Transitional Justice* (Oxford University Press 2000).

Tigroudja Helène, *Conflits armés et droit international des droits de l'homme*, Recueil des cours de l'Académie de droit international de La Haye, vol. 444, 2025.

*Transitional Justice in Albania*, Papers compiled by OSCE Presence in Albania and Konrad-Adenauer-Stiftung, 2020.

*Truth Commissions: A Comparative Assessment. An Interdisciplinary Discussion Held at Harvard Law School in May 1996*, Organized by the Human Rights Program Harvard Law School and the World Peace Foundation (Harvard Law School Human Rights Program, 1997).

Turgis Noémie, *La justice transitionnelle en droit international* (Bruylant 2014).

Van der Merwe Hugo and Jasmina Brankovic (eds), *Advocating Transitional Justice in Africa. The Role of Civil Society* (Springer, 2018).

Van Ness W Daniel and Gerry Johnstone (eds), *Handbook of Restorative Justice* (Willan Publishing 2007).

Van Ness W Daniel and Karen Heetderks Strong, *Restoring Justice: An Introduction to Restorative Justice* (5th edn, Routledge 2015).

Vázquez Guevara Valeria, *Truth Commissions and International Law: Jurisdiction, Representation, Authority* (Cambridge University Press 2026).

Virgilli Fabrice and François Rouquet, *Les Françaises, les Français et l'Épuration* (Gallimard 2018).

Wallis Joanne and Lia Kent (eds), *Reconceiving Civil Society and Transitional Justice Lessons from Asia and the Pacific* (Routledge 2020).

Werle Gerhard and Moritz Vormbaum, *Transitional Justice: The Legal Framework* (Springer 2022).

Yadav Philbrick, *Yemen in the Shadow of Transition. Pursuing Justice Amid War* (Hurst & Company 2022).

Yusuf O Hakeem and Hugo Van der Merwe (eds), *Transitional Justice. Theories, Mechanisms and Debates* (Routledge 2022).

Zartmann I William et Victor Kremenyuk (eds), *Peace Versus Justice. Negotiating Forward -and Backward- Looking Outcomes* (Rowman and Littlefield Publishers 2005).

## 2 Articles

'Dossier: Le jus post bellum – nouveau cheval de Troie du droit des conflits armés ?' (2011) *Revue Belge de Droit International.*

'Special Issue: Race, Racism and Transitional Justice' (2024) 18(1) *International Journal of Transitional Justice* 1.

Abrams Bradley, 'The Politics of Retribution: The Trial of Josef Tiso in the Czechoslovak Environment' in István Deák, Jan T. Gross, and Tony Judt (eds), *The Politics of Retribution in Europe: World War II and Its Aftermath* (Princeton University Press 2000).

Akhtarkhavari Afshin and Fiona Lubett, 'Nature's Access to Water in Post-conflict Peacebuilding Efforts in South Sudan' in Natalia Szablewska Sascha and Dominik Bachmann (eds), *Current Issues in Transitional Justice. Towards a More Holistic Approach* (Springer 2015).

Albon Mary, The Charter Seventy-Seven Foundation – New York, Project on Justice in Times of Transition (Report of the Project's Inaugural Meeting, Salzburg, March 7–10, 1992).

Albon Mary, 'Project on Justice in Times of Transition: Report of the Project's Inaugural Meeting' in Neil J Kritz (ed), *Transitional Justice, How Emerging Democracies Reckon with Former Regimes*, vol. 1 (United States Peace Institute 1995).

Alexander Mayer-Rieckh, 'Vetting' in Carsten Stahn and Jens Iverson (eds), *Just Peace After Conflict* (Oxford University Press 2020).

Ambos Kai, 'The Legal Framework of Transitional Justice: A Systematic Study with a Special Focus on the Role of the ICC' in Kai Ambos, Judith Large and Marieke Wierda (eds), *Building a Future on Peace and Justice: Studies on Transitional Justice, Peace and Development* (Springer 2009).

Andrieu Kora, 'Political Liberalism after Mass Violence: John Rawls and a 'Theory' of Transitional Justice' in Susanne Buckley-Zistel, Teresa Koloma Beck, Christian Braun and Friederike Mieth (eds), *Transitional Justice Theories* (Routledge 2013).

Arbour Louise, 'Economic and Social Justice for Societies in Transition' (2007) 40 *New York University Journal of International Law and Politics* 1.

Arthur Paige and Christalla Yakinthou, 'Refocusing on Civil Society: How to Make – Not Miss – Connections' in Paige Arthur and Christalla Yakinthou (eds), *Transitional Justice, International Assistance, and Civil Society: Missed Connections* (Cambridge University Press 2018).

Bačanovikj Oliver, 'Transitional Justice between Retributive and Restorative Justice', *Dialogues Security*, 2015.

Backer David, 'Civil Society and Transitional Justice: Possibilities, Patterns and Prospects' (2003) 2(3) *Journal of Human Rights* 297.

Banungana Christian Tshiamala, 'La judiciarisation des atteintes environnementales: la cour pénale internationale à la rescousse?' (2018) *Revue québécoise de droit international* 205.

Bassiouni Cherif (Project director), Daniel Rothenberg (Executive editor), Etelle Higonnet and Michael Hanna (Contributors), 'The Chicago Principles on Post-conflict Justice' (International Human Rights Law Institute 2007).

Bassiouni Cherif and Daniel Rothenberg, "Facing Atrocity: The Importance of Guiding Principles on Post-conflict Justice" in Bassiouni Cherif (Project director), Daniel Rothenberg (Executive editor), Etelle Higonnet and Michael Hanna (Contributors), 'The Chicago Principles on Post-conflict Justice' (International Human Rights Law Institute 2007).

Bassiouni Cherif, 'Perspectives on International Criminal Justice' (2010) 50(2) *Virginia Journal of International Law* 269.

Bell Christine and Catherine O'Rourke, 'Does Feminism Need a Theory of Transitional Justice? An Introductory Essay' (2007) 1 *The International Journal of Transitional Justice* 23.

Bernabeu Almudena and Carolyn Patty Blum, 'The Road to Spain: The Jesuit Massacre and the Struggle against Impunity in El Salvador' (2012) 18(1) *Peace and Conflict: Journal of Peace Psychology* 96.

Bílková Veronika, 'Lustration: the Experience of Czechoslovakia/The Czech Republic', Conference paper, *Past and Present-Day Lustration: Similarities, Differences, Applicable Standards*, Hosted by the Ministry of Foreign Affairs of the Czech Republic, Prague, Czech Republic, 7 September 2015.

Bilsky Leora, 'The Right to Truth in International Criminal Law' in Kevin Jon Heller, Frédéric Mégret, Sarah M H Nouwen, Jens David Ohlin, and Darryl Robinson (eds), *The Oxford Handbook of International Criminal Law* (Oxford University Press 2020).

Binder Christina, 'Introduction to the Concept of Transitional Justice' in Walter Feichtinger, Gerald Hainzl and Predrag Jurekovic (eds), *Transitional Justice: Experiences from Africa and the Western Balkans* (Landesverteidigungsakademie, 2013).

Bojarski Łukasz, 'Civil Society Organizations for and with the Courts and Judges – Struggle for the Rule of Law and Judicial Independence: The Case of Poland 1976–2020' (2021) 22 *German Law Journal* 1344.

Boraine Alex, 'Transitional Justice as an Emerging Field', Presentation at the symposium, *Repairing the Past: Reparations and Transition to Democracy*, Ottawa, Canada, 11 March 2004.

Bosdriesz Hanna and Sander Wirken, 'An Imperfect Success – The Guatemalan Genocide Trial and the Struggle against Impunity for International Crimes' (2014) 14(6) *International Criminal Law Review* 1067.

Brady P James, 'The Talking Stone: Evolution and Action of People's Criminology' (1975) 5(4) *Insurgent Sociologist* 73.

Buergenthal Thomas, 'The United Nations Truth Commission for El Salvador' (1994) 27(3) *Vanderbilt Law Review* 497.

Buszka J Alexander, 'When Alternative Dispute Resolution Works: Lessons Learned from the Bashingantahe' (2019) 67 *Buffalo Law Review* 165.

Cahin Gérard, 'L'Impact Des Tribunaux Pénaux Internationalisés Sur La (Re)Construction de L'État de Droit' in Hervé Ascensio, Elisabeth Lambert-Abdelgawad and Jean-Marc Sorel (ed), *Les juridictions pénales internationalisées (Cambodge, Kosovo, Sierra Leone, Timor Leste)* (Société de législation comparée 2006).

Camilo Sánchez Nelson and Rodrigo Uprimny Yepes, 'Transitional Justice without Transition? The Colombian Experience in the Implementation of Transition Measures' in *Contribution of Truth, Justice, and Reparation Policies to Latin American Democracies* (Inter-American Institute of Human Rights 2011).

Cassese Antonio, 'Clemency Versus Retribution in Post Conflict Situations' (2007) 46(1) *Columbia Journal of Transnational Law* 1.

Clamp Kerry and Jonathan Doak, 'More than Words: Restorative Justice Concepts in Transitional Justice Settings' (2012) 12 *International Criminal Law Review* 339.

Clark Natalya Janine, 'Transitional Justice and the Significance of More-Than-Human Worlds: Some Reflections from the Russia-Ukraine War' (2025) 17(3) *Journal of Human Rights Practice*.

Collins Cath, "Paraguay: Accountability in the Shadow of Stroessner" in Elin Skaar, Jemina Garcia-Godos and Cath Collins (eds), *Transitional Justice in Latin America: The Uneven Road from Impunity towards Accountability* (Routledge 2016).

Conway Martin, 'Justice in Postwar Belgium: Popular Passions and Political Realities' in István Deák, Jan T. Gross, and Tony Judt (eds), *The Politics of Retribution in Europe: World War II and Its Aftermath* (Princeton University Press 2000).

Corradi E Juan, 'Toward Societies without Fear' in Juan E Corradi, Patricia Weiss Fagen, and Manuel Antonio Garretón (eds), *Fear at the Edge: State Terror and Resistance in Latin America* (University of California Press 1992).

Corradi E Juan, Patricia Weiss Fagen, and Manuel Antonio Garretón, 'Introduction: Fear: A Cultural and Political Construct' in Juan E. Corradi, Patricia Weiss Fagen, and Manuel Antonio Garretón (eds), *Fear at the Edge: State Terror and Resistance in Latin America* (University of California Press 1992).

Cotte Bruno and Julien Seroussi, 'La manifestation de la vérité en droit pénal international' (2010) 53 *Archives de philosophie du droit* 86.

Courtney Jung Courtney, 'Canada and the Legacy of the Indian Residential Schools: Transitional Justice for Indigenous Peoples in a Non-transitional Society', April 8, 2009.

Crocker A David, 'Truth Commissions, Transitional Justice, and Civil Society' in Robert I. Rotberg and Dennis Thompson (eds), *Truth v. Justice. The Morality of Truth Commissions* (Princeton University Press 2000).

Dankwart A Rustow, 'Transitions to Democracy: Toward a Dynamic Model' (1970) 2(3) *Comparative Politics* 337.

De Frouville Olivier, 'Towards Global Transitional Justice?' (2022) Working Papers, Geneva Academy 5.

De Greiff Pablo, 'Theorizing Transitional Justice' (2012) 51 *Nomos* 31.

Decaux Emmanuel, 'Droit International Et Expériences Nationales', Commission Nationale Consultative Des Droits de L'Homme Et Commission Internationale Des Juristes, *L'impunité des auteurs de violations graves des droits de l'homme* Rencontres internationales, 2–5 novembre 1992 (Dijon-Chenôve 1993) 27–66.

Di Palma Giuseppe, 'Italy: Is There a Legacy and Is It Fascist?' in Herz H. John (ed), *From Dictatorship to Democracy: Coping with the Legacies of Authoritarianism and Totalitarianism* (Greenwood 1982).

Diamandouros Nikiforos, 'Regime Change and the Prospects for Democracy in Greece' in Neil J Kritz (ed), *Transitional Justice, How Emerging Democracies Reckon with Former Regimes*, vol. II (United States Peace Institute 1995).

Dugard John, 'Is the Truth and Reconciliation Process Compatible with International Law? An Unanswered Question' (1997) 13 *South African Journal on Human Rights* 258.

Dugard John, 'Possible Conflicts of Jurisdiction with Truth Commissions' in Antonio Cassese, Paola Gaeta and John R. W. D. Jones (eds), *The Rome Statute of the International Criminal Court: A Commentary* (Oxford University Press 2002).

Dyzenhaus David, 'Review Essays: Transitional justice' (2003) 1(1) *International Journal of Constitutional Law* 163.

Easterday S Jennifer, Jens Iverson and Stahn Carsten, "Exploring the Normative Foundations of Jus Post Bellum: An Introduction" in Jennifer S. Easterday, Jens Iverson, and Stahn Carsten (eds), *Jus post bellum: Mapping the normative foundations* (Oxford University Press 2014).

Ellen Lutz and Kathryn Sikkink, 'The Justice Cascade: The Evolution and Impact of Foreign Human Rights Trials in Latin America' (2001) 2 (1) *Chicago Journal of International Law* 1.

Ellis S Mark, 'Purging the Past: The Current State of Lustration Laws in the Former Communist Bloc' (1996) 59(6) *Law and Contemporary Problems* 181.

Engelmann C Frederick, 'How Austria Has Coped with Two Dictatorial Legacies' in Herz H. John (ed), *From Dictatorship to Democracy: Coping with the Legacies of Authoritarianism and Totalitarianism* (Greenwood 1982).

Fichter Michael, 'Non-state Organizations and the Problems of Redemocratization' in Herz H. John (ed), *From Dictatorship to Democracy: Coping with the Legacies of Authoritarianism and Totalitarianism* (Greenwood 1982).

Givskov Carl Christian, 'The Danish 'Purge-Laws'' (1948) 39(4) *Journal of Criminal Law and Criminology (1931–1951)* 447.

Goldberg Eliot and Mary C Theisen (Rapporteurs), 'Post-conflict Justice: The Role of the International Community: Report of a Vantage Conference' in (Stanley Foundation, April 4–6 1997).

Goldstone Richard, 'Past Human Rights Violations: Truth Commissions and Amnesties or Prosecutions' (2000) 51(2) *Northern Ireland Legal Quarterly* 164.

Goldstone Richard, 'Peace versus Justice' (2006) 6 *Nevada Law Journal* 421.

Gonzalez Eduardo, 'The end of transitional justice? Potentials and limitations of our position in the decolonization debate', 21 November 2022, online: https://frient.de/en/artikel/the-end-of-transitional-justice/.

González-Enríquez Carmen, 'De-Communization and Political Justice in Central and Eastern' in Alexandra Barahona de Brito, Carmen González-Enríquez and Paloma Aguilar (eds), *The Politics of Memory. Transitional Justice in Democratizing Societies* (Oxford University Press 2001).

Gordon S Gregory, 'The Trial of Peter Von Hagenbach: Reconciling History, Historiography and International Criminal Law' in Kevin Jon Heller and Gerry Simpson (eds), *The Hidden Histories of War Crimes Trials* (Oxford University Press 2013).

Gready Paul and Simmons Robins, 'Rethinking Civil Society and Transitional Justice: Lessons from Social Movements and 'New' Civil Society' (2017) 21(1) *The International Journal of Human Rights* 956.

Gready Paul, ' 'You're Either with Us or Against Us': Civil Society and Policy Making in Post-genocide Rwanda' (2010) 109(437) *African Affairs* 637.

Gutmann Amy and Dennis Thompson, 'The Moral Foundations of Truth Commissions' in Robert I. Rotberg and Dennis Thompson (eds), *Truth v. Justice. The Morality of Truth Commissions* (Princeton University Press 2000).

Harith Al-Dabbagh, 'Débaathification en Irak: Justice Transitionnelle ou Simple Vengeance' (2014) 27 *Revue Québécoise de Droit International* 31.

Hayner B Priscilla, 'Fifteen Truth Commissions-1974 to 1994: A Comparative Study' (1994) 16(4) *Human Rights Quarterly* 597.

Helen Gyr, 'Transitional Justice Process and the Justice Theory of Roland Dworkin' (2023) 12(3) *Laws* 35.

Henkin H Alice, 'Conference Report' in *State Crimes: Punishment or Pardon* (The Aspen Institute 1989).

Henry Nicola, 'From Reconciliation to Transitional Justice: The Contours of Redress Politics in Established Democracies' (2015) 9 *International Journal of Transitional Justice* 199.

Herman Schwartz, 'Lustration in Eastern Europe' (1994) 1(2) *Parker School of East European Law* 141.

Hermet Guy, 'Rethinking Transitology' in Aurel Braun and Zoltan Barany (eds), *Dilemmas of Transition: The Hungarian Experience* (Rowman and Littlefield 1999).

Herz H John, 'Denazification and Related Policies' in John Herz (ed), *From Dictatorship to Democracy: Coping with the Legacies of Authoritarianism and Totalitarianism* (Greenwood 1982).

Horne M Cynthia, 'International Legal Rulings on Lustration Policies in Central and Eastern Europe: Rule of Law in Historical Context' (2009) 34(3) *Law & Social Inquiry* 713.

Hourquebie Fabrice, 'La notion de justice transitionnelle a -t-elle un sens' (2009) 398(90) *Les petites affiches* 6.

Hourquebie Fabrice, 'La justice transitionnelle a bien un sens' (2014) 250(2) *Afrique contemporaine* 86.

Ingelaere Bert, 'The Gacaca Courts in Rwanda' in Luc Huyse and Mark Salter (eds), *Traditional Justice and Reconciliation after Violent Conflict. Learning from African Experiences* (IDEA, 2008).

Ingelaere Bert, 'Reparation in Rwanda's Gacaca Courts' (2019) *Témoigner. Entre histoire et mémoire* 84.

Jackson M Miles, 'The Customary International Law Duty to Prosecute Crimes against Humanity: A New Framework' (2007–2008) 16(1) *Tulane Journal of International and Comparative Law* 117.

Jackson-Meyer Kate, 'A Clergy Abuse Truth and Reconciliation Commission' (2023) 3 *Journal of Moral Theology* 230.

Jacquelin Mathieu, 'International Law' (2018) 1(1) *Journal of Criminal Science and Comparative Criminal Law* 229.

Jakobsen Line Jespersgaard, 'Colombia as the 'Laboratory' for Transitional Justice: Consolidation and Innovation of Global Formulas' (2024) 18(3) *International Journal of Transitional Justice* 422.

Karsi Laszlo, 'The People's Court and Revolutionary Justice in Hungary, 1945–1946' in István Deák, Jan T. Gross, and Tony Judt (eds), *The Politics of Retribution in Europe: World War II and Its Aftermath* (Princeton University Press 2000).

Kemp Susan, 'Guatemala Prosecutes Former President Ríos Montt: New Perspectives on Genocide and Domestic Criminal Justice' (2014) 12(1) *Journal of International Criminal Justice* 133.

Kim Joon Hun, 'Transitional Justice in South Korea' in Renée Jeffery and Hun Joon Kim, *Transitional Justice in Asia-Pacific* (Cambridge University Press 2014).

Kim Jung Myung, 'Transitional Justice in North Korea' (2015) *Yonsei Journal of International Studies* 91.

Klinsky Sonia and Jasmina Brankovic, *The Global Climate Regime and Transitional Justice* (Routledge 2018).

Kohlhagen Dominik, 'Le Bushingantahe Au Burundi: Transformations Et Réminiscences D'Un Concept Judiciaire Ancien' in Laboratoire D'Anthropologie Juridique de Paris, Cahiers D'Anthropologie Du Droit 2009, *Dire le droit, rendre la justice* (Karthala 2010).

Kora Andrieu, 'Transitional Justice: A New Discipline in Human Rights, Mass Violence & Resistance' (2010), online, http://bo-k2s.sciences-po.fr/mass-violence-war-massacre-resistance/fr/document/transitional-justice-new-discipline-human-rights, ISSN 1961–9898.

Lambourne Wendy, 'Transitional Justice after Mass Violence: Reconciling Retributive and Restorative Justice' in Helen Irving, Jacqueline Mowbray and Kevin Walton (eds), *Julius Stone: A Study in Influence* (Federation Press-Annandale 2010).

Lambourne Wendy, "Transformative Justice, Reconciliation and Peacebuilding" in Susanne Buckley-Zistel, Teresa Koloma Beck, Christian Braun and Friederike Mieth (eds), *Transitional Justice Theories* (Routledge 2013) 21.

Landsman Stephan, 'Alternative Responses to Serious Human Rights Abuses: of Prosecution and Truth Commissions' (1996) 59(4) *Law and Contemporary Problems* 81.

Lange-Quassowski Jutta-B, 'Coming to Terms with the Nazi Past: Schools, Media, and the Formation of Opinion' in Herz H John (ed), *From Dictatorship to Democracy: Coping with the Legacies of Authoritarianism and Totalitarianism* (Greenwood 1982).

Lanni Adriaan, 'Transitional Justice in Ancient Athens: A Case Study' (2010) 32 *University of Pennsylvania Journal of International Law* 551.

Latigo Ojera James, 'Northern Uganda: Tradition-Based Practices in the Acholi Region' in Luc Huyse and Mark Salter (eds), *Traditional Justice and Reconciliation after Violent Conflict. Learning from African Experiences, Stockholm* (IDEA 2008).

Lenta Patrick, 'Transitional Justice and Retributive Justice' (2019) 22(2) *Ethical Theory and Moral Practice* 385.

Lessa Francesca, 'Beyond Transitional Justice: Exploring Continuities in Human Rights Abuses in Argentina between 1976 and 2010' (2011) 3(1) *Journal of Human Rights Practice* 25.

Llewellyn L Jennifer and Robert Howse, 'Institutions for Restorative Justice: The South African Truth and Reconciliation Commission' (1999) 49(3) *The University of Toronto Law Journal* 355.

Ludwin King B Elizabeth, 'Transitional Justice and the Legacy of Child Sexual Abuse in the Catholic Church' (2018) 81(1) *Albany Law Review* 121.

Lundy Patricia and Mark McGovern, 'Whose Justice? Rethinking Transitional Justice from the Bottom Up' (2008) 35(2) *Journal of Law and Society* 265.

Lutz L Ellen, 'Understanding Human Rights Violations in Armed Conflict' in Julie Mertus and Jeffrey W Helsing (eds), *Human Rights and Conflict. Exploring the Links between Rights, Law, and Peacebuilding* (United States Peace Institute 2006).

Lykes M Brinton and Colleen Murphy, 'Decolonizing Transitional Justice: Soft, Radical or Beyond Reform' (2023) 17(3) *International Journal of Transitional Justice* 361.

Macridis C Roy, 'France: from Vichy to the Fourth Republic' in Herz H. John (ed), *From Dictatorship to Democracy: Coping with the Legacies of Authoritarianism and Totalitarianism* (Greenwood 1982).

Mair Theresa, 'Transforming Transitional Justice to Address Colonial Crime. The Nama's and Herero's Claim for Justice for Germany's Colonial Genocide in Namibia' in Norman Weiß (ed) *Transitional Justice Theoretical and Practical Approaches* (Universitätsverlag Potsdam 2022).

Malamud-Goti Jaime, 'Transitional Governments in the Breach: Why Punish State Criminals?' (1990) 12(1) *Human Rights Quarterly* 1.

Malamud-Goti Jaime, 'Trying Violators of Human Rights: the Dilemma of Transitional Democratic Governments' in *State Crimes: Punishment or Pardon* (The Aspen Institute 1989).

Malefakis Edward, 'Spain and Its Francoist Heritage' in Herz H. John (ed), *From Dictatorship to Democracy: Coping with the Legacies of Authoritarianism and Totalitarianism* (Greenwood 1982).

Mallinder Louise, 'Can Amnesties and International Justice be Reconciled ?' (2007) 1 *International Journal of Transitional Justice* 208.

Mandela Nelson, 'Foreword' in Neil J Kritz, *Transitional Justice, How Emerging Democracies Reckon with Former Regimes*, vol. 1 (United States Peace Institute 1995).

Mani Rama, 'Dilemmas of Expanding Transitional Justice, or Forging the Nexus between Transitional Justice and Development' (2008) 2(3) *International Journal of Transitional Justice* 253.

Maxwell Kenneth, 'The Emergence of Portuguese Democracy' in Herz H. John (ed), *From Dictatorship to Democracy: Coping with the Legacies of Authoritarianism and Totalitarianism* (Greenwood 1982).

Mazower Mark, 'The Cold War and the Appropriation of Memory: Greece after Liberation' in István Deák, Jan T. Gross, and Tony Judt (eds), *The Politics of Retribution in Europe: World War II and Its Aftermath* (Princeton University Press 2000).

McEvoy Kieran, "Letting Go of Legalism: Developing a 'Thicker' Version of Transitional Justice" in Kieran McEvoy and Lorna McGregor (eds), *Transitional Justice from Below: Grassroots Activism and the Struggle for Change* (Hart Publishing 2008).

McGaughey Fiona, Rachel Rafferty and Amy Maguire, 'Transitional Justice from Above and Below: Exploring the Potential Glocalising Role of Non-governmental Organisations through a Northern Ireland Case Study' (2023) 74(3) *Northern Ireland Legal Quarterly* 472.

McGregor Lorna, "International Law as a 'Tiered Process': Transitional Justice at the Local, National and International Level" in Kieran McEvoy and Lorna McGregor (eds), *Transitional Justice from Below: Grassroots Activism and the Struggle for Change* (Hart Publishing 2008).

Meerts W. Paul, 'Turning Point Westphalia: Negotiation Processes Establishing a New Political and Legal Order in Europe' in Zartmann I William et Victor Kremenyuk (eds), *Peace Versus Justice. Negotiating Forward -and Backward- Looking Outcomes* (Rowman and Littlefield Publishers 2005).

Melich S Jiri, 'Transitology' in *Encyclopedia of Political Science* 5 (2011) 1683.

Mezarobba Glenda, 'Between Reparations, Half Truths and Impunity: The Difficult Break with the Legacy of the Dictatorship in Brazil' (2010) 7(13) *International Journal on Human Rights* 7.

Mignone F Emilio, Cynthia L Estlund and Samuel Issacharoff, 'Dictatorship on Trial: Prosecution of Human Rights Violations in Argentina' (1984) 10(1) *Yale Journal of International Law* 118.

Mihr Anja, 'An Introduction to Transitional Justice', in Olivera Simić (ed), *An Introduction to Transitional Justice* (2nd edn, Routledge 2021).

Moyo Khanyisela, 'Feminism, Postcolonial Legal Theory and Transitional Justice: A Critique of Current Trends' (2012) 1(2) *International Human Rights Law Review* 237.

Mwaka Deogratius Amos and Willy Obol Olango, 'Reconciliation Among the Central Luo of Northern Uganda: The Ingredients and Process of Mato Oput' (2023) 9(1) *Cogent Social Sciences* 1.

Naftali Patricia, 'Crafting a "Right to Truth" in International Law: Converging Mobilizations, Diverging Agendas?' (2013) XIII *Champ pénal/Penal field*, online: http://journals.openedition.org/champpenal/9245.

Naniwe-Kaburahe Assumpta, 'The Institution of Bashingantahe in Burundi', in Luc Huyse and Mark Salter (eds), *Traditional Justice and Reconciliation after Violent Conflict. Learning from African Experiences* (IDEA 2008).

Niclauss Karlheinz, 'Political Reconstruction at Bonn' in John Herz (ed), *From Dictatorship to Democracy: Coping with the Legacies of Authoritarianism and Totalitarianism* (Greenwood 1982).

Niebur Eisnaugle J Carrie, 'An international truth commission: Utilizing restorative justice as an alternative to retribution' (2003) 36 *Vanderbilt Journal of Transnational Law* 209.

Nino S Carlos, 'The Duty to Punish Human Rights Violations of a Prior Regime: The Case of Argentina' (1991) 100 *The Yale Law Journal* 2619.

Orentlicher F Diane, 'A Reply to Professor Nino' (1991) 100 *The Yale Law Journal* 2641.

Orentlicher F Diane, 'Settlings Accounts: The Duty to Prosecute Human Rights Violations of a Prior Regime' (1991) 100 *Yale Law Journal* 2537.

Paige Arthur, 'How "Transitions" Reshaped Human Rights: A Conceptual History of Transitional Justice' (2009) 31(2) *Human Rights Quarterly* 321.

Parmentier Stephan, 'The South African Truth and Reconciliation Commission. Towards Restorative Justice in the Field of Human Rights' in Ezzat Fattah and Stephan Parmentier (eds) *Victim Policies and Criminal Justice on the Road to Restorative Justice. Essays in Honour of Tony Peters* (Leuven University Press 2001).

Pinto Costa Antonio, 'The Radical Right in the Contemporary Portugal', in Neil J Kritz, *Transitional Justice, How Emerging Democracies Reckon with Former Regimes*, vol. II (United States Peace Institute 1995).

Pinto Monica, 'Awakening the Leviathan through Human Rights Law – How Human Rights Bodies Trigger the Application of Criminal Law' (2018) 34 *Utrecht Journal of International and European Law* 161.

Plotniko Oleksii, 'Defining Transitional Justice: Scholarly Debate and UN Precision' (2017) 1(3) *Lex Portus* 50.

Politis Nicolas, 'Les commissions internationales d'enquête' (1912) *Revue générale de droit international public* 149.

Popkin Margaret and Naomi Roht-Arriaza 'Truth as Justice: Investigatory Commissions in Latin America' (1995) 20(1) *Law & Social Inquiry* 79.

Posner A Eric and Adrian Vermeule, 'Transitional Justice as Ordinary Justice' (2004) 117(3) *Harvard Law Review* 761.

Prusin V Alexander, 'Poland's Nuremberg: The Seven Court Cases of the Supreme National Tribunal, 1946–1948' (2010) 24(1) *Holocaust and Genocide Studies* 1.

Psomiades J Harry, 'Greece: from the Colonels' Rule to Democracy' in Herz H. John (ed), *From Dictatorship to Democracy: Coping with the Legacies of Authoritarianism and Totalitarianism* (Greenwood 1982).

Quinn R Joanna, 'Whither the Transition of Transitional Justice' (2014–2015) 8 *Interdisciplinary Journal of Human Rights Law* 64.

Rodman A Kenneth, 'Peace versus Justice' in *Encyclopedia of Global Justice* (Springer 2011).

Rogers A P V, 'War Crimes Trials under the Royal Warrant: British Practice 1945–1949' (1990) 39(4) *International and Comparative Law Quarterly* 780.

Roht-Arriaza Naomi, 'Criminal Prosecutions for Genocide in Guatemala: Advances and Obstacles in Transnational and Domestic Cases' in Etelle Higonnet (ed), *Quiet Genocide. Guatemala 1981–1983* (Routledge 2009).

Roht-Arriaza Naomi, 'Making the State Do Justice: Transnational Prosecutions and International Support for Criminal Investigations in Post-armed Conflict Guatemala' (2008), 9 *Chicago Journal of International Law* 79.

Roht-Arriaza Naomi, 'State Responsibility to Investigate and Prosecute Grave Human Rights Violations in International Law' (1990) 78 *California Law Review* 449.

Romijn Peter, 'Restoration of Confidence': The Purge of Local Government in the Netherlands as a Problem of Postwar Reconstruction' in István Deák, Jan T. Gross, and Tony Judt (eds), *The Politics of Retribution in Europe: World War II and Its Aftermath* (Princeton University Press 2000).

Sandrine Lefranc, 'La justice transitionnelle n'est pas un concept' (2008) 53(1) *Mouvements* 61.

Schabas William, 'Transitional Justice and the Norms of International Law', Presentation to the Annual Meeting of the Japanese Society of International Law, Kwansei Gakuin University, 8 October 2011.

Schabas William, 'La Place de La Coutume Dans Les Travaux Des Commissions Vérité, Justice Et Réconciliation: Le Cas de La Sierra Leone' in Paul Tavernier and Jean-

Marie Henckaerts (eds), *Droit international coutumier: Enjeux et défis contemporains* (Bruylant 2008).

Schabas William, 'The Relationships between Truth Commissions and International Courts: The Case of Sierra Leone' (2003) 25(4) *Human Rights Quarterly*1035.

Schabas William, 'War Economics, Economic Actors, and International Criminal Law' in Karen Ballentine and Heiko Nitzsshke (eds), *Profiting from Peace. Managing the Resource Dimensions of Civil War* (Lynne Rienner Publishers 2005).

Schmitter C Philippe and Terry Lynn Karl, 'The Conceptual Travels of Transitologists and Consolidologists: How Far to the East Should They Attempt to Go?' (1994) 53(1) *Slavic Review* 173.

Schwartz Hermann, 'Lustration in Eastern Europe' in Neil J Kritz, *Transitional Justice, How Emerging Democracies Reckon with Former Regimes*, vol. II (United States Peace Institute 1995).

Segovia Alexander, 'The Reparations Proposals of the Truth Commissions in El Salvador and Haiti: a History of Noncompliance' in Pablo De Greiff, *The Handbook of Reparations* (Oxford University Press 2006).

Seibert-Fohr Anja, 'Transitional Justice in Post-conflict Situations' in *Max Planck Encyclopedia of Public International Law* (Oxford University Press 2019).

Sharp N Dustin, 'Addressing Economic Violence in Times of Transition: Toward a Positive-Peace Paradigm for Transitional Justice' (2012) 35(3) *Fordham International Law Journal* 780.

Sharp N Dustin, 'Transitional Justice and 'Local' Justice' in Cheryl Lawther and Luke Moffett (eds), *Research Handbook on Transitional Justice* (Edward Elgard 2017) 143.

Sikkink Kathryn and Carrie Booth Walling, 'The Impact of Human Rights Trials in Latin America' (2007) 24(4) *Journal of Peace research* 427.

Simon L Robert, 'Global Justice and the Authority of States' (1983) 66(4) *The Monist* 557.

Sirleaf V S Matiangai, 'Palestine as a Litmus Test for Transitional Justice' (2024) 18(1) *International Journal of Transitional Justice* 162.

Sissons Miranda and Abdulrazzaq Al-Saiedi, 'A Bitter Legacy: Lessons of De-Baathification in Iraq', International Center for Transitional Justice, 2013.

Skaar Elin and Eric Wiebelhaus-Brahm, 'The Drivers of Transitional Justice: An Analytical Framework for Assessing the Role of Actors' (2013) 31(2) *Nordic Journal of Human Rights*, 127.

Smith Duryea Charles, 'Introduction' in Neil J Kritz, *Transitional Justice, How Emerging Democracies Reckon with Former Regimes*, vol. 1 (United States Peace Institute 1995).

Son A Sarah, Nazanin Zadeh-Cummings, and Danielle Chubb, 'Participatory Transitional Justice as Anticipatory Project: North Korea, Diasporas and Uncertain Futures' (2025) 19(2) *International Journal of Transitional Justice* 296.

Stoll David, 'How the Guatemalan Civil War Became a Genocide: Revisiting the 2013 Trial of General Efraín Ríos Montt' (2022) 27 *The Journal of Latin American and Caribbean Anthropology* 528.

Sullo Pietro, 'Taking Colonialism Seriously. A Decolonial Approach to International Law, Transitional Justice and the Restitution of Cultural Heritage' (2025) 16 *Deusto Journal of Human Rights* 275.

Sweeney A James, 'The EU's Promotion of Transitional Justice: External and Internal Dimensions of a Patchwork of Policies' (2026) *International Journal of Human Rights*.

Swoboda Sabine, 'Paying the Debts – Late Nazi Trials before German Courts: The Case of Heinrich Boere' (2011) 9(1) *Journal of International Criminal Justice* 243.

Teitel G Ruti, "Transitional Jurisprudence: The Role of Law in Political Transformation" (1997) 106 *Yale Law Journal* 2029.

Teitel G. Ruti, 'Paradoxes in the Revolution of the Rule of Law (Symposium: Constitutionalism in the Post-Cold War Era)" (1994) 19(239) *Yale Journal of International Law* 241.

Teitel Ruti, 'Editorial Note-Transitional Justice Globalized' (2008) 2(1) *International Journal of Transitional Justice* 1.

Teitel Ruti, 'Globalized Transitional Justice' (2010) Working paper n°8, Center for Global Studies, 1.

Teitel Ruti, 'How are the New Democracies of the Southern Cone Dealing with the Legacy of the Past Human Rights Abuses' (Paper presented to the Council on Foreign Relations Latin America Project, New York, 17 May 1990).

Theisen Mary (Rapporteur), 'Accountability and Judicial Response: Building Mechanisms for Post-conflict Justice', 38th Strategy for Peace, US Foreign Policy Conference, Warrenton, Virginia, October 23–25, 1997, 4–5.

Tiedemann E Arthur, 'Japan Sheds Dictatorship' in Herz H. John (ed), *From Dictatorship to Democracy: Coping with the Legacies of Authoritarianism and Totalitarianism* (Greenwood 1982).

Unger Thomas and Marieke Wierda, 'Pursuing Justice in Ongoing Conflict: a Discussion of Current Practice' in Ambos Kai, Large Judith, and Wierda Marieke (eds), *Building a Future on Peace and justice. Studies on Transitional Justice, Peace and Development* (Springer 2009).

Valls Andrew, 'Racial Justice as Transitional Justice' (2003) 36(1) *Polity* 53.

Van Der Merwe Hugo and M Brinton Lykes, 'Racism and Transitional Justice' (2020) 14(3) *International Journal of Transitional Justice* 415.

Van Der Merwe Hugo and Richard Chelin, 'Impartial Versus Selective Justice: How Power Shapes Transitional Justice in Africa' (2020) 10(1) *African Conflict and Peacebuilding Review* 99.

Van Schaack Ben, 'Transitional Justice without Transition: the International Community's Efforts in Syria' in Hilli Moodrick-Even Khen H, Nir T. Boms and Sareta

Ashraph (eds), *The Syrian War: Between Justice and Political Reality* (Cambridge University Press 2020).

Viaene Lieselotte, Peter Doran and Jonathan Liljeblad, 'Editorial Special Section: Transitional Justice and Nature: A Curious Silence' (2023) 17(1) *International Journal of Transitional Justice* 1.

Walusimbi Senkungu Dinah, *Mato Oput: The Drinking of a Bitter Potion Made from the "Oput" Tree* (AuthorHouse 2012).

Wanjala Tecla Namachanja, 'Transitional Justice in Post-conflict Societies: A Call for Decolonization and Peace Sustainability' in Elias O Opongo, David Kaulem, Susan M. Kilonzo and Sarah Njeri (eds), *The Palgrave Handbook of Peace, Conflict and Security Studies in Africa* (Palgrave Macmillan 2025).

Webber Jeremy Webber, 'Forms of Transitional Justice' (2012) 51 *Nomos* 98.

Weeraratne Suranjan, 'Assessing the Many Faces of Transitional Justice in Timor-Leste' in Ajlina Karamehić-Muratović, and Laura Kromják (eds), *Remembrance and Forgiveness. Global and Interdisciplinary Perspectives on Genocide and Mass Violence* (Routledge 2020).

Wiebelhaus-Brahm Eric, 'Transitional Justice, Civil Society and the Development of the Rule of Law in Post-conflict Societies' (2007) 9(4) *International Journal of Not-for-Profit Law.*

Winter Stephen, 'Theorising Transitional Justice in Ongoing Conflict' in Tine Destrooper, Line Engbo Gissel and Kerstin Bree Carlson (eds), *Transitional Justice in Aparadigmatic Contexts Accountability, Recognition, and Disruption* (Routledge 2023).

Winter Stephen, 'Towards a Unified Theory of Transitional Justice' (2013) 7(2) *International Journal of Transitional Justice* 224.

Yahaya Ubale Jibrin, 'Conflict, Mass Atrocities, and the Quest for Transitional Justice in Darfur' (2025) 1(5) *African Research Reports* 447.

Yusuf O Hakeem, 'Origin, Context and Development of Transitional Justice' in Hakeem O. Yusuf and Hugo Van der Merwe (eds), *Transitional Justice. Theories, Mechanisms and Debates* (Routledge 2022).

Yusuf O Hakeem, 'Transitional Justice and Colonialism' in *Research Handbook on Transitional Justice* (Edward Elgar Publishing 2023).

Zalaquett José, 'Confronting Human Rights Violations Committed by Former Governments: Principles Applicable and Political Constraints' in *State Crimes: Punishment or Pardon* (The Aspen Institute, 1989).

Zinn M Cherish, 'Consequences of Iraqi De-Baathification' (2016) 9(2) *Cornell International Affairs Review* 80.

# 3 Jurisprudence

## 3.1 African Commission on Human and Peoples' Rights

ACOmHPR, *Commission nationale des droits de l'homme et des libertés v. Chad*, Communication n° 74/92, October 1995.

AComHPR, *Organisation des droits de l'homme du Soudan v. Sudan* and 296/05, *Centre on Housing Rights and Evictions v. Sudan*, communications 279/03, May 2009.

AComHPR, *Organisation des droits de l'homme du Soudan v. Sudan* and 296/05, *Centre on Housing Rights and Evictions v. Sudan*, communications 279/03, May 2009.

AComHPR, *Thomas Kwoyelo v. Uganda*, communication n°431/12, February 2018.

## 3.2 African Court on Human and Peoples' Rights

ACtHPR, *African Commission on Human and Peoples' Rights v. Libya*, No. 004/2011 (Provisional Measures), 25 March 2011.

ACtHPR, *African Commission on Human and Peoples' Rights v. Libya*, (Merits), 3 June 2016, 1 *AfCLR* 153.

## 3.3 ECOWAS Court of Justice

ECOWAS Court of Justice, *Hissein Habré v. République du Sénégal*, Doc. No. ECW/CCJ/APP/07/08 ARRET NO: ECW/CCJ/JUD/06/10, 18 November 2010.

ECOWAS Court of Justice, *The Global Justice & Research Project and al. v The Republic of Liberia*, Complaint to ECOWAS Court of Justice, 29 September 2022.

ECOWAS Court of justice, *The Global Justice & Research Project & 3 ORS v. The Republic of Liberia*, Application No: ECW/CCJ/APP/48/22, Ruling No: ECW/CCJ/RUL/04/24, 17 October 2024.

## 3.4 European Court of Human Rights

ECtHR [GC], *Broniowski v. Poland*, No. 31443/96, 22 June 2004.

ECtHR [GC], *Georgia v. Russia* (II), No. 38263/08, 21 January 2021.

ECtHR [GC], *Janowiec and Others v. Russia*, n° 55508/07 29520/09, 21 October 2013.

ECtHR [GC], *Korbely v. Hungary*, No. 9174/02, 19 September 2008.

ECtHR ([GC], *Malhous v. Czech Republic*, No. 33071/96, 13 December 2000.

ECtHR [GC], *Marguš c. Croatie*, No. 4455/10, 27 May 2014.

ECtHR [GC], *Mocanu and Others v. Romania*, No. 10865/09, 45886/07, 32431/08, 17 September 2014.

ECtHR [GC], *Salman v. Turkey*, No. 21986/93, 27 June 2000.
ECtHR [GC], *Ukraine v. Russia (Re Crimea)*, No. 20958/14 38334/18, 25 June 2024.
ECtHR, *Gülbahar Özer and others v. Turkey*, No. 44125/06, 2 July 2013.
ECtHR, *Ivanovski v. the former Yugoslav Republic of Macedonia*, No. 29908/11, 21 January 2016.
ECtHR, *Mahmut Kaya c. Turkey*, No. 22535/93, 28 March 2000.
ECtHR, *Matyjek v. Poland*, No. 38184/03, 24 April 2007.
ECtHR, *Palić v. Bosnia-Herzégovina*, No. 4704/04, 15 February 2011.
ECtHR, *Pincová and Pinc v. The Czech Republic*, No. 36548/97, 5 November 2002.
ECtHR, *Tunaitis v. Lithuania*, No. 42927/08, 24 November 2015.
ECtHR, *Turek v. Slovakia*, No. 57986/00, 14 February 2006.
ECtHR, *Velikovi and Others v. Bulgaria*, No. 43278/98 45437/99 48380/99, 15 March 2007.
ECtHR, *Wolf-Sorg v. Turkey*, No. 6458/03, 8 June 2010.

## 3.5 Human Rights Committee

HRC, *Edgardo Dante Santullo Valcada v. Uruguay*, Communication No. R.2/9, 1980.
HRC, *Gilboa de Reverdito v. Uruguay*, UN doc. CCPR/C/26/D/147/1983, 1 November 1985. HRC, *Ornar Berterretche Acosta v. Uruguay*, Communication No. *162/1983*, 25 October 1988.
HRC, *M.K., V.G., M.T. and J.Z. v. Slovakia*, No. 2062/2011, UN doc. CCPR/C/116/D/2062/2011, 23 March 2016.
HRC, *Rodriguez v. Uruguay*, UN doc. CCPR/C/51/D/322/1988, 19 July 1994.

## 3.6 Interamerican Court of Human Rights

IACtHR, *Almonacid-Arellano et al. v. Chile*, Judgment (Preliminary Objections, Merits, Reparations and Costs), 26 September 2006.
IACtHR,*Anzualdo-Castro v. Peru*, Judgment (Preliminary Objection, Merits, Reparations and Costs), 22 September 2009.
IACtHR,*Bámaca Velásquez v. Guatemala*, Judgment (Merits), 25 November 2000.
IACtHR,*Case of Barrios Altos v. Peru*, Judgment (Merits), 14 March 2001.
IACtHR, *Case of Contreras et al. v. El Salvador*, Judgment (Merits, Reparations and Costs), 31 August 2011.
IACtHR, *Case of Gelman v. Uruguay*, Judgment (Merits and Reparations), 24 February 2011.
IACtHR, *Case of Gomes Lund et al. ("Guerrilha Do Araguaia") v. Brazil*, Judgment (Preliminary Objections, Merits, Reparations, and Costs), 24 November 2010.

IACtHR,*Case of Ibsen Cárdenas and Ibsen Peña v. Bolivia*, Judgment (Merits, Reparation, and Costs), 1st September 2010.
IACtHR, *Case of Massacres of El Mozote and neighboring villages v. El Salvador*, Judgment (Merits, Reparations and Costs), 25 October 2012.
IACtHR,*Case of Myrna Mack-Chang v. Guatemala*, Judgment (Merits, Reparations and Costs), 25 November 2003.
IACtHR, *Case of Rochac Hernández et al. v. El Salvador*, Judgment (Merits, Reparations and Costs), 14 October 2014.
IACtHR, *Case of Zambrano Vélez et al v. Ecuador*, Judgment (Merits, Reparations and Costs), 4 July 2007.
IACtHR, *Chitay-Nech et al. v. Guatemala*, Judgment (Preliminary Objections, Merits, Reparations and Costs), 25 May 2010.
IACtHR,*Contreras et al. v. El Salvador*, Judgment (Merits, Reparations and Costs), 31 August 2011.
IACtHR,*Ibsen-Cárdenas and Ibsen-Peña v. Bolivia*, Judgment (Merits, Reparations and Costs), 1 September 2010.
IACtHR,*La Cantuta v. Peru*, Judgment (Merits, Reparations and Costs), 29 November 2006.
IACtHR,*Maritza Urrutia v. Guatemala*, Judgment (Merits, Reparations and Costs), 27 November 200.
IACtHR,*Myrna Mack Chang v. Guatemala*, Judgment (Merits, Reparations and Costs), 25 November 2003.
IACtHR, *Plan de Sánchez Massacre v. Guatemala*, Judgment (Reparations and Costs), 19 November 2004.
IACtHR,*Serrano-Cruz Sisters v. El Salvador*, Judgment (Merits, Reparations and Costs), 1st March 2005.
IACtHR, *The "Las Dos Erres" Massacre v. Guatemala*, Judgment (Preliminary Objection, Merits, Reparations and Costs), 24 November 2009.
IACtHR, *Zambrano-Vélez et al. v. Ecuador*, Judgment (Merits, Reparations and Costs), 4 July 2007.
IACtHR,*'Street Children' (Villagrán-Morales et al.) v. Guatemala*, Judgment (Reparations and Costs), 26 May 2001.

## 3.7 International Court of Justice

Application Instituting Proceedings, Questions Relating to the Obligation to Prosecute or Extradite (*Belgium v. Senegal*), filed in the Registry of the Court on February19, 2009.

Application of the Convention on the Prevention and Punishment of the Crime of Genocide (*Bosnia and Herzegovina v. Serbia and Montenegro*), Judgment, I.C.J. Reports 2007.

Factory at Chorzow (*Germany v. Poland*), 1928 P.C.I.J. (ser. A, No. 17).

Questions Relating to the Obligation to Prosecute or Extradite (*Belgium v. Senegal*), Judgment, I.C.J. Reports 2012.

## 4 Concluding Observations of Human Rights Bodies

### 4.1 Committee against Torture

CAT, *Suleymane Guengueng et al. v. Senegal*, UN doc. CAT/C/36/D/181/2001, 17 May 2006.

CAT, Concluding observations on the second periodic report of Ethiopia, UN doc. CAT/C/ETH/CO/2, 10 May 2023.

CAT, Concluding observations on the third periodic report of Burundi, UN doc. CAT/C/BDI/CO/3, 12 November 2023.

CAT, Concluding observations on the seventh periodic report of Spain, UN doc. CAT/C/ESP/CO/7, 27 July 2023.

CAT, Concluding observations on the sixth periodic report of Colombia, UN doc. CAT/C/COL/CO/6, 8 May 2023.

CAT, Concluding observations on the third periodic report of El Salvador, UN doc. CAT/C/SLV/CO/3, 23 November 2022.

CAT, Concluding observations on the second periodic report of South Africa, UN doc. CAT/C/ZAF/CO/2, 14 May 2019.

CAT, Concluding observations on the seventh periodic report of Peru, UN doc. CAT/C/PER/CO/7, 29 November 2018.

CAT, Concluding observations on the initial report of Timor-Leste, UN doc. CAT/C/TLS/CO/1, 4 December 2017.

CAT, Concluding observations on the seventh periodic report of Ecuador, UN doc. CAT/C/ECU/CO/7, 28 November 2016.

CAT, Concluding observations on the third periodic report of Kenya, UN doc. CAT/C/KEN/CO/3, 11 May 2022.

CAT, Concluding observations on the second periodic report of South Africa, UN doc. CAT/C/ZAF/CO/2, 14 May 2019.

CAT, Concluding observations on the initial report of Timor-Leste, UN doc. 4 December 2017.

CAT, Concluding observations on the seventh periodic report of Paraguay, UN doc. CAT/C/PRY/CO/7, 8 August 2017.

CAT, Concluding observations on the initial report of Maldives, UN doc. CAT/C/MDV/CO/1, 6 December 2018.

## 4.2 Committee for the Elimination of Racial Discrimination

CERD, Concluding observations on the combined ninth to eleventh periodic reports of South Africa, UN doc. CERD/C/ZAF/CO/9-11, 6 December 2023.

CERD, Concluding observations on the combined twenty-fourth to twenty-sixth periodic reports of Uruguay, UN doc. CERD/C/URY/CO/24-26, 24 August 2023.

CERD, Concluding observations on the combined fifth to eleventh periodic reports of Zimbabwe, UN doc. CERD/C/ZWE/CO/5-11, 26 August 2022.

CERD, Concluding observations on the combined eighteenth and nineteenth periodic reports of Togo, UN doc. CERD/C/TGO/CO/18-19, 6 December 2016.

CERD, Concluding observations on the combined ninth to fourteenth periodic reports of Croatia, UN doc. CERD/C/HRV/CO/9-14, 23 August 2023.

CERD, Concluding observations on the combined twenty-second to twenty-fifth periodic reports of Iraq, UN doc. CERD/C/IRQ/CO/22-25, 10–11 December 2018.

CERD, Concluding observations on the combined tenth to twelfth reports of the United States of America, UN doc. CERD/C/USA/CO/10-12, 24 August 2022.

CERD, Concluding observations on the combined twentieth to twenty-third periodic reports of Mauritius, UN doc. CERD/C/MUS/CO/20-23, 24 August 2018.

CERD, Concluding observations on the combined twenty-first to twenty-third periodic reports of Canada, UN doc. CERD/C/CAN/CO/21-23, 23–24 August 2017.

## 4.3 Committee on Economic, Social and Cultural Rights

CESCR, Concluding observations on the seventh periodic report of Sweden, UN doc. E/C.12/SWE/CO/7, 1 March 2024.

CESCR, Concluding observations on the third periodic report of Yemen, UN doc. E/C.12/YEM/CO/3, 3 March 2023.

CESCR, Concluding observations on the sixth periodic report of the Democratic Republic of the Congo, UN doc. E/C.12/COD/CO/6, 4 March 2022.

CESCR, Concluding observations on the initial report of Mali, UN doc. E/C.12/MLI/CO/1, 12 October 2018.

CESCR, Concluding observations concerning the initial report of the Central African Republic, UN doc. E/C.12/CAF/CO/1, 29 March 2018.

CESCR, Concluding observations on the fifth periodic report of Sri Lanka, UN doc. E/C.12/LKA/CO/5, 23 June 2017.

## 4.4 Committee on Enforced Disappearances

CED, Concluding observations on the additional information submitted by Uruguay under article 29 (4) of the Convention, UN doc. CED/C/URY/OAI/1, 23 September 2022.

CED, Concluding observations on the report submitted by Mali under article 29 (1) of the Convention, UN doc. CED/C/MLI/CO/1, 22 September 2022.

CED, Concluding observations on the additional information submitted by Spain under article 29 (4) of the Convention, UN doc. CED/C/ESP/OAI/1, 22 September 2021.

CED, Concluding observations on the report submitted by Brazil under article 29 (1) of the Convention, UN doc. CED/C/BRA/CO/1, 23 September 2021.

CED, Concluding observations on the additional information submitted by Colombia under article 29 (4) of the Convention, UN doc. CED/C/COL/OAI/1, 12 April-7 May 2021.

CED, Concluding observations on the additional information submitted by Iraq under article 29 (4) of the Convention, UN doc. CED/C/IRQ/OAI/1, 7 September–25 November 2020.

CED, Concluding observations on the report submitted by Honduras under article 29 (1) of the Convention, UN doc. CED/C/HND/CO/1, 31 May 2018.

CED, Concluding observations on the report submitted by Albania under article 29 (1) of the Convention, UN doc. CED/C/ALB/CO/1, 31 May 2018.

CED, Concluding observations on the report submitted by Ecuador under article 29 (1) of the Convention, UN doc. CED/C/ECU/CO/1, 15 March 2017.

CED, Concluding observations on the report submitted by Tunisia under article 29 (1) of the Convention, UN doc. CED/C/TUN/CO/1, 15 March 2016.

CED, Concluding observations on the report submitted by Montenegro under article 29 (1) of the Convention, UN doc. CED/C/MNE/CO/1, 16 September 2015.

CED, Concluding observations on the report submitted by Japan under article 29 (1) of the Convention, UN doc. CED/C/JPN/CO/1, 14 November 2018.

## 4.5 Committee on the Elimination of Discrimination against Women

CEDAW, Concluding observations on the fourth periodic report of Timor-Leste, UN doc. CEDAW/C/TLS/CO/4, 9 May 2023.

CEDAW, Concluding observations on the fourth periodic report of Côte d'Ivoire, UN doc. CEDAW/C/CIV/CO/4, 30 July 2019.

CEDAW, Concluding observations on the fourth periodic report of Timor-Leste, UN doc. CEDAW/C/TLS/CO/4, 9 May 2023.

CEDAW, Concluding observations on the ninth periodic report of Peru, UN doc. CEDAW/C/PER/CO/9, 1 March 2022.

CEDAW, Concluding observations on the fourth periodic report of Côte d'Ivoire, UN doc. CEDAW/C/CIV/CO/4, 30 July 2019.

CEDAW, Concluding observations on the sixth periodic report of Nepal, UN doc. CEDAW/C/NPL/CO/6, 14 November 2018.

CEDAW, Concluding observations on the ninth periodic report of Peru, UN doc. CEDAW/C/PER/CO/9, 1 March 2022.

CEDAW, Concluding observations on the fourth periodic report of Côte d'Ivoire, UN doc. CEDAW/C/CIV/CO/4, 30 July 2019.

CEDAW, Concluding observations on the combined sixth and seventh periodic reports of Ireland, UN doc. CEDAW/C/IRL/CO/6-7, 9 March 2017.

CEDAW, Concluding observations on the eighth periodic report of the Republic of Korea, UN doc. CEDAW/C/KOR/CO/8, 14 March 2018.

CEDAW, Concluding observations on the combined seventh and eighth periodic reports of Japan, UN doc. CEDAW/C/JPN/CO/7-8, 10 March 2016.

CEDAW, Concluding observations on the fourth periodic report of Côte d'Ivoire, UN doc. CEDAW/C/CIV/CO/4, 30 July 2019.

CEDAW, Concluding observations on the sixth periodic report of Nepal, UN doc. CEDAW/C/NPL/CO/6, 14 November 2018.

CEDAW, Concluding observations on the sixth periodic report of the Gambia, UN doc. CEDAW/C/GMB/CO/6, 1 November 2022.

CEDAW, Concluding observations on the eighth periodic report of Kenya, UN doc. CEDAW/C/KEN/CO/8, 2 November 2017.

CEDAW, Concluding observations on the seventh periodic report of Iraq, UN doc. CEDAW/C/IRQ/CO/7, 12 November 2019.

CEDAW, Concluding observations on the fourth periodic report of Côte d'Ivoire, UN doc. CEDAW/C/CIV/CO/4, 30 July 2019.

CEDAW, Concluding observations on the eighth periodic report of the United Kingdom of Great Britain and Northern Ireland, UN doc. CEDAW/C/GBR/CO/8, 14 March 2019.

CEDAW, Concluding observations on the eighth periodic report of Sri Lanka, UN doc. CEDAW/C/LKA/CO/8, 9 March 2017.

CEDAW, Concluding observations on the combined sixth and seventh periodic reports of Mali, UN doc. CEDAW/C/MLI/CO/6-7, 15 July 2015.

## 4.6 Committee on the Rights of Persons with Disabilities

CRPD, Concluding observations on the initial report of Colombia, UN doc. CRPD/C/COL/CO/1, 31 August 2016.

## 4.7 Committee on the Rights of the Child

CRC, Concluding observations on the combined fifth and sixth periodic reports of El Salvador, UN doc. CRC/C/SLV/CO/5-6, 5 October 2018.

CRC, Concluding observations on the combined fifth and sixth periodic reports of Sri Lanka, UN doc. CRC/C/LKA/CO/5-6, 2 February 2018.

CRC, Concluding observations on the combined third to fifth periodic reports of Nepal, UN doc. CRC/C/NPL/CO/3-5, 3 June 2016, para. 29 (b).

CRD, Concluding observations on the combined fifth and sixth periodic reports of Canada, UN doc. CRC/C/CAN/CO/5-6, 3 June 20222.

## 4.8 Human Rights Committee

HRC, Concluding observations of the Human Rights Committee, Guatemala, U.N. doc. CCPR/C/79/Add.63, 3 April 1996.

HRC, Concluding observations on the third periodic report of Brazil, UN doc. CCPR/C/BRA/CO/3, 20 July 2023.

HRC, Concluding observations on the sixth periodic report of Peru, UN doc. CCPR/C/PER/CO/6, 20 March 2023.

HRC, Concluding observations on the fourth periodic report of Croatia, UN doc. CCPR/C/HRV/CO/4, 18 July 2024.

HRC, Concluding observations on the fourth periodic report of Suriname, CCPR/C/SUR/CO/4, 22 July 2024.

HRC, Concluding observations on the seventh periodic report of Chile, UN doc. CCPR/C/CHL/CO/7, 22 March 2024.

HRC, Concluding observations on the second periodic report of Indonesia, UN doc. CCPR/C/IDN/CO/2, 26 March 2024.

HRC, Concluding observations on the fourth periodic report of Serbia, UN doc. CCPR/C/SRB/CO/4, 26 March 2024.

HRC, Concluding observations on the eighth periodic report of Colombia, UN doc. CCPR/C/COL/CO/8.

HRC, Concluding observations on the fourth periodic report of Panama, UN doc. CCPR/C/PAN/CO/4, 21 March 2023.

HRC, Concluding observations on the fifth periodic report of Ireland, UN doc. CCPR/C/IRL/CO/5, 22 July 2022.

HRC, Concluding observations on the sixth periodic report of Uruguay, UN doc. CCPR/C/URY/CO/6, 20 July 2022.

HRC, Concluding observations on the sixth periodic report of Iraq, UN doc. CCPR/C/IRQ/CO/6, 23 March 2022.

HRC, Concluding observations on the third periodic report of Cambodia, UN doc. CCPR/C/KHM/CO/3, 22–23 March 2022.

HRC, Concluding observations on the fifth periodic report of Togo, UN doc. CCPR/C/TGO/CO/5, 23 July 2021.

HRC, Concluding observations on the third periodic report of the Central African Republic, CCPR/C/CAF/CO/3, 27 March 2020.

HRC, Concluding observations on the sixth periodic report of Tunisia, UN doc. CCPR/C/TUN/CO/6, 27 March 2020.

HRC, Concluding observations on the fourth periodic report of Paraguay, UN doc. CCPR/C/PRY/CO/4, 22 July 2019.

HRC, Concluding observations on the Gambia in the absence of its second periodic report, UN doc. CCPR/C/GMB/CO/2, 19 July 2018.

HRC, Concluding observations on the initial report of Liberia, UN doc. CCPR/C/LBR/CO/1, 23 July 2018.

HRC, Concluding observations on the seventh periodic report of El Salvador, CCPR/C/SLV/CO/7, 28–29 March 2017.

HRC, Concluding observations on the fourth periodic report of the Democratic Republic of the Congo, UN doc. CCPR/C/COD/CO/4, 6 November 2017.

HRC, Concluding observations on the initial report of Burkina Faso, UN doc. CCPR/C/BFA/CO/1, 11 July 2016.

HRC, Concluding observations on the sixth periodic report of Ecuador, UN doc. CCPR/C/ECU/CO/6, 27–28 June 2016.

HRC, Concluding observations on the fifth periodic report of Argentina, UN doc. CCPR/C/ARG/CO/5, 11 July 2016.

HRC, Concluding observations on the fourth periodic report of Rwanda, UN doc. CCPR/C/RWA/CO/4, 24 March 2016.

HRC, Concluding observations on the initial report of South Africa, UN doc. CCPR/C/ZAF/CO/1, 23 March 2016.

HRC, Concluding observations on the sixth periodic report of Spain, UN doc. CCPR/C/ESP/CO/6, 20 July 2015.

HRC, Concluding observations on the third periodic report of Croatia, UN doc. CCPR/C/HRV/CO/3, 31 March 2015.

HRC, Concluding observations on the initial report of Côte d'Ivoire, UN doc. CCPR/C/CIV/CO/1, 31 March 2015.

HRC, Concluding observations on the initial report of Haiti, CCPR/C/HTI/CO/1, 27 October 2014.

HRC, Concluding observations on the initial report of Montenegro, UN doc. CCPR/C/MNE/CO/1, 28 October 2014.

HRC, Concluding observations on the third periodic report of the Plurinational State of Bolivia, UN doc. CCPR/C/BOL/CO/3, 29 October 2013.

HRC, Concluding observations on the third periodic report of the Central African Republic, UN doc. CCPR/C/CAF/CO/3, 27 March 2020.

HRC, Concluding observations on the Gambia in the absence of its second periodic report, UN doc. CCPR/C/GMB/CO/2, 19 July 2018.

HRC, Concluding observations on the initial report of Sierra Leone, UN doc. CCPR/C/SLE/CO/1, 25 March 2014.

HRC, Concluding observations on the fifth periodic report of Ireland, UN doc. CCPR/C/IRL/CO/5, 22 July 2022.

HRC, Concluding observations on the fourth periodic report of the Democratic Republic of the Congo, UN doc. CCPR/C/COD/CO/4, 6 November 2017.

HRC, Concluding observations on the third periodic report of the Central African Republic, CCPR/C/CAF/CO/3, 27 March 2020.

HRC, Concluding observations on the initial report of Liberia, UN doc. CCPR/C/LBR/CO/1, 23 July 2018.

HRC, Concluding observations on the second periodic report of Honduras, UN doc. CCPR/C/HND/CO/2, 24 July 2017.

## 5 Reports/Resolutions and Other Documents of International Organisations

### 5.1 African Union and African Commission on Human and Peoples' Rights

AComHPR, 'Study on Transitional Justice and Human and Peoples' Rights in Africa', 28 April 2019.

AcomHPR, Resolution on the Appointment of a New Commissioner for the Transitional Justice Study in Africa, doc. ACHPR/Res.326(LVII)2015, 28 November 2015.

AcomHPR, Resolution on the fight against impunity in Africa, doc. ACHPR/Res. 344 (LVIII) (2016).

AcomHPR, Resolution on Transitional Justice in Africa, doc. ACHPR/Res.235(LIII) 2013, 23 April 2013.

African Union, *Strategic Programs on Transitional Justice*, Transitional Justice Unit, Democracy, Election and Constitutionalism Division (DEC) Directorate of Governance and Conflict Prevention (GCPD) Department of Political Affairs, Peace and Security African Union Commission, Addis Ababa, Ethiopia, 2025.

AU, *Transitional Justice Policy*, 2019.

## 5.2 Council of Europe

CE, 'Eradicating Impunity for Serious Human Rights Violations. Guidelines and Reference Texts', 30 March 2011.

## 5.3 European Union

EU, 'The EU's Policy Framework on support to transitional justice', 2015.

## 5.4 Interamerican Commission on Human Rights

IACHR, Compendium of the Inter-American Commission on Human Rights on Truth, Memory, Justice and Reparation in Transitional Contexts, OEA/Ser.L/V/II., Doc. 121, 12 April 2021.

## 5.5 United Nations

'Annual Report of the United Nations High Commissioner for Human Rights and Reports of the Office of the High Commissioner and the Secretary-General, Analytical study on human rights and transitional justice', UN doc. A/HRC/12/18, 6 August 2009.

'From Justice for the Past to Peace and Inclusion for the Future. A Development Approach to Transitional Justice Lessons Learned from UNDP Policy and Practice', November 2020.

'Guidance Note of the Secretary-General on Transitional Justice', 2023.

'Guidance Note of the Secretary-General, United Nations Approach to Transitional Justice', 2010.

'Independent Study on Best Practices, Including Recommendations, to Assist States in Strengthening Their Domestic Capacity to Combat All Aspects of Impunity', by Professor Diane Orentlicher, UN doc. E/CN.4/2004/88, 27 February 2004.

'Memorialization processes in the context of serious violations of human rights and international humanitarian law: the fifth pillar of transitional justice', Report of the Special Rapporteur on the Promotion of Truth, Justice, Reparation and Guarantees of Non-recurrence, UN doc. A/HRC/45/45, 9 July 2020.

'Question of Human Rights of All Persons Subjected to Any Form of Detention or Imprisonment, in Particular: Question of Missing and Disappeared Persons', Report of the Working Group on Enforced or Involuntary Disappearances, UN doc. E/CN.4/1435, 26 January 1981.

'Question of the Impunity of Perpetrators of Human Rights Violations (Civil and Political)', Revised Final Report Prepared by Mr. Joinet Pursuant to Sub-commission Decision 1996/119', UN doc. E/CN.4/Sub.2/1997/20/Rev.1, 2 October 1997.

'Report of the Special Rapporteur on the Promotion of Truth, Justice, Reparation and Guarantees of Non-repetition', UN doc. A/67/368, 13 September 2012.

'Revised Set of Basic Principles and Guidelines on the Right to Reparation for Victims of Gross Violations of Human Rights and Humanitarian Law', prepared by Mr. Theo van Boven pursuant to Sub-commission decision 1995/117, Annex Basic Principles and Guidelines on the Right to Reparation for Victims of Gross Violations of Human Rights and Humanitarian Law, UN doc. E/CN.4/SUB.2/1996/17, 24 May 1996.

'Rule of Law and Transitional Justice in Conflict and Post-conflict Societies', Report of the Secretary-General, UN doc. S/2004/616, 23 August 2004.

'Study by the Office of the United Nations High Commissioner for Human Rights on Human Rights and Transitional Justice Activities Undertaken by the Human Rights Components of the United Nations System', UN doc. E/CN.4/2006/93, 7 February 2006.

'Study Concerning the Right to Restitution, Compensation and Rehabilitation for Victims of Gross Violations of Human Rights and Fundamental Freedoms', Final report submitted by Mr. Theo van Boven, Special Rapporteur, UN doc. E/CN.4/Sub.2/1993/8, 2 July 1993.

'Study on Amnesty Laws and Their Role in the Safeguard and Promotion of Human Rights', Report by Louis Joinet, Special Rapporteur of the Sub-commission on Prevention of Discrimination and Protection of Minorities, UN doc. E/CN.4/SUB.2/1985/16, 21 June 1985.

'The Right to Restitution, Compensation and Rehabilitation for Victims of Gross Violations of Human Rights and Fundamental Freedoms', Final report of the Special Rapporteur, Mr. M. Cherif Bassiouni, submitted in accordance with Commission resolution 1999/33, Annex, Basic Principles and Guidelines on the Right to a Remedy and Reparation for Victims of Violations of International Human Rights and Humanitarian Law, UN doc. E/CN.4/2000/62, 18 January 2000.

'Uniting Our Strengths: Enhancing United Nations Support for the Rule of Law', Report of the Secretary-General, UN doc. A/61/636-S/2006/980, 14 December 2006.

OHCHR, 'Rule-of-Law Tools for Post-conflict States. Vetting: An Operational Framework', 2006.

OHCHR, 'Rule-of-Law Tools for Post-conflict States: Amnesties', 2009.

OHCHR, 'Rule-of-Law Tools for Post-conflict States: Archives', 2015.

OHCHR, 'Rule-of-Law Tools for Post-conflict States: National Consultations on Transitional Justice', 2009.

OHCHR, 'Rule-of-Law Tools for Post-conflict States: Prosecution Initiatives', 2006.

OHCHR, 'Rule-of-Law Tools for Post-conflict States: Reparations Programmes', 2008.

OHCHR, 'Rule-of-Law Tools for Post-conflict States: Truth Commissions', 2006.
Resolution 18/7 of the Human Rights Council, Special Rapporteur on the Promotion of Truth, Justice, Reparation and Guarantees of Non-recurrence, UN doc. A/HRC/RES/18/7, 25 September 2011.

## 6 Texts/International and Hybrid Criminal Tribunals

Cambodia, Agreement between the United Nations and Cambodia for the Prosecution of Crimes Committed during the Period of Democratic Kampuchea, 6 June 2003.
Cambodia, Law on the Establishment of the Extraordinary Chambers in the Courts of Cambodia, 27 October 2004.
Central African Republic, Loi organique No. 15–003 portant création, organisation et fonctionnement de de la Cour Pénale Spéciale, 3 June 2015.
Former Yugoslavia (ICTY), UN doc. S/RES/827 (1993) 25 May 1993.
Gambia (Special Accountability Mechanism), Special Prosecutor's Office Act, 2024.
Germany (Nuremberg), Agreement by the Government of the United States of America, the Provisional Government of the French Republic, the Government of the United Kingdom of Great Britain and Northern Ireland and the Government of the Union of Soviet Socialist Republics for the Prosecution and Punishment of the Major War Criminals of the European Axis, Agreement signed at London, 8 August 1945, with charter of the International Military Tribunal, Entered into force 8 August 1945.
International Criminal Court, Rome Statute of the International Criminal Court, 17 July 1998.
Japan (Tokyo), Special Proclamation by the Supreme Commander for the Allied Powers at Tokyo, 19 January 1946.
Kosovo, Law No. 04/L-274 on Ratification of the International Agreement between the Republic of Kosovo and the European Union on the European Union Rule of Law Mission in Kosovo, 23 April 2014.
Kosovo, Law No.05/L-053 on Specialist Chambers and Specialist Prosecutor's Office, 3 August 2015.
Kosovo, UNMIK Regulation 2000/34, UN doc. UNMIK/Reg/2000/6, 27 May 2000.
Kosovo, UNMIK Regulation 2000/6, UN doc. UNMIK/Reg/2000/6, 15 February 2000.
Rwanda (ICTR), UN doc. S/RES/955 (1994), 8 November 1994.
Senegal/Chad, Agreement between the Republic of Senegal and the African Union on the Establishment of Extraordinary African Chambers in the Courts of Senegal, 22 August 2012.

Senegal/Chad, Statute of the Extraordinary African Chambers in the Courts of Senegal for the Prosecution of Crimes Committed in Chad during the Period from 7 June 1982 to 1st December 1990.

Sierra Leone, Agreement between the United Nations and the Government of Sierra Leone, 16 January 2002.

Sierra Leone, Statute of the Special Court for Sierra Leone, 16 January 2002.

South Sudan, Signed Revitalized Agreement on the Resolution of the Conflict in South Sudan (R-ARCSS), Addis Ababa, 12 September 2018, Section 5.3 Hybrid Court for South Sudan (HCSS).

Timor (East Timor), Regulation No. 2000/15 on the Establishment of Panels with Exclusive Jurisdiction over Serious Criminal Offences, UN doc. UNTAET/REG/2000/15, 6 June 2000.

Ukraine, Agreement between the Council of Europe and Ukraine on the Establishment of the Special Tribunal for the Crime of Aggression Against Ukraine, Strasbourg, 25 June 2025.

## 7 Acts Establishing Truth Commissions/Final Reports of Truth Commissions

Argentina, 'Nunca Más (Never Again), Report of Conadep (National Commission on the Disappearance of Persons)', 1984.

Argentina, Decreto 187, *Comisión Nacional sobre la Desaparición de personas*, 15 de diciembre de 1983.

Australia (Victoria), Yoorook Justice Commission, Summary Report, 2025.

Bangladesh, Commission of Inquiry on Enforced Disappearances, *Unfolding the Truth: A Structural Diagnosis of Enforced Disappearance in Bangladesh, Final Report*, vol. 1, 2026.

Bolivia, Comisión de la verdad, 'Memoria histórica de las investigaciones, Estado plurinacional de Bolivia, Informe ejecutivo', 2021.

Bolivia, Decreto Supremo No. 19241, *Comisión Nacional de Investigación de Ciudadanos Desaparecidos*, 28 de Octubre de 1982.

Bolivia, Ley n° 879, Ley de la comisión de la verdad, 23 de diciembre de 2016.

Brazil, 'Comissão nacional da verdade, Relatório', 3 vol., 2014.

Brazil, Lei N° 12.528, 18 de Novembro de 2011.

Burkina Faso, Loi organique n° 003-2015/CNT portant attributions, composition, organisation et fonctionnement de la commission de la réconciliation nationale et des réformes, 23 January 2015.

Burundi, Loi n°1/ 18 portant création, mandat, composition, organisation et fonctionnement de la commission vérité et réconciliation, 15 mai 2014.

Canada, 'Truth and reconciliation Commission of Canada, Canada's Residential Schools, Report', 6 vol., 2015.

Canada, Indian Residential Schools Settlement Agreement (2006b, May 8); Schedule "N" Mandate for the Truth and Reconciliation Commission.

Canada, Order-in-Council P.C. no. 2008–0793, 25 April 2008a.

Central African Republic, Loi n° 20.009 portant création, organisation et fonctionnement de la commission vérité, justice, réparation et réconciliation (CVJRR), 07 avril 2020.

Chad, Decree No. 014/P.CE/CJ/90 establishing the Commission of Inquiry into the crimes and misappropriations committed by the former President, his co-authors and/or accomplices, 29 December 1990.

Chad, *Les crimes et détournements de l'ex-président Habré et de ses complices. Rapport de la commission nationale d'enquête du ministère tchadien de la Justice* (L'Harmattan 1993).

Chile, 'Informe de la Comisión Nacional de Verdad y Reconciliación', 3 tomos, 1996.

Chile, Decreto 355 crea comisión de verdad y reconciliación, Ministerio del interior; Subsecretaria del interior, 25 de abril de 1990.

Colombia, Comisión para el Esclarecimieto de la Verdad, la Convivencia y la No Repetición, 'Hay futuro si hay verdad. Informe Final, 2022.

Colombia, Final Agreement to End the Armed Conflict and Build a Stable and Lasting Peace, Part. 5.1.1.1. Truth, Coexistence and Non-Recurrence Commission (Comisión para el Esclarecimiento de la Verdad, la Convivencia y la No Repetición), 24 November 2016.

Côte d'Ivoire, 'Commission Dialogue, vérité et réconciliation, Rapport final, 2014.

Côte d'Ivoire, Ordonnance n° 2011-167 portant création, attributions, organisation et fonctionnement de la commission dialogue, vérité et réconciliation, 13 juillet 2011.

Democratic Republic of Congo, Loi n°/04/018 portant organisation, attributions et fonctionnement de la commission vérité et réconciliation, 30 juillet 2004.

Democratic Republic of the Congo (Kasaï-Central), Edit N°006/KC/2021 portant création, organisation et fonctionnement de la commission provinciale vérité, justice et réconciliation dans la province du Kasaï Central, 15 juillet 2021.

Ecuador, 'Informe de la comisión de la verdad, Sin verdad, no hay justicia', 5 tomos, 2010.

Ecuador, Ministerial Accord No. 012, 17 September 1996.

Ecuador, Presidente Constitucional de la República, Se creó la Comisión de la Verdad "para impedir la impunidad", 3 de mayo de 2007.

El Salvador, 'Report of the Commission on the Truth for El Salvador, From Madness to Hope. The 12-Year War in El Salvador', UN doc. S/25500, 1 April 1993, Annex.

El Salvador, Peace Accords signed by representatives of the Government of El Salvador and the Frente Farabundo Martí para la Liberacíon Nacional (FLMN) in Mexico City on 27 April 1991, UN doc. A/46/553, S/23130, 9 October 1991, Annex, 16, 'Commission on the Truth'.

Finland, Establishing a truth and reconciliation commission concerning the Sámi people, Government of Finland in cooperation with the Sámi Parliament and the Skolt Village Assembly.

Gambia, 'Truth, Reconciliation and Reparations Commission. Report', 16 vol., 2021.

Gambia, Truth, Reconciliation and Reparations Commission Act, 2017.

Germany, Deutscher Bundestag, Drucksache 12/7820, Bericht der Enquete-Kommission "Aufarbeitung von Geschichte und Folgen der SED-Diktatur in Deutschland", 31 May 1994.

Germany, Deutscher Bundestag, Drucksache 13/1535, Enquete-Kommission, "Überwindung der Folgen der SED-Diktatur im Prozeß der deutschen Einheit", 30 Mai 1995.

Germany, Drucksache 12/2597, Enquete-Kommission, "Aufarbeitung der Geschichte und Folgen der SED-Diktatur", 13 Mai 1992.

Germany, Drucksache 13/11000, Deutscher Bundestag, Schlußbericht der Enquete-Kommission "Überwindung der Folgen der SED-Diktatur im Prozeß der deutschen Einheit", 10 June 1998.

Germany, Materialien der Enquete-Kommission "Überwindung der Folgen der SED-Diktatur im Prozeß der Deutschen Einheit" (13. Wahlperiode des Deutschen Bundestages): acht Bände in 14 Teilbänden, Baden Baden, Nomos, 1999.

Germany, Materialien der Enquete-Kommission "Aufarbeitung von Geschichte und Folgen der SED-Diktatur in Deutschland" (12. Wahlperiode des Deutschen Bundestages): neun Bände in 18 Teilbänden 3, Baden-Baden: Nomos, 1995.

Ghana, National Reconciliation Commission Report, 2004.

Ghana, The National Reconciliation Commission Act, Act 611, 11 January 2002.

Grenada, 'Truth and Reconciliation Report, Redeeming the Past. A Time for Healing', 3 vol., 2006.

Guatemala, Agreement on the establishment of the Commission to clarify past human rights violations and acts of violence that have caused the Guatemalan population to suffer, signed by the Government of Guatemala and the Unidad Revolucionaria Nacional Guatemalteca (UNRG) in Oslo on 23 June 1994 (UN doc. A/48/954, S/1994/751, 1 July 1994, Annex II).

Guatemala, Comisión para el Esclarecimiento Histórico, *Guatemala Memoria Del Silencio*, 12 vol. (Guatemala: Oficina de Servicios para Proyectos de las Naciones Unidas, 1999).

Haiti, Arrêté créant la Commission Nationale de Vérité et de Justice, 17 décembre 1994. Haïti, Arrêté créant la Commission Nationale de Vérité et de Justice, 28 Mars 1995.

Haiti, Commission nationale de Justice et de Vérité, 'Si m pa rele', 29 septembre 1991–14 octobre 1994, Institute of Haïtian Studies, University of Kansas, 1998.

Honduras, 'Para que los hechos no se repitan: Informe de la Comisión de la Verdad y la Reconciliación', 2 tomos, julio de 2011.

Honduras, Decreto Ejecutivo Nùmero PCM 011-2010, 13 de abril de 2010.

Indonesia/Timor, Agreement to establish a Commission of Truth and Friendship between Indonesia and Timor-Leste, 14 December 2004.

Indonesia/Timor, Terms of Reference for The Commission of Truth and Friendship Established by The Republic of Indonesia and The Democratic Republic of Timor-Leste, 5 August 2006.

Indonesia-Timor-Leste, 'Final Report of the Commission of Truth and Friendship (Ctf)', 2008.

Kenya, 'Report of the Truth, Justice and Reconciliation Commission', 4 vol., 2013.

Kenya, Truth, Justice and Reconciliation Commission Bill, 9 May 2008.

Liberia, 'Report of the Truth and Reconciliation Commission', Monrovia, 2009.

Liberia, An Act to Establish Truth and Reconciliation Commission of Liberia, 12 May 2005.

Liberia, Art. XIII, Peace Agreement between the Government of Liberia, the Liberians United for Reconciliation and Democracy, the Movement for Democracy in Liberia and the Political Parties, Accra, Ghana, 18 August 2003, UN doc. S/2003/850, Annex.

Libya, Law No. 29 on Transitional Justice, 2 December 2013.

Mali, Décret No 2014 0013 P-RM portant organisation et modalités de fonctionnement de la Commission vérité, justice et réconciliation, 15 January 2014.

Mali, Ordonnance No. 2014-003 P-RM portant création de la Commission vérité, justice et réconciliation, 15 January 2014;

Mauritius, 'Report of the Truth and Justice Commission', 4 vol., November 2011.

Mauritius, Truth and Justice Commission Act, 22 August 2008.

Morocco, 'Instance Equité et Réconciliation. Rapport', 6 vol., 2009.

Morocco, Dahir n° 1.04.42 Du 19 safar 1425, 10 avril 2004, portant approbation des Statuts de l'Instance Equité et Réconciliation.

Nepal, Comprehensive Peace Agreement concluded between the Government of Nepal and the Communist Party of Nepal (Maoist), 21 November 2006.

Nepal, The Enforced Disappearances Enquiry, Truth and Reconciliation Commission Act, 2071 (2014), Nepal Gazette 2071/01/28, 11 May 2014.

Nigeria, 'Human Rights Violations Investigation Commission: Aka Oputa Panel Report', 9 vol., 2002.

Nigeria, Instrument Constituting Judicial Commission of Inquiry for the Investigation of Human Rights Violations, 8 June 1999.

Norway, Innst. 408 S (2017–2018) Innstilling til Stortinget fra Stortingets presidentskap, 12. juni 2018.

Norway, Innst. 493 S (2016–2017), Innstilling til Stortinget fra kontroll- og konstitusjonskomiteen, Dokument 8:30 S (2016–2017).

Norway, Sannhet og forsoning, – grunnlag for et oppgjør med fornorskingspolitikk og urett mot samer, kvener/norskfinner og skogfinner, Rapport til stortinget fra sannhets- og forsoningskommisjonen, 01. juni 2023.

Panama, 'Informe Final de la Comisión de la Verdad de Panamá', 2002.

Panama, Ministerio de Gobierno y Justicia, Decreto Ejecutivo n° 2, 18 de enero de 2001.

Paraguay, Comisión de verdad y justicia, 'Informe Final, Anive haguã oiko' 3 tomos, 2008.

Paraguay, Ley nº 2225, Por la cual se crea la Comisión de Verdad y Justicia, 16 de octubre de 2003.

Peru, Comisión de la Verdad y Reconciliación, 'Informe Final', 9 tomos, Lima, 2003.

Peru, Decreto Supremo No. 065-2001-PCM, Crean Comisión de la Verdad, 2 de junio de 2001.

Philippines (The), OP Executive Order No. 1, S. 2010, *Creating the Philippine Truth Commission*, July 30, 2010.

Serbia and Montenegro, Truth and Reconciliation Commission for Serbia and Montenegro: Presidential Decree, 30 March 2001.

Sierra Leone, 'Report of the Truth and Reconciliation Commission of Sierra Leone: Witness to Truth', 3 vol. and appendices, 2004.

Sierra Leone, Art. XXVI of the Peace Agreement signed between the Government of Sierra Leone and the Revolutionary United Front, Lomé, 7 July 1999, UN doc. S/1999/777, 12 July 1999, Annex.

Sierra Leone, The Truth and Reconciliation Commission Act 2000, Supplement to the Sierra Leone Gazette, vol. CXXXI, No. 9, 10 February 2000.

Solomon Islands, Truth and Reconciliation Commission Act 2008.

Solomon Islands, Truth and Reconciliation Commission, 'Confronting the Truth for a better Solomon Islands, Final Report', 5 vol., 2012.

South Africa, 'Truth and Reconciliation Commission of South Africa Report', 7 vol., 1998.

South Africa, Promotion of National Unity and Reconciliation Act, No. 34, 1995.

South Korea, 'The National Committee for Investigation of the Truth about the Jeju April 3 Incident, Jeju 4·3', Peace Foundation, 2003.

South Korea, *A Hard Journey to Justice: First Term Report by the Presidential Truth Commission on Suspicious Deaths of the Republic of Korea* (10.2000–10.2002) (Samin Book 2004).

South Korea, Framework Act on Clearing Up Past Incidents for Truth and Reconciliation Enacted by Law No. 7542, 31 May 2005.

South Korea, Framework Act on Settling Past Affairs Truth and Reconciliation (Amended on June 9, 2020)

South Korea, Special Act to Reveal the Truth regarding Suspicious Deaths, Act n°6170, 15 January 2000 (Amended by Act no. 6496, 24 July 2001; Act no. 6670, 25 March 2002; Act n°6750, 5 December 2002).

South Korea, The Special Law for Truth Investigation about the Jeju 4·3 Incident and Honoring Victims, Law no. 6117, 12 January 2000 (Revision Law no. 8264, 24 January 2007; Partial Revision Law no. 8435, 17 May 2007).

South Korea, Truth and Reconciliation Commission, 'Comprehensive Report', 4 vol., 2010.

South Sudan, Signed Revitalized Agreement on the Resolution of the Conflict in South Sudan (R-ARCSS), Addis Ababa, 12 September 2018, Section 5.2 Commission of Truth, Reconciliation and Healing (CTRH).

Sri Lanka, 'Report of the Commission of Inquiry on Lessons Learnt and Reconciliation', 2011.

Sri Lanka, Charter 855/19, 1995, Ref. P.O. No. SP/6/N/193/94; Charter 855/20, 1995, Ref. P.O. No. SP/6/N/192/94.

Sri Lanka, The Gazette of the Democratic Socialist Republic of Sri Lanka (Extraordinary), Charter 855/18, 1995, Ref. P.O. No. SP/6/N/191/94.

Sri Lanka, The Gazette of the Democratic Socialist Republic of Sri Lanka (Extraordinary). Charter 1060/13, 1998, Ref. No. SP/6/N/21/97.

Taiwan, Act on Promoting Transitional Justice CH, Executive Yuan (Creation and Statute of the Transitional Justice Commission), 27 December 2017.

Timor Leste, '*Chega*, The Report of the Reception, Truth, and Reconciliation Timor Leste', 5 vol., 2005.

Timor, Regulation No. 2001/10, On the Establishment of a Commission for Reception, Truth and Reconciliation in East Timor, UN doc. UNTAET/REG/2001/10, 13 July 2001.

Togo, Décret n° 2009/046/PR portant création de la commission vérité, justice et réconciliation, 25 février 2009.

Togo, Rapport final de la Commission vérité, justice et réconciliation, 2012.

Tunisia, 'Instance Vérité et Dignité, Rapport final global', 2019 (translated from Arabic to French).

Tunisia, Loi organique 2013–53 relative à l'instauration de la justice transitionnelle et à son organisation, 24 décembre 2013.

Uganda, 'The Report of the Commission of Inquiry into Violations of Human Rights', Kampala, 1994.

Uganda, Charter, Legal Notice No. 2 of 1974.

Uganda, Commission of Inquiry Act Legal Notice No. 5, 16 May 1986.

Uganda, Commission of Inquiry into Disappearances, 'Final Report', 1975.

Uruguay, 'Informe final de la comisión para la paz', 10 de abril de 2003.

Uruguay, Resolución de la Presidencia de la República No. 858/200, 9 de agosto de 2000.

## 8 Other Selected National Legislation and Reports

Belgium, *Loi du 5 août 2003 relative aux violations graves du droit international humanitaire.*

Brazil (reparation), Lei nº 10.536, de 14 de Agosto de 2002.

Brazil (reparation), Lei nº 9.140, de 04 de Dezembro de 1995;

Rwanda, Organic Law No. 13/2008 of 19 May 2008 Amending and Supplementing Organic Law No. 16/2004 of 19 June 2004 on the Organisation, Jurisdiction and Operation of the Gacaca Courts Responsible for Prosecuting and Trying Offences Constituting the Crime of Genocide and Other Crimes Against Humanity Committed Between 1 October 1990 and 31 December 1994.

Spain, Ley Orgánica 6/1985, de 1 de julio.

USA, Alien Tort Claims Act, 1789.

USA, The Torture Victim Protection Act, 1991.

Olivier Bercault (Écrit en collaboration avec Reed Brody), *La Plaine des Morts. Le Tchad de Hissène Habré 1982–1990*, Basé sur les recherches de Olivier Bercault, Reed Brody, Maria Koulouris, Martien Schotsmans, Human Rights Watch; Avec la participation de: Fédération Internationale des ligues des Droits de l'Homme, Association des Victimes des Crimes du Régime de Hissène Habré, Association Tchadienne pour la Promotion et la Défense des Droits de l'Homme, Human Rights Data Analysis Group (Black Print Cpi Ibérica, Human Rights Watch, 2013).

REMHI, *Informe del Proyecto Interdiocesano de Recuperación de la Memoria Histórica Guatemala: Nunca Más*, IV Tomos (Oficina de Derechos Humanos del Arzobispado de Guatemala 1998).

# Index



HTTPS://DOI.ORG/10.1163/9789004766655-020

www.ingramcontent.com/pod-product-compliance
Lightning Source LLC
LaVergne TN
LVHW011216150926
848065LV00003B/29

* 9 7 8 9 0 0 4 7 6 6 6 2 4 *